Whose Tradition?

In seeking to answer the question *Whose Tradition?* this book pursues four themes: Place: Whose Nation, Whose City?; People: Whose Indigeneity?; Colonialism: Whose Architecture?; and Time: Whose Identity?

Following Nezar AlSayyad's Prologue, contributors addressing the first theme take examples from Indonesia, Myanmar and Brazil to explore how traditions rooted in a particular place can be claimed by various groups whose purposes may be at odds with one another. With examples from Hong Kong, a Santal village in eastern India and the city of Kuala Lumpur, contributors investigate the concept of indigeneity, the second theme, and its changing meaning in an increasingly globalized milieu from colonial to post-colonial times. Contributors to the third theme examine the lingering effects of colonial rule in altering present-day narratives of architectural identity, taking examples from Guam, Brazil, and Portugal and its former colony, Mozambique. Addressing the final theme, contributors take examples from Africa and the United States to demonstrate how traditions construct identities, and in turn how identities inform the interpretation and manipulation of tradition within contexts of socio-cultural transformation in which such identities are in flux and even threatened. The book ends with two reflective pieces: the first drawing a comparison between a sense of 'home' and a sense of tradition; the second emphasizing how the very concept of a tradition is an attempt to pin down something that is inherently in flux.

Nezar AlSayyad, President of the International Association for the Study of Traditional Environments, is Professor of Architecture, Planning, Urban Design and Urban History, at the University of California, Berkeley, USA.

Mark Gillem, Professor at the University of Oregon, USA, teaches architecture and urban design through a joint appointment in the Departments of Architecture and Landscape Architecture. He is the Director of the International Association for the Study of Traditional Environments (IASTE).

David Moffat is an architect and planner in Berkeley, California, USA. He is currently Managing Editor of *Traditional Dwellings and Settlements Review*.

Whose Tradition?
Discourses on the Built Environment

Edited by

Nezar AlSayyad
Mark Gillem
David Moffat

LONDON AND NEW YORK

First published 2017
by Routledge
2 Park Square, Milton Park, Abingdon, Oxon OX14 4RN

and by Routledge
711 Third Avenue, New York, NY 10017

Routledge is an imprint of the Taylor & Francis Group, an Informa business

© 2017 Selection and editorial material: Nezar AlSayyad, Mark Gillem and David Moffat; individual chapters: the contributors

The right of the authors has been asserted in accordance with sections 77 and 78 of the Copyright, Designs and Patents Act 1988.

All rights reserved. No part of this book may be reprinted or reproduced or utilized in any form or by any electronic, mechanical or other means, now known or hereafter invented, including photocopying and recording, or in any information storage or retrieval system, without permission in writing from the publishers.

The publisher makes no representation, express or implied, with regard to the accuracy of the information contained in this book and cannot accept any legal responsibility or liability for any errors or omissions that may be made.

Trademark notice: Product or corporate names may be trademarks or registered trademarks, and are used only for identification and explanation without intent to infringe.

British Library Cataloguing in Publication Data
A catalogue record of this book is available from the British Library

Library of Congress Cataloging in Publication Data
Names: AlSayyad, Nezar, editor.
Title: Whose tradition? : discourses on the built environment / [editors] Nezar Alsayyad, Mark Gillem, David Moffat.
Description: New York : Routledge, 2017. | Series: Planning, history and environment series | Includes bibliographical references and index.
Identifiers: LCCN 2017011643 | ISBN 9781138192072 (hardback) | ISBN 9781315640112 (ebook)
Subjects: LCSH: Architecture and society. | Identity (Psychology) in architecture.
Classification: LCC NA2543.S6 W498 2017 | DDC 720.1/03—dc23
LC record available at https://lccn.loc.gov/2017011643

ISBN: 978-1-138-19207-2 (hbk)
ISBN: 978-1-315-64011-2 (ebk)

Typeset in Aldine and Swiss by PNR Design, Didcot

Contents

Preface   vii

The Editors and Contributors   ix

Prologue

Whose Tradition?   1
   Nezar AlSayyad

Part I: Place: Whose Nation, Whose City?

1 Tradition and Its Aftermath: Jakarta's Urban Politics   21
   Abidin Kusno

2 Tradition as an Imposed and Elite Inheritance: Yangon's Modern Past   41
   Jayde Lin Roberts

3 Mega-Events, Socio-Spatial Fragmentation, and Extraterritoriality in the City of Exception: The Case of Pre-Olympic Rio de Janeiro   62
   Anne-Marie Broudehoux

Part II: People: Whose Indigeneity?

4 Revamping Tradition: Contested Politics of 'the Indigenous' in Postcolonial Hong Kong   85
   Shu-Mei Huang

5 Their Voice or Mine? Debating People's Agency in the Construction of Adivasi Architectural Histories   111
   Gauri Bharat

6 Malaysianization, Malayization, Islamization: The Politics of Tradition in Greater Kuala Lumpur   128
   Tim Bunnell

Part III: Colonialism: Whose Architecture?

7   How the Past and the Future Have Influenced the Design of
    Guam's Government House   147
    Marvin Brown

8   The Missing 'Brazilianness' of Nineteenth-Century Brazilian
    Art and Architecture   168
    Pedro Paulo Palazzo and Ana Amélia de Paula Moura

9   Empire in the City: Politicizing Urban Memorials of
    Colonialism in Portugal and Mozambique   188
    Tiago Castela

Part IV: Time: Whose Identity?

10 Whose Neighbourhood? Identity Politics, Community
    Organizing, and Historic Preservation in St. Louis   213
    Susanne Cowan

11 Cosmopolitan Architects and Discourses of Tradition and
    Modernity in Post-Independence Africa   236
    Jennifer Gaugler

12 New Traditions of Placemaking in West-Central Africa   258
    Mark Gillem and Lyndsey Deaton

Reflections

13 The Agency of Belonging: Identifying and Inhabiting Tradition 285
    Mike Robinson

14 Process and Polemic   301
    Dell Upton

Index   311

Preface

Tradition has been the subject of many books and much research by scholars from many disciplines. Tradition's relationship to the built environment has been the focus of researchers and scholars who present their work at the meetings and in publications of the International Association for the Study of Traditional Environments (IASTE), which I co-founded in 1988. Recent IASTE conferences have dealt with tradition's relationship to development, utopia, and myth, and these conferences have advanced multiple perspectives regarding the construction of tradition and sustained IASTE's long-term position that tradition is not the static legacy of a past, but rather a contemporary project for a dynamic reinterpretation of this past in the service of the future. To understand how traditions are tied to notions of time and space, we asked the question 'Traditions of Whom?'. We went further to ask whose interests are present in the invocations of tradition, particularly in the making of the built environment. This question 'Whose Tradition?' was the theme of the 2014 IASTE conference held in Kuala Lumpur, Malaysia in December of that year. As in past IASTE conferences, scholars and practitioners from architecture, architectural history, art history, anthropology, geography, planning, and urban studies submitted papers that addressed the theme. This book contains a few of these papers revised as chapters to fit the different parts of the book and complemented by a few others that were not presented at the conference.

As part of passing on the baton and hence sustaining a tradition, I have asked Mark Gillem and David Moffat, my long time associates and IASTE fellows, to join me in editing this volume. Many individuals deserve thanks for their effort to make this book a reality. First, I must acknowledge Jennifer Gaugler, the IASTE Conference Coordinator in Kuala Lumpur, for her excellent management of the conference. Victoria Duong, the IASTE Executive Coordinator, deserves special recognition for her effort in corresponding with the authors, managing the submission process, maintaining all the records and acquiring the proper releases. Lyndsey Deaton, the IASTE Liaison in Eugene, was ably responsible for revising the papers and turning them into chapters according to the publisher's guidelines in collaboration with David Moffat. Finally, I must thank Ann Rudkin, my long time editor. This book marks our sixth collaboration over a fifteen-year period, and I am grateful for all of her guidance on these book projects.

Nezar AlSayyad
Berkeley, 2017

The Editors and Contributors

The Editors

Nezar AlSayyad is an architect, planner, urban historian, and public intellectual. He is Professor of Architecture, Planning, and Urban Design at the University of California at Berkeley where he currently serves as the Faculty Director of the Center for Arab Societies and Environments Studies (CASES). He is the Co-founder of the International Association for the Study of Traditional Environments (IASTE), and currently its President and Editor of its journal, *Traditional Dwellings and Settlements Review (TDSR)*. AlSayyad is the recipient of many grants for his research, books, films, and projects from the US National Endowment of the Arts (NEA), the Graham Foundation, the Getty Foundation, the Ford Foundation, the Woodrow Wilson Center in Washington DC, the Doris Duke Foundation, and the US Department of Education. Among AlSayyad's numerous awards are the *Pioneer America Society Best Book Award* in 1988, the *American Institute of Architects Education Honors* in 1991, and more recently a *Distinguished Guggenheim Fellowship* for 2014–2015. In 2008, the University of California recognized his work with the *Distinguished Teaching Award*, the highest recognition given to a faculty member on the Berkeley campus. AlSayyad is the author, co-author, editor, or co-editor of many books, among them *Streets of Islamic Cairo* (1981); *Dwellings, Settlements and Tradition* (1989); *Cities and Caliphs* (1991); *Forms and Dominance* (1992); *Consuming Tradition, Manufacturing Heritage* (2001); *Hybrid Urbanism* (2001); *Muslim Europe or Euro-Islam* (2002); *The End of Tradition* (2004); *Making Cairo Medieval* (2005); *Cinematic Urbanism* (2006); *The Fundamentalist City? Religiosity and the Remaking of Urban Space* (2010); *Cairo: Histories of a City* (2011); and *Traditions: The Real, the Hyper, and the Virtual in the Built Environment* (2014).

Mark Gillem is Professor of Architecture, Landscape Architecture, and Urban Design at the University of Oregon. His book *America Town: Building the Outposts of Empire* (2007) draws on a decade in the US Air Force, both as an architect and planner and as a faculty member of the Air Force Institute of Technology. *America Town* examines the forces behind the exportation of the American lifestyle to military bases abroad and explores the impact of this approach on foreign lands. He also contributed an essay on this topic to *Indefensible Space: The Architecture of the National Insecurity State*, edited by Michael Sorkin (2007). Gillem addresses sustainability, social responsibility, and historic preservation through his research and his professional practice. He received recognitions from the American Planning Association for air base master plans in Korea and Texas. Other honours include a Design Excellence Award from the US Air Force and the Crocker Award for Teaching Excellence at the Air Force Institute of Technology. Gillem is the Director of the International Association for the Study of Traditional Environments (IASTE). He is Principal of his practice, The Urban Collaborative. Gillem is also a fellow of both the American Institute of Architects (FAIA) and the American Institute of Certified Planners (FAICP).

David Moffat is an architect and planner in Berkeley, CA, and editor of numerous environmental-design publications over the last 25 years. He is currently Managing Editor of *Traditional Dwellings and Settlements Review (TDSR)*, the journal of the International Association for the Study of Traditional Environments (IASTE), with which he has been affiliated since its founding in 1988. He has played a major role in planning and producing many of the edited volumes that have emerged from conferences and other initiatives of the Association since its inception. He also served as Managing Editor of the journal, *Places*, from 2002 to 2009.

The Contributors

Gauri Bharat is Assistant Professor of Architecture at CEPT University in Ahmedabad, India. In both research and teaching, she is primarily interested in exploring how people engage with built environments. In teaching humanities and architectural research, she similarly focuses on exploring everyday life and environments using discursive frameworks of popular culture, politics and marginality. She also practises with Analog Studio where they have designed and executed several private residences.

Anne-Marie Broudehoux is Associate Professor at the School of Design of the University of Quebec at Montreal, where she has been teaching since 2002. She is the author of *Mega-Events and Urban Image Construction: Beijing and Rio de Janeiro*, published by Routledge in 2017. She has given several conference papers and published multiple articles on the socio-spatial impacts of large-scale urban transformations. Her book, *The Making and Selling of Post-Mao Beijing*, was awarded the International Planning History Society book prize in 2006.

Marvin Brown has been an architectural historian in the field of cultural resources management, primarily on the American East Coast, for 35 years. His study of Rosenwald Schools, built for African-American children in the South in the early twentieth century, received the Vernacular Architecture Forum's Buchanan Award for Excellence in Field Work in 2008. He served on the Board of Directors of the VAF for many years, edited its quarterly newsletter for a decade, and co-organized its 2016 national conference in North Carolina. He has written three books on that state's architecture. For the past 25 years, Marvin Brown has been a Senior Architectural Historian with AECOM and its predecessors in Raleigh, North Carolina. An AECOM assignment gave him the opportunity to encounter Richard Neutra and Ricardo Bordallo on Guam.

Tim Bunnell is Professor of Geography and the Deputy Head of the Department of Geography at the National University of Singapore. He also holds a joint appointment with the Asia Research Institute where he leads the Asian Urbanism Research Cluster. His research is focused on urban studies, urban aspirations, urban theory, and decentralized governance, specifically in Southeast Asia with a focus on Malaysia and Indonesia. He has authored many publications including books and journal articles, most significantly *Malaysia, Modernity, and the Multimedia Super Corridor: A Critical Geography of Intelligent Landscapes* (2004).

Tiago Castela is a Research Associate at the Centre for Social Studies of the University of Coimbra in Portugal. He has also recently served as Principal Investigator of the exploratory research project 'Urban Aspirations in Colonial/Postcolonial Mozambique' at the same centre. His research explores the history of the political dimension of spatial planning and architecture, with a focus on urban peripheries in southwestern Europe and southern Africa in the twentieth century.

Susanne Cowan is Assistant Professor of Architectural History in the School of Architecture at Montana State University. Her research focuses on the relationship between urban design and the social conditions of cities, particularly regarding participatory democracy as a method for urban policy-making. In her most recent work, she has been tracing the ways that planning policies in deindustrializing cities have shaped the process of urban decay and/or gentrification, and what positive or negative impacts urban design interventions have had on social and economic conditions of residents. Much of the research for her chapter took place in her former capacity as a Post-Doctoral Fellow at Washington University in St. Louis.

Lyndsey Deaton is a PhD candidate in architecture and the Associate Director of the Urban Design Lab in the School of Architecture and Allied Arts at the University of Oregon, Eugene. Her research explores how contemporary social phenomena, such as social media and neoliberalization, influence people's perception and use of the urban environment. She is a practising, licensed architect and urban designer and has completed projects across the United States as well as in Europe, the Middle and Far East, and Africa. Her most recent publications include a study of social cohesion in tiny house communities of homeless Americans published in a chapter in collaboration with Mark Gillem in *Ethnographic Architecture*, (2016) 'Security, Surveillance, and the New Landscapes of Migration'.

Jennifer Gaugler is a PhD candidate in architecture at the University of California, Berkeley. Her research focuses on the historic and contemporary architecture and urbanism of Rwanda and neighbouring countries in East Africa, including both vernacular building traditions and formal architectural projects. She is trained as an architect and has experience working in architecture in both the United States and Rwanda. She coordinated the 2014 IASTE conference, 'Whose Tradition?', in Kuala Lumpur.

Shu-Mei Huang is Assistant Professor at the Graduate Institute of Building and Planning, National Taiwan University. Her research interests include postcolonial urbanism, trans-nationalization of care and space, and dark heritage. She has carried out research into defunct prisons built by the colonial regimes in several East Asian cities, including Taipei, Seoul, Singapore and Lushun. In collaboration with one of her Korean colleagues, she is preparing for a book project on remembering of punishment in post-colonial Asian cities. She is author of *Urbanizing Carescapes of Hong Kong: Two Systems, One City* (2015).

Abidin Kusno is Professor in the Institute of Asian Research and Director of the Centre of Southeast Asia Research at the University of British

Columbia. His research examines the roles of cities in shaping the political cultures of decolonization, nation building, and development, with a particular focus on exploring the historical and contemporary conditions of urban politics and city life in Indonesia. Kusno has held multiple distinguished academic positions. He currently serves as the Canada Research Chair in Asian Urbanism and Culture at the University of British Columbia. He has authored several books, including *After the New Order: Space, Politics, and Jakarta*; *Appearances of Memory: Mnemonic Practices of Architecture and Urban Form in Indonesia*; and *Behind the Postcolonial: Architecture, Urban Space and Political Cultures in Indonesia*.

Ana Amélia de Paula Moura is an architect, PhD candidate at the University of Brasilia, and an Assistant Professor at Goiás State University. Her research focuses on modern architectural history and historic preservation.

Pedro Paulo Palazzo is an architect and Assistant Professor at the University of Brasilia School of Architecture. His primary research fields include the history and historiography of Brazilian art and architecture in the nineteenth and twentieth centuries; interactions between the classical tradition and the Modern Movement in monumental and civic architecture; and representations of architecture in painting.

Jayde Lin Roberts is a tenured Lecturer in Asian Studies at the University of Tasmania, Australia. She is an interdisciplinary scholar of the built environment and a Burma Studies specialist who was awarded a Fulbright US Scholar grant for 2016–2017. Her book, *Mapping Chinese Rangoon: Place and Nation among the Sino-Burmese*, was published in June 2016. Her current research focuses on discourses of development and urbanization in Yangon and Myanmar.

Mike Robinson is Professor and the Chair of Cultural Heritage at the University of Birmingham, UK, and is Director of the Ironbridge International Institute for Cultural Heritage. He is Founder and Editor-in-Chief of the *Journal of Tourism and Cultural Change* and of the *Tourism and Cultural Change Book Series*. His work focuses on the relations between heritage, culture, and tourism, and he has published numerous books, articles and chapters on the various ways in which these realms collide. His recent research focuses upon conceptions of heritage in Taiwan and upon the heritage, tourism and collective memory relating to World War I.

Dell Upton is Professor at the University of California, Los Angeles, where he teaches courses on American and world architecture and urbanism, art- and architectural-history theories and methods, material culture, and cross-cultural spatial formation in the postcolonial world. His books and articles treat subjects ranging from pre-Revolutionary American architecture to critiques of New Urbanism and heritage tourism. They include *Another City: Urban Life and Urban Spaces in the New American Republic* (2008), *Architecture in the United States (1998), and Holy Things and Profane: Anglican Parish Churches in Colonial Virginia* (1986). Upton served as a consultant and chief catalogue essayist for the Metropolitan Museum of Art's 2000 exhibition Art and the Empire City: New York, 1825–1861.

Prologue

Whose Tradition?

Nezar AlSayyad

A number of scholars, especially those from the International Association for the Study of Traditional Environments (IASTE), have to date advanced multiple perspectives regarding the construction of traditions in space and place. Yet behind the construction or deconstruction of any tradition also lies the subject, whose interests in the present are often hidden. To reveal this process of agency, one may therefore also ask: Tradition, by whom? In examining themes of authorship and subjectivity, contributors to this book seek to uncover in what manner, for what reason, by whom, to what effect, and during what intervals traditions have been deployed with regard to the built environment.

Our current period of globalization has led to the flexible reinterpretation of traditions via the mass media in pursuit of power and profit. A proliferation of environments, for example, adapt the traditional forms of one place and period to a completely different contextual setting, while new design traditions may privilege image over experience. At the same time the advent of new mobile technologies, with the power to compress and distort traditional configurations of space and time, have allowed new empowering practices to flourish. Such practices have led to new traditions of urban resistance and uprisings that travel fluidly between diverse locales and give voice to certain populations previously excluded. Questions of power and the changing configurations of time and space thus open up discussion of the ways in which traditional practices shape the histories and futures of built environments.

This volume reflects ongoing work by scholars of IASTE, as originally presented at the organization's fourteenth biennial conference in Kuala Lumpur, in December 2014. It may be considered part of an ongoing dialogue within this international and interdisciplinary forum, established in 1988, about the role, value, and operation of tradition as a validating discourse within the built environment. The authors of each chapter engage with ideas and arguments put forth in previous IASTE publications, including my own authored or edited volumes *Traditions: The 'Real', the Hyper, and the Virtual in the Built Environment* (2014), *The End of Tradition?* (2004), and *Consuming Tradition, Manufacturing Heritage: Global Forms and Urban Norms in an Age of Tourism* (2001). Together this body of work expresses an interpretive trajectory that has sought to document, evaluate, and finally critique the workings of tradition as a constitutive element in the creation and interpretation of both Western and non-Western built environments.

Past IASTE discourses have described how the advent of modernism as a mode of thinking and colonialism as a political project were underpinned by the simultaneous invention of the 'traditional environment' as a complementary other. The study of traditional identities thus provided both a new arena for knowledge production and a validation of the modernist teleology. However, under increasingly global economic and social conditions, the consumption of traditional environments, especially in the arena of tourism and mass media, has often elevated them to the status of hyper-environments. More recently, their portrayal in both the virtual realm and heritage discourses has also resulted in creative and divergent articulations that could not have been imagined just a few decades ago. It has been IASTE's mission for over three decades to explore this evolving interpretive frame and raise important questions about such foundational notions as authenticity, hybridity, and displacement.

The present volume advances this project by seeking to better understand the increasingly complex question of agency inherent in contemporary claims to traditionality. Such claims are rarely without purpose. Instead, they reflect the situated interests of a host of actors for whom particular definitions of tradition may impart political power, financial profit, or cultural legitimacy. In the second decade of the twenty-first century, as change seems to happen ever more rapidly and globalization makes the world seem ever smaller, it is critical to reflect upon these emerging new connections between people, heritage, and tradition.

In seeking to answer the question 'Whose tradition?' our effort must address three essential aspects of tradition in the built environment: who, what, and where? In asking 'Who?' we question the ownership and authority of dominant traditions deployed in the making of space. Traditions of agency have been created, adopted, or invoked by certain social groups and/or governments for specific purposes. Which narratives become privileged in spatial practices and to what end? What are the politics of 'choosing' traditions, or transmitting them and to whom? Further, what is omitted, negated, or silenced in the interest of those in power at a given moment? Next, we ask 'What?' because in order to examine how traditions are manifest in space and time, it is important to consider which versions, particularities, or specificities of tradition emerge and are subsequently anchored in specific places. Understanding how traditions are established in built form and practice is just as important as understanding whose traditions are privileged. We must explore a variety of hegemonic spatial practices and their alternatives that either adopt or challenge standard configurations of power and authority. How have disadvantaged groups, those that are often left out of dominant spatial traditions, created their own traditions? And how do they subvert established norms, allowing new voices to enter and gain legitimacy? Finally, in considering 'Where?' we seek to understand the mobility and the re-imagination of traditions. In a rapidly changing post-global world, traditions cease to be fixed or attached to given places for very long. The mobile nature of contemporary traditions creates the possibility for both disruption and foreclosure, and it can therefore negate past forms of ownership and authorship that assumed a top-down power structure that privileged an elite. The modern technologies of reproducibility have undermined the placed-based nature of traditions, allowing flexible interpretations as well as the creation of new cyber meanings. In fact, mass media and the Internet have created their own traditions with flexible temporalities in space.

Past IASTE projects have called on scholars to consider tradition's relationship to development, utopia, and most recently, myth. In response, scholars have advanced multiple perspectives regarding the construction of traditions in space and place. As these show, utopia implies the construction of a future ideal, whether religious or philosophical, while myth attempts to discover the origins of history, whether in the imagination or in reality. Myth thus usually invokes an invented past, and utopia imagines an alternative future. But in both cases the dimension of time is paramount. Above all, this condition reveals how traditions are never the static legacy of the past, but rather a project for its dynamic reinterpretation in the service of the present and the future. To understand how traditions are tied to notions of time and space, it is thus important to consider their subjectivity, authorship, and power. Behind the construction or deconstruction of any tradition lies the subject, whose interests in the present are often hidden. To pursue these issues, the chapters in this volume reflect four broad themes: 'Place: Whose Nation, Whose City?'; 'People: Whose Indigeneity?'; 'Colonialism: Whose Architecture?'; and 'Time: Whose Identity?'.

Place: Whose Nation, Whose City?

The chapters in this section explore how traditions that are rooted in a particular place can be claimed by various groups whose purposes may be at odds with one another. These competing claims may indeed make the same place the site of multiple traditions and hence multiple spatial practices. Thus, hegemonic spatial practices may adopt or reinforce standard configurations of power and authority, while subversive ones may challenge or contest them. How have disadvantaged groups, left out of dominant spatial traditions, created their own traditions? How are these spatial practices transmitted? And how do they subvert established norms, allowing new voices to enter and gain legitimacy?

In the first chapter, 'Tradition and Its Aftermath: Jakarta's Urban Politics', Abidin Kusno looks into how a new configuration of political practices entails an invention of tradition, as well as disputes over 'Whose tradition?'. Kusno illustrates this point by discussing the rise to power of the populist Joko 'Jokowi' Widodo, first as governor of Jakarta and then president of Indonesia, and of his successor Basuki 'Ahok' Purnama as governor of Jakarta. During their respective administrations, the two men have sought to expose and undermine traditions of power established in the later decades of the twentieth century under the authoritarian New Order government of Suharto. Kusno explains how these traditions worked through a systematic informalization of social, political, and economic relations. These created conditions of urban life that Jokowi identified in a May 2014 speech as 'corruption, intolerance of differences, greed, selfishness, the tendency to use force to settle matters, law violations, and opportunism'.

As part of the New Order system, traditions operated at various levels both inside and outside the government to conceal the workings of power, while at the same time creating a structure for its implementation. Kusno identifies five in particular, each maintained and performed by different social groups. At the top, all affairs in the city were guided by a ruling oligarchy, which combined large commercial interests with state military power. The right to exercise influence within this structure was then subcontracted to successively smaller organizations, brokers, and street enforcers. This patronage chain was overlaid by an underfunded government bureaucracy, dependent on graft and corruption for its functioning. A fourth tradition was that of the *rakyat*, or common people, whose right to anonymity and powerlessness were assumed together. And fifth, Kusno describes as the *kampung* tradition, one of self-building and community organization, which both moderated alienation and conflict and supported the formal economy through a comprehensive network of informal services. Against this system, the new tradition of Jokowi/Ahok has emphasized the formalization of civil and economic relations through such programmes as slum upgrading, health-services access cards, and an accountable bureaucracy. However, undoing old traditions of urban order also means eliminating the *rakyat* tradition of anonymity, forcing all residents to identify themselves to the state. And it means eliminating some forms of local autonomy and control. According to Kusno, Jokowi and Ahok's campaign of urban transformation nevertheless is 'intended to show how the poor were mistreated or poorly served in the past, not because they were less fortunate, but because they formerly lived according to unjust traditions created in part by the government'.

The second contribution in the section, 'Tradition as an Imposed and Elite Inheritance; Yangon's Modern Past', by Jayde Lin Roberts, examines the pending transformation of Myanmar's capital. As Roberts argues, 'the downtown core of Yangon (formerly Rangoon) stands as an odd inheritance – not so much bestowed as cast aside by the British Empire, and not so much affirmed as acquiesced to by the independent Burmese state'. For a variety of reasons related to the economic isolation of the Burmese state for much of the last half century, the downtown's imposing colonial buildings remain today largely unaltered. As such, the city stands in stark contrast to such nearby metropolises as Bangkok and Singapore, which have surrendered much of their historic identity to become modern.

As the country reopens to outside influence, the preservation of this downtown has been hailed by elite cultural groups both inside and outside the country as a way to retain a sense of local authenticity. As Roberts points out, claiming a former colonial modernity as a local tradition 'turns the linear liberatory discourse of modernity back on itself, rendering it cyclical and therefore more traditional'. However, it also ignores the reality these buildings once embodied. No doubt, preservationists are correct that they are beautiful. 'Yet what they fail to mention is that these buildings once excluded most Burmese people. Instead, they housed a colonial and then a military bureaucracy that treated the local population as potential enemies of the state.' As Roberts writes: 'Burmese expatriates and the country's educated elite are rallying to resist the negative effects of modernization – that is, the rampant reproduction of "faceless" or "placeless" high-rise towers such as those that have produced a globalized Southeast Asia... The idea is that Yangon, the first city to be modern in Southeast Asia, can now recover its modernity as a way of maintaining its past, its tradition'.

Yet, to fund these dreams, plans call for the repurposing of the buildings as hotels and tourist destinations. Thus, as Myanmar seeks to rejoin the world economy, 'neoliberal capitalism is poised to reshape Yangon, much as colonial capitalism created it… However, the built environment of Yangon is a paradoxical legacy that has once, and could again, exclude its local population based on class and ethnicity'. For Roberts, the colonial architecture of downtown Rangoon 'is more like the inheritance passed down within a wealthy family; it remains private property, not a public good'. And yet, 'Downtown Rangoon, seen as an integrated social and physical fabric, is Burmese. Imposing colonial architecture has not suffocated the vitality of everyday life; life has happened in between the buildings. The Burmese people are well practised in making do and circumventing technologies of power, but the tide of neoliberalism could push current residents out of the city'.

The third chapter in this section, Anne-Marie Broudehoux's 'Mega-Events, Socio-Spatial Fragmentation, and Extraterritoriality in the City of Exception: The Case of Pre-Olympic Rio de Janeiro', discusses the transformation of Rio de Janeiro in the years leading up to hosting the 2014 FIFA World Cup and the 2016 Olympics. In particular, Broudehoux explores the effect of such mega-events on the production of 'a new urban territoriality, marked by the creation of spaces of exception, which are both spatially and legally located outside the normal urban order'. As she explains, 'mega-events are at the root of increasingly fragmented and polarized urban topographies, which are the material expression of growing social, political, and economic inequality'. Furthermore, 'hosting mega-events reinforces a spatial hierarchy of the urban landscape that considers some spaces more worthy than others and reinforces the construction of a geography of segregation and exclusion'.

Broudehoux's investigation looks first at the ability of the self-imposed 'state of emergency' surrounding sporting mega-events to create exceptional moments for neoliberal growth. At these times, ordinary legal and civic controls may be bypassed, and elite groups may reframe public debate or even institute new, lasting forms of authoritarian governance. Meanwhile, the effect during the event is to create territories of exception – physically, legally, and commercially separate from the surrounding urban fabric. Such areas are rigidly policed and surveilled; traditional commercial activities are forbidden in order to create a captive market for powerful international sponsors; and attendees must relinquish all rights to political expression. The hosting of a mega-event may also be linked to a radical restructuring of a city's residential and entertainment districts to benefit wealthy real estate interests. And, as a consequence, they typically result in further diminishment of the right of the poor to occupy urban space, in some cases through their brutal expulsion from key territories. According to Broudehoux, 'In spite of their reputation as great social unifiers and celebrations of togetherness, mega-event spectacles are powerful instruments in concealing the growing fragmentation of the urban territory into pockets of privatized enclaves that increasingly escape local legal and spatial norms'. Nevertheless, she also concludes that the series of demonstrations that marked the lead-up to the 2014 World Cup and the 2016 Olympics potentially indicate they may likewise provide 'a platform for the expression of dissent and … an umbrella cause around which collective resistance can be organized'.

People: Whose Indigeneity?

The second section of the book explores the concept of indigeneity and its changing meaning in an increasingly globalized milieu. In the past, indigeneity derived its reliable value as an 'other' to modern globalized practices. However, from a number of perspectives, the indigenous can now be understood as a self-serving construction within this discourse. Indeed, the very concept of indigeneity is in some cases now being exploited within these same circuits by the 'indigenous' themselves. The chapters in this section investigate some of the many ways the notion of the indigenous is used to create social and monetary value.

In the first chapter here, 'Revamping Tradition: Contested Politics of "the Indigenous" in Postcolonial Hong Kong', Shu-Mei Huang writes that the notion of 'tradition' is complicit in establishing the special privileges of the indigenous. Key among these is the right of indigenous males in the New Territories to each build one 'small house' on designated village lands during their lifetimes. This privilege distinguishes this population from all other residents of Hong Kong, including all women and all other inhabitants of the New Territories. Yet, while this traditional right was originally intended to preserve specific practices of village-based agriculture, it has now been almost completely monetized. As a result, those who today actually build and occupy such houses, which may take the form of gated enclaves, bear little resemblance to the local farmers the tradition was originally designed to protect.

Understanding the workings of the small house policy (SHP) requires appreciating the dualism at work in Hong Kong's territorial origins. At the time the New Territories were joined to the colony under treaty with

China in 1898, residents of its 642 existing villages were accorded special protection by the colonial government. At the time, Huang explains, this was a paternalistic gesture, largely derived from the colonial gaze. However, the New Territories have since become the site of vast public housing estates. They are likewise dotted with the settlements of more recent migrants from China, which lack protection and may be easily removed to make way for government development projects. The value of the tradition today is primarily embodied in its guarantee to participate in the SHP. This creates two systems of development, privileging those who can claim to be descended from New Territories villagers over those descended from migrants who arrived later (many of whom were seeking refuge from the Chinese Revolution of 1949 and may be closely related in every way to the former group). Huang's examination of how this policy originated and how it has been refined, enhanced, and fiercely defended over the years by powerful political interests is intended to shed light on the processes of agency and authorship that frequently support notions of tradition. She further argues that the time has come to question the right of those it benefits to continue to profit from it, without due respect for its negative effects on the surrounding ecology and village heritage – or on the establishment of new agricultural practices that might protect a much-needed greenbelt between Hong Kong and neighbouring Shenzen. As she writes, 'The invention of the indigenous and of their privilege to build small houses serves as a living embodiment of how tradition may create privileges and cleavages within a given population'.

The next chapter in the section, Gauri Bharat's 'Their Voice or Mine? Debating People's Agency in the Construction of Adivasi Architectural Histories' deals with the disconnect between local and 'expert' perceptions of indigenous environmental values. When the residents of one Santal village in Jharkhand State, eastern India, where Bharat was conducting research, did not select the images she expected they would as being most representative of their local environment, she began to question her bias as a Western-trained architect-researcher. On the one hand, the villagers' selections revealed how they viewed the environment from within a different set of values, one which registered both their spiritual and cultural investment in their surroundings and their aspiration for a more modern, prosperous life. On the other, it pointed to her own bias for built forms, especially the houses that Santal women spend considerable time decorating, and which are a recognized characteristic of Santal culture. The apparent lack of importance the villagers accorded to these built forms was distressing because it made her question the very relevance of her work on historical change in Santal dwelling form. Bharat eventually discovered that considerable change had occurred in Santal dwelling form since the mid-nineteenth century. It was related to larger social, economic, political, and environmental changes in the region, primarily owing to the arrival there of nontribal people seeking to exploit its abundant resources. As a result, a thickly forested landscape had been replaced by one of paddy cultivation and heavy industry. Dispossessed of their old habitats and mobile ways of living, the Santal had gradually resettled in villages, and their houses had become more internally differentiated, complex, and permanent. The same ethnographic, architectural-historical gaze that allowed Bharat to construct this narrative, however, also separated her from the 'lived' perspectives of the village inhabitants. And the very device of the photo exhibition compounded this divide by phenomenologically framing the village as a series of isolated images pulled from the totality of their experience. However, instead of remaining resigned to the inseparability of these realities, Bharat decided to investigate ways in which the two views might inform each other. While she theorized this would have benefits for both sides, it also highlighted how historical narratives of architecture need not be singular, and that they may be constructed both *about* and *from within* a particular subject position.

The following chapter is Tim Bunnell's 'Malaysianization, Malayization, Islamization: The Politics of Tradition in Greater Kuala Lumpur'. In it, Bunnell describes the experience of modernity for a group of men who left the Malay region (*alam Melayu*) as merchant seamen in search of a better life in the middle decades of the twentieth century. After years of seafaring, they settled in the British city of Liverpool, which they took to be a prime seat of the modern world they aspired to belong to. However, in the years they had been 'away', profound changes had taken place in both the material and discursive circumstances of Liverpool and their native Southeast Asia. As Bunnell writes, 'While post-imperial Liverpool and its wider urban region experienced profound commercial demise; postcolonial Malaysia and Singapore experienced a correspondingly miraculous economic rise'. The result was that the modern they had left to seek overseas, in *Eropah*, had become installed in dramatically new and different form 'back home'. Nevertheless, when they returned for visits, many of its signature monuments, such as the skyscrapers on the skylines of burgeoning Southeast Asian cities, did not register as such. Instead, 'In interview after interview with elderly ex-seafarers in Liverpool, it was the shift from *jamban* [open latrines] to *tandas* [modern bathrooms] that was used to encapsulate half a century of modern progress'.

According to Bunnell, the seafarers' view of the relative deficiency of the newly built modernity of their native lands may be partly attributed to their own mid-twentieth-century perspective. Since their departure, modernity had been achieved there through three processes that never figured in the secular, colonial view of it with which they grew up. The first was a period of 'Malaysianization', involving independence, architecture and national infrastructure development. The second, 'Malayization', saw the proliferation of traditional Malay symbols, both as the result of a search for a visibly distinct national identity and 'the enflamed ethno-cultural politics of identity and indigeneity'. The third period of 'Islamization', Bunnell writes, 'drew on Islamic elements from beyond the Malay world as part of the efforts to identify suitably great civilizational traditions upon which a global Islamic modernity may be constructed'. While the seafarers may have been able to fit the built environment of the first period into their mid-twentieth-century view, they had few referents with which to incorporate the second two. As a result of this reconfiguration of the conceptual divide between tradition and modernity, they were more likely to find credible evidence of modernity in more mundane domestic transformations.

Colonialism: Whose Architecture?

The third section of the book explores the lingering effects of colonial rule in altering present-day narratives of architectural identity. The colonial influence may be present today in diverse and unpredictable ways. In some cases, it may involve overt political choices between forms and styles; in others, the influence may be related to more subtle notions of metropolitan superiority. The lasting impacts of colonial domination are evident today in many forms: from continuing cultural influence between former colonial and colonized lands, to impulses to reaction and efforts to revalue built heritage.

The section opens with Marvin Brown's 'How the Past and the Future Have Influenced the Design of Guam's Government House', which examines the successive transformations of Government House on the Pacific island of Guam as a case of how architectural forms may be recast to serve different purposes over time. One people's tradition may thus be constructed partly out of the pieces of others, reframed to express new cultural and political purposes. 'Architectural forms and styles are inherently ambiguous as cultural signifiers, open to appropriation and imitation for many purposes', Brown writes. In this case, the condition allowed 'a building that at first blush seems to represent the architecture of a land's two principal colonial occupiers [to] transform those styles into the symbols of a modern and (semi-) independent place'.

Guam's native residents, known as the Chamorro, originally resided in rectangular houses with thatch, reed, or board walls and steeply pitched, thatched, gabled roofs. These were raised on broad platforms and extended to a number of exterior spaces where much domestic life took place. With Spanish colonization, however, a new style of formal architecture was introduced, marked by thick, plastered walls, arches, and red-tiled, hipped roofs. Guam became a US territory in 1898 following the Spanish-American War. Initially, the US did little to change architecture on the island. But after World War II, a US military governor, in rebuilding the island, set out to honour what he saw as Chamorro traditions, while simultaneously seeking to update its built environment to modern standards. One of his first steps was to hire the modernist architecture and planning firm of Neutra & Alexander. Richard Neutra's design for a new Government House to replace its Spanish Colonial predecessor, though non-traditional in appearance, attempted to retain what the architect saw as the open-air quality of traditional Chamorro space. These design qualities were subverted, however, in the actual construction of the building by a succeeding governor and his wife, who wanted it to reflect more traditional, commonsense American values. The final redesign of Government House took place under the administration of Governor Ricardo Bordallo, a native Chamorro and populist. Over two terms in the 1970s and 1980s he expanded the structure to include a second floor, and added many details designed to give it the appearance of a hipped-roof, Spanish Colonial dwelling. Brown argues that Bordallo's view of authentic Chamorro architecture following three hundred years of colonization should not be dismissed. His redesign declared that colonial forms need not be viewed as a sign of oppression if they are selectively and knowingly embraced and transformed. 'It declares that such architecture can stand as a symbol of resoluteness and determination. It calls out: "We're still here. Where are you?"'

Next, Pedro Paulo Palazzo and Ana Amélia de Paula Moura's 'The Missing "Brazilianness" of Nineteenth-Century Brazilian Art and Architecture' moves the discussion to early-twentieth-century Brazil, where leading members of the cultural establishment took great interest in the matter of national character in art and architecture. Most importantly, in their writings, they explored the purported lack of such character in the work of those born in the generations immediately preceding them. As Palazzo and de Paula Moura point out, this view has largely been refuted in Portuguese language scholarship since the 1960s. Yet the discourses constructed to argue for this position, though largely discredited today, have much to tell about the role of tradition in the construction of national identity.

The chapter examines the writings of a number of important intellectual figures of the time: the academic art critic Gonzaga Duque, the engineer and neocolonial advocate Ricardo Severo, the physician José Marianno Filho, the Beaux-Arts architect Adolfo Morales de los Ríos Filho, the writer Monteiro Lobato, and the modernist architect Lucio Costa. As Palazzo and de Paula Moura describe, from a variety of perspectives and using a variety of arguments, these figures all decried the lack of Brazilian character in nineteenth-century art and architecture. In doing so, one of their primary motives was to establish a teleology of Brazilian national identity. Its starting point 'was invariably a timeless period of formation of the national identity, followed by a clearly circumscribed period of decay'. However, as they continue, 'Th[is] starting point did not need to be an exemplary or admirable stage. The essential point was that it provided fundamentals of national identity that could be later reworked and improved: Portuguese language and way of life, adaptation to climate and geography, simplicity, and rationality'. As they then point out, 'Disagreements among these authors revolved mostly around which social group claimed the authority to define national character and, therefore, whose tradition was to be held up as the true architectural image of Brazil'. Regardless, the form of the narrative remained constant, its purpose being to establish a mythic sense of inner moral strength. And, of course, 'the contribution of South American Indians and enslaved Africans was entirely disregarded, despite growing evidence of their fundamental role in shaping Brazilian culture'.

The section ends with Tiago Castela's 'Empire in the City: Politicizing Urban Memorials of Colonialism in Portugal and Mozambique', which explores the differential management, in the postcolonial era, of memorials to Portuguese colonialism in Mozambique and Portugal. Castela details how in the years since the last territories of the Portuguese empire in Africa achieved their independence in 1975, these memorials have been treated in ways that both contest and perpetuate the colonial legacy. This can be seen both in Maputo (the present-day capital of Mozambique) and in major cities of Portugal such as Porto and Lisbon. Following independence in Mozambique, figures of Portuguese colonial heroes and subject natives that had been installed in important urban nodes in Maputo were torn down and taken to the Fortaleza, a museum built in the 1940s on the site of a former colonial military installation. Here they were reframed as elements of an anti-colonial exhibition – in a space originally conceived by colonial architects as a site of 'unchanging memoriality' to the superiority of Africans of European origin. However, the way this space has been established and managed, Castela writes, continues to perpetuate the built legacy of colonialism. The same may be said for other aspects of state urban planning, including the curtailment of markets in urban space, interventions in the so-called 'peripheries', and the design of major streets and public spaces – all originally intended to foster a postcolonial identity. Meanwhile, in Portugal, Castela argues, the place of African colonial memorials has, at best, not been addressed. This failure continues to allow the unequal representation of Africans to appear in several major public as well as private spaces. The result is that the legacy of colonialism, today considered to represent ahistoric artistic production, has failed to receive proper political attention.

According to Castela both situations display the persistence of a 'postcolonial rationality of rule'. While this may be typical of contemporary modes of valuing built heritage, it involves a continuing 'pedagogy' of inequality, because the designers and patrons of state memorials originally envisioned them as explicit instruments by which to instruct citizens. Political democratization requires both the interrogation of such urban forms as well as the development of expert, technical knowledge and practice that can mitigate the conditions leading directly or indirectly to state-sanctioned spatial violence.

Time: Whose Identity?

The last section of the book explores how traditions construct identities, and in turn how identities inform the interpretation and manipulation of tradition within contexts of socio-cultural transformation in which such identities are in flux and even threatened. These chapters ask several questions. How are traditions used to bolster existing identity? Alternatively, how are they transformed to reflect new identities in new circumstances? And how do changing identities lead to new or revised interpretations of tradition? The chapters thus acknowledge that all traditions, no matter how resilient, must face processes of change and modernization as time marches relentlessly on.

Using a neighbourhood in St Louis, MO, as a case study, Susanne Cowan's 'Whose Neighbourhood? Identity Politics, Community Organizing, and Historic Preservation in St. Louis', engages here with the issue of agency in the definition of architectural heritage. Soulard was originally built to house the European immigrants who formed a key component of the city's nineteenth- and early-twentieth-century working class. However, mirroring a more general exodus from US cities, most of this population moved to the suburbs following World War II, and its built fabric was left to decay. The area was subsequently rediscovered as part of a back-to-the-city movement by a new, young population in the late 1960s and 1970s, who valued it for its multiethnic heritage. However, two groups within this population of largely white, middle-class returnees to the city were soon battling over issues such as the content of historic district legislation, the creation of infill public housing, and the scope and nature of city code-enforcement.

As the restoration of Soulard proceeded through the 1970s and 1980s, two different views emerged as to what constituted its heritage value, representing a cultural divide between 'yuppies' and 'hippies', respectively. As Cowan writes, 'the Soulard Restoration Group (SRG) reflected a nostalgic, bourgeois vision of re-inhabiting a multiethnic nineteenth-century urban village, and its members championed a purist preservation programme celebrating the neighbourhood's "French"-style row houses'. On the other hand, 'the Soulard Neighbourhood Improvement Association (SNIA) saw itself as preserving working-class culture and economic practices by protecting the interests of the neighbourhood's remaining ethnic immigrant population and more recent rural migrants'. As the process of Soulard's gentrification advanced, the divergence between the two groups became more pronounced. According to Cowan, the battles represented their view of heritage as primarily either a physical or social construct. To support their positions, the two groups advanced competing narratives of tradition to justify their claims as rightful heirs to its nineteenth-century built fabric and former ethnic, immigrant identity. Ultimately, Cowan writes, neither group was able to prevail completely in setting an agenda for the revitalization of the district. But its current residents, many of whom claim its diversity as a type of cultural capital, are unaware how this value was born out of decades of class conflict. These situated struggles 'concerned whose neighbourhood it really was, and who had the power to define how and for whom its history would be preserved'.

The next chapter, Jennifer Gaugler's 'Cosmopolitan Architects and Discourses of Tradition and Modernity in Post-Independence Africa', explores the work of several African architects who participated in attempts to construct a two-way dialogue between tradition and modernity in the years immediately following independence from colonial rule on the continent. The architects – Demas Nwoko in Nigeria, and Anthony

Almeida and Beda Amuli in Tanzania – used their cosmopolitan training in Europe, the US, and other developed nations to try to fashion modern buildings that reflected traditional African qualities. As Gaugler writes, their designs showed how, unlike conditions across much of the continent today, 'modernism in the post-independence period was *not* simply a Eurocentric diaspora – a linear flow from the West into the "Third World". It was a multifaceted conversation in which influence flowed in multiple directions'.

Gaugler recounts how a sense of cultural nationalism among Africans in the 1960s split into two competing views on the arts and architecture. 'One advocated that traditional buildings should be referenced as precedents for a new African architecture, while the other argued that, to move towards the future, traditional buildings should be left behind as remnants of the past'. As representatives of the former view, Nwoko, Almeida and Amuli, recognized that it was impossible to return to traditional construction practices; however, neither did they simply want to mimic imported modernist styles. Their approach would later be reflected in writings about critical regionalism. According to Gaugler, '[their approach] combined the native and imported in a way that allowed for growth and modernization, and it related back to traditional culture, but without relying on imitation or kitsch'. Today, this can be seen in such buildings as Nwoko's Akenzua Cultural Centre in Benin City, and Almeida's Central Library and Joint Christian Chapel and Amuli's Kariakoo Market in Dar es Salaam. Gaugler believes that the true success of such designs from the late 1960s and early 1970s came from their participation in a global dialogue which considered tradition and modernity 'not as a binary but as a dialectic'. However, in the years since, repressive political regimes, misinformed work by foreigners, and a desire to attract foreign capital have combined with other factors such as loss of respect for architecture as an important cultural practice to render such work a largely forgotten legacy. The result is the generic cityscape of many African cities today.

The last chapter in this section, Mark Gillem and Lyndsey Deaton's 'New Traditions of Placemaking in West-Central Africa', explores how the relatively new nations of west-central Africa have sought to establish themselves as respected players in the globalized economy, and how they have increasingly turned to China as a source of development aid. In China, they have found a partner willing to buy their abundant natural resources (in particular, oil) without questioning their often murky political systems. In return, China is currently 'building infrastructure to support resource extraction, and … erecting buildings to flatter visions of national grandeur'.

This essentially neocolonial oil-for-infrastructure development model provides China with essential inputs for its growing industrial economy, while boosting the fortunes of African elites by providing them with the trappings of modern society.

As Gillem and Deaton point out, the problem with this arrangement is that the current surge of high-profile new development in countries like Gabon, Angola, and the Republic of Congo is in many ways largely symbolic. Despite its association with the promise of modernity, the governments it supports remain rife with corruption and nepotism, as the benefits of resource extraction continue to support primarily a narrow ruling elite. Meanwhile, the promise of a middle class to fill the new residential districts and shiny office parks remains elusive without a broadening of local economic opportunity. Further, the opportunity for technology and skills transfer from the experience of constructing such spaces is also largely lost because the projects are mostly being designed, and even built, by foreign (primarily Chinese) companies. The evolution of oil-for-infrastructure currently driving such development thus provokes the question of whose tradition is being pursued in the construction of these new African states. In formal terms, the developments evince a symbolic modernism whose image is drawn from the shiny new hubs of international capitalism; but this is unrelated to existing local urban patterns or climatic concerns. And without an educated, economically engaged local population to occupy or benefit from them, they are unlikely to serve as agents of change for their underlying societies. The current oil-for-infrastructure model thus raises significant concerns about how tradition, modernity, and power are being constructed in west-central Africa.

Reflections

The book ends with two reflective pieces, one by Mike Robinson and another by Dell Upton. Robinson's chapter, 'The Agency of Belonging: Identifying and Inhabiting Tradition', engages in a comparison between a sense of 'home' and a sense of tradition. His aim is to point out how 'Over the years the discussion around tradition and the idea of the traditional has begun to move to a more flexible and discursive place that recognizes the subjectivity of its uses and the complexity of the environments it is used within'.

Upton's contribution, 'Process and Polemic', emphasizes how the very concept of a tradition is an attempt to pin down something that is inherently in flux. What is currently seen as tradition may thus better be understood as a process of adapting to changing social and environmental conditions, rather than establishing fixed markers of cultural identity. This is indeed the tradition of this globalized era, one whose nature and constituency are both fleeting and ever changing in a time whose history is always the present.

Part I

Place: Whose Nation, Whose City?

Chapter 1

Tradition and Its Aftermath: Jakarta's Urban Politics

Abidin Kusno

The question 'Whose tradition?' is one of authorship, subjectivity, and recognition of the work of intellectuals in the field of traditions. It also acknowledges the modernity of tradition, as contemporary practices are reworked or reconstituted to create ruptures with, or renew, older cultural regimes (AlSayyad, 2014). If the built environment is a representation of such work by social groups struggling for hegemony, then the question also recognizes it as an arena of contestation among different cultural agencies. In this chapter, I contribute to this discussion by looking at urban politics in Jakarta, where the local state, represented by a governor (often under pressure from different sections of the population), today has broad power to make decisions affecting urban form and life.

Urban politics are well known in Western societies, but the phenomenon has not, historically, been present everywhere, especially in Indonesia. Indeed, the Indonesian term for urban politics, *politik kota*, only emerged after the collapse of Suharto's authoritarian rule in 1998, because it was only then that the central government granted cities the power to determine their own policies and promote public participation through the election of governors and local councils. This point was made by Suryono Herlambang, a researcher of urban planning, in his introduction to *Politik Kota dan Hak Warga Kota* (*Urban Politics and the Rights of Urban Citizens*) (2006), a collection of newspaper essays from 2000 to 2006. With new laws guaranteeing regional autonomy, the direct election of local council members and governors, and a proliferation of critical commentary about daily life in the metropolitan press (*Kompas*), Herlambang asked, '[Has] urban politics … returned to the city?'

Since colonial times, a hierarchical tradition of central government prevented municipalities in Indonesia from gaining power over their own affairs. Decentralization, however, now means that local/city governments may make decisions that affect urban form and life. The new policy, which started after the end of Suharto's authoritarian regime, has also allowed local elections to choose the head of local government and with this a new style of local politics has emerged where an unexpected individual outside the circle of the political elites, could be elected governor. It has allowed, for instance, Joko Widodo (known as Jokowi) and Basuki Tjahaja Purnama (known as Ahok, and a member of the Christian Chinese minority), neither of whom had any previous connection to Jakarta, to become Governors of the city. The new policy has also given rise to new civic and democratic values which are often translated into populist politics and programmes such as 'good governance', the practice of which ranges from transparency and accountability to free bus travel and free health care. Urban politics thus has become more popular than national politics as the city has replaced the state as the arena for the representations of popular values. While it may still be difficult to separate the effects of municipal from national decision-making (especially in the capital of Jakarta), as disputes surface regularly over authorities, jurisdictions, and competencies, urban politics nevertheless are now an essential part of life in Indonesia and have come to play an increasing role in the production of space.

Any new configuration of political practices, however, also entails an invention of tradition, as well as disputes over 'Whose tradition?'. To explore these issues, I will focus on a particular period in the history of Jakarta: the Jokowi-Ahok era. This began when Joko 'Jokowi' Widodo was elected governor in 2012, and it has continued through the term of his successor, Basuki 'Ahok' Purnama.[1] Yet, while I use the policies of Jokowi and Ahok as a main frame of reference, the chapter's focus (including its temporal frame) is not intended to limit discussion. Indeed, as far as the themes of this book are concerned, I hope to raise the issue of how a new agent of social order may create entirely new claims to tradition in the production of the built environment (in this case, in a place where most important economic and political decisions were once made at a national, or even an international, level).

Further, the chapter is not intended to document, either comprehensively or in detail, the dynamics of the whole era. It simply seeks to tease out some components of urban politics to encourage further research, not only on the given timeframe but also on the increasingly important role of urban politics in (Southeast) Asian societies. As urban politics becomes a new site for the production of cultural hegemony and physical form in the region, there is much to learn from the way Jokowi and Ahok have sought to constitute a new tradition of urban politics. In particular, I will show how the two men have legitimized their rule through a 'politics of time', which has problematized previous political practices.

Mental Revolution

On 10 May 2014, the then-presidential candidate Jokowi outlined a vision for how he would lead the country in the next 5 years, if elected:

The reforms implemented in Indonesia since the fall of Suharto's New Order regime in 1998 were merely directing towards an institutional revamp. None has yet focused on the paradigm, mindset, or the culture of politics in Indonesia in the context of nation-building. In order for a meaningful and sustainable change to take into effect, and in accordance with Indonesia's Proclamation of Independence ... a mental revolution is much required ... there is still a large number of traditions (*tradisi*) or a kind of culture (*budaya*) that is evolving and growing rapidly creating repression as in the New Order. These range from corruption, intolerance of differences, greed, selfishness, a tendency to use violence in problem solving, legal harassment, and opportunism. These are still going on, with some growing more rampant... It is time for Indonesia to take corrective action ... by imposing a mental revolution which creates a new paradigm, political culture, and nation-building approach which is more humane, suitable to the Nusantara cultural traits, easy and coherent... The use of the term 'revolution' is not excessive. This is because Indonesia needs a breakthrough in its political culture to wholesomely put an end to all the bad practices that have long been left to spread since the era of the New Order till the present... I have started this movement when leading Surakarta and since 2012 as the Governor of Jakarta... *Insya Allah* [God willing], this effort will develop further and expand to become a truly national movement as mandated by Bung Karno [a reference to Sukarno, the first President of Indonesia], as the revolution itself has not ended. Indonesian Mental Revolution has just begun.[2]

I quote this statement at length because it indicates how the term 'mental revolution' became a manifesto for Jokowi's presidential campaign. It also shows clearly how the need for such a 'mental revolution' was defined by the practices of its enemies – that is, by those who profited from traditions that flourished during the repressive era of the New Order (and which still remain). Jokowi was suggesting that only after Indonesians combated these traditions could they restore 'the original character of the nation', which he defined as '*santun, berbudi pekerti, ramah dan bergotong royong*' (*Kompas*, 2014). These words are impossible to translate accurately, but they suggest everything that is good, from 'grace' and 'kindness' to 'mutual help'. Of course, Indonesians intrinsically know that if one can be all these things, one will have no enemies. But what is important here is that these are terms for human relations, which, in the language of governance, refer to an ideal relation between the ruler and the ruled.

During his campaign, Jokowi also occasionally used the term 'corruption', and related it to mentality and traditions. While it is not easy to unravel the relation between *tradisi* and *sikap mental* (mental attitude), Jokowi has argued that a corrupt work ethic evolved under the former regime into a *tradisi* (tradition) and *budaya* (culture). Any Indonesian bureaucrat would likely acknowledge that corruption is wrong, and that it is often caused by a wrong *sikap mental* (Server, 1996; Smith, 1971). But Jokowi was in effect explaining that corruption, collusion, and nepotism had taken root in the nation because they had grown into a tradition and culture.[3] For Jokowi, a tradition may be formed over time, and when it is allowed to run as deep as in Indonesia under the New Order, a *'revolusi mental'* is needed to uproot it.

Jokowi has thus sought to combat the New Order's traditions – that is, the whole practice associated broadly with corruption. It may be useful here to note that Jokowi's vision, or mission, is consistent with the populism that has marked the politics of Southeast Asia since the financial crisis of the late 1990s and the collapse of authoritarian regimes in many parts of the region (Mizuno and Phongpaichit, 2009). 'Populist politics' – as one can learn, for instance, from Ernesto Laclau (2005) – are based on two propositions (Anderson, 2009). First is the sense that a society ought to be based on the principle of equality – an idea similar to that of the nation. For Jokowi, this is represented by the 'original character' of the nation, attained through a quest for what he understands as 'balanced development'. Second, the force of a populist movement is based on its opposition to an enemy, which, in the case of Jokowi, is represented by the former New Order regime. Jokowi's war against the legacy of Suharto, then, must be understood as taking place not only at the level of performance but, more substantially, at the level of mentality – of culture and traditions. The question of 'Whose tradition?' thus lies at the centre of politics in Jakarta and Indonesia today.

It is useful also to recognize that the traditions Jokowi seeks to combat to restore the nation's mentality are associated with conditions of 'informality' developed in both state and civil society. Nezar AlSayyad and Ananya Roy (2004) conceptualized informality as a 'mode', a 'modality', a 'method', and a 'way of being' that governs the life of cities in both developed countries and the Global South. In so doing, they raised two important points.

First, they called attention to informality as a practice involving both the ruler and the ruled, the elite and the underclass. In terms of the built environment, informality thus covers both shantytowns and upper-class gated compounds, for both are based on violations, such as of land-use regulations. This means the relevant conceptual divide needs to be revised as 'not between formality and informality but rather [as] a differentiation *within* informality' (Roy, 2005, p. 149). Second, AlSayyad claimed that informality may be produced by the state. And in this sense, the range of informality can be stretched to include the list of terms identified by Jokowi as *traditions* of Suharto's regime: 'corruption, intolerance of differences, greed, selfishness, a tendency to use violence in problem solving, legal harassment, and opportunism'. Jokowi's 'mental revolution' thus is a call for a direction opposite to, or different from, the traditions of informality of the Suharto era.

For the sake of analysis, I have repacked the list Jokowi has identified as traditions of the Suharto era (which continue today) in the following section as five urban traditions of informality – each of which is governed and performed by different social groups.

The Five Traditions of Urban Politics

The Oligarchic Tradition

In one of the very few works on urban governance in Jakarta, Manasse Malo and Peter Nas (1996) described (at the height of Suharto's authoritarian regime) the workings of power in the city as follows:

> The most important groups operating in the Jakarta urban arena are central and local administration, the military, the business community, and the common people. The military and the administration form one governmental strategic group that is very dominant in administrative affairs and urban planning. The business community, including the banks, industry, and large developers also has strategic resources at its disposal, and in co-operation with the government strategic group it effectively determines the development of Jakarta by the construction of offices, malls and houses. (Malo and Nas, 1996, p. 130)

Malo and Nas indicated that these three elements – business groups, the state, and the military – determined the development of Jakarta, because they possessed the power to shape the city. The city, then, was not simply run by business groups, because the military colluded with the head of state to make sure there were businesses and assets to share. It should therefore be possible to understand much of the city's history during this period by researching the actions (or collaborations) of these three groups (Cowherd, 2002; Leaf, 1991). Such an investigation would surely also uncover a story of urban informality as conducted by the elites. This is the very tradition that Jokowi wishes to overcome, for corruption, legal harassment, and using force to settle matters are clearly products of this elite alliance.

This emphasis on the power of the elites in the work of Malo and Nas is understandable, as the object of their analysis is the authoritarian state.[4] They thus assume that power operates only top-down. Yet, by focusing only on an elite coalition behind the transformation of space in the city, they overlook a peculiar (or not so peculiar?) tradition of Indonesian politics – namely, the role of middlemen, often operating as thugs (*preman*), shadowy officials (*oknum*), and brokers (*perantara*). These individuals or groups operate as a hinge between the top and the bottom, and their authority in many cases is 'subcontracted' to them by the powerful to administer to the common people at the local level (Onghokham, 2003; Simone, 2014).

The Subcontracted Tradition

Contrary to dominant perception (as represented by Malo and Nas), the city of Jakarta has never been completely run from the top. Such a perception typically relies on an obsession with the central power of the state to integrate the urban population to achieve unity (*manunggal*) (a concept I will discuss later). But it is equally important to note that power in Jakarta is commonly subcontracted to civilian organizations, civilian militias, local leaders, or headmen (Barker, 1999; Lindsey, 2001; Ryter, 1998). Indeed, these micro-powers are a 'necessary component in the maintenance of state power and the collection of taxes' (Barker, 1999, p. 122).

Subcontracted power moves within the structure of governance and may take many forms – as in the figures mentioned above. Such figures may appear to act with relative autonomy, even though they are tied to, or harnessed by, powerful groups and the ruling elite. Just such a situation was reported in a newspaper story from the time of Suharto describing a case of land dealing that involved developers, state agencies, local *oknum*, and independent '*preman*' brokers:

It appears that brokers have established very close working relationships with local officials. In addition to supplying information, such officials help establish the 'legitimacy' of the broker... In the case of disputes or uncertainty about ownership, these same officials are called upon to resolve the problem. They are not uninterested parties in such matters, since the fees and commissions they receive for witnessing land transactions and other services are a significant part of their income. (*Jakarta Post*, 1990)

Local elements thus operate as contractors or subcontractors to the ruling groups, maintaining and shaping order at the local level. Yet they do not necessarily work together, as each has its own discursive domain. And they may further subcontract their tasks to even more local organizations, to the point that the originating centre of power may have little idea what is going on at the local level. The city, then, may accommodate many players, many brokers, and many deals with or without direct acknowledgement by the central government. This may be seen as an example of the decentralized 'patron–client' political tradition of Southeast Asia (Scott, 1972), or the 'one-and-the-many' authority of Indonesia (Reid, 1998).

This form of decentralized tradition can be traced back to the precolonial era (Onghokham, 2003). Indeed, as a 'tradition', it was appropriated and nurtured by the colonial administration, which had run into problems governing the societies it had conquered. Under the Suharto regime, patron–client relationships took a more direct form. It was thus quite common for the Suharto government to subcontract with thugs or civilian militias to control the *rakyat* (common people). The government also subcontracted with loosely organized civilian and youth groups, such as Pemuda Pancasila (shown in the documentary *The Act of Killing*), to terrorize specific communities for political and commercial gain (Ryter, 1998). These organizations appeared to be both inside and outside the military; they were civilians, yet they were also connected to the state apparatus to form the 'New Order Racket state' (Wilson, 2010; Lindsey, 2001).

To sum up, a 'tradition' of decentralized power developed in Jakarta and Indonesia over a long period of time, continuously being reinvented as a mode of governance. This tradition survived the collapse of the Suharto regime, yet its many layers have now splintered into fragments. The paramilitary civil organizations of the Suharto era, for instance, have become freelancers looking for new contracts, while new groups have been invented. There are thus many more *preman* today, who continue to control the streets – for example, providing security for street vendors. Such figures can operate independently, or they can be supported by politicians and business groups. Yet it is precisely this tradition of power sharing, strategic alliances, and subcontracting that has sustained the oligarchic tradition.

Closely connected to this tradition of subcontracted power is another tradition, located in the bureaucracy, known as *pungli pungutan liar* (illegal fee extortion) or *korupsi* (corruption).

The Bureaucratic Tradition

'Corruption' has long been considered a tradition of Indonesian bureaucracy.[5] Historians have traced it back through the colonial and precolonial eras to what is known as the era of kingdoms (for Java, this would include the Hindu-Buddhist Majapahit, the Islamic Mataram, and other sultanates) (Onghokham, 2003).

During this time, no civil servant of the kingdom (of any rank, from minister to district head to guard) received a salary (*Ibid.*). Instead, their income derived from their right to collect taxes and receive tribute from the common people.[6] This practice of making commoners cover the living expenses of civil servants prevailed down to the level of local government and the household. Thus, the staff or servants of a district head would accept 'fees', or a certain percentage (*persenan*), from those who needed their services. As far as the *rakyat* were concerned, every man in the bureaucracy was a tax collector, and they were much disliked (*Ibid.*). In modern times, such dislike has been expressed by the term *pungli* (extortion).

One consequence of this tradition within the contemporary bureaucracy is that it costs almost nothing to appoint new staff, because individual positions have no (or little) salary implications. In fact, it may be beneficial to appoint new staff, because each such position may be sold to its new occupant. For individual bureaucrats, the ultimate goal is to buy a position with good prospects for receiving tributes or fees. 'Money politics' – to buy access and position – is thus recognized as a tradition.[7] To the extent that corruption continues today, then, it has much to do with the fact that civil servant salaries are too low. But the continuance of such practices also relies on the assumption of extortion as a tradition.

This is certainly not a tradition that is popular among the common people. How do they react to it?

The Rakyat Tradition

As a capital city, Jakarta concentrates many things, including wealth and power; and it is precisely this quality that continues to make it attractive to migrants. A large percentage of Jakarta's contemporary population belongs to a social group Malo and Nas (1996) identified as the *rakyat* or *wong cilik* (common people). Yet, they rightly describe this group as powerless, because 'migrants who settle on empty space are not organized and do not promote common plans' (*Ibid.*, p. 130). Nonetheless, the *rakyat* are important because they are a majority, and because they are simply too numerous and diverse to control effectively. Governments, from precolonial to colonial to postcolonial times, have had a hard time administering this 'urban majority' (Simone, 2014). Such efforts are further hampered by unresolved issues of who the *rakyat* are, where they come from, and what they are doing – all of which translate into questions of control.

The *rakyat* are further important because their relationship with the ruler is supposed to embody a particular and historically important ideology, referred to in the Javanese language as *kawula gusti*. The *rakyat*, too, are the foundation of Indonesian nationalism. The ideal of any Indonesian government is thus to achieve *manunggaling kawula gusti*: the union of the one and the many (or the ruler and the ruled). In practice, this means the submission of the subjects to the ruler, who, in turn, must commit himself to advancing their interests. Failure to achieve this relationship would result in the ruler losing the divine authority (*wahyu*) that underlies sovereign power.

All Indonesian governments have sought to achieve union with the *rakyat*. Consider, for example, Sukarno's '*penyambung lidah rakyat*' ('the tongue of people') or Suharto's '*dwi tunggal*' ('two and yet one'). The populist 'pro-*rakyat*' programmes of the post-Suharto era are essentially another attempt to bring the government and the *rakyat* back into a *kawula-gusti* relation. Thus, as Jokowi has said, 'Fixing the life of the marginal will give a positive atmosphere to the life in the center' (Endah, 2012, pp. 189–190). All leadership concepts include the *rakyat*, as attending to it constitutes the moral economy of the state.

The moral economy of the state – a concept Jokowi has distilled as 'the poor should be helped' – has been a notion widely shared by previous rulers, but it has gained new prominence in the era of populist politics. The *rakyat* share this understanding, and know (or at least the elites fear they *might* know) when power is being abused. Signs of disintegrating power can take many forms, from economic to environmental to political crises, but they are all read as a general cultural crisis (often understood as *zaman edan* [a time of madness]).[8] As an essentially powerless group, the *rakyat* had few options when confronted with such a situation. But historically (and arguably also today), the *rakyat* simply fled when they felt oppressed, making flight a form of protest.[9] Alternatively, the *rakyat* could resist by not listening to a ruler's order, or they could pretend not to understand, or to misrecognize, his commands.

Ignoring power is a familiar action of the *rakyat*, often associated with a particular vocabulary. The intent here is to give authority a headache, and its articulation is associated with words such as *nekat* (taking risks), *keras kepala* (stubborn), *anarkis* (anarchic), and *dan tunggal* (autonomous). These are all terms used by the ruling class to describe situations in which the subaltern expresses a desire not to be governed. Here, the performance of informality (as a violation of law) by the underclass is conditioned by the *rakyat*'s idea about the nature of power and its applications. The *rakyat* thus invents a tradition of resistance within its own perception of power.[10] Therefore, in a period of political transition such as during a power vacuum or an economic crisis, the *rakyat* may become *mobokrasi*, a term for anarchism and disregard for social norms. The reciprocal view, however, is of the state as irresponsible and having failed in its obligation to improve the life of the people.[11]

The Kampung *Tradition*

The fifth tradition (more directly related to the study of the built environment) involves the vast area of the city called the *kampung* – often (mis)translated as the 'urban-village'. The *kampung* may be seen as an expression of the informality of the life of the *rakyat*, but it may also be conceptualized as a product of the state and the capital in externalizing the cost of housing. In other words, the *kampung* can be seen as the spatial expression of informality that involves the state, the capital, and society at large. A simple statement by an Indonesian bureaucrat, in 1991, captured well the complicity of the state and the capital in the production of *kampung*; without it, he said, '(formal) workers would simply be unable to survive on the level of salary they are receiving' (Wirosardjono, 1991, p. 61).

In the *kampung* there is a great mix of land tenure, some of which is considered illegal. There is informal leadership (the platform for exercising subcontracted power) and a mix of urban and rural practices. It is also a 'space of tradition', often misinterpreted as a 'space of transition'. Thus, the complex presence of the *kampung* has routinely been dismissed by policy-makers as something that will eventually disappear or become gentrified (by way of gradual land certification) into formalized housing. Yet some scholars argue that the *kampung* is a permanent feature of Indonesian cities – one that existed prior to colonialism, and that will continue to exist even after the end of the capitalist world economy. Whatever the case, the *kampung* characterizes the city as a 'big village', and this is not a condition modernizers wish to celebrate.

Consider for a moment Georg Simmel's 'The Metropolis and the Mental Life' (1971[1903]) and Louis Wirth's 'Urbanism as a Way of Life' (1938). These two classic essays characterized the city in terms of its density, heterogeneity, and anonymity – qualities the authors saw as offering the experience, simultaneously, of individual liberation and alienation. In a place like Jakarta, however, the contrast between city and countryside is not as clear. Jakarta is filled with a variety of *kampungs*, where rural traditions are still found, and where the dominant cultural attitudes and socialization patterns are associated with the countryside. Indeed, one can say that migrants to Jakarta may find in the *kampung* components of their former rural lives.[12]

The *kampung* thus serves to moderate alienation and conflict, as well as gradually to socialize rural folk to urban conditions. Thus, while the state and the capital may seem to want to demolish the *kampung*, they are really more intent on maintaining it as a space of exception (to a certain point) – as far as it benefits them. All governments see the *kampung* ambiguously, for they see in it the *rakyat* (or the labour) they need. And they see a space in which to resolve housing problems (through the residents' own cheap labour) and other urban conflicts – even as they (very slowly) try to modernize it.

Overcoming Traditions?

I have spent much of this chapter attempting to describe some of the informal urban traditions of Jakarta – both those of the elite and those of the common people. These traditions have a long history as a modality of life, which became well developed under the oligarchic regime of Suharto. Jokowi and Ahok's urban programmes can be seen as a critical response to these traditions – some of which produced 'corruption, law violation and opportunism'. I will next outline some of the urban programmes (associated with the idea of 'mental revolution') that they have advocated as part of their populist agenda.[13]

Prior to the tenure of Jokowi and Ahok as governors of Jakarta, city hall was seen as the embodiment of an old, bureaucratic apparatus operated behind closed doors by the elite. Today, it is seen as a place open to public scrutiny. This is largely due to initiatives of Governor Ahok (who took over from Jokowi in 2014 after Jokowi was appointed President of Indonesia).

As governor, Ahok has brought a performance-based managerial style to the municipality and insisted that city governance be conducted in public. To enhance transparency and accountability, he has occasionally recorded and uploaded videos of meetings with staff and city council members to YouTube – a decision applauded by the public. He has transformed the municipality from being a haven for corrupt and lazy staff through a new emphasis on competitive performance; cut the number of middle-ranking officials by 20 per cent and streamlined departments for efficiency; instituted an open-recruitment process that requires civil servants to compete for the limited positions in each office; and rewarded the meritorious while firing unproductive department heads and staff. Such bureaucratic downsizing has already saved millions of dollars, which Ahok has used to raise allowances for productive officials. He has also eliminated budget mark-ups and ineffective programmes and streamlined project proposals and reports. And he has replaced cash transactions with bank transfers, to ensure proper accounting. Together, such reforms (influenced by a neoliberal work ethic) have minimized the practices of extortion and corruption that were part of the old bureaucratic tradition. Under Ahok and Jokowi it has become increasingly difficult for city hall to continue the tradition of 'business as usual'. Their reformation of city hall has placed municipal government *under the public gaze*, where it may serve as an agent of change and a site for the invention of a new tradition. The governor thus has retained strong popular support – in large measure because of his anti-corruption stance and his ability to reform bureaucratic culture.

This drama of bureaucratic reform is regularly reported on by the media, making city hall one of the most interesting spectacles in Jakarta. Residents have followed the disciplining of public servants and become fascinated by stories of resistance among the old guard. City hall is thus seen as embodying a kind of hope, precisely because its bureaucratic tradition is being shaken, scrutinized, and reformed. Thus, although Ahok and Jokowi's reforms may be primarily explained as an anti-corruption drive and an exercise of 'mental revolution', they have also created a new image for city hall. Such measures, we should note, have slighted some senior bureaucrats and politicians as well as business groups who have been benefitting from the old tradition. It is reasonable to imagine that they wish Ahok would not be re-elected so that the old tradition could be restored.

The new administration has likewise registered its presence on the street. Ahok and Jokowi have targeted the much disliked *preman* and challenged their domination of the streets. The power of the *preman*, as discussed above, embodies the tradition of subcontracting on which oligarchic power has relied. Like bureaucratic culture, it has a long history and is not easily discarded; nevertheless, city government must deal with it if it is to register its influence on the *rakyat*. Toward this end, Ahok has sought to remove patronage control over street vendors by relocating them to proper buildings and marketplaces. The municipality also plans to build more shopping malls for vendors and revitalize traditional markets. In these efforts, the city has tried to make clear that its enemy is not the vendor. Following the humane approach Jokowi introduced when he served as mayor of Solo, the Jakarta administration has attempted to befriend vendors. It has repaired their carts (or offered them new ones), while providing permits to operate at no cost. By removing the influence of the *preman*, and thus undermining the subcontracting tradition, Jokowi and Ahok have sought to bring the *rakyat* back into the government fold. This may be seen as populist politics, but it may also be interpreted as a necessary step to achieve *kemanunggalan kawula gusti* (unification of the ruler and the ruled).

Finally, to win the hearts of *kampung* folk, Jokowi and Ahok have launched a number of other programmes. Among these is the issuance of Jakarta Health Cards (Kartu Jakarta Sehat [KJS]) and Jakarta Education Cards (Kartu Jakarta Pintar [KJP]) to enable access by the poor to health care and education. And since the beginning of the Jokowi-Ahok tenure, some thirty-eight *kampung* locations have been designated as sites for the construction of new, decent *per-kampung-an* (settlements with a *kampung* environment). The Kampung Deret Program, as it is called, envisions a wide-ranging reconstruction and renovation of existing low-income settlements. In Jokowi's words:

The *kampung* residents should have a clean public space. Their neighbourhoods should have good sanitation, good septic tank system, good streets, and good green space... How beautiful it would be if in the slum-like *kampung* of Cilincing, we could build centres for the arts, spaces for IT, small libraries, and parks, among others. (Endah, 2012, pp. 189, 191)

This may sound like a middle-class dream for the underclass. Furthermore, as part of the effort, the governor has said he is willing to give tenure and certification to some lands informally occupied by *kampung* dwellers. Yet, as part of the modernization effort, *kampung* traditions will be both assumed and simultaneously transformed. Thus, while the re-enactment of traditions may give a sense of continuity and improvement, it also makes possible the relocation of the urban poor (including the recent violence associated with the eviction of communities in Kampung Pulo) to new low-rise *kampung deret* (row villages), *kampung susun* (elevated villages), and high-rise rental apartments.

Ultimately, the new *kampung* programme is set up in favour of change – but not without limit. For example, it requires the city to classify *kampung* into different categories. According to Sita W. Dewi in the *Jakarta Post* (2014), the Jakarta Housing and Administrative Buildings Agency identified '392 community units across the capital ... [as] slum areas', and estimated that '50 percent of the capital's population of 10 million are ... low income or poor'. Yet he also cautioned that 'houses built on riverbanks or public roads' would not be eligible for renovation funding (*Ibid.*).

Categories come with the power to exclude, but those who are eligible for slum-upgrading initiatives will have no choice but to reckon with the governor's desire to formalize and transform existing *kampung*. In keeping with Ahok and Jokowi's aspiration to modernize and formalize housing in Jakarta (a consistent policy among all governors to date), the same news report cited a gubernatorial decree that every private developer acquiring a plot larger than 5,000 square metres must allocate 20 per cent of new building space for affordable housing. Meanwhile, it reported that the Housing and Administrative Buildings Agency was compiling a list of city properties that could be developed into low-cost apartments (even though such accommodation may be unsuitable to *kampung* traditions).

Ultimately, by the end of Ahok's term in 2017, the city administration's aim is no less than to achieve 'Jakarta without slums'. On the one hand, this can be seen as reflecting UN Habitat's 'Cities without Slums' campaign. But it is also inseparable from Ahok's desire to transform Suharto's traditions of urban politics, within which the *kampung* played an important part. From eradicating corruption in local government to integrating the *rakyat* through housing, the new municipal programmes seek to dissolve the legacy of informality that characterized Jakarta during the previous era.

This rationale likewise underpins Ahok's obsession with rules, permissions, and the formal registration of all Jakarta residents. The ultimate representation of this are plans for a Jakarta One Card, which would contain comprehensive information about its holder, from family ties to work and financial status. Through this single card, Ahok would not only ensure legitimacy for workers in the informal sector but also resolve questions of who the *rakyat* are, where they come from, what they are doing, and how to control them. And while this move can be interpreted as creating urban citizens, it can also be seen as seeking to overturn the *rakyat* tradition of fleeing from power.

The populist policies of the Jokowi-Ahok administration are intended to show how the poor were mistreated or poorly served in the past, not because they were less fortunate, but because they formerly lived according to unjust traditions created in part by the government. They also intend to show that no one need be marginalized within a new tradition that seeks to distribute the fruits of development to all (even as some have been forcibly evicted from *kampung* along the riverside). The administration similarly believes that when the lower class is cared for, and when its needs are assumed to be not that different from those of the middle class, Jakarta will be freed from anxiety over the possibility of class rage and envy.

Politics of Time

The question of 'whose traditions' is intimately related to politics of time. Much of the politics sketched out thus far, at root, entail criticism of certain practices of Indonesian political culture reified under the previous regime of Suharto. Yet the time of Jokowi and Ahok is also the time of neoliberal populism, in which moving fast is crucial to the legitimization of their electoral success. This performative time, while different from the time of 'order and stability' characteristic of the previous regime, delineates certain priorities. Specifically, these emphasize projects strategically identified as capable of speedy completion and quick results, even as they might not present the entire solution to problems.

The administrations of Jokowi and Ahok came to power at a time when the city was highly divided and the nation was in the grip of powerful oligarchs. They arrived at the height of urban informality – when city government, political parties, private developers, urban residents, and bureaucratic elites ruled by means of corruption, greed, selfishness, law violation, and opportunism. Had the city continued on this course, it could have exploded into violent conflict. Even the old forces seemed to know that new leadership and a different urban imaginary were needed (at least temporarily or symbolically) to stabilize conditions in the city. It has been in this context that Jokowi and Ahok – neither with previous ties to big business, the military, or elite families – have sought to relieve pressures and articulate a new urban agenda. Thus, while Jokowi and Ahok have sought to combat Suharto-era traditions and pursue a path of genuine reform, they have also played a stabilizing role.

Considering this situation, one could claim that the city's traditions of informality (especially the oligarchic and militaristic ones) are simply too deep to uproot, and that all Jokowi and Ahok have done is innovate *within* the reach of the old order. For instance, Ahok has made considerable effort to harness private developers to put aside a certain percentage of their assets and profits for the city government to build low-cost apartments and public facilities. He is willing to issue permits, as in the case of the land reclamation project in North Jakarta, as long as the developers are willing to share its profit with the city even though such a project is considered as ecologically unsustainable. His view that capitalism should be allowed to prosper in Jakarta as long as its profit is shared with the city recalls a legacy of Suharto's regime. To defend North Jakarta's land reclamation project, Ahok thus refers to the legal document set up by Suharto's 1995 Presidential Decree regardless of the fact that the decree was established with the explicit purpose of accumulating capital for Suharto's own families and cronies.

Furthermore, Ahok's aspiration for a 'Jakarta without slums' is only part of a larger urban 'beautification' agenda which includes not only efforts to prevent flooding but also to relocate the urban poor to what he considers proper housing (i.e. non-*kampung* low-cost apartments). And in pursuit of these goals, Ahok has shown no hesitation in forcibly evicting residents from riverbank neighbourhoods and relocating them in high-rise apartments. Indeed, the manner in which evictions have been conducted – with a thousand-strong security force armed with tear gas, water cannons, and riot gear – recalls the era of authoritarianism.

So what appears new may soon become old; the 'new traditions' established under Jokowi and Ahok could be negated, displaced, or crushed, not least by traditional forces. Ahok's tenure ends in October 2017, and there have been more than murmurs that his legacy is not secure. The recent massive protest by Islamic hardliners against Ahok (who is charged with insulting Islam and is now on trial for blasphemy) is an indication of just how vulnerable Ahok's position can be. The incident can be seen as a gift for politicians vying against Ahok's new urban politics. Should Ahok fail to be re-elected, Jakarta's next governor will no doubt once again raise the question of 'Whose tradition?' The arrival of a new administration could lead either to a furthering of the Jokowi-Ahok legacy or a retrieval of New Order-like traditions of urban politics.

In Indonesia, the granting of power by the state to cities has created a groundswell for reimagining traditions. And this chapter has raised the question whether urban identity can be formed on the basis of citizen participation in politics. Benedict Anderson (1991) never theorized the location of his 'imagined communities'. He thus left open the question of whether such a collective identity could be popularly formed in a city – where 'urban imaginaries', in Andreas Huyysen's (2008, p. 3) words, 'differ depending on a multitude of perspectives and subject positions'. Through a focus on the populist programmes of the last two governors of Jakarta, this chapter has suggested that urban politics may serve as a site for the formation and contestation of urban-based 'imagined communities' – and along with them, new claims to traditionality and new investments of meaning in the built form of the city.

Notes

1. Joko Widodo served 2 years as Governor of Jakarta before becoming Pesident of Indonesia in 2014. When he departed, he was replaced by the Vice Governor, Basuki 'Ahok' Purnama, whose term will end in 2017.
2. Joko Widodo, 'Indonesian Mental Revolution', first published in *Kompas*, 10 May 2014, as 'Revolusi Mental'. Available at: http://nasional.kompas.com/read/2014/05/10/1603015/revolusi.mental. The English version was posted on 20 May 2014. Available at: http://www.establishmentpost.com/indonesia-mental-revolution/.
3. Joko Widodo: 'korupsi, kolusi, nepotisme, etos kerja tidak baik, bobroknya birokrasi, hingga ketidaksiplinan. Kondisi itu dibiarkan selama bertahun-tahun dan pada akhirnya hadir di setiap sendi bangsa'. Available at: http://nasional.kompas.com/read/2014/10/17/22373441/Jokowi.dan.Arti.Revolusi.Mental.
4. Malo and Nas (1996) did not mention the 'middle class', and they did not see much difference between the central and local government. They were just teasing out a tradition of urban governance peculiar (or maybe not so peculiar) to a city like Jakarta.
5. *Pungli* and *korupsi* (extortion and corruption) are major keywords in Indonesia today. Indonesians all remember that the stepping down of Suharto was accompanied by rallies against KKN (*kolusi, korupsi, and nepotisme*) (collusion, corruption, and nepotism), which refer to the oligarchic tradition of the government.
6. If a particular servant impressed the king, he might be paid with lands and farms. But the kingdom did not generally seek to control how its agents generated income as long as they continued to produce tribute for the king. This system of low salary but high income through extortion sustained the kingdom (Onghokham, 2003).
7. When the colonial state was established in the nineteenth century, its first governor-general instituted a salary system based on rank. However, in practice, illegal extortion continued, especially by local chiefs, because their salaries were not high enough to cover the need to maintain extended patron–client networks. Below the level of the regents (*bupati*), extortion thus continued. However, small corruptors and their petty corruptions/extortions (below the *bupati* level) were often caught and punished by the colonial state (Onghokham, 2003).
8. One can think of how people in Jakarta, or in Indonesia generally, have learned to doubt the power of the state to distribute fairly the necessities of life. They may even have learned to doubt the location of power if experience tells them that local chieftains and thugs (*preman*) are more important to their daily lives than the government. Thus, historically, they may have learned that the government is powerless without the help of local chieftains or civil leaders – including the thugs who often appear to rule without supervision or control. Knowing the government was unreliable and that they couldn't trust thugs, they informally and continuously set up their own (temporary) networks to cope with the conditions of uncertainty – a condition that often found expression in the built environment.
9. Malo and Nas (1996, p. 130) described the *rakyat* as 'the common people ... the

migrants who settle on empty space (and) ... are not organized and do not promote common plans'. But they did not describe why they were not organized and have no common plan. It is also generally accepted that organized protests and rallies on the streets or in front of government buildings have not been part of the *rakyat* tradition – even as NGOs and middle-class activists have hailed the importance of street protests, especially since the fall of Suharto. Instead, street protests or riots, organized under the name of the *rakyat*, are understood to represent cases of the *rakyat* being used, bought, or appropriated by powerful groups for political gain. In any case, the politics of the *rakyat* cannot be formalized under the concept of a 'right to the city'. This doesn't mean that the *rakyat* do not care about the context of their struggle to work and live in the city, but they have their own way of doing politics.

10. The *rakyat* seem to invent their traditions of action in relation to the 'looseness in the centre', or the disappearance of the state – a condition in which the face of the state is not clear, or in which its political culture cannot be grasped. The other condition in which action by the *rakyat* may arise is when the state (to make itself present or legitimize its power) oppresses the *rakyat* through evictions and violence. These two conditions – emphasizing alternatively the absence or presence of the state – may be responded to by anarchy and disobedience.

11. But what kind of situation is likely to stimulate such behaviours? The context for such behaviour, one could speculate, may be recognition that the moral economy of the state (since independence) has been based on an aspiration to achieve social justice for the *rakyat* (*keadilan sosial bagi seluruh rakyat Indonesia*), and that any deviation from this mission would result in resistance. Related to this is a sense of uncertainty. In his work on Jakarta, AbdouMaliq Simone (2014) described this condition of uncertainty as a stage for acts that give at least a sense of certainty: building a house on occupied land, building a mosque, forming an identity-based group, and so on. One could add the restoration of selfhood, which often implies a condition of not being governed.

12. The city's connection to the village also takes place in the practice of *mudik*, an annual returning to the village during the Ramadhan New Year. *Mudik* combines the words *mulih* (healing) and *udik* (village), implying a return to the village for healing, before moving back to the city. The notion of healing here suggests a recovery and acceptance of one's rural roots after a whole year of struggling in a city characterized by density, heterogeneity, and (relative) anonymity (yet a place that nevertheless offers opportunities for progress). *Mudik* is an important annual event, invented by migrants, and it has become a central way to register the presence of the village in the minds of urban folk. *Mudik* has replaced circular (or seasonal) migration (*perantauan musiman*), which was more common in the past when farmers went to the city to work while waiting for the planting and harvest season in the village. The current condition therefore does not suggest a world of linear time and space, as suggested by the term 'urbanization'. The city of Jakarta has a great mix of rural and urban patterns of tradition.

13. Data from the section below are based on a variety of 'middle-class' metropolitan newspapers and journal reports.

References

AlSayyad, N. (2004) Urban informality as a 'new' way of life, in AlSayyad, N. and Roy, A. (eds.) *Urban Informality: Transnational Perspectives from the Middle East, South Asia and Latin America*. Lanham, MD: Lexington Books, pp. 7–30.

AlSayyad, N. (2014) *Traditions: The 'Real', the Hyper, and the Virtual in the Built Environment*. London: Routledge.
Anderson, B. (1991) *Imagined Communities*. London: Verso (revised edition).
Anderson, B. (2009) Afterword, in Mizuno, K. and Phongpaichit, P. (eds.) *Populism in Asia*. Honolulu: Hawaii University Press, pp. 217–220.
Barker, J. (1999) Surveillance and territoriality in Bandung, in Rafael, V. (ed.) *Figures of Criminality in Indonesia, the Philippines and Colonial Vietnam*. Ithaca, NY: Cornell University, pp. 95–127.
Cowherd, R. (2002) Cultural Construction of Jakarta: Design, Planning and Development in Jabotabek, 1980–1997. PhD dissertation, Department of Architecture, MIT.
Dewi, S.W. (2012) Jakarta administration aiming to clear all slum housing by 2017. *Jakarta Post*, 21 November. Available at: http://www.thejakartapost.com/news/2014/11/21/jakarta-administration-aiming-clear-all-slum-housing-2017.html.
Endah, A. (2012) *Jokowi: Memimpin Kota Menyentuh Jakarta* [Jokowi: Leading the City, Touching Jakarta]. Jakarta: Metagraf.
Herlambang, S. (2006) *Politik Kota dan Hak Warga Kota*. Jakarta: Gramedia.
Huyysen, A. (2008) World cultures, world cities, in Huyysen. A. (ed.) *Other Cities, Other Worlds: Urban Imaginaries in a Globalizing Age*. Durham, NC: Duke University Press.
Jakarta Post (1990) Operation of land brokers upsets mayor. *Jakarta Post*, 14 May.
Kompas (2014) Jokowi dan arti 'Revolusi Mental'. *Kompas*, 17 October.
Laclau, E. (2005) *On Populist Reason*. London: Verso.
Leaf, M. (1991) Land Regulation and Housing Development in Jakarta, Indonesia: From the 'Big Village' to the 'Modern City'. PhD dissertation, University of California, Berkeley.
Lindsey, T. (2001) The criminal state: premanisme and the new Indonesia, in Lloyd, G. and Smith, S. (eds.) *Indonesia Today: Challenges of History*. Singapore: ISEAS, pp. 283–297.
Malo, M. and Nas, P. (1996) Queen City of the East and symbol of the nation: the administration and management of Jakarta, in Ruland, J. (ed.) *The Dynamic of Metropolitan Management in Southeast Asia*. Singapore: ISEAS, pp. 99–132.
Mizuno, K. and Phongpaichit, P. (eds.) (2009) *Populism in Asia*. Honolulu: Hawaii University Press.
Onghokham (2003) *Wahyu yang Hilang, Negeri yang Guncang* [The Loss of Divine Power, the Shock of the Nation]. Jakarta: Tempo and the Freedom Institute.
Reid, A. (1998) Political 'tradition' in Indonesia: the one and the many. *Asian Studies Review*, **22**(1), pp. 23–38.
Roy, A. (2005) Urban informality: towards an epistemology of planning. *Journal of the American Planning Association*, **71**(2), pp. 147–158.
Ryter, L. (1998) 'Pemuda Pancasila': the last loyalist freemen of Suharto's Indonesia. *Indonesia*, **66**, pp. 44–73.
Server, O.B. (1996) Corruption: a major problem of urban management: some evidence from Indonesia. *Habitat International*, **20**(1), pp. 23–41.
Scott, J. (1972) Patron-client politics and political change in Southeast Asia. *American Political Science Review*, **66**(1), pp. 91–113.
Simmel, G. (1971[1903]) The metropolis and mental life, Levine, D. (ed.) *Georg Simmel on Individuality and Social Forms*. Chicago. IL: University of Chicago Press.
Simone, A.M. (2014) *Jakarta: Drawing the City Near*. Minneapolis, MN: University of Minnesota Press.
Smith, T.M. (1971) Corruption, tradition and change. *Indonesia*, **11**, pp. 21–40.
Wilson, I. (2010) Reconfiguring rackets: racket regimes, protection and the state in post-

new order Jakarta, in Aspinall, E. and van Klinken, G. (eds.) *The State and Illegality in Indonesia*. Leiden: KITLV, pp. 239–260.

Wirosardjono, S. (1991) The informal sector: victims of a double standard. *Prisma*, **51**, pp. 61–63.

Wirth, L. (1938) Urbanism as a way of life. *American Journal of Sociology*, **44**(1), pp. 1–44.

Chapter 2

Tradition as an Imposed and Elite Inheritance: Yangon's Modern Past

Jayde Lin Roberts

If tradition is something that is handed down from the past to the present, the downtown core of Yangon (also known as Rangoon) stands as an odd inheritance – not so much bestowed as cast aside by the British Empire, and not so much affirmed as acquiesced to by the independent Burmese state.[1] Having fought against the rapacious rule of the British, the independent governments of Burma (also known as Myanmar) have maintained a critical stance towards all things foreign.[2] From 1948, when Burma gained its independence, to the present, Rangoon's imposing colonial buildings have been generally neglected and periodically repurposed. The new Union of Burma had first to rebuild itself from the devastation of World War II before it could address the maintenance of colonial heritage, however grand. This nation-building project has continued under all the various governments of independent Burma. Both civilian and military rulers have grappled with questions of national identity, vacillating between anti-colonial rhetoric and assertions of indigenous unity, despite the undeniable ethnic diversity within the national territory.

Until recently, Burma and its former capital were rarely thought of outside the country. Military rule from the early 1960s to 2011 and international sanctions after 1988 effectively closed off the country, resulting in a period of isolation that has been interpreted by the national elite and Burma-watchers as an unfortunate interlude in the march towards modernity. However, after President Thein Sein initiated national reforms in 2011, the world quickly returned through diplomatic visits, trade missions and international aid. The current reframing of the country through a neoliberal development agenda has represented it as a virgin market with untapped resources, a nation needing capacity-building in order to fulfil its unmet potential, and a place as yet untainted by the homogenizing forces of modernization and globalization.

Such characterizations are typical of a well-worn trope about 'developing' countries, which continues to be deployed despite the clearly unequal outcomes of, and contradictions inherent in, development discourse (Escobar, 2011; Rankin, 2009). In the case of Yangon, this trope has been adopted by Burmese expatriates and the educated elite as a useful, if wilfully naive, tool to save the British-designed downtown. Colonial modernity can thus be claimed as a tradition to counter the post-2011 tide of globalized modernization. In the words of Thant Myint-U, founder of the Yangon Heritage Trust and grandson of the former UN Secretary General U Thant, '[The] colonial era landscape downtown is where the Burmese people first learned to be modern, to interact with the world' (Brown, 2014). Thant Myint-U (2014) also predicted that Yangon stands on the cusp of a new relevance, and can retrieve its fin-de-siècle cosmopolitanism from more than 60 years ago.

Calling on the former modernity of Rangoon to save a modernizing Yangon is a laudable manoeuvre. It turns the linear liberatory discourse of modernity back on itself, rendering it cyclical and therefore more traditional. Until colonial rule, history in Burma was conceived as cycles that originated with the reign of the Mahasammatha, the mythical king who ruled over a perfect moral kingdom (Jordt, 2007, pp.176, 218). However, this deployment of modernity also suffers from 'post-coloniality', which Kwame Anthony Appiah (1991, p. 348) defined as 'the condition of what we might ungenerously call a comprador intelligentsia: a relatively small, Western-trained group of writers and thinkers, who mediate the trade in cultural commodities of world capitalism at the periphery'.

Yangon's Neoclassical, Victorian, Queen Anne and eclectic Western-influenced architecture are undeniably beautiful and infinitely marketable. In campaigning for the conservation of downtown Yangon, the Burmese elite describe the city as a rare gem in a globalized Southeast Asia, one in which the colonial building stock stands largely unadulterated. But what they fail to mention is that these buildings have excluded most Burmese people. They housed a colonial and then a military bureaucracy that treated the local population as potential enemies of the state (Callahan, 2005).

The elite have also defined the downtown as an opportunity to showcase how development can proceed without destroying its heritage. As Thant Myint-U has stated, 'If we can make Yangon the most attractive, beautiful and liveable city in Southeast Asia, this is an asset worth billions of dollars' (Linthicum, 2014). However, this representation of Yangon privileges external and globalized discourses of architectural aesthetics. It also obscures a history of rule by force and coercion that excluded common people – whether they were of the dominant ethnicity (Burman), belonged to one of the nation's ethnic minorities (Mon, Karen, and others), or resident aliens (Indian and Chinese).[3] Adopting this narrative of economic development renders conservationists complicit in perpetuating existing inequalities because the restoration of colonial-era buildings will further exclude local residents who neither remember nor benefitted from the city's period of modernity.

This chapter examines the 'tradition of modernity' in Yangon as an imposed and elite inheritance, which was first instigated by the English East India Company, and then perpetuated by the city's elite. In this retelling, modernity is both the past and the future of Yangon, while the present – often understood as not only the current period of transition from overt military rule to a civilian government but also the preceding five decades of decline – is shunted aside in favour of the teleology of progress. However, what this modernity is and how it is a part of Yangon's tradition is only suggested, never defined. This elision allows the colonial-era buildings to be placed in the same category as the Shwedagon Pagoda and other Buddhist monuments, which elicit unmistakable devotion from Yangon's residents and fall more easily into the category of Burmese tradition.[4] Thus urban heritage is rendered broadly, apparently encompassing any building that existed before the 1950s. Such a campaign to save Yangon's colonial-era buildings takes maximum advantage of the romance of the ruin, with grand but crumbling building façades captured in the golden glow of sunset. But within such a discourse, not all buildings are accorded equal value. Indeed, worthiness is often dictated by universalized standards as set by organizations such as the UNESCO World Heritage Centre and the World Monuments Fund.

Beyond the aesthetic representations in global media and appeals to international experts, Burmese expatriates and elite have yet to engage with local residents or to evaluate the nature and consequences of their British-designed city. Beginning with a re-examination of the design of Rangoon, therefore, this chapter analyzes changes in the urban fabric and recent discourses about the city to consider the failed promise of colonial modernity and the problem of its retrieval as a tradition capable of putting Yangon back on the world stage.

Rangoon: A Modern and Foreign City

The narrative of modernity usually begins in 1852 with the founding of Rangoon as the capital of the British territory of Burma, and it cites as evidence the rational design of the city. This representation was promoted by colonial rulers such as Arthur Purves Phayre, the first commissioner, and was subsequently popularized by colonialists such as Bertie Reginald Pearn, who wrote *A History of Rangoon* in 1931, the one and only English-language book on the history of the city.[5] In this book, Pearn called the construction of British Rangoon, 'Planning the Modern City'. Modernity was seen as a linear, liberating force capable of perfecting the world through rational human effort, a project that would inevitably spread around the globe via free-market trade.[6]

Rangoon and Lower Burma as a whole were seized by British forces during the Second Anglo-Burmese War in 1852. Soon after, Phayre declared all land in and around Rangoon government property, citing the destruction of the town before the 1852 war as just cause for assuming state ownership. Through British eyes, the native topography appeared wild and devoid of value. Company men such as F.O. Oertel and painters such as Colesworthey Grant described Rangoon as a place of flimsy huts and dishevelled markets, sadly unimpressive with nothing to recommend it but the Shwedagon Pagoda (Oertel, 1995). Grant even published a book titled *Rough Pencillings of a Rough Trip to Rangoon* (1995). Much like the Black Town of Calcutta, the native landscape did not deserve careful attention because there was nothing important in the native town (Chattopadhyay, 2005). Only after colonial intervention through their pure analytic vision would places such as Rangoon and Calcutta become worthy of consideration.

On this conveniently blank slate, Phayre and Lieutenant Alexander Fraser designed a rational Cartesian city composed of straight, wide streets and rectilinear lots. Phayre and Fraser, like other elite in the empire, saw the need to discourage the spread of bodily disease (illness) and societal disease (crime) through the proper planning of their conquered territories. Straight and wide streets were seen as the primary instrument to flush out Rangoon's miasma-filled swampland and inculcate proper English civility in its residents.[7] A hierarchical grid of streets (with major streets at 100 feet wide, intermediary streets at 50 feet and minor streets at 30 feet [30.5 m, 15.25 and 10.2 m. respectively]) was thus systematically laid out in the designated urban core (figure 2.1). This allowed central Rangoon to be divided into twenty-five blocks that were then subdivided into 172 lots per block, resulting in 4,300 lots that became available for sale, taxation, and regulation.

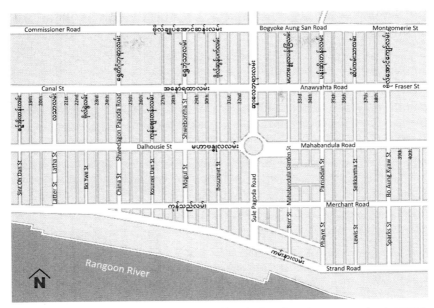

Figure 2.1. Map of central Rangoon with historical and contemporary street names. (*Drawing*: Luo Lishi)

Under colonial rule, Burmese people were excluded from the city through economic and political measures. The 4,300 lots devised by Phayre were divided into five different classes with the lots closest to the Rangoon River, along Strand Road, commanding the highest prices. The riverfront, the most valuable property, was reserved for official buildings that would present a majestic face to Europeans arriving by sea.[8] The next three classes of property were valued according to their distance from the river and proximity to existing wharves. In addition, specific requirements were dictated for different classes. All building on first-class lots near Strand Road and in the business district had to be made of brick with *pukka* or tiled roofs.[9]

Regardless of class, all owners of all lots had to build 'a good and substantial bona fide dwelling house or warehouse' within one year of purchase or the property would be confiscated (Maxim, 1992, p. 66). This latter regulation was initially implemented to prevent speculative buying, but also served to mandate a particular kind of physical and social environment. Specifically, it meant only the wealthy could afford both to buy a lot and build on it. Local Burmese were excluded from the planned city because the pricing of the lots combined with the building requirements and taxation rendered property prohibitively expensive.

In theory, the parcels in the northernmost area near Montgomerie (now Bogyoke Aung San) Road were priced for commoners, but no Burmese could afford to buy them. Instead, they squatted on unoccupied land in the urban periphery, now part of Sanchaung, Kamaryut, and Kyimyindaing Townships.

By the early part of the twentieth century, Rangoon was usually described by British officials as a model of modern urban development and 'the only large Indian city which ha[d] grown up on a scientific plan' (Maxim, 1992, p. 322). Burma was incorporated into the Empire as a province of British India and administered from Calcutta. Indians could move freely between India and Burma as if travelling from one district to another (Chakravarti, 1971). Therefore, from the perspective of colonial officials, Rangoon was an Indian city, albeit one located in the newer territory of Burma. As in other British territories such as Calcutta and Singapore, 'the distinctive European architectural vocabulary enabled one to recognize the space occupied by the colonizers, setting out in easily observable material terms distinctions between the rulers and the ruled' (Chattopadhyay, 2005, p. 29). Initially, Neoclassical architecture, as seen in the Court House completed in 1868, was deployed to proclaim the British right to rule. Later, English dominance over the urban landscape was solidified through buildings such as the Queen Anne-style High Court by James Ransome, Consulting Architect to the Government of India (figure 2.2). As an outpost of British India, architecture in Rangoon was largely made up of 'Indianized' European buildings designed by Scottish and Western-trained architects. There was little of Burma in the colonial port city.

Figure 2.2. The High Court. (*Photo*: Jayde Lin Roberts)

The built environment of Rangoon was not meant to make manifest its *genius loci* [spirit of place] but to spread the British vision of modernity. That is, Rangoon was a foreign city designed to declare British superiority and to reform the native population and landscape. Through critical eyes, Rangoon was a doubly colonized city that had been artificially implanted. Passing through Rangoon in 1916, the Indian intellectual, Rabindranath Tagore (1940) wrote: 'This city has not grown like a tree from the soil of the country … [it] floats like foam on the tides of time… I have seen Rangoon, but it is mere visual acquaintance, there is no recognition of Burma in this seeing … the city is an abstraction'. Tagore lamented the fact that colonial commerce had dominated and determined the character of the city and noted that Indians, as the overwhelming majority, had essentially colonized the Burmese once more, almost in lockstep with the British Raj. The Indian population not only dominated numerically, but also economically and spatially. 'The Indian middle class had the strongest hold on foreign [and domestic] trade of any group in Burma' (Taylor, 1987, p. 135). By 1911, over half of the urban population was Indian and the *lingua franca* was Hindi, not English or Burmese (Chakravarti, 1971, p. 19; Pearn, 1939, p. 287).

The local Burmese elite also recognized the foreignness of Rangoon even as they worked within the British colonial system to access power. There is considerable scholarship about Burmese nationalism and anti-imperial sentiments, but generally, the analyses do not draw connections between the built environment and the rise of political activism. Thus, except for discussions about Rangoon University and the Shwedagon Pagoda, there is but one documented protest against the British design of the city. This concerned the new Rangoon City Hall in 1925. Although a design by L.A. McClumpha had been chosen by the Municipal Committee in 1913, World War I delayed its construction, and the project was not reinitiated until 1925. By then, anti-imperial sentiment had become more organized, and nationalists demanded a city hall with Burmese architectural features. U Ba Pe, then a leading voice of Burmese middle-class nationalism, spoke at the Burma Legislative Council calling for a new design that would feature the ornamentations seen in Pagan, the capital of an ancient Burman kingdom and a sacred Buddhist site. European members of the council disagreed, citing the inappropriateness of religious-inspired architecture for a civic building because in the modern era, state and religion were supposed to be separate. However, U Ba Pe responded, 'No civic architecture in the world can be found that is not founded on either ecclesiastical, monumental or other religious architecture' (Roony, 2013, p. 41).

U Ba Pe won the debate and Burmese architectural features, such as a three-tiered *pyatthat* roof and traditional iconography such as peacocks and *nagas* (serpents), were added (figure 2.3).[10] However, the change to City Hall was superficial. It remained a neoclassical building with Burmese makeup added by a Burmese architect, Sithu U Tin, who had been trained in Bombay. The foreign quality of Rangoon's urban fabric was barely disturbed.

Modernizing the Burmese Way

For many, if not most, observers within and beyond Burma, the British-instigated modernization of Rangoon appeared to stop dead in its tracks in 1962 and even rolled backwards towards more 'primitive' and 'superstitious' ways of living and governing. However, this interpretation is from the standpoint of linear modernity, which presumes colonial or Western rule to be more rational and scientific than indigenous Burmese rule. It further erroneously equates modernity with progress. In the colonial era, the country was targeted as a cheap source of raw materials and a market for British goods – a capitalist orientation that clearly resulted in inequality and abuse. Burma's experience under colonial rule, compounded with the threat of politico-economic intrusion by the superpowers during the Cold War, rendered all foreign influence suspect. With this suspicion, the various

Figure 2.3. City Hall. (*Photo*: Jayde Lin Roberts)

post-independence governments attempted to modernize the country on their own terms. Until 1988, they chose socialism as an ideology more in alignment with traditional Burmese values.

U Nu, the first prime minister of independent Burma, endeavoured to establish a moral bureaucracy and society based on the idea of Buddhism as a scientific practice (Jordt, 2007; Tinker, 1967). However, armed rebellion by several ethnic and ideological groups, and the challenge of rebuilding the war-torn economy preoccupied the fledgling state, delaying national reform. The British government that had returned at the end of World War II had left permanently by 1948, with most of the country in disarray, and with ethnic minority groups challenging central Burman rule. For a period, the government of U Nu was known as 'the Rangoon government', as that was the only part of the country it effectively controlled. Burma had to first weather the many trials of postwar reconstruction and nation-building before it could turn to modernizing the urban environment, as a secondary, or even tertiary, concern.[11] Thus the capital of British Burma had to serve as the capital of independent Burma, with no attempt to design a new city to signify the founding of a new nation.

In 1958, General Ne Win assumed temporary control from U Nu. At the time, the military considered the political struggle within the ruling Anti-Fascist People's Freedom League and continuing conflicts in ethnic minority regions to be imminent threats to national security. It also saw itself as the only organization capable of stabilizing the country. In 1960, U Nu was reinstated by popular vote; but a second *coup d'état* in 1962 put Ne Win back in command. Ne Win and his supporters first established the Revolutionary Council, then the Burmese Socialist Programme Party, and tried to create a modern secularist nation-state without deviating from Buddhist phenomenology and morality (Jordt, 2007). In their conception, this path required building a self-sufficient Burma based on Buddhism and Marxism. Unfortunately, the socialist government's attempt to break from Burma's colonial past and construct a uniquely Burmese future ended in failure. By 1987, the United Nations placed Burma in the category of Least Developed Country (LDC), and in 1988, the Burmese people rose up in mass protest after years of inflation, severe shortages in basic goods and political oppression.[12]

Popular discourse about Burma depicts the socialist period as one of irrationality and ineptitude, effectively a deviation from the path of modernity. General Ne Win was said to have based his decisions for the nation on numerology, and his staff was described as paranoid and uneducated.[13] There were glaring shortcomings in the Revolutionary

Council, who proved to be soldiers unprepared to lead a nation. However, their effort to establish an economy and society based on Burmese Buddhist values rather than exchange value should be understood as an ideologically driven response to colonialism and neocolonialism. They did not subscribe to the colonial discourse of modernity and were not interested in selling Burma to the world.

Rangoon, as designed by the British, remained almost unaltered from 1948 to 1988. In the downtown core, institutional buildings constructed by the British and other foreigners maintained their functions or were repurposed as headquarters for various government departments. The Irrawaddy Flotilla Company became the Inland Waterways Department; Grindlay's Bank became the Burma Agricultural Development Bank; and others such as the Port Authority and Telegraph Office continued to serve as the port authority and other government offices. More modest buildings such as the townhouses built by Indian and Chinese merchants remained residences but were gradually sold off by their owners in order to generate income (figure 2.4). The configurations and uses within these buildings

Figure 2.4. Townhouses in Tayout Tan (Chinatown). (*Photo*: Jayde Lin Roberts)

changed, but their structures remained constant except for weathering and gradual decay. Likewise, the urban fabric of the downtown core endured because the country was in economic decline and few could afford to build new (or maintain existing) buildings. Meanwhile, beyond the downtown, the Revolutionary Council helped establish government housing blocks and satellite towns. New towns such as Thuwanna were planned in the periurban area to relocate residents to the periphery. As a part of the socialist campaign, people were promised the right to homeownership if they built their houses with their own hands.[14]

Lost Opportunities, Lost Modernity

In the news, Burma is usually characterized as a resource-rich country that has squandered its riches. Some pundits even lament the 'fact' that Burma failed to capitalize on the civil and physical infrastructure bequeathed by the British and somehow let the country fall into ruin.[15] By the late 1980s, the low levels of health care, education, income, and other measures of development made the failure of the socialist state undeniable. Lost opportunities, a lost modernity, and the need to catch up are well-rehearsed refrains that have haunted and continue to haunt the country. In contemporary Yangon, the local elite like to think of their home as a city that was once more advanced than Singapore. They cite as evidence the fact that Rangoon had the first international airport in Southeast Asia, which served as a regional hub in the 1950s. Some also say that Lee Kuan Yew, the former prime minister of Singapore, travelled to Rangoon to study how a modern city works.[16] However, this praise is usually offered apologetically, as a counter-argument to the obvious deterioration of the contemporary urban environment.

In the eyes of typical Yangon residents, little is modern in the city's urban fabric. Until about 2012, they pointed to the Sakura Tower and the Traders Hotel (now the Shangri-la) as the only *khit hmi de* [translated as 'modern' but literally 'of the times'] buildings because they employed concrete in their construction. They define modern buildings as high-rise towers, which are above eight storeys and require elevators.[17] However, even with the dramatic influx of foreign investment after national reform, there are still few high-rises in downtown Yangon. In this city, modernity is an idea more defined by its absence than its presence. It is alluring because of the promise of something better: something more scientific and technologically advanced, something with more freedom and democracy, something that allows Burmese people to be *khit hmi de*.

In reality, downtown Yangon remains the colonial city abandoned by the British – with its buildings, building heights, lot sizes, street widths, and infrastructure mostly unaltered. International news reporting, television documentaries, and tourism literature refer to Yangon as a 'forgotten city' and 'a city trapped in time', seeing romance and beauty in the frozen colonial landscape. Recently, heritage conservationists have tried to capitalize on this romanticized image to increase the perceived value of Yangon. They have highlighted the character and quality of construction in the old buildings, while emphasizing the city's former modernity. They have sought to re-create the image of Yangon as Rangoon in its heyday, when the city was still a busy regional port and its neoclassical, Queen Anne, and other Western-derived architecture was still modern.

By retrieving that lost modernity, conservationists hope to render Yangon more relevant in the eyes of the world, and thereby more valuable to Burmese people, particularly those with direct access to power and money. Although Yangon's residents see nothing modern in their city and want to modernize in order to catch up with the world, a contrary perspective could prove persuasive. The Yangon Heritage Trust (YHT) has appealed to international organizations such as the UNESCO World Heritage Centre and the World Monuments Fund to seek external validation for Yangon as a city whose value extends beyond the borders of Myanmar and which holds universal significance. This global recognition is supposed to convince developers and their contacts within the upper echelon of the military to invest the billions of dollars necessary to save the downtown core. However, this is the tactic of the 'comprador intelligentsia', identified by Appiah, who play by the rules of neoliberalism and see the sale and preservation of Yangon's built environment as key to the city's renewal. Their intimate knowledge of the West enables their voices to be heard on the world stage, but that knowledge often blinds them to their own complicity in perpetuating the unequal trade of cultural commodities. This is inequality not only at the international level, where Yangon as a romanticized tourist destination is once again a commodity to be consumed, but also at the local level, where everyday Yangon residents have no voice in determining what is valuable in their city.

Sun Oo, a member of the YHT, has said that many Burmese once viewed the colonial-era buildings as a vestige of British imperialism but now realize they are a part of the city's cultural heritage (Brady, 2012). Similarly, Thant Myint-U equivocated, 'No one has a positive view of colonialism as colonialism, but what I try to say is that this colonial era landscape downtown is also where the Burmese people first learned to be modern' (Brown, 2014). These statements reveal the dissonance between the priorities of the conservationists and the concerns of everyday residents. To date, Burmese have not rallied to save colonial-era buildings but have publicly protested to preserve the sanctity of the Shwedagon Pagoda and save the Ayeyawady [Irrawaddy] River. When this author queried residents on five different streets in November 2014, they were largely unconcerned about architectural heritage but specifically asked for a cleaner, more orderly and affordable city, and modern infrastructure. As summarized by Maitrii Aung-Thwin, an associate professor of Myanmar history at the National University of Singapore, '[W]hen you look at the social and economic issues that are facing the country, health and education, these things are going to have to take a priority at the moment over the preservation of some of these buildings' (Holmes, 2012).

Claiming Modernity as Tradition

Indeed, it is difficult to justify the conservation of colonial-era buildings when Yangon still lacks potable water and a reliable sanitation system. Open sewage channels remain a common sight because the broken sidewalk pavers that cover them are only sporadically repaired. In such a situation, calling for the conservation of grand buildings sounds like the folly of the rich or at least a case of mistaken priorities. It is as if the Western-educated Burmese elite are seeking to assume the colonial mantle, looking to impose their will on Yangon.

However, the actions and discourse of the conservationists have also emerged at a time of unprecedented uncertainty and possibility. Like most people in the country, members of the YHT are searching for ways to identify themselves, their city, and their nation in a reforming Myanmar suddenly thrown onto the world stage. The problem is not that the YHT is trying to save colonial-era buildings in the hope that these buildings will become the image of post-reform Yangon. The problem is that Yangon's municipal government has consistently failed to deliver basic services and still has few professional planners, leaving a vacuum to be filled by any organization with skilled employees. In this context, the YHT has become the only voice speaking for the city, and its perspective is dominated by a globalized standard of architectural value. The YHT's dedication to the preservation of colonial architecture could thus become the focal point around which more urgent planning issues could be appended. Problems such as sanitation, public transportation, and basic livelihood are less photogenic and do not generally have members of a Western-educated, media-savvy elite as their spokespeople. On this unequal playing field, the needs of the poorest could be drowned out by the concerns of the elite.

By claiming modernity as Yangon's tradition, the YHT has identified a discourse with both international and national appeal. As aptly analyzed by Anthony Giddens, Southeast Asia still abides by the concept of linear modernity (Giddens and Peirson, 1998). Aid and loans from institutions such as the Asian Development Bank flow to projects that can 'prove' measureable progress, while ASEAN (the Association of Southeast Asian Nations) remains intent on making Southeast Asian Nations competitive by the rules of capitalism. Further afield, the European Union, the United States, and other developed states provide funding to help developing nations rationalize their governments on the model of the West. Within Myanmar, the experience of being named as a least-developed country is a source of national embarrassment that has made Burmese people eager to become modern at almost any cost.

However, the genius of the YHT lies not in their invocation of modernity as linear progress. Rather, it is their attempt to make Yangon modern *again*, a step forward that ingeniously requires cycling back to the colonial past. Burma has yet to reconcile itself with its colonial experience. The exigencies of Burma left the first independent government with little capacity to reform the nation, thereby perpetuating British law and other means of control. The socialist government led by General Ne Win completely rejected colonial history, but in that denial failed to find a viable alternative path. In contemporary Myanmar, the failures of the socialist state, followed by the abuses of the military junta between 1988 and 2011, seem to have opened the floodgates to global capitalism and neoliberalism. Myanmar appears ready to charge forward, to break away from its embarrassing 'undeveloped' past, in order to catch up. Common residents and government leaders are worried about measuring up to more developed neighbouring countries. As a member of ASEAN, the free-trade area that was supposed to be fully implemented in December 2015 looms like a ticking time-bomb, threatening to crush the Myanmar economy. However, in the haste to become more competitive, modernity is pursued as a rupture, an antithesis to tradition, leaving no room for contradictions and reconciliation. A middle ground cannot be achieved if there is only one right position.

By narrating a modernity that is both of the past and the future, the YHT is unintentionally creating an opening wherein Yangon's and Burma's tattered history can be reconsidered and perhaps accepted as an imperfect whole. To date, portions of the country's past have been either rejected or sublimated in order to write an unproblematic story of triumph. Just as the socialist government tried to erase the colonial past, the post-1988 military junta glorified precolonial warrior kings such as Anawyata and Bayint Naung, claiming Burma's historical victory over neighbouring kingdoms as evidence of Myanmar's strength in the postcolonial period. The abuses of the colonial state are irrefutable but expunging that portion of Burma's history robs Burmese people of critical details and significant places that can become the basis for reinterpreting the nation. The country does not have to be either traditional or modern; it can be both. Similarly, Myanmar's sovereignty does not have to stand in opposition to its colonial past; it can build upon it. Indeed, the rise of Burman nationalism took place in organizations such as the Young Men's Buddhist Association (which was inspired by the Young Men's Christian Association) and Western institutions such as Rangoon University. The colonial experience, and by extension the colonial built environment that still remains in Yangon, are integral to Burma's history.

Unlike cities such as Jakarta and Chandigarh where High Modernist structures declared the rise of a new order, Yangon marched into the modern era with no supporting evidence in its built environment.[18] The generals in charge did not deploy architecture as a tool for nation-building. A new capital for the Union of Myanmar was not built until 2005 when Nay Pyi Taw was suddenly constructed near Pyinmina, a remote, inland town in Mandalay Region. Therefore, the position and meaning of Yangon have yet to be reconciled with national history. How does a British port city designed to generate profit for the Empire and once seen as a direct threat to the sovereignty of the Burman kingdom become a Burmese city?[19] How does the built environment of downtown Yangon become local tradition?

In practice, everyday life in the spaces left by the British has been Burmese for decades. Vendors sell betel nut, *lahpet-yei* (Burmese tea), and *mohinga* (fish noodle soup) on the street, and their customers dine happily on the sidewalks, sitting on tiny chairs and benches (figure 2.5). The social life of downtown Yangon is Burmese regardless of the architecture. Although grand buildings such as Rowe and Company Department Store and Grindlay's Bank are unmistakably colonial in their appearance, they are mainly beautiful if decaying surfaces that do not impinge on daily life. Under British rule, most Burmese people did not enter institutional buildings, and after independence, they only entered out of absolute necessity. As convincingly argued by Mary Callahan (2005), the independent state saw many of the people within its territory as potential enemies who threatened the unity of the vulnerable nation-state. Therefore, state institutions

Figure 2.5. Street life in Yangon. (*Photo*: Jayde Lin Roberts)

did not welcome its people as citizens but dealt with them as necessary inconveniences. As such, entering one of the institutional buildings on Pansodan or Strand Road to apply for a Myanmar passport or obtain other government documents was countenanced with dread. In fact, until 2012, no one could enter City Hall without an official invitation. Before the initiation of reform, the grand edifices left by the British had not been integrated into everyday Burmese life. They were aloof monuments that precluded personal attachment. How they can become an integral part of the everyday Yangon remains to be seen, and the process will require direct participation from local residents. If international developers are given free rein in the name of development, Yangon's inhabitants will again be priced out and excluded from the downtown core.

A Valuable, Paradoxical Legacy

It is perhaps ironic that a city once designed to mimic other colonial port cities in function and appearance has become unique through the vagaries of time. Between 1962 and 2011, the built environment of Yangon changed so little that it still looks like a fin-de-siècle British colonial city, unlike its model and predecessor, Singapore. By re-entering the world five decades after other Southeast Asian cities, Yangon is able to turn its late entry into a strength and claim the former modernity of Rangoon as its authentic heritage. But this heritage is more like the inheritance that is passed down within wealthy families; it remains private property, not a public good. Burmese expatriates and the country's educated elite are rallying to resist the negative effects of modernization – that is, the rampant reproduction of 'faceless' or 'placeless' high-rise towers that have produced a globalized Southeast Asia. The cautionary tales are Singapore and Bangkok, which have surrendered much of their historic identity to become modern. The idea is that Yangon, the first city to be modern in Southeast Asia, can now recover its modernity as a way of maintaining its past, its tradition.

However, this tradition is an imposed and problematic inheritance built upon the political economy of empire. In the colonial era, British rule tied Burma into the world economy as a supplier of raw materials. Burma was once the rice bowl of the world, but it never regained this position of prominence after demand dropped during the Great Depression. Today, the country is once again entering the world economy as a barely tapped source of natural resources, thereby resuming its vulnerable position on the bottom rung in the global market. The value of Rangoon as a praiseworthy city was determined by the British, and reasserting its value today requires recognition from the outside world. The current effort to put Yangon back on the world map through marketing its colonial architecture is an attempt to raise the self-esteem of Burmese people after a long period of isolation and economic decline.

As the Myanmar government aggressively pursues economic growth through foreign direct investment, neoliberal capitalism is poised to reshape Yangon, much as colonial capitalism created it. The preservation of the colonial-era architecture in the downtown core is a viable gambit against the onslaught of accelerated modernization. However, the built environment of Yangon is a paradoxical legacy that has and could once again exclude its local population based on class and ethnicity. Downtown Rangoon, seen as an integrated social and physical fabric, is Burmese. Imposing colonial architecture has not suffocated the vitality of everyday life; life has happened in between the buildings. Burmese people are well practiced in making do and circumventing technologies of power, but the tide of neoliberalism could push current residents out of the city. If grand colonial-era buildings are repurposed as hotels and tourist destinations, common Burmese people will not only have little space to transform those buildings into their traditional built environment, but they will also be driven out of the spaces in between those buildings that are already Burmese.

Notes

1. In the field of Burma studies, nomenclature has been a persistent problem and has at times served as a symbol of political allegiance: for or against the military government, the State Law and Order Restoration Council, or SLORC (renamed the State Peace and Development Council, or SPDC, in 1997). Burmese people use Burma and Myanmar, Rangoon and Yangon interchangeably. All four names are historically legitimate. But for the sake of clarity, I will use Rangoon to refer to the colonial-era capital (that is, the city between 1852 and 1948) and Yangon to refer to it in the years since independence. As for Burma and Myanmar, I use Burma in general but Myanmar in particular to refer to the country under the post-1990 government, even if its rule remains contested.
2. Burma Studies is still rebuilding itself after a dormant period from about the late 1960s to late 1990s. Therefore, many areas of study await investigation. Research on military rule and the politics of the nation-state are more complete, but as a whole analyses of Burma are limited. For studies of the built environment, there are no English-language sources that discuss the city of Yangon or the country as a whole for the socialist period (1962 to 1988) and only two or three master's level works for the period after 1988. Since the initiation of reform in 2011, international organizations such as Japanese International Cooperation Agency have undertaken quantitative analysis of Yangon and proposed a master plan. The author is currently researching the history and development of Yangon from the colonial era to the present through Burmese language sources, but this project is in its early stages. Therefore, broad characterizations as presented in this chapter should be understood as partial representations.
3. Among Burma Studies scholars, 'Burmese' refers to everyone within the nation-state of Burma/Myanmar, while 'Burman' and 'Bamar' refer to the dominant ethnic group. Burmans have been and remain the dominant ethnic population at about 70 per cent of the total national population – and the country is named after this dominant group. Limitations on word count do not permit discussion here of persistent ethnic conflicts in the nation-building project, but it must be noted that the tremendous ethnic diversity in Burma remains a key and volatile issue. In this discussion of Yangon, 'Burmese' does not include resident Indian and Chinese populations, who continue to live with uncertain citizenship status. This use of nomenclature does not indicate my stance with regard to so-called 'alien' or 'migrant' populations within Myanmar. My analysis of their predicament is discussed in my book, *Mapping Chinese Rangoon: Place and Nation among the Sino-Burmese* (2016). Also, the generalized term 'Burmese' is adequate in this chapter because, until the 1990s, the population of Yangon was mainly Burman, Mon, Karen, Indian and Chinese.
4. The language used by Burmese conservationists does not seem to distinguish between tradition and heritage. My fieldwork indicates that the Burmese word *yoya yinkyehmu* (tradition) is used for common customs and is often equated with culture. Heritage appears to be a newer concept for everyday people, and might gain relevance based on its association with tradition.
5. There is one Burmese-language book on the history of Yangon, written by U Thein Maung (1963).
6. One could easily argue that this doctrine of modernity is still operative, particularly in developing nations that still feel a need to catch up. However, in the globalized, millennial world, there is less faith in modernity, as made evident through protests against global capitalism such as the WTO Protest in Seattle in 1999 and the Occupy Wall Street Movement of 2011.

7. Colonial urbanism has been discussed in works such as Chattopadhyay (2005), Hosagraher (2005), and King (1976).
8. Of course, this is not unique to Rangoon. Other colonial port cities such as Calcutta and Singapore were designed from the perspective of Europeans arriving by sea. The riverfront was the first opportunity to declare the majesty of the British Empire to other colonial powers.
9. *Pukka*, or *pucka*, was a term borrowed from British India that meant solid, substantial, or properly constructed.
10. *Pyatthat* is the name for the multi-tiered and spired roof found in Burmese royal and Buddhist architecture. There are three primary types of *pyatthat*: three-tiered, five-tiered, and seven-tiered – with the greater number of tiers representing greater sanctity.
11. In addition to these internal threats to national security, external pressures from the Eastern and Western Blocs of the Cold War demanded Burma's allegiance. Along with India, Indonesia and other newly independent states that felt threatened by the superpowers, Burma participated in the Bandung Conference of 1955 and joined the Non-Aligned Movement.
12. In August 1988, the people's uprising forced the socialist government out of power, but soon a military junta took over, continuing the rule of generals. Initially, there was hope for a transition toward a democratic government, as the junta promised and delivered popular elections. However, after the National League of Democracy (NLD), led by Aung San Suu Kyi, won the election in June 1990, the junta refused to hand over power.
13. Ne Win was said to be fixated on numerology and introduced the 45- and 90-kyat banknotes, which incorporated his favourite number nine. He also demonetized Burmese currency with little or no warning in 1964, 1985, and 1987. The last of these actions rendered 75 per cent of the country's currency worthless, thereby robbing most people of their savings.
14. Some Burmese scholars, such as Than Than Nwe (1998), have begun to analyze the growth of the city beyond the colonial plan. However, to date, there are still few studies.
15. See, for example, Mark Tallentire: http://www.theguardian.com/world/2007/sep/28/burma.uk.
16. This 'fact' about Lee Kuan Yew was told to me by approximately five Yangon residents during my PhD fieldwork between 2007 and 2009. However, I have not been able to locate a newspaper report or other documents verifying this trip.
17. This is based on the municipal government's definition of high-rise buildings.
18. Scholars such as Abidin Kusno (2000) and James Scott (1998) have discussed the contradictions in asserting local identity through deploying universalizing modernity. See also Giddens and Peirson (1998).
19. In his unpublished doctoral thesis, Francois Tainturier (2010) provided a clear analysis of how Mandalay, the last capital of the last Burmese kingdom, was designed and built as a sanctuary against British invasion.

References

Appiah, K.A. (1991) Is the post- in postmodernism the post- in postcolonial? *Critical Inquiry*, **17**(2), pp. 336–357.

Brady, B. (2012) Economic Growth Could Imperil Yangon's Colonial-Era Buildings. *Public*

Radio International, 15 October. Available at: http://www.pri.org/stories/2012-10-15/economic-growth-could-imperil-yangons-colonial-era-buildings.

Brown, J. (2014) Will development overshadow Myanmar's rich cultural heritage? *PBS News Hour*, 15 April. Available at: http://www.pbs.org/newshour/bb/will-development-overshadow-myanmars-rich-cultural-history/.

Callahan, M.P. (2005) *Making Enemies: War and State Building in Burma*. Ithaca, NY: Cornell University Press.

Chakravarti, N.R. (1971) *The Indian Minority in Burma: The Rise and Decline of an Immigrant Community*. Oxford: Oxford University Press.

Chattopadhyay, S. (2005) *Representing Calcutta: Modernity, and the Colonial Uncanny*. London: Routledge.

Escobar, A. (2011) *Encountering Development: The Making and Unmaking of the Third World*. Princeton, NJ: Princeton University Press.

Giddens, A. and Peirson, C. (1998) *Conversations with Anthony Giddens: Making Sense of Modernity*. Stanford, CA: Stanford University Press.

Grant, C. (1995) *Rough Pencillings of a Rough Trip to Rangoon in 1846* (Vol.2). Bangkok: White Orchid Press (reprint of 1853 edition).

Holmes, S. (2012) Myanmar's Yangon fights city sprawl. Asia News. *The Wall Street Journal*, 18 November. Available at: http://www.burmanet.org/news/2012/11/19/the-wall-street-journal-myanmars-yangon-fights-city-sprawl-%E2%80%93-sam-holmes/.

Hosagrahar, J. (2005) *Indigenous Modernities: Negotiating Architecture and Urbanism*. New York: Routledge.

Jordt, I. (2007) *Burma's Mass Lay Meditation Movement: Buddhism and the Cultural Construction of Power*. Athens, OH: Ohio University Press.

King, A.D. (1976) *Colonial Urban Development: Culture, Social Power and Environment*. London: Routledge and Kegan Paul.

Kusno, A. (2000). *Behind the Postcolonial: Architecture, Urban Space and Political Cultures in Indonesia*. London: Routledge.

Linthicum, K. (2014) Myanmar's untold stories: a scholar is racing to save colonial-era buildings as change sweeps the country. *Los Angeles Times*, 7 January, p. 4.

Maxim, S. (1992) Resemblance in External Appearance: The Colonial Project in Kuala Lumpur and Rangoon. PhD Dissertation, Cornell University.

Oertel, F.O. (1995) *Note on a Tour in Burma in March and April, 1892*. Bangkok: White Orchid Press (Originally published in 1892 by Government Printing, Rangoon).

Pearn, B.R. (1939) *A History of Rangoon*. Rangoon: American Baptist Mission Press.

Rankin, K.N. (2009) Critical development studies and the praxis of planning. *City*, **13**(2/3), pp. 219–29.

Roberts, J.L. (2016) *Mapping Chinese Rangoon: Place and Nation among the Sino-Burmese*. Seattle, WA: University of Washington Press.

Roony, S. (2013) *30 Heritage Buildings of Yangon: Inside the City that Captured Time*. Chicago, IL: Shane Suvikapakornkul [Serindia Publications].

Scott, J.C. (1998) *Seeing Like a State: How Certain Schemes to Improve the Human Condition have Failed*. New Haven, CT: Yale University Press.

Tagore, R. (1940) *Japane-Parashye in Japan and Persia*. Calcutta: Granthalay.

Tainturier, F. (2010) The Foundation of Mandalay by King Mindon. PhD Dissertation, School of Oriental and African Studies, University of London.

Taylor, R.H. (1987) *The State in Burma*. Honolulu: University of Hawaii Press.

Than Than Nwe (1998) Yangon: the emergence of a new spatial order in Myanmar's capital city. *Sojourn: Journal of Social Issues in Southeast Asia*, **13**(1), pp. 86–113.

Thant Myint-U. (2014) Polishing Myanmar's colonial gem. *The Irrawaddy*. Published electronically 14 October. Available at: http://www.irrawaddy.com/contributor/polishing-myanmars-colonial-gem.html.

Tinker, H. (1967) *The Union of Burma: A Study of the First Years of Independence*. London: Oxford University Press.

U Thein Maung (1963) *A History of Rankon (Rangoon)*. Yangon: Zwe Sarpay Press.

Chapter 3

Mega-Events, Socio-Spatial Fragmentation, and Extra-territoriality in the City of Exception: The Case of Pre-Olympic Rio de Janeiro

Anne-Marie Broudehoux

This chapter examines the role of sporting mega-events in the legal and spatial reconfiguration of the urban landscape. It explores their effect on the production of a new urban territoriality, marked by the creation of spaces of exception, which are both spatially and legally located outside the normal urban order. The chapter seeks to demonstrate that mega-events are at the root of increasingly fragmented and polarized urban topographies, which are the material expression of growing social, political, and economic inequality. It argues that hosting mega-events reinforces a spatial hierarchy of the urban landscape that considers some spaces more worthy than others and reinforces the construction of a geography of segregation and exclusion. In spite of their reputation as great social unifiers and celebrations of togetherness, mega-event spectacles are powerful instruments in concealing the growing fragmentation of the urban territory into pockets of privatized enclaves that increasingly escape local legal and spatial norms.[1]

The chapter centres specifically on the transformation of Rio de Janeiro in the years leading up to hosting two of the world's greatest events: the 2014 World Cup and the 2016 Olympics. Urban fragmentation is not foreign to the city of Rio de Janeiro; it has long been inscribed into its genetic code. Built on narrow strips of flatland caught between the mountains and the sea, Rio's unique geography has always been highly fragmented. Rio's history has imposed a pattern of segregation and exclusion onto this already discontinuous landscape and has been marked by struggles over the boundaries that separate distinct urban sectors and social realities. The chapter argues that in Rio the recent hosting of mega-events has exacerbated fragmentation by creating new territories of exception and further isolating existing spaces of exclusion while promoting the privatization of vast urban sectors.

Neoliberal Planning, Mega-Events, and the City of Exception

In recent decades, mega-events have come to be seen as major disruptors in a city's development and catalysts for great urban transformations (Hiller, 2012; Gold and Gold, 2017; Chalkey and Essex, 1999). Neoliberal civic leaders, who have long learned to harness a discourse of crisis to generate popular consensus for major urban interventions, have seized the opportunity offered by these events to push forward their own urban programmes (Vainer, 2011; Arantes, 2009). Coalitions of political and economic agents thus exploit the artificial crisis engineered by their fixed deadline and exceptional nature to galvanize large urban projects, override other priorities on the urban agenda, and facilitate the adoption of neoliberal urban policies (Vanwynsberghe et al., 2012; Hayes and Horne, 2011; Peck and Tickell, 2002). It is in part through their capacity to generate a generalized sense of urgency – what Stavros Stavrides (2010) has called an 'Olympic state of emergency' – that mega-events legitimize the adoption of an exceptional politico-institutional framework, often in total disregard for existing legal and spatial realities, to help reshape the urban landscape and restructure its territory.

This state of emergency has created unique planning conditions and legitimated an extraordinary set of exceptions and exemptions, leading Carlos Vainer (2011) to describe the sporting event host city as a 'city of exception', and Isaac Marrero-Guillamon (2012) to talk of an 'Olympic state of exception'. Such conceptualizations draw upon Giorgio Agamben's (2005) notion of the 'state of exception', which describes the suspension of laws in times of crisis and emergency in order to face an unexpected necessity, such as a war or national catastrophe. Agamben (2005) defined the 'state of exception' as the state bypassing the pre-existing juridical order in the interest of expediency, a unilateral process which he qualified as the 'suspension of law by law'. And he warned that, rather than being a provisional measure developed to cope with an emergency situation, the state of exception has a tendency to impose itself permanently and to become a regular, autocratic, technique of government, increasingly used in a range of non-war situations such as financial crises or general strikes.

Much like with the 'shock doctrine' described by Naomi Klein (2008), where disasters are used to push local economies to adapt to the needs of a neoliberal agenda, local politicians and their economic allies instrumentalize mega-events to advance policies they could never institute under normal political circumstances. Jules Boykoff (2013) thus differentiated between 'celebration capitalism' (that which rests upon an exuberant state of exception) and 'disaster capitalism' (that which occurs during a catastrophic state of exception). For him, disaster capitalism exploits the collective vulnerability caused by social trauma to institute neoliberal policies rooted in privatization and deregulation. Celebration capitalism is backed by mass-media-supported political spectacle, festive commercialism, consensual claims of social and environmental sustainability and benefits for the security industry.

While disaster capitalism weakens the state with the adoption of neoliberal policies that allow the market to override the state, celebration capitalism deploys state actors as strategic partners in public-private partnerships, where the public assumes most of the costs and risks (Boykoff, 2013). In the process, the state's role is co-opted and appropriated to provide assistance to private accumulation. In the Olympic city of exception, the state thus coordinates and directs investments and uses public resources to make the city attractive to developers and investors through infrastructure upgrading and public service provision so that private capital can capitalize on the revamped city.

With their tremendous symbolic weight, global visibility, massive construction programmes, and hefty price tags, mega-events represent exceptional moments in a city's historical development. Their constrained timeframe, which allows little time for public criticism or in-depth analysis, helps to create a political climate that will permit the realization of large urban projects that in normal circumstances may not have appeared acceptable. The heightened civic pride and collective euphoria that result from over-enthusiastic media coverage also make them perfect opportunities to manipulate public opinion in favour of policy changes. Together, these exceptional factors grant event-promoting coalitions considerable leeway in reshaping the city for the needs of the event, its sponsors, and their local partners. The 'event-city of exception' is thus characterized by a radical transformation of the city's legal and spatial landscape, both of which are marked by a high level of exceptionalism (Marrero-Guillamon, 2012).

Mega-Events as Sites of Legal Exceptionalism

Megan Corrarino (2014) has described in detail the extraordinary legal regime adopted to facilitate mega-event preparations. The unique circumstances offered by hosting mega-events gives event organizers licence to suspend the pre-existing legal order and to impose new rules and sanctions that circumvent the normal decision-making process. This legal exceptionalism has allowed the introduction of highly restrictive regulatory instruments that govern speech, the use of public space, employment, housing, and numerous other facets of life in ways that would normally be unfeasible, while also diverting the normal protection of rights. The notion that extraordinary measures are necessary to the timely realization of the event also justifies lifting normal workplace protections including safety standards and labour negotiation rights (Corrarino, 2014).

For example, throughout Brazil, the urgency of mega-event projects has justified the suspension of collective bargaining rights of construction workers at World Cup sites (Articulaçao, 2012). The Fédération Internationale de Football Association (FIFA), the world governing body for the sport, also imposed a strict construction pace and threatened to force work around-the-clock at several stadia in order to ensure that the sites were completed in time for the event. Other forms of legal exemptions were used to legitimate free-speech bans or to evict or displace people without due process. Likewise, it has become common practice for Olympic host cities to introduce restrictive legislation specifically directed at population groups considered undesirable to the city's image (COHRE, 2007). Here the case of Olympic Beijing is a perfect example: more than 1.5 million people were displaced and countless migrant workers were expelled from the city for the duration of the event, while a vast state-led 'civilizing' campaign banned a host of public behaviours and criminalized informal practices (Broudehoux, 2010, 2011).

In this 'regime of legal exceptionalism' (Corrarino, 2014), laws are not applied equally for all citizens. Actors involved in event preparations enjoy preferential treatment and are allowed to bypass the competitive bidding process, suspend established procedures (like public consultation and participation), reformulate planning regulations, and lift safety standards. Not only do such legal exceptions benefit some more than others, but many new laws, passed in exceptional circumstances to protect the rights and interests of private corporations, are in direct violation of local citizen's rights. This exceptional legal regime leads to a great power imbalance between local and foreign interests and results in uneven rights protections in favour of international organizations and their sponsors. It also facilitates the fast-tracking of special laws to ensure compliance with the stipulations of local and global organizers and to better serve investor interests (Hayes and Horne, 2011; Lima, 2010).

The exceptional circumstances that characterize mega-event planning thus affect government and city management. Event promoters and elite interests take advantage of mega-events to reframe the political debate using diverse rhetorical strategies to promote a culture that undermines respect for normal rights protections and to create a policy environment in which legal exceptionalism becomes acceptable, and is even encouraged (Corrarino, 2014). Therefore, by allowing the emergence of extralegal forms of governance, mega-events are at the source of great ruptures in the local political process.

One of the direct consequences of the legal exceptionalism that has come to characterize mega-event preparations is the establishment of, or consolidation of, an authoritarian form of urban governance marked by the direct interference of executive powers in the act of legislation and in silencing dissent. Nelma Gusmão de Oliveira (2013) has claimed that in the run-up to World Cup Brazil, the distinction between legislative, executive, and judicial power all but disappeared. Decisions were made behind closed doors, without normal participatory processes, and in contravention of the normal human rights protections enshrined in both national and international law. The symbolic appeal of mega-events limited popular resistance and facilitated the adoption of substantial legal changes without much opposition. In Rio de Janeiro, a total lack of transparency and tight filtering of information – even deliberate misinformation – about event-related projects marked preparations for the two mega-events. Private citizens and civil-society groups seeking details about project implementation were often denied access to this information, in violation of Brazilian and international laws. Mega-events can thus be seen as essential tools to help bypass the normal democratic political process.

A last aspect of the legal exceptionalism that characterizes mega-events is the establishment of a new institutional framework in which nonelected agents, including beneficiaries of international sponsorships like the International Olympic Committee (IOC) and FIFA, play a key role in local decision-making (Gusmão de Oliveira, 2011; Alegi, 2008). Gusmão de

Oliveria (2013) went so far as to talk of the emergence of a parallel form of government and a parallel form of justice.[2] Organizations like FIFA and the IOC enjoy an unprecedented political and judicial autonomy, while public-private coalitions responsible for the realization of the event are given extraordinary powers and privileged access to public funds, without any form of accountability. They are thus able to remake the city by imposing their own timeframe and agendas on urban development. In short, mega-events allow for the creation of a state within the state, where political and ethical responsibilities are blurred and sovereign law is suspended (Gusmão de Oliveira, 2013).

Territories of Exception

Not only has the state of exception produced a legal vacuum, marked by indeterminacy and legal exceptionalism, but it has also allowed the emergence of new territorialities, in the form of self-governing enclaves, which can be seen as the spatial manifestation of the city of exception. These pockets of extraterritoriality echo Eyal Weizman's (2005) 'archipelagos of exception', defined as discontinuous territorial fragments where sovereign power is deposed or challenged. They are considered extraterritorial because of their position outside local and national jurisdiction. According to Weizman (2005), in international law, the term 'extraterritoriality' refers to those instances where a state extends its jurisdiction or effective control over zones, individuals, or activities beyond its borders. The concept applies to military movements on foreign soil as well as to embassies or diplomats in the form of diplomatic immunity (Weizman, 2005).

In the Olympic city of exception, territorial enclaves are constituted as special autonomous zones, controlled and regulated by corporate or intergovernmental entities, where normal legal processes do not apply. For example, Olympic parks as well as areas surrounding stadia and other venues are often isolated, both physically and legally, from their immediate context. Designated as special legal zones where political and ethical responsibilities are lifted, they function in certain respects as colonized territories, benefitting from an altered form of sovereignty and aspects of 'diplomatic immunity'. These zones of exception are not governed by the laws of the land but by the laws of corporate intergovernmental entities, which allow them to operate by their own rules. Although publicly funded and benefitting from generous fiscal conditions, these newly created territories are often privately owned and managed. They mainly serve to protect the exclusive rights and privileges of major stakeholders like the IOC and FIFA, their sponsors, and associated developers. The intent is to help these entities generate profits from the mega-event and limit their risk.

If these territories of exception are characterized by the suspension of the normal legal process, it does not mean that they are unregulated spaces. Quite the contrary, they have become some of the city's most regulated areas. For example, many territories of exception rely on stringent antiterrorist-like regulations to provide security for capital and protect the rights and privileges of major stakeholders. The fact that mega-events' revenues rely on exclusive broadcasting and sponsorship contracts explains some of the extreme measures deployed to protect the sponsors' acquired monopoly rights, especially against widely bedevilled ambush marketing. So vast is the sovereignty of these territories of exception that they are immune to the rules of the free market. Indeed, many of them could be qualified as zones of protected monopoly, and represent places where market rules of fair competition no longer apply.

Among different types of territories of exclusion that have emerged in the city of exception are 'brand-exclusion zones', which are areas surrounding event venues designated as special legal zones where commercial product placement for approved branded sponsors is protected (Hall, 2012). Exceptional legislation adopted in advance of the coming mega-events thus allows the conversion of areas of public space in a city into privatized, exclusive, and monopolistic commercial territories. These exclusive zones typically correspond to an area delimited by a one-kilometre radius from event venues. Inside, commercial and advertising rights are restricted to event sponsors, while the sale of products and the placement of publicity from companies other than official sponsorship-rights holders is prohibited.

Within the perimeter, local businesses are banned from displaying event-related symbols, logos, slogans, or images, and guards patrol the territory to discourage ambush marketing. No food or drinks can be brought onto the site by visitors, refreshments are confiscated upon entry, and water bottles are emptied. Even the clothes worn by supporters may be prohibited because of the presence of logos or colours associated with competitors. At the 2010 South African World Cup a group of Dutch women were expelled from a match because they were dressed in orange (a colour associated with a non-sponsor beer company), and they were arrested on charges of ambush marketing. Within the zones, in shops and in restaurants, noncash transactions are restricted to credit transactions from official sponsoring companies. And non-official commerce activities are strictly prohibited, including street vending, even if it is an important part of the event experience and represents an important source of livelihood for the local population.

At the 2012 London Olympics, an interesting example of brand exclusion were the 'adiZones', Adidas-branded, outdoor multisport gyms built throughout the United Kingdom in the year before the event. More than a temporary, promotional support or an opportunity for positive brand reinforcement, the adiZones proved to be clever publicity stunts that outlasted the Olympic event. Adidas purchased both the naming rights for the gyms as well as exclusive advertising rights. By promising a three-year maintenance contract as part of the deal, Adidas managed to secure access to advertising space for a prolonged period. The company thus extended its sponsorship opportunity beyond the event timeline, establishing what Duman (2012) has called 'permanent branding'.

This kind of reality has led Boykoff (2013) to describe mega-events not as a strictly neoliberal affair, marked by growing deregulation and privatization, but as a stringent regime of rules and regulations emanating from mega-event franchise owners like the IOC or FIFA. He thus charged that these remarkably powerful institutions are actually opposed to free markets. For example, by enforcing stringent brand protections they force host cities to bend local laws to accommodate commercial imperatives (Boykoff, 2013).

Rio's Brand Exclusion Zones

In Rio de Janeiro, one of these brand-exclusion zones surrounded the mythical Maracanã stadium, a symbol of Brazilian identity and an emblem of Rio's popular culture, where the World Cup's final match and the Olympics' opening and closing ceremonies were held. The exclusion zone was part of the renovations required by FIFA for the World Cup, which deeply altered the stadium's architectonic qualities and spatial organization (Winterbottom, 2016).

The creation of the brand-exclusion zone around the Maracanã was backed by special federal legislation. And while Brazilian law prohibits the sale of alcohol within a vast perimeter surrounding all sporting arenas, this rule was lifted for the duration of Rio's two mega-events, specifically to allow the sale of beer by exclusive sponsors. Non-sponsor vendors were forced out of their usual workplaces, and established food-sellers were banned from areas where they had long held the right to work, and where generations of families have enjoyed traditional *churrascos* (barbecues) on their way to the game. In Gusmão de Oliveira's words (2013, p. 224), during the World Cup and the Olympics, 'people could not consume beer that was not Budweiser's, soft drinks that were not Coca-Cola's, sandwiches that were not McDonald's or hygiene products that were not Johnson & Johnson's'.

Such restrictions were greatly contested. Fan associations and members of the general public accused FIFA of denaturing the Maracanã by forbidding the kinds of popular appropriations that had marked its history and had become an integral part of the Brazilian football experience (Mascarenhas *et al*., 2011). Other social groups contested interventions that threatened the integrity of both the material and the immaterial heritage of the stadium. Several judicial actions were taken against the state's plan to privatize this beloved public institution after the state spent more than half a billion dollars of taxpayers' money to bring the stadium up to the FIFA's standards. Conflicts also erupted with regard to the planned demolition of several public facilities in the stadium's vicinity, especially the historic Museu do Indio (Aboriginal Museum), to establish a safety perimeter and create open-air parking lots (Sánchez and Broudehoux, 2013).[3]

In March 2013 Rio's riot police brutally evicted dozens of indigenous squatters from the abandoned museum, near the Maracanã. Since 2006 native people from across Brazil had used it as a safe haven when visiting Rio to study, sell crafts, or receive medical attention, renaming it Aldeia Maracanã (Maracanã Village). The eviction took place on the day of the revamped stadium's inauguration. More than one hundred unarmed protesters were dispersed by shock troops using pepper spray and tear gas. Few journalists could witness the demonstration and report on the subsequent clash with the police because they had, conveniently, been taken directly into the arena in government vans to attend a demonstration of the stadium's new light and sound capabilities. The Maracanã was also at the heart of the June 2013 protest movement that rocked all urban Brazil, and it was the site of many actions denouncing the high social and economic price of hosting mega-events, both during the 2013 Confederations Cup and the 2014 World Cup.

Olympic Parks as Territories of Exception

A second spatial manifestation of event-related extraterritoriality is found in the design of Olympic parks and other large multi-venue spatial entities. Generally marked by a particular form of urbanism that is at once introverted, aggressive, and slightly paranoid, these territories of exception are characterized by a defensive architecture and a spatial layout that is inspired by military urbanism. A fortress-like design and tightly controlled borders limit physical access to event sites. They are protected by a multilayered, safety perimeter composed of a series of barriers in the form of gates, fences, moats, or waterways, through which there are only a few, easily monitored entry points. Event venues are thus isolated by the creation of a *cordon sanitaire* (an unbuilt buffer zone), keeping them a safe distance from nearby urban districts. Other means of filtering access include airport-like security checkpoints and a vast array of surveillance technologies. A striking example was the heavily secured downtown site at the Vancouver 2010 Winter Olympics, where even the Olympic flame was guarded like a military zone.

Such a military-inspired infrastructure of defence is generally supplemented by extensive patrols of municipal police officers, private security guards, and military police. Fussey *et al.* (2011) have described security measures at Olympic parks as a militarization of urban space that relies heavily on a policing model which emphasizes zero-tolerance orthodoxies and exceptional forms of penalty. Although actual security threats are difficult to assess, Olympic security consultants use a martial discourse replete with war metaphors that help to create a sense of collective insecurity; this justifies the state's recourse to extreme surveillance tactics and what appears to be excessive policing (Kennelly and Watt, 2011).

Fussey *et al.* (2011) warned of the risk associated with provisional security regimes transforming into permanent norms and practices of control. Pointing to the extraordinary municipal by-laws regulating public behaviour and the right to assembly that were retained in Sydney after the Olympics, they underlined the possibility that these extreme restrictions would become the 'new normal'. Tokyo (1964) and Seoul (1988) inherited a similar legacy of private policing after their respective Olympics.

These spaces of exception are generally removed from the normal political realm and are shielded from the local political reality. They are turned into apolitical territories from which all forms of political expression and representation are banned and criminalized. On entry, citizens must surrender their right to express themselves freely, except to cheer their favourite team. The only ideologies that can be openly expressed without fear of expulsion are the official slogans of event propaganda and the consensual jingles of their exclusive commercial sponsors. Venues are conceived as absolutist spaces, marked by the radical negation of political space, where only the voice of those in control can be heard, and in which all forms of dissent have been silenced.

Thanks to such complex security regimes and filtering tactics, territories of exception are thus closed to the general public. Admittance is only granted to a select few who are either part of the organization or have the rare privilege to hold event tickets. This population enjoys preferential treatment and is granted temporary citizenship on the basis of their close contact with event sponsors or organizers, their status as members of the press, or their capacity to pay. In the context of Rio's 2007 Pan-American Games, Curi et al. (2011, p. 13) wrote that ticket prices were so high that the walls around the Olympic park acted as a 'border between the colorful, modern spectacle that met international standards and the normal city with its Third World grievances'.

Privatized Urban Districts

A third category of territories of exception created in sight of mega-events consists of large-scale redevelopment projects not directly related to the event itself but which are conceived as a showcase for the city. They are often controversial, image-driven projects that seek to transform derelict neighbourhoods into profitable leisure and entertainment districts for international tourists and local elites. Their realization benefits from the event's tight deadline because they are typically fast-tracked through planning and development, allowing them to bypass the public consultation process. Often built in public-private partnership, they are modelled after Business Improvement Districts found in cities like New York, London, and Los Angeles, where entire urban neighbourhoods may come under private management.

An example of such consumption-oriented territories of exception is the renovation of Beijing's Qianmen district in the years leading to the 2008 Olympics (Meyer, 2008). This popular shopping and nightlife neighbourhood, known as the birthplace of Peking Opera and located next to Tiananmen Square, was transformed into a new festive consumption and entertainment hub with up-to-date tourist facilities. Inaugurated on the eve of the 2008 Olympic opening ceremonies, the project accelerated the transformation of this historically and socially sensitive area, resulting in the eviction and displacement of hundreds of families and the disappearance of a rich urban fabric (Bristow, 2011).

In Rio de Janeiro, Porto Maravilha epitomizes such exceptional, event-related urban privatization projects. Launched in June 2009 as the flagship of Rio's vast Olympic facelift, this expansive port revitalization will raze five million square metres of devalued housing and industrial buildings to create an upscale leisure, consumption, and entertainment centre. As the largest public-private partnership in Brazilian history, this real estate project will put five urban neighbourhoods under private management. As part of this effort public infrastructure provision was contracted out to a private consortium made up of three of Brazil's largest engineering and construction firms, who were made responsible for clearing the land, upgrading urban infrastructure, and providing basic services such as street lighting, drainage, traffic management, and garbage collection.

Although Rio's port was not part of the original Olympic bid, the project capitalized on its association with the Olympic brand when it came to raising money from investors, and in establishing itself as one of Rio's great Olympic legacies (Ferreira, 2010, p. 21). The redevelopment process was facilitated by extraordinary political interventions, creative financial innovations, and legal decrees passed in exceptional circumstances, all supposedly intended to comply with binding promises made to the IOC. However, research has unveiled evidence of collusion between the state and private enterprises in the reconfiguration of the legal framework that allowed the project's realization (Gusmão de Oliveira, 2011 and 2013). Entire sections of the municipal decree that defined the legal and territorial makeup of the PPP were identical to a private-sector proposal for the port's redevelopment submitted in 2009. And the three enterprises behind this proposal were the same companies that would later be selected as unique contenders for the realization of Porto Maravilha. The same companies (who were among the largest donors to the government's campaign) were also involved in the construction of FIFA's twelve stadia and most of Brazil's Olympic projects.[4]

Another example of the exceptionalism that characterizes Porto Maravilha's realization concerns the adoption of innovative instruments to finance the second phase of the project. These took the form of titles that allow private interests to build beyond the legal height limit (at times going from six- to fifty-storey heights) and maximize land use to increase profit. Regulated by the commission of real estate values, these titles became a subject of speculation because they could be traded on the stock market. Such financial instruments thus sought to capture, in advance, the increased property value created by revitalization, so as to help finance infrastructure projects, and their use has been denounced as a form of real estate speculation (Rolnik, 2011). Porto Maravilha's economic success relies on the transformation of this devalued part of town into prime real estate, which is contingent on the evacuation of its lower income residents. The project has already had a drastic impact upon the port district's socioeconomic makeup, with the expulsion of more than 700 families by 2013, or close to 2,500 residents (Broudehoux, 2013).

Informal Spaces of Exclusion

Another type of territory of exception that must be considered in the framework of mega-event planning are the informal settlements of the poor – whose exceptional nature is exacerbated by the hosting of such events. In contrast to the first three territories of exception, defined from within as sovereign spaces enjoying extraordinary legal exemptions, these extraterritorial enclosures are determined from without as spaces of exclusion, separation, and confinement that mainstream society refuses to incorporate.

Rio de Janeiro is no stranger to this type of extraterritoriality, which has long been a central part of its urban reality. Created through the illegal occupation of hills and marshlands by poor and often black residents, the *favela* (as informal urban settlements are known in Brazil) is construed as a 'special' territory existing outside the formal city. Demonized as a dangerous city-within-a-city, it has been perceived as unruly, outlaw territory – a rogue area that must be reigned in, conquered, and incorporated into the formal domain (Zaluar and Marcos, 1998). *Favelas* have also been described as spaces of transgression, where established rules do not apply, and where normative life is suspended. The most recent census (2010) produced by the Brazilian statistics bureau (IGBE) classified *favelas* as 'subnormal settlements', thereby legitimizing their non-adherence to social norms.

For years, *favelas* did not exist in formal imagery; nor did they appear on city maps. Instead they appeared as an absence in the formal landscape. They were construed as 'refuse spaces', negatively connoted landscapes, and interruptions in the urban fabric (Wright, 1997).[5] Their residents paid no taxes, received few public services, were deprived of the same civil rights as other Brazilians, and were basically refused urban citizenship. Moreira Salles (2013) has defined *favelas* as essentially 'mini failed states' within the city of Rio, where the only form of state presence is police repression.

Hosting Rio de Janeiro's two mega-events has exacerbated the differential treatment given to *favelas*, increased the government's indifference toward their residents (*favelados*), and consolidated their status as territories of exception. In the years preceding these events, *favelados* were subjected to a series of extralegal measures that confirmed their lack of citizen status. Many illegal actions and housing-rights violations were perpetrated by the state to ensure that the poor were removed from desirable land as required for event-related projects. The most widespread actions consisted of coercive tactics developed by city officials to facilitate speedy slum eviction and convince residents to sign away their homes. Denounced as 'strategies of war and persecution' (Articulaçao, 2011, p. 8), such intimidation tactics included infrastructure denial, public-service cuts, misappropriation and destruction of property, home invasions without court orders, *in absentia* marking of houses slated for demolition, and curtailed notice-and-comment periods.

In 2010 such tactics were used by the state to speed up the clearance of the Metrô-Mangueira *favela* and to force residents to abandon their homes to allow construction of parking lots for the adjacent Maracanã stadium (Campbell-Dollaghan, 2013). After being presented with a take-it-or-leave-it offer, residents who refused to leave were cut off from state services and left in unbearable living conditions amidst the debris of their neighbours' demolished homes and exposed to the increased risk of disease. The United Nations criticized these evictions on human-rights grounds in 2010, causing Rio's government to somewhat moderate its approach (Campbell-Dollaghan, 2013).

Similar strategies were deployed in Vila Autódromo, a *favela* located on the edge of the future Olympic park in the western suburb of Barra da Tijuca. Having survived waves of expulsion, especially before the 2007 Pan-American Games, Vila Autódromo is a symbol of resistance to forced evictions in Rio de Janeiro. The westward expansion of exclusive shopping malls and luxury condominiums in Barra da Tijuca and the proximity of the future Olympic park, with views over a lagoon, made the community's land extremely valuable. Initial plans for the Olympic park preserved the community intact; but pressure to vacate the land began after the project was handed over to a private consortium, which was promised the land in exchange for providing infrastructure and Olympic facilities. Despite having been granted a 99-year 'concession of use' land title from the state government in 1994, the community was threatened by a series of eviction orders from the municipal government. And the tactics used to enforce it ranged from generous compensation proposals to acts of persecution whose brutality and psychological violence were unprecedented.

Legal experts have underlined several violations in these eviction procedures. Many state actions were found to run counter to the constitutional protection of informal settlements and denounced as violations of the Statute of the City, a national law passed in 2001 to protect the right to housing and recognize the social function of urban property (Heck, 2013; Caldeira and Holston, 2005). Environmental-framing tactics, which justified expulsion on spurious environmental-protection grounds were also found to violate existing housing rights. This was especially the case when such tactics were applied to historically established *favelas*, many of which had been legalized as zones for upgrading in 2000 (Heck, 2013, Campbell-Dollaghan, 2013).

In the years leading to hosting the World Cup and the Olympics, *favelados* were also subjected to a differential security regime that reconfirmed and exacerbated their status as territories of exception. *Favelas* have long been familiar with a mode of policing in which the police and other institutions of criminal justice act like border patrols to guard the elite against the poor (Pinheiro, 2000). Much like other Olympic territories of exception unprecedented security measures were deployed around the *favelas* in preparation for mega-events to protect visitors from the presumed violence within. Following a logic of containment, many *favelas* located near event sites, and major tourist attractions were circled by heavily militarized buffer zones. Thus Morro da Providência, a small *favela* that sits at the heart of the newly developed Porto Maravilha, found itself surrounded by a disproportionate number of police units – an act that Zibechi (2010) denounced as a 'militarization of the poor'.

Part of the exceptional security regime recently imposed on the *favela* is the new 'police pacification' state programme, initiated in 2009, weeks after Rio was chosen to host the Olympics. The rhetoric that surrounds this programme portrays the *favela* as a warring enemy territory. Pacification is carried out through the 'reconquest of *favela* territory' by the Batalhão de Operações Policiais Especiais (BOPE) (Special Operations Battalion), known as one of the best-trained urban fighting forces in the world. According to this policy, before a *favela* is 'pacified', it must first be 'invaded' using a 'clear and hold' strategy and 'shock treatment' to demilitarize the drug trade (Yutzy, 2012). Once the *favela* has been cleared of drug-gang affiliates, a Police Pacification Unit enters the reconquered territory, symbolically planting both a state and a national flag, and settling permanently in a highly visible building dominating the *favela*. This permanent police presence is experienced as an occupying force by local residents, a militarized body ruling over them and limiting their ability for self-determination (Freeman, 2012). Far from marking the *favela*'s integration into the formal city, the presence of the Police Pacification Unit only reinforces its status as a marginal enclave and a territory of exception that must be treated and maintained as a separate urban entity (Yutzy, 2012). The widely televised and sensationalized police invasion of the Complexo of Alemão in 2010 was described by Maria Clara Dias and Luis Eslava (2013, p. 190) as a 'true act of war'.

Redefining Traditions of Power

This chapter has explored the effect of mega-events on the production of a new urban territoriality, marked by the creation of archipelagos of exception, which are both spatially and legally located outside the normal urban order. It has identified four types of spaces of extraterritoriality: commercially defined brand-exclusion zones, fortress-like event sites, privatized urban districts, and informal spaces of exclusion. These may come to exist as a result of impending mega-events, or their situation may be exacerbated by planning for these events. The examples given demonstrate how mega-events facilitate the construction of an event city of exception, based on the implementation of new regimes of legal exceptionalism that serve neoliberal interests, exacerbate social and territorial polarization, and accelerate the appropriation of urban space by private capital. By providing opportunities for local elite interests to reframe domestic political debates in a way that erodes rights protection, mega-events also reinforce power inequality.

This initial examination of the relationship between mega-events and the spatialization of neoliberal exceptionalism leaves many questions unanswered, however. Further investigation is needed, for example, to evaluate conditions that determine the longevity of this state of exception. Are these new forms of extraterritoriality temporary, lasting only for the duration of a mega-event, or are they irrevocable? Fussey *et al.* (2011), drawing on Agamben (2005), have claimed that provisional and exceptional measures established in preparation for mega-events can be transformed into lasting techniques of government. These may later be incorporated into the design and management of these places, producing norms and practices of control that often become permanent. It is clear that, in spite of their assumed temporary nature, many exceptional laws, new urban regimes, and semiautonomous zones can have a lasting impact. These may be registered in terms of the production of polarized topography, the deterritorialization of existing population, and the emergence of new forms of enclaves. Will they ultimately be part of the 'legacy' that event promoters so adamantly promise once the event is over?

Continued research on the spatial dimension of mega-events is needed to further current understanding of their long-term spatial and legal ramifications. The series of demonstrations that have rocked Brazil since June 2013 have proved that mega-events may also provide a platform for the expression of dissent and create an umbrella cause around which collective resistance can be organized. As a result of public pressure exerted by these social movements, the creation of many territories of exception planned in preparation for Rio's recent mega-events have been reconsidered, and some of their legal ramifications have been re-examined and revisited by local authorities and defenders of civil rights.

Notes

1. This notion resonates with Debord's (1967, p. 7) assertions that, although the spectacle presents itself as a *means of unification*, the appearance of unity is in fact an illusion, as the spectacle instead leads to 'universal separation' and intensified fragmentation.
2. For example, a new Brazilian law, if passed, would allow for the creation of fast-track tribunals to expedite prosecution linked to mega-event offences, thus creating a parallel system of justice for the duration of mega-events. See Projeto de Lei do Senado, no.728 de 2011. Available at: http://www.senado.gov.br/atividade/materia/detalhes.asp?p_cod_mate=103652.
3. Other threatened public institutions include the Fredenreich municipal school, the Célio de Barros track-and-field stadium, and the Julio Delamare aquatic park. As a result of public outrage, only the track-and-field stadium was demolished and the space was used as a parking lot during both the World Cup and the Olympic Games. But athletes and local community members deplored losing access to this essential training facility.
4. The three enterprises are Norberto Odebrecht, Carioca Christiani-Nielsen Engenharia, and OAS Ltd.
5. In his typology of urban spaces, Tamaldge Wright (1997) distinguished between 'pleasure space' (spaces of entertainment and relaxation) associated with middle-class users and 'refuse space' (spaces of neglect, violence, and abandonment) often taken over by marginal population groups.

References

Acioly, C. (2001) Reviewing urban revitalisation strategies in Rio de Janeiro: from Urban project to urban management approaches. *Geoforum*, **32**(4), pp. 501–530.
Agamben, G. (2005) *State of Exception*. Chicago, IL: University of Chicago Press.
Alegi, P. (2008) A nation to be reckoned with: the politics of World Cup Stadium construction in Cape Town and Durban, South Africa. *African Studies*, **6**(3), pp. 397–422.
Arantes, O. (2009) Uma estratégia fatal. A cultural nas novas gestoes urbanas, in Arantes, O., Vainer, C. and Maricato, M. (eds.) *A cidade do pensamento unico: desmachando consensus*. Petrópolis: Vozes, pp. 11–74.
Articulação Nacional Dos Comitês Populares Da Copa (National Network of Popular Committees on the World Cup) (2012) *Megaeventos E Violações De Direitos Humanos No Brasil* (2nd ed.), pp. 37–41.
Boykoff, J. (2013) *Celebration Capitalism and the Olympic Games*. London: Routledge.
Bristow, M. (2011) Beijing's Qianmen district: rebuilt for better or worse. *BBC News*, 15 February. Available at: http://www.bbc.co.uk/news/world-asia-pacific-12344304.
Broudehoux, A.M. (2010) Civilizing Beijing: social beautification, civility, and citizenship at the 2008 Olympics, in Hayes, G. and Karamichas, J. (eds.) *The Olympics, Mega-*

events and Civil Societies: Globalization, Environment, Resistance. Basingstoke: Palgrave Macmillan.

Broudehoux, A.M. (2011) The social and spatial impacts of Olympic image construction: the case of Beijing 2008, in Wagg, S. and Lenskyj, H. (eds.) *A Handbook of Olympic Studies*. Basingstoke: Palgrave Macmillan.

Broudehoux, A.M. (2013) Sporting mega-events and urban regeneration: planning in a state of emergency, in Leary. M.E. and McCarthy, J. (eds.) *The Routledge Companion to Urban Regeneration*. London: Routledge.

Caldeira, T. and Holston, J. (2005) State and urban space in Brazil: from modernist planning to democratic interventions, in Ong, A. and Collier, S.J. (eds.) *Global Assemblages: Technology, Governmentality, Ethics*. Oxford: Blackwell, pp. 393–416.

Campbell-Dollaghan, K. (2013) Make way for the Olympics: the paramilitary clearance of Rio's slums. *The Guardian*, 11 October. Available at: http://www.gizmodo.in/news/Make-Way-For-the-Olympics-The-Paramilitary-Clearance-of-Rios-Slums/articleshow/23991312.cms.

Chalkey, B.S. and Essex, S.J. (1999) Urban development through hosting international events: a history of the Olympic Games. *Planning Perspectives*, **14**(4), pp. 369–394.

COHRE (Centre on Housing Rights and Eviction) (2007) *Fair Play for Housing Rights: Mega-Events*. Geneva: COHRE Special Report.

Corrarino, M. (2014) Law exclusion zones: mega-events as sites of procedural and substantive human rights violations. *Yale Human Rights and Development Law Journal*, **17**, pp. 180–204.

Curi, M., Knijnik, J. and Mascarenhas, G. (2011) The Pan American Games in Rio de Janeiro 2007: consequences of a sport mega-event on a BRIC country. *International Review for Sociology of Sport*, **46**(2) pp. 1–16.

Debord, G. (1967) *La société du spectacle*. Paris: Gallimard.

Dias, M.C. and Eslava, L. (2013) Horizons of inclusion: life between laws and developments in Rio de Janeiro. *University of Miami Inter-American Law Review*, **44**(2), pp. 177–218.

Duman, A. (2012) AdiZones: rewriting the 2012 Olympic legacy as permanent branding, in Powell, H. and Marrero-Guillamón, I. (eds.) *The Art of Dissent: Adventures in London's Olympic State*. London: Marshgate Press, pp. 56–64.

Ferreira, A. (2010) O projeto 'Porto Maravilha' No Rio De Janeiro: inspiração de Barcelona e produção a serviço do capital? *Revista Bibliográfica de Geografía y Ciencias Sociales* (Universidad de Barcelona), **15**(895). Available at: http://www.ub.edu/geocrit/b3w-895/b3w-895-21.htm.

Freeman, J. (2012) Neoliberal accumulation strategies and the visible hand of police pacification in Rio de Janeiro. *Revista de Estudos Universitários*, **38**(1), pp. 95–126.

Fussey, P., Coaffee, J., Armstrong, G. and Hobbs, D. (2011) *Securing and Sustaining the Olympic City: Reconfiguring London for 2012 and Beyond*. Farnham: Ashgate.

Gold, J. and Gold, M. (2017) *Olympic Cities: Urban Planning, City Agendas and the World's Games, 1896–2020*. London: Routledge.

Gusmão de Oliveira, N. (2011) Força-de-lei: rupturas e realinhamentos institucionais na busca do 'sonho olímpico' carioca. Paper presented at the 14th annual meeting of the National Association of Researchers in Urban and Regional Planning (ANPUR), Rio de Janeiro.

Gusmão de Oliveira, N. (2013) O Poder Dos Jogos e Os Jogos De Poder: Os Interesses Em Campo Na Produção De Uma Cidade Para O Espetáculo Esportivo. PhD Dissertation, IPPUR, Federal University of Rio de Janeiro.

Hall, E. (2012) London outdoes China in brand crackdown at Summer Olympics:

restrictions to protect sponsors even stricter than Beijing Games. *Ad Age*, 4 June. Available at: http://adage.com/article/global-news/brand-police-full-force-london-olympics/235136/.

Hayes, G. and Horne, J. (2011) Sustainable development: shock and awe? London 2012 and civil society. *Sociology*, **45**(5), pp. 749–764.

Heck, C. (2013) The 'area of risk' justification for favela removals: the case of Santa Marta. *Rio on Watch*, 29 October. Available at http://rioonwatch.org/?p=11410.

Hiller, H.H. (2012) *Host Cities and the Olympics: An Interactionist Approach.* London: Routledge.

Kennelly, J. and Watt, P. (2011) Sanitizing public space in Olympic host cities: the spatial experiences of marginalized youth in 2010 Vancouver and 2012 London. *Sociology*, **45**(5), pp. 765–781.

Klein, N. (2008) *The Shock Doctrine: The Rise of Disaster Capitalism.* Harmondsworth: Penguin.

Lima, P.N. Jr (2010) *Uma estratégia chamada 'planejamento estratégico'.* Rio de Janeiro: 7 Letras.

Marrero-Guillamon, I. (2012) Olympic state of exception, in Powell, H. and Marrero-Guillamon, I. (eds.) *The Art of Dissent: Adventures in London's Olympic State.* London: Marshgate Press, pp. 20–29.

Mascarenhas, G., Curi, M. *et al*. (2011) The Pan American Games in Rio de Janeiro 2007: consequences of a sport mega-event on a BRIC country. *International Review for the Sociology of Sport*, **46**(2), pp.140–156.

Meyer, M. (2008) The death and life of old Beijing. *Architectural Record*, **196**(7), pp. 73–76.

Moreira Salles, J.P. (2013) One Rio, two Brazils. *Brown Political Review*, 22 October. Available at: http://www.brownpoliticalreview.org/2013/10/one-rio-two-brazils/.

Peck, J. and Tickell, A. (2002) Neoliberalizing space. *Antipodes*, **34**(3), pp. 380–404.

Pinheiro, P.S. (2000) Democratic governance, violence, and the (un) rule of law. *Daedalus*, **129**(2), pp. 119–143.

Rolnik, R. (2011) Porto Maravilha: custos públicos e benefícios privados? Blog posted 13 June. Available at: https://raquelrolnik.wordpress.com/.

Sánchez, F. and Broudehoux, A.M. (2013) Mega-events and urban regeneration in Rio de Janeiro: planning in a state of emergency. *International Journal of Urban Sustainable Development*, **5**(2), pp. 132–153.

Stavrides, S. (2010) The Athens 2004 Olympics: Modernization as a State of Emergency. Paper presented at the International Conference on Mega-events and the City. Federal Fluminense University, Niterói.

Vainer, C.B. (2009) Pátria, empresa e mercadoria: notas sobre a estratégia discursiva do Planejamento Estratégico Urbano, in Arantes, O., Vainer, C. and Maricato, E. (eds.) *A cidade do pensamento único: Desmanchando consensos*. Petrópolis: Vozes, pp. 75–103.

Vainer, C.B. (2011) Megaeventos e a Cidade de Exceção. Paper presented at the 14th annual meeting of the National Association of Researchers in Urban and Regional Planning (ANPUR), Rio de Janeiro.

Vanwynsberghe, R. *et al*. (2012) When the Games come to town: neoliberalism, mega-events and social inclusion in the Vancouver 2010 Winter Olympic Games. *International Journal of Urban and Regional Research*, **36**(2), pp. 3–23.

Weizman, E. (2005) On Extraterritoriality. Conference lecture at the symposium Archipelago of Exception: Sovereignties of Extraterritoriality, Centre for Contemporary Culture, Barcelona.

Winterbottom, T. (2016). *A Cultural History of Rio de Janeiro after 1889: Glorious Decadence*. Basingstoke: Palgrave Macmillan.

Wright, T. (1997) *Out of Place: Homeless Mobilizations, Subcities, and Contested Landscapes*. Albany, NY: State University of New York Press.

Yutzy, C. (2012) Increased state presence through the Unidade De Polícia Pacificadora in Santa Marta, Rio De Janeiro: the creation of the city's theme park and resulting social issues. *Revista de Estudos Universitários*, **38**(1), pp. 127–146.

Zaluar, A. and Marcos, A. (1998) *Um seculo de Favela*. Rio de Janeiro: Fundaçao Getulio Vargas.

Zibechi, R. (2010) *Rio de Janeiro: Control of the Poor Seen as Crucial for the Olympics*. Washington DC: Americas Program, Center for International Policy. Available at: http://sociologias-com.blogspot.ca/2010/01/rio-de-janeiro-control-of-poor-seen-as.html.

Part II

People: Whose Indigeneity?

Chapter 4

Revamping Tradition: Contested Politics of 'the Indigenous' in Postcolonial Hong Kong

Shu-Mei Huang

> *[Yet] it was unthinkable that anyone not of the village clan could build a house in a village.*
>
> Denis Bray (2001, p. 164)
>
> *Using the past, present, and future to emphasize each other is common in commemorations.*
>
> John Carroll (2005, p. 165)

On lunar New Year's Eve, 2012, the chairman of the Heung Yee Kuk (HYK), Wong-fat Lau, made a drawing in the Che Kung Temple in the presence of many of the elite in the New Territories (NT) – a symbolic gesture to welcome the New Year in Hong Kong. The poem in the drawing read, 'What is evil and what is divine? It's so hard to differentiate the evil from the divine'. Chairman Lau was subsequently bombarded by questions from the media about whether the poem alluded to the then-serious competition for Chief Executive of the Hong Kong Special Administrative Region (HKSAR). Lau laughed, without giving any explicit message.

About 2 years earlier, during mid-October 2010, I had happened to attend a community meeting in the soon-to-be-demolished village of Choi Yuen. Some sixty people had gathered to witness a significant phone call to Lau, in which the villagers were trying to obtain his assistance in negotiating a right-of-way to enable their relocation plan. 'Did Lau own the land?' I asked. 'No', I was told. 'But he is the king of the NT!'

The mystic power represented by Lau raises several questions. What are the longstanding traditions in the NT that make politics – and the politics of land, in particular – so different from urban Hong Kong? And, specifically, how has the privilege of the indigenous been translated into a 'small-house policy' (SHP) that continues to produce low-density development in the rapidly urbanizing landscape of the New Territories? In addressing these questions, this chapter will explore how the notion of 'tradition' is complicit in establishing the special privileges of 'the indigenous' in Hong Kong.

The SHP, and the indigenous communities which qualify for it, have been much criticized in recent years. Indeed, abuse of the small-house policy is not unheard of. Yet no criminal case related to it had ever been brought before a court until a recent housing scam in which eleven indigenous villagers and a developer were to be jailed for defrauding the authorities. Not surprisingly, the HYK opposed the sentence, pointing out that the policy of allowing each male indigenous villager to build a three-storey villa was a traditional right protected by the Basic Law – Hong Kong's mini-constitution (*SCMP*, 2015).

To understand the idea and practice of traditional rights in postcolonial Hong Kong it is first necessary to appreciate the dualism at work in accounting for Hong Kong's territorial origins. On the one hand, official history stresses the political and cultural break that took place with the formation of the British colony (Carroll, 2005, pp.164–167). On the other, strategic recognition of precolonial tradition has been reinforced in many matters in the NT. This binary is embodied in the landscape, where walled villages (*poon choi* – also the term used for a Cantonese dish served in big bowls) and three-storey 'village houses' have been closely associated with the lives of those descended from the NT's original inhabitants (figure 4.1). Indeed, though less celebrated than other aspects of the global city, the power of the indigenous has become a key feature of land and identity politics in Hong Kong – especially since, in recent years, the NT became the frontier of economic integration with mainland Shenzhen.

Among other rights, since 1972, indigenous males have been allowed to build small houses, in the name of tradition. This privilege distinguishes them from other residents, especially those descended from migrants who arrived in the NT after the Chinese revolution in 1949. These non-indigenous villagers, despite having contributed to the survival of agriculture in Hong Kong, have mostly been considered landless farmers without an ancestral settlement or officially recognized tradition. Their settlements and leased farmlands have thus been vulnerable to takeover

Figure 4.1. Three-storey 'village houses' in the New Territories. (*Photo*: Shu-Mei Huang)

as sites for development of new towns and infrastructure projects. Meanwhile, the privileged indigenous, who dominate with respect to land rights, have continued to expand their presence in the NT. The power granted by 'indigeneity' and 'tradition' thus seems to reinforce the dualism embedded within the rural landscape of Hong Kong.

By examining the origin and nature of this unequal condition, this chapter seeks to advance understanding of processes of agency and authorship that frequently support notions of tradition. The interpretation and commercialization of tradition for power and profit, as the editors of this volume suggest, have been a potent force in both the transformation and preservation of built environments. What is of particular interest here is how tradition and the authors of tradition transform and constitute one another, and how these processes may lend legitimacy to, and leverage power from, indigenous claims to space and place. The chapter begins by introducing the colonial gaze that produced the indigenous inhabitants of Hong Kong.

Building for and of the Great Difference

It was only in 1972, on the occasion of the institutionalization of the SHP, that the term 'indigenous inhabitants' was officially adopted by the Hong Kong Executive Council (Chan, 1996). Ethnically speaking, indigenous residents of Hong Kong are indeed Han Chinese, the majority in China. Yet they have been differentiated from the non-indigenous population, Han and otherwise, on the basis of a shared tradition defined at a specific moment, i.e. when the British colony was expanded to include the New Territories. As Chan (1998) has noted, 'Tradition is interpreted as the sharing of a place of origin and rural customs by the villagers, and [in Hong Kong] the year 1898 has assumed significance in the interpretation of shared native place (*xinangxa*) by the inhabitants'. To be more precise, the indigenous community was differentiated along with the demarcation of the New Territories, and their tradition was explicitly recognized in 1899 when the British forced Qing China to grant them a 99-year lease to the area through 'The Convention for the Extension of Hong Kong Territory'.

James Stewart Lockhart, the Cadet Officer of the Hong Kong Civil Service at the time, called the distinction between native villagers and the colonial population 'the great difference', to be respectfully managed (Hayes, 2006). And for more than a century this instance of the colonial gaze has left its imprint on the way the NT have been governed. It persists today despite the reality that contemporary development has massively changed the area and diluted the original difference between its urban and rural populations. As a consequence, since 1980, many have challenged the necessity of separating land policies in the NT from those in the rest of Hong Kong (Hayes, 2006, p. 159). Yet the indigenous leadership has managed to maintain their paramount power, even though, according to the 2011 Census, indigenous inhabitants now comprise less than 10 per cent of the population of the NT.

The New Territories today make up 86 per cent of Hong Kong's land area. When the area was initially taken over by the British Crown, it was demarcated into 355 survey districts according to the New Territories (Land Court) Ordinance of 1900 (the Ordinance 1900). This law also stipulated premiums and certificates of land ownership and use between 1904 and 1905 that changed the prevailing system of tenure from freehold to leasehold (Sit, 2011; Lau, 1999). The ordinance further discontinued the practice of 'bottom-soil right', reshaping the relationship between tenant farmers and landlords.[1] Significantly, since that time, the use of land cannot be changed without official permission. Moreover, the Ordinance 1900 allowed the government to expropriate properties in the interest of public good (Sit, 2011, p. 58).

Considering this history, it may be fair to say that the establishment of indigeneity in the former colony was itself a colonial product, rendered by what Renato Rosaldo (1989) has called 'imperialist nostalgia'. As one former district officer, Denis Bray (2001, p. 37), wrote in a memoir, 'In the 1950s, the New Territories were terra incognita for urban dwellers – and that included everyone of any seniority in the government'. Thus, despite celebrating the centenary of its governance of Hong Kong in 1941, in the eyes of the British colonial administration the NT were still a place where farmers grew rice and '… village life continued in very much the way that it had done for generations' (Bray, 2001, p. 37). According to Jones (1995, p. 180), the lack of understanding of the NT by the British contributed to the romantic goal of preserving village life. Interestingly, however, this nostalgic reading of life did not extend to similar historical villages in New Kowloon and on Hong Kong Island (figure 4.2).[2] In effect, therefore, the century-old discourse surrounding tradition in the NT has emphasized both connections and disconnections: it has connected people of shared origin with their lands, while simultaneously disconnecting them from their motherland and from the urbanized territory of the colony.

Indigenous communities have, in general, been characterized by their connection to the land, by traditions embedded in place, and by the ways place-making involves multiple acts of remembering and imagining

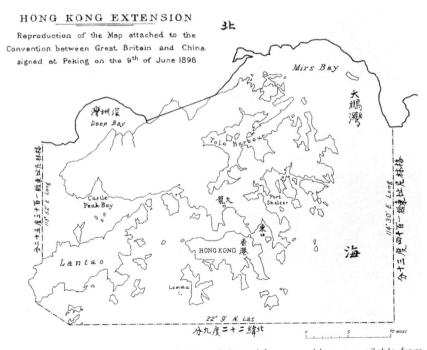

Figure 4.2. The New Territories. (*Source*: Adapted from an old map available from Wiki Commons)

(Casey, 1987). If tradition is to continue, philosophers have argued, the fact that '... its transmission is carried in the ebb and flow of everyday life makes it indispensable that it be presented not in a description or theory but instead instantiated as thus embedded' (Marshall, 2005, p. 2). Yet the kind of tradition referred to in the NT has been largely reduced to a continuation of the right from one generation to the next to occupy land with the approval of the government no matter what is built there or what activities are practised. Today, it is thus not a surprise to find non-indigenous inhabitants residing in rented small houses built on village lands next to stacks of shipping containers. Arguably, when the state introduced itself into the act of transmission – when tradition was first translated into the colonial policy of small houses, and then written into the Basic Law prior to the handover of Hong Kong to China in 1997 – tradition as an embedded *process* was essentially transformed into a commodifiable land grant. It is thus important to historicize the commodity chain and reveal the political agency hidden within it.

Nezar AlSayyad's treatment of tradition as a regime is helpful here. He has suggested that tradition is 'deployed, resisted, and reworked through hegemonic struggles that seek to create both built environments and citizen-subjects' (2004, p. 19). The colonial creation of the SHP exemplifies this thesis, particularly as it related to the perpetuation of aspects of the colonial landscape in postcolonial Hong Kong. Before elaborating further on this relation, let me provide a brief history of the policy.

The most dedicated advocate of the small-house policy is the HYK. Even though it was only given formal status by the Heung Yee Kuk Ordinance (Chapter 1097) in 1959 (Lee, 1984, pp. 166–167), it has been the most important political organization in the NT since the 1920s. The HYK initially rose to importance as a result of a political crisis, when the colonial government promulgated the 'crown lands resumption ordinance' in 1922, and followed it with a plan to regulate the conversion of farmland to building sites (Sit, 2011, p. 191). Numerous protests organized by the HYK eventually forced the government to exempt the indigenous villagers from paying a differential premium when they built houses for their own use. And since then, the HYK has served as an important consultation group. As mentioned above, its status was formalized after World War II, at a time when an elective system of village representatives and rural committees was also created to establish a local political system. Yet, especially in light of the rapid demographic change in the New Territories from the 1950s to the 1970s, this patrilineal system was never meant to cover the whole population of the area (Bray, 2001, p. 97).

The SHP emerged in November 1972 from a two-decade-long negotiation of rights between villagers and the colonial government. Following the war, the Building Ordinance of 1950 required villagers to submit their plans for approval before constructing houses. And a subsequent policy change in 1955 required owners of concrete houses to pay an extra premium. Furthermore, anyone who planned to build a new such house had to convert their leasehold to a site from farmland to residential land at a value ratio of 3 to 1. From 1959 to 1971, numerous debates emerged over deregulation and premium exemption with regard to such issues as materials, area, and building height.

The constant changes upset the indigenous population, and the resentment grew into an unprecedented village uprising between 1971 and 1972. With 1,000 signatures collected from village representatives, the HYK called a rally against the increasing regulation of housing construction in the existing villages.[3] The government gave in, and within six weeks it passed the 'Building Ordinance [New Territory], 1972', which gave birth to the SHP. The SHP allowed any certified indigenous male (of at least eighteen years of age, descended through the male lineage from a male resident of an officially recognized indigenous village in 1898 or earlier) to build one small house in his lifetime in the rural development zone or in an extension area. Moreover, as long as owners complied with certain criteria, they were exempted from submitting formal building plans to the government.

At the time, the government also provided a list of 642 indigenous villages recognized as having existed prior to 1898. Small houses could be built on private land, or they could be built on government land at a concessionary premium – but only within the Village Environs (VE) (typically defined as an area 300 feet [91 metres] from the outermost corner of the outermost house built before December 1972), or within the VEA (Village Extension Area). The SHP was therefore intended to codify the allegedly traditional practice whereby the family head could build for himself and for each of his sons upon marriage a house within the village area, either on his own land or on village building lots acquired through auction among certified residents of a particular village.

Why is the footprint of a small house set today at 700 square feet (65 square metres)? In fact, the measurement of small houses has changed over time – as if tradition could be sized and negotiated. The preliminary sizing dates to 1905, when the British decided, based on their observations, that a traditional village house would be defined as occupying 436 square feet (40.5 square metres and one-hundredth of an acre, also known as one 'traditional division' of land). This was important because buildings were taxed based on such units.

The contemporary area of 700 square feet is halfway between 436 square feet (one 'traditional division') and 872 square feet (two 'traditional divisions'), rounded to the nearest hundred feet. Some have additionally suggested that 700 square feet is simply the maximum building footprint the government felt comfortable permitting. An important reference here were publicly funded houses built to accommodate residents of traditional villages displaced by government projects. The first prototype was an approximately 700 square foot, gabled, two-storey structure built for the residents of Kwan Mun Hau village. Later, such houses were built to two-and-a-half storeys, including the cockloft, or three storeys with a flat roof (Hopkinson and Lei, 2003, p. 8). Indeed, over the years the building height restriction has gradually been increased from two, to two and a half, and finally three storeys (not to exceed 25 feet [7.6 metres]) by 1975. Furthermore, flat roofs gradually came to dominate new buildings, since the wooden beams required for pitched roofs became less available (figure 4.3).

It is worth noting here that the term 'small house' was only instituted as a replacement for 'village-type house' on the advice of Denis Bray, when he served as district officer (Bray, 2001, p. 164). This new, pragmatic definition eliminated guidelines that had previously addressed traditional

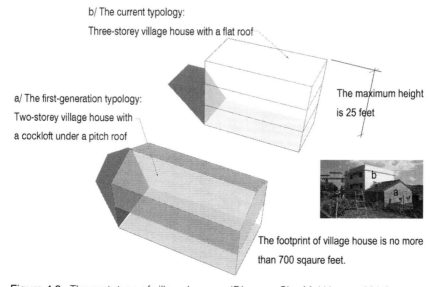

Figure 4.3. The prototype of village houses. (*Diagram*: Shu-Mei Huang, 2014)

styles, replacing them with a simple dimensional standard. A juxtaposition of the official English name for the structure, however, with the colloquial Cantonese term, *ting uk* (literally, 'the male's house') is also revealing. While colonial policy-makers focused on the SHP as a convenient way to control village sprawl, indigenous residents focused on the exclusive nature of the grant as a male right. The different wordings thus reflect the ambiguousness of tradition. As Bray, the architect of the SHP, noted in retrospect (2001, p. 166): 'I knew perfectly well that it would not be long before some enterprising architect would design pleasant little buildings that fitted the rules but looked nothing like a traditional village house. Sure enough, a Spanish-style house began to appear with lovely tiled half roofs'.

Bray also wrote that the policy was never meant to be permanent: 'I do not see these measures as anything more than interim measures which will complement the major job of producing a comprehensive development plan for the rural New Territories' (2001, p. 166). Nevertheless, the indigenous villagers saw the policy differently; for them the land grant was *ting*, a 'right'.

Today, small houses appear as no small privilege among Hong Kongers, most of whom live in cramped conditions (Lai and Ho, 2001). 'By definition it is wrong', the property-management expert Roger Nissim (2012, p. 130) has noted. Compared to the traditional 436 square foot, two-storey Old Schedule house prevailing in the NT in 1898, small houses today are far from small (Nissim, 2012). Indeed, they are quite spacious compared to the limited area available to the non-indigenous population, who live in informal cottages, or to those NT residents who have been relocated to public housing. The exclusive nature of the policy and the conduct of the qualification process also leave considerable room for abuse. To certify a grant applicant's indigenous status, a small-house applicant must submit a declaration, signed either by the representative of the applicant's village or by a chairman (or vice-chairman) of the relevant rural committee. It is often difficult for outsiders to verify these claims, and cases of corruption have been reported. In retrospect, then, it is possible to see how the exclusive grant has been naturalized out of what originated as short-term thinking about how to meet the indigenous population's housing demand.

Gender also matters. When the colonial government passed the original ordinance related to land ownership in the New Territories in 1902, it allowed only males to inherit property. James Stewart Lockhart, who delineated the boundaries of the NT, suggested that the most efficient and cheapest way to deal with land matters was to follow the then existing male-oriented inheritance system. Though the ordinance was soon abandoned, in 1903, the article that stipulated 'the tradition' was continued in the New Territories Ordinance, 1910 (article 13), and it remained in effect until the 1990s.[4] As mentioned earlier, it was only in 1972, following the institutionalization of the SHP, that the term 'indigenous inhabitants' was officially adopted (Chan, 1996). However, it was also at this time that the Hong Kong government started to expand its public housing programme and the building of urban infrastructure in the NT to ease congestion in other areas of the colony (Nissim, 2012, p. 127). These parallel policies eventually led to the coexistence in the NT of two contrasting housing forms: small houses and high-rise public housing blocks.

Today, the disappearing distinction between the urban and the rural in the NT, as mentioned earlier, has destabilized the discourse of 'great difference' that once provided a basis for the grant of special housing status to indigenous inhabitants. In fact many indigenous inhabitants who enjoy 'traditional rights' do not even reside in the NT. According to Dell Upton (2001, p. 299), manufactured traditions are not inherently pernicious. Nevertheless, the use of manufactured traditions and their consequences are worthy of concern. What is of particular interest here is how the use of tradition has led to a deterioration in the relationship between the indigenous community of the NT and its neighbours and fellow citizens. The increasing sense of disconnection is two-fold: on the one hand, the indigenous have disconnected themselves from their neighbours in both geographical and political terms; on the other, they have largely disconnected themselves from the place itself through the commodification of the small houses the law has allowed them to build.

Arguably, the SHP may be considered compensatory in nature – a privilege rather than a right, granted in response to the villagers' demand for housing (Lai, 2000). As of the end of 2011, according to statistics provided by the Secretary for Development, since it was instituted in 1972, a total of 36,912 small-house applications had been approved by the Lands Department. By the end of 2011 the additional number of applications being processed and waiting to be processed stood at 6,895 and 3,360, respectively. Each application requires land, and as of 2012, the Planning Department noted that about 3,147 hectares had been set aside as Village Zone for the continuing construction of small houses (Man-Lei, 2013). Yet the land available for small house development cannot be open-ended, and this means the policy is inherently unsustainable.

Meanwhile, the resale of small houses has also been a subject of controversy. In January 1978, the then secretary for the NT, Sir David Akers-Jones, almost cancelled the SHP over this issue. After negotiation, however, resale was formally permitted in August 1978. The rules today stipulate that, upon resale, an owner must pay a differential premium if the house was built on public land. However, if a house is built on private land, the owner must only pay such a differential if the transaction occurs within 5 years of initial construction. Resale is further not limited to other members of the indigenous population.[5]

Such stipulations represented the beginning of a formal commodification of traditional rights. A small house can today be divided into three, one-storey units (of three bedrooms each) and sold to three buyers at HK$2.5 to HK$4.5 million (US$322,600 to US$709,200) each. According to an audit conducted in October 2002, nearly all such flats were sold within about five months of the removal of the restriction on alienation (Hopkinson and Lei 2003). In the name of indigenous villagers, some developers are also building and selling luxury houses on SHP land, providing a share of the proceeds to the villagers. According to one source I interviewed in November 2015, 'There are middle-class professionals who purposely seek tranquillity by living in small houses to disconnect themselves from the urban chaos'.

Additionally, the issue of resale surfaced at a time when at least 80 per cent of indigenous male villagers had migrated abroad to work – a fact in seeming conflict with the claim of increased indigenous-village housing demand. Indeed, the indigenous population in 1987 was about 460,000, of whom 260,000 (more than a half) resided overseas (Committee on the Right, Wellbeing…, 1987). Nevertheless, the HYK has now ensured that the SHP and other rights be extended to indigenous males overseas. This, however, created an invitation for developers to abuse the SHP. Indeed, some have even sent scouts to the UK to look for indigenous villagers with entitlements. Thus, instead of responding to real housing need, the SHP is primarily valuable today because it creates a profitable commodity such as those structures built by developers and shown in figures 4.4 and 4.5.

In the late 1980s, when it came to drafting the Sino-British Joint Declaration and the Basic Law in the lead-up to the 1998 handover of Hong Kong to China, it also became clear that, in the name of tradition, the indigenous elite was determined to maintain the two systems of land rights in the NT (Committee on the Right, Wellbeing…, 1987). In this regard, indigenous representatives refused to consider the SHP a privilege; it was rather framed as a form of compensation that could hardly make up for the historical loss they incurred when their freehold rights had been transmuted to leasehold following the annexation of the NT to Hong Kong.

Figure 4.4. The developers built small houses as collective housing by soliciting 'ting rights' from the indigenous inhabitants. (*Photo*: Shu-Mei Huang, 2014)

Figure 4.5. Village houses built as gated communities by private developers. (*Photo*: Shu-Mei Huang, 2015)

In the end, Article 40 of the Basic Law recognized that '*The lawful traditional rights and interests* of the indigenous inhabitants of the "New Territories" shall be protected by the Hong Kong Special Administrative Region' (emphasis added). Moreover, out of respect for 'traditional rights', all leases that were to expire on 30 June 1997 were extended until 30 June 2047, with the exception of the new annual rent applicable to other land leaseholders. It is further worth noting here that the wording of an older draft of the article had referred to 'the legitimate traditional rights and interests…', but the word 'legitimate' was ultimately replaced with 'lawful' (Hopkinson and Lei, 2003). The subtle change avoided the need to address the debatable legitimacy of legislating a privilege. Tradition may now thus be taken for granted, since no clear definition of 'traditional rights and interests' appears in the document. Furthermore, the continued traditional character of the given society where the law is embedded is left unquestioned.

Over the years male indigenous leaders in the NT have lobbied government officials to protect their 'rights'. But there has been no shortage of criticism of the exclusion of indigenous women from the benefits of the SHP and related inheritance laws. A movement during the late 1980s and early 1990s advocating for female inheritance in Hong Kong reached its peak in 1994, when a report by the Hong Kong Council of Women pointed to the patrilineal practice as a form of gender discrimination that contravened the colony's newly passed Bill of Rights. In 1995, echoing the movement, the United Nations Committee on Economic, Social and Cultural Rights also made its concern with the policy official. This was met by a campaign by the HYK, 'Why are you killing our culture?' (Merry and Stern, 2005). Eventually, however, the movement did lead to a successful amendment to the New Territories Land (Exemption) Ordinance allowing women to inherit property. Significantly, however, this also left the SHP intact.

Tradition is (Dis)connection

As Selina Chan has pointed out, the ethnicity of the indigenous inhabitants of the NT villages represents a clear case of the politicization of identity. At the outset this identity was constructed in a way that homogenized the diverse ethnicities living in the area, including at least Punti and Hakka, before 1898 (Chan, 1998). However, the lineage organization of the villages, which so intrigued anthropologists in the 1960s and 1970s, now consists mainly of 'virtual kinship' (Watson, 2004). Nevertheless, it is by these means that an exclusive distribution system operates. And it is by means of this system that tradition has been produced and consumed in the NT.

Tradition, as Ananya Roy (2004, p. 64) has noted, 'only becomes authentic in the act of consumption', and 'the consumption of tradition is the production of tradition'. Simultaneous consumption and production may be partially the case with regard to the construction of small houses. But the fact that each small house also requires a piece of land makes the act of its construction more than merely performative. For instance, the lack of comprehensive planning has encouraged village sprawl and created environmental impacts in such areas as drainage, water quality, and transportation. The exercise of traditional 'rights' has, ironically, also resulted in the loss of old village houses as indigenous heritage.

The granting of such rights obviously represents an inefficient and unsustainable use of a scarce resource, in which the greater society of Hong Kong should have a say. The continuous growth of small houses cannot be contained; they establish claims that simultaneously produce and consume territory. Thus, while others may lament that tradition is ending, the power of tradition in this case seems very much to have progressed in new directions, ones that arguably enable continuing processes of exclusion and dispossession. As AlSayyad (2004, p. 23) has argued, 'so it would seem that what has ended, in the end, is not tradition itself, but the idea of tradition as a harbinger of authenticity, and as a container of specific cultural meaning'. By transforming itself into a distribution system that serves the self-displaced indigenous, tradition has thus displaced the issue of 'authenticity' altogether in the NT.

With reference to the spread of Western cultural dominance, Jane M. Jacobs (2004, p. 31) has pointed to 'the embedded teleology and geography of the modern making of tradition'. Moreover, to describe their twinned etiology, she described tradition and modernity as 'a vibrating couplet within which the terms are *both* co-dependent and mutually exclusive' (Jacobs, 2004, p. 33). Thus, in understanding processes of deterritorialization and reterritorialization under globalization, she argued for a formulation of relationship whereby 'tradition is (not) modern'.

Of related concern here are the processes of disconnection and reconnection that may appear in the name of tradition when tradition is extended to a new cultural regime. Jacobs appreciated the inevitable inventiveness of continuations of tradition, and, in particular, of attempts to amplify indigenous authority through productive processes enabled by hybrid architecture. The indigenous authority in Hong Kong, however, has not sought to connect different actors in the extension of tradition.

Rather, it has acted more as if engaged in a bidding game, where the indigenous inhabitants have now disconnected themselves from their place and tradition. Literally speaking, they are not necessarily there. However, the fact that an increasing share of the consumption and production of tradition is now carried out in the absence of the indigenous villagers raises questions about the fundamental meaning of being indigenous and of the authority of the indigenous when its authors are no longer in place. To paraphrase Jacobs's productively unstable formula, it may be fair to say that tradition can sometimes be considered a (dis)connection. And in this case, the sense of disconnection is completely materialized in the emerging gated communities being created through the construction of new small houses (see figure 4.5).

It was within this context that the indigenous population originally sought to lobby Chinese authorities to continue the two land-tenure systems developed during colonial times into post-handover Hong Kong (Chan, 1998, pp. 39–54). And they attempted to find justification, by association, in the differential treatment granted to Hong Kong under the principle of 'One Country, Two Systems' by which the territory was to be reincorporated with the mainland (Chan, 1998, pp. 39–54). In other words, they sought to formalize the special system of indigenous rights through a condition of 'Two systems in One Hong Kong' (Lau, 1999, p. 119). However, beneath the discourse of tradition, 'the great difference' in the NT has been translated into a particular kind of social order, land politics, and built form. And the HYK was not totally unaware of the problems created by this system. They therefore encouraged proposals for alternative ways to sustain tradition – for example, by a doubling or tripling of the volume of small houses (in six- to ten-storey blocks) to address the issue of an insufficient supply of land (Ng, 2000).

At the same time as the indigenous population has sought to extend its rights, interest has also been revived in farming in the now rapidly urbanizing NT. This movement has been led by non-indigenous farmers, who have organized protests to keep the territories green, agrarian, and unbuilt. Ironically, this group would never have been considered a legitimate claimant under the colonial gaze.

The postcolonial thinker Ashis Nandy has provided some thoughts that may be relevant here. Nandy (1983, p. ix) has argued that 'Modern colonialism won its great victories not so much through its military and technological prowess as through its ability to create secular hierarchies incompatible with the traditional order'. Seemingly, it is precisely in this sense that the invention of the small-house policy created a political hierarchy that served the interest of colonial governance. The colonial regime did not deny, but rather it transformed the traditional order. And this has resulted in a unique form of urbanization in the NT in which tradition is simultaneously disabled and augmented. While ordinary indigenous people were thus encouraged to leave their farmland behind, the indigenous elite gained a new form of power and authority in a political system certified by the British, who ironically came to function as the upholders of Chinese tradition. By accepting indigenous status, as governable imperial subjects, one gained the 'privilege' to have one's agricultural lands expropriated in exchange for a small house. Yet this has now led to a loss of the very unbuilt territory where the tradition was originally grounded.

This interpretation of historical events raises several important questions. Is it possible that tradition might once again serve as a connecting device, rather than one that displaces people from lands, and that disconnects people from other people? And, is there an alternative to the gradual 'ungrounding' of tradition?

For his part, Nandy (2014, p. 12) has called for recognition of the creativity of everyday life and the possibilities opened by 'the partly mnemonic traditions of healing and agronomy'. That tradition is translated into a tradable property right has gradually led to a loss of the land where the mnemonic traditions were embedded. In the following section I will describe actions by the non-indigenous population of the NT that demonstrate their determination to sustain the mnemonic traditions embedded there.

Non-indigenous Communities Acting for and against 'Tradition'

Some of the aforementioned gated communities that have been developed with small-house grants are located in the proximity of the Kam Sheung Road station. The same area contains many non-indigenous villages originally formed in the 1950s and 1960s, when many mainlanders fled to Hong Kong from southern China to avoid political turmoil and famine. Their arrival coincided with the colonial government's policy to promote local agriculture to reduce Hong Kong's dependence on China for its food supply. Many migrants took on the important role of being farmers, cultivating lands leased to them by the indigenous villagers. Yet, because they were considered 'non-indigenous inhabitants', they were excluded from local politics, which were dominated by the HYK. Next

Figure 4.6. Typical one- or two-story houses in non-indigenous villages. (*Photo*: Shu-Mei Huang, 2014)

to their gardens, they mostly lived in self-built farmhouses, which have been categorized under the law as 'temporary structures' if they were built before 1980 (figure 4.6).

Following the initial period of growing agricultural production, however, a decline closely followed the relaxing of control over agricultural imports from China starting in the late 1980s. One consequence, for example, is there has been no production of rice since 1990. Hong Kong's self-sufficiency in vegetables, which stood at 13.9 per cent in 1997, had also fallen to only 2.3 per cent by 2012 (Local Research Community, 2013). Overall, agriculture now accounts for less than 0.5 per cent of GDP in Hong Kong. Likewise, in the past decade, 30 per cent of farmland has been transformed into other uses. Currently, there are only 4,575 hectares of farmland remaining in Hong Kong, and about 80 per cent of agricultural land is idle (most of it having been bought up by developers).

In a territory where farming has become a marginal activity, the case of Choy Yuen village (among others) illustrates the birth of a new awareness of how farming may connect tradition to a more sustainable way of life. The name Choy Yuen literally means 'vegetable garden'. A typical non-indigenous village formed in the 1950s, it comprised roughly 500 people in 2009. During the 1970s and 1980s, vegetable- and flower-growing were the predominant activities there. This was exemplified by the 'veggie station' at its entrance – one of two government-run stations associated with the Vegetable Market Organization, through which villagers could sell their produce through a public entity.

In the mid-2000s, plans were announced to demolish the village to allow construction of the controversial Guangzhou-Hong Kong Express Rail Link (hereafter XRL). Once this plan was announced, many questions arose. For example, why was it necessary to demolish this village in particular? And why was it even necessary to carry out such a plan, which would cost US$9 billion? From 2008 onwards, however, the village's resistance to displacement evolved into a general anti-high-speed-rail movement, and between 2009 and 2011 thousands of people took to the streets to urge the HKSAR to adequately rehouse village inhabitants and allow them to continue farming and living in an integrated landscape.

Some in mainstream Hong Kong society have questioned why the village opted to fight for collective relocation instead of accepting an immediate monetary compensation or rehousing in public estates. It was largely forgotten that there had been previous instances of entire villages being relocated in both the 1960s and 1980s. In both the case of Tsuen Wan and Ha Kwai Chung, two indigenous villages, the colonial government had forcedly expropriated village lands and built new housing for the villagers at public expense. Interestingly, in the Ha Kwai Chung case, the government had built new two-storey houses with 675 square foot (62.7 square metre) footprints. The size and form of these new houses implicitly recognized the example of the SHP (Yiu, 2015).

The Choy Yuen village mobilization was augmented by the emerging social activism of the so-called post-80 and post-90 Hong Kongers, whose numerous rallies pressured the Legislative Council to temporarily hold back funding for the XRL. Throughout 2009 and into early 2010, several reports were also published by civic groups questioning planning for the project, including overly optimistic claims of transportation speed, poor analysis of cost-benefit return, inflated ridership estimates, and inadequate concern for immigration control. Despite growing opposition, funding was eventually approved, however, and Choy Yuen village was dismantled in 2012. The notable level of social discontent did force the government to partially accommodate the villagers' appeal for collective relocation.

With the help of social workers and student volunteers, the villagers organized themselves to purchase a parcel of land where they could build houses together as a cooperative. However, this seemingly simple effort at collective relocation proved much more challenging than expected. Major difficulties arose when it came to obtaining building permits, land, rights-of-way, and access to water and utilities. For example, the government did not provide the assistance it would have in the case of the relocation of an indigenous village. And the villagers were not granted permits through the SHP. Instead, they could only apply, through the less generous Land Rehabilitation Scheme, to build two-storey structures with footprints of 400 square feet (37 square metres) next to their farmlands.[6]

Farmland, obviously the key to the relocation plan, was also not easy to obtain. After more than sixty failed attempts the village still had not been able to acquire a suitable site. Across the NT, available land often suffered from serious pollution and soil degradation due to the practice of 'destroy first, build later' – for example, by dumping construction waste on abandoned farmland or in fish ponds to preclude future efforts to farm them.

Another problem, hinted at earlier, is the requirement that villagers secure the consent of local indigenous leaders to buy or develop properties. This is why, as I mentioned at the beginning of the chapter, the Choy Yuen villagers had to phone the then HYK chairman, Wong-fat Lau. At the end of 2010 the villagers had finally been able to obtain a suitable site from one landlord and an agreement for a right-of-way to it from another. But their excitement was soon dashed when the price for the right-of-way was subsequently raised from an initial US$25,800, to US$387,000, and then US$645,000 – that is, twenty-five times the original offer. Faced with this situation, the villagers had no other alternative than to appeal to Lau, who then surprisingly announced that an anonymous donor had agreed to settle the deal for them. The entire drama seemed to have been created for the express purpose of reaffirming the power of the indigenous leadership.[7]

'There are no ancestral halls or temples in the non-indigenous villages', noted Y.C. Chen, one of the village activists, in a 15 June 2011, interview. 'But the belief in farming as an integrated way of living serves as our temple to anchor the new village.' Indeed, some third-generation villagers I interviewed in May 2011 told me they considered their village to be *heung ha*, a Cantonese term used by early mainlander migrants literally to mean 'hometown'. To assert their way of life next to their farms was to some extent a search for an alternative tradition that might empower the non-indigenous population.

In effect, the lack of a longstanding patrilineal leadership structure within the indigenous community had left a space for families with different backgrounds and interests to negotiate, cooperate, and even fight one another for access to resources. As P.F. Chen, one of the organizers of the village relocation effort pointed out, the social network in the village has been largely developed based on their lived experiences over five decades. This has, among other things, involved battling floods, building houses, and selling vegetables together (Yu, 2013, p. 95). And with the help of activists and planners, these villagers had ultimately managed to reconcile their diverse opinions in the relocation struggle through an exhaustive participatory planning and building process (Wang, 2014). The result was a project for a new village comprising forty-seven low-cost 'eco-village houses', along with a sustainable plan for fish ponds, orchards, a rainwater garden, and wastewater recycling.

Interestingly, farming as a way of life has also gradually attracted the interest of young activists from outside the village community. Several of them even launched a project entitled 'Choy Yuen Life', and moved into a vacant village house to continue working with the villagers from 2010 to 2012. Gradually, the project evolved into a combination of community organizing, organic farming, and experimental art. In a way, these young people became part of the village, and in so doing expanded, if not redefined, the villagers' traditional way of life. As one of the young activist-farmers told me in a 22 May 2011, interview: 'Initially it was indeed a way to establish trust among the activists and the villagers. But it has been changing. Now I see us doing this more for our own interest in farming and living together than serving the social movement'. Another implication of this transformative process, however, is that it has implicitly extended the notion of tradition and the boundary of the village within which it operates.

Following in the footsteps of Choy Yuen village, other cases of the struggle of the non-indigenous population for land rights have now increased awareness of the endangered nature of farming in the NT. Another non-indigenous village threatened by development is Ma Shi Po. Its case appeared in the press as the result of a controversial plan to rezone the Northeast New Territories (NENT) (Cheung et al., 2014). In fact, this village is one of fifteen in the south of Yuen Long, the north of Fanling, and in Kwu Tung North, which were all slated to be dismantled as a consequence of the plan. The rezoning was designed to develop and urbanize the greenbelt area between Hong Kong and Shenzhen. Supposedly, the redevelopment would upgrade the regional economy to advance tertiary industry, attract new talent to the area, and ease competition for jobs and housing in overpopulated urban Hong Kong. But eliminating the greenbelt would ultimately affect 250 million people living in an area of 7,000 square kilometres.

There is not room here to give a detailed report of this ongoing project.

Yet the fact that more and more young Hong Kongers have joined the non-indigenous villagers to oppose it over the past 3 years sends an important message. Opponents have sought to highlight the significance of the area as the only remaining greenbelt between Hong Kong and Shenzhen. And their action has discursively expanded the meanings and geographies of tradition.

Interestingly, with respect to the rezoning of the NENT, the indigenous elite has not talked about farming as a tradition. Rather, they have encouraged the would-be-displaced communities to compromise their personal interest in the name of the public good, just as the indigenous population was encouraged to give up their ownership rights to the land a century ago. But in return there is no potential new 'traditional right' being offered to the non-indigenous villagers in this case.

Juxtaposing this struggle by the non-indigenous population to continue farming with the longstanding effort by the indigenous villagers to maintain their traditional rights raises significant issues that reflect on the themes of agency and tradition that underlie this book. In particular, it shows the contemporary power of tradition to serve as an instrument of (dis)connection. On the one hand, the indigenous elites are now insisting on perpetuating their special right to exclude others from developing lands in the NT designated for village use, in the interest of 'villagers' who may no longer even reside there. On the other, non-indigenous farmers are inviting people to join them in sustaining the borderlands as a productive greenbelt between two globalizing cities, and in the process they are extending the 'grounded' tradition of farming to a new generation of Hong Kong residents. It is worth asking whose practices offer a better case for safeguarding 'the great difference' identified by the former colonial authorities as the basis for traditional rights in the first place.

Towards Unearthing Tradition

[T]radition itself is lost, or transmuted into traditionalism, when it ceases to move forward.

Susan Felch (2005)

A friend of mine, who is a university teacher and who rents one floor in a typical three-storey small house, generously shared with me the view of the serene NT countryside framed from her window. My friend and most of her neighbours in the gated neighbourhood where they live are not indigenous to the NT, nor are they necessarily aware of the ongoing changes brought about by the houses in which they reside. What exactly is this tradition, then, when the small houses built in its name are simply tradable properties?

One cannot but recall the colonial gaze of the British officers who established the basis for this condition. They believed it was crucial to allow the indigenous inhabitants to sustain the dwelling practices that differentiated them from the urbanized population of Hong Kong. And they believed that colonial governance would work more effectively and efficiently if two systems of land tenure were allowed to coexist in the colony. Today, however, it is often the non-indigenous middle-class that buys or rents space in the small houses to benefit from the colonial gaze, and so perpetuate the two systems in the postcolonial city. Considering this underlying reality, one has to question the reason for continuing to disconnect the inhabitants of small houses from the rest of Hong Kong.

This chapter has reviewed the historical context behind the creation of the SHP, which was supposedly enacted in an effort to protect the traditional social organization embedded in access to village lands as part of an ancestral trust. It has also revealed how, within a rather short period of time, the SHP has produced a privilege among the indigenous male inhabitants to continue to build and profit from their right as if it were a commodity, without due respect for the negative effects it might have on the surrounding ecology and village heritage.

It should be clear by now that the specific policy measure that found its source in tradition was never equal to the tradition. However, the indigenous elite has not let anyone question the formula. Indeed, in mid-December 2015, several reports revealed that, due to political pressure, the government had shelved for at least 10 years an effort to review the SHP. Recently, the HYK also stated that it might bring the case of 'traditional rights' to the Standing Committee of the National People's Congress, a symbolic move seen as challenging the autonomy of the HKSAR. Both developments suggest that the use of tradition remains central to politics in postcolonial Hong Kong (Ng, 2015). Today they indicate that 'the nation-state' is now being asked to legitimize selectively the source of the tradition, even though the nation-state – as the arbiter of official built tradition (AlSayyad, 2004, p. 5) – in this case continues its unstable relation with the postcolonial territory. Tradition, again, is used strategically as a (dis)connection to, at once separate and connect, and ultimately to produce the somewhat arbitrary differences that legitimize the tradition.

The invention of the indigenous and of their privilege to build small houses serves as a living embodiment of how tradition may create privileges and cleavages within a given population. In this case, practices related to the SHP separate the privileged indigenous not only from the urbanites of Hong Kong but also from the descendants of farmers who were largely identical to them, but who migrated to the colony later as a result of historical events in south China. When the colonial authority demarcated the NT from the mainland, the communities there were differentiated from those living across the border, and in some cases villages that occupied the borderlands were cut in two and became populated by two kinds of people. A privilege, compensation, or a right (as the villagers would have it) was created by this act of arbitrary separation, without consideration for how the colonial project might eventually have an equally profound effect on people on the other side of the border. When the farmers living there migrated to the NT, they suddenly became non-indigenous villagers, as if the historical connection and mnemonic traditions of agronomy did not exist. That the invented tradition had been used to create a disconnect with the past inevitably made its goal self-conflicting.

This chapter has described how certain indigenous residents of Hong Kong have translated their tradition into a claim for special rights. However, this claim was founded on a presumption that the NT would be kept a distinct territory from urban Hong Kong. Ironically, this claim may now present a challenge to the ongoing top-down project to connect the cities of the region across the border between Hong Kong and mainland China. In a way, then, the indigenous communities and the non-indigenous farmers are not necessarily without common interest, although it would be quite difficult to imagine the two camps working together in the near future. The case of Cascadia presented by Matthew Sparke (2004, pp. 112–13) suggests that challenges to national sovereignty may succeed if claims from different communities can together 'landscape' the end of the nation-state. Success in this case, however, may engage the indigenous population instrumentally without necessarily providing justice for those who have suffered from being excluded from access to the land in the same territory. Among these groups are both indigenous women and non-indigenous communities, which arguably share a very similar ethnic background and lifestyle with the indigenous inhabitants.

This chapter has also examined the ways in which farming as a mnemonic tradition may help revamp the notion of tradition. To unearth tradition, it is not necessary to negate or oppose its authenticity but to seek out coeval existing traditions that may connect rather than disconnect or disinherit lived memories across borders. Authenticity, as Colin Graham (2001, p. 63) has argued, is concurrent with the rise of the nation, and arises out 'of contexts in which the nation becomes an active arbiter between the past and a "people"... [It thus] combines the prioritization of "origins" with the "pathos of incessant change"'. The invention of the NT and of its indigenous inhabitants serves this purpose, and it continues to strengthen the nation-state even if it took place literally outside the regime of postcolonial Hong Kong. It is such a continuation of governance from the outside that disallows different people from negotiating for themselves to connect their multiple pasts with the future. By contrast, the non-indigenous farmers' resistance, as the case of Choy-Yuen village demonstrates, unearths the mnemonic tradition embedded in farming in the NT, to conceive an alternative future of connection rather than separation. Yet, the fact that the urban development agenda they are fighting is a nationalist one, designed to connect people across the ambiguous border between postcolonial Hong Kong and the mainland further complicates the context in which tradition serves as a (dis)connection.

The question of how to sustain a productive greenbelt that can be meaningful to multiple parties and their understanding of tradition remains a theoretical and political challenge that can only be explored in future research. In particular, it raises the additional question of how to accommodate similarly disadvantaged farmers living in mainland areas across the Shenzhen River. Will it likewise be possible to include them in the remaking of tradition, so that their plea to also farm the borderlands will not be reduced to one of nationalism or traditionalism?

Perhaps it is necessary to review how tradition operates by examining 'Whose tradition?' is at work and on what grounds. The ongoing task then would be to search for a more inclusive process of engaging tradition in a way that might be generative rather than deadening (Felch, 2005, p. 55). It would enable multiple communities to participate in and, more importantly, to ensure that the ground of tradition remains fertile and productive.

Notes

1. The land practice allowed for 'bottom-soil' rights, which gave the owner a fixed rent from a plot of land without any right to remove the renter or control use. See more in Watson and Watson (2004).
2. For example, Pokfulam is such a village, dated to at least the eighteenth century. See more in Caritas Communities (2012).
3. Minutes of DOO Meeting of 10 June 1971, in Hong Kong Record Service (HKRS 563-2-39), p. 2.
4. Legislative Council Sitting Record, 27 November 1902, pp.70–71. Available at: http://www.legco.gov.hk/1902/h021127.pdf.
5. The resale soon led to an additional clause being added in 1976 to prevent villagers selling to outsiders within 5 years of obtaining a Certificate of Compliance. An

amendment in 1979 permitted this non-assignment clause to be waived as long as the full market premium was paid.
6. The Agriculture, Fisheries, and Conservation Department created the Agricultural Land Rehabilitation Scheme in 1988 to encourage use of otherwise idle agricultural land for productive farming.
7. See another recent case documented by Elaine Yau (2014).

References

AlSayyad, N. (2004) The end of tradition, or the tradition of endings? in AlSayyad, N. (ed.) *The End of Tradition?* London: Routledge.
Bray, D. (2001) *Hong Kong Metamorphosis*. Hong Kong: Hong Kong University Press.
Caritas Communities (2012) *Pokfulam Village: A Historical Settlement Below Victoria Peak*. Hong Kong: Sanmin Publisher.
Carroll, J. (2005) *Edge of Empires: Chinese Elites and British Colonials in Hong Kong*. Hong Kong: Hong Kong University Press.
Casey, E.S. (1987) *Remembering: A Phenomenological Study*. Bloomington, IN: Indiana University Press.
Chan, S.C. (1996) Negotiating Coloniality and Tradition: The Identity of Indigenous Inhabitants in Hong Kong. Working Paper no. 131, Department of Sociology, National University of Singapore.
Chan, S.C. (1998) Politicizing tradition: the identity of indigenous inhabitants in Hong Kong. *Ethnology*, **37**, pp. 90–91.
Cheung, T., Chan, S. and Lee, A. (2014) Chaos as initial funding for new towns in New Territories approved by Legco Panel. *South China Morning Post*, 27 June.
Committee on the Right, Wellbeing, and Responsibility of the Residents and Others (1987) *The Legal Rights of the Indigenous People in the New Territory*. CCBL-SG/RDI-INTI-01-RP01-861220. Hong Kong.
Felch, S. (2005) In the chorus of others, in Marshall, D. (ed.) *The Force of Tradition: Response and Tradition in Literature, Religion, and Cultural Studies*. Lanham, MD: Rowman & Littlefield, pp. 55–77.
Graham, C. (2001) *Deconstructing Ireland: Identity, Theory, Culture*. Edinburgh: Edinburgh University Press.
Hayes, J. (2006) *The Great Difference: Hong Kong's New Territories and Its People, 1898–2004*. Hong Kong: Hong Kong University Press.
Hopkinson, L. and Lei, M.L.M. (2003). *Rethinking the Small House Policy*. Hong Kong: Civic Exchange.
Jacobs, J.M. (2004) Tradition is (not) modern: deterritorializaing globalization, in AlSayyad, N. (ed.) *The End of Tradition?* London: Routledge, pp. 29–44.
Jones, C. (1995) New Territories inheritance law: colonization and the elites, in Pearson, V. *et al.* (eds.) *Women in Hong Kong*. Hong Kong: Oxford University Press, pp. 167–192.
Lai, L.W.C. (2000) Housing indigenous villagers in a modern society – an examination of the Hong Kong Small House Policy. *Third World Planning Review*, **22**, pp. 207–230.
Lai, L.W.C. and Ho, K.O. (2001) Small is beautiful: a probit analysis of development control of small houses in Hong Kong. *Environment and Planning B*, **28**, pp. 611–622.
Lao, M.M.L. (2013) *Small House Policy II: An Update*. Hong Kong: Civic Exchange.
Lau, Y. (1999) *The Brief History of New Territories*. Hong Kong: The Commercial Press.
Lee, M.K. (1984) The evolution of the Heung Yee Kuk as a political institution, in Faure, D.

et al. (eds.) *From Village to City*. Hong Kong: Centre of Asian Studies, University of Hong Kong, pp. 164–177.

Local Research Community (2013) *Not a Problem of Land Supply*. Hong Kong: Local Research Community.

Man-Lei, M.L. (2013) *Small House Policy II: An Update*. Hong Kong: Civic Exchange. Available at: https://designingvillages.files.wordpress.com/2014/09/2013-4-civic-exchange-shp-update.pdf.

Marshall, D.G. (ed.) (2005) *The Force of Tradition: Response and Resistance in Literature, Religion, and Cultural Studies*. Lanham, MD: Rowman & Littlefield.

Merry, S.E. and Stern, R.E. (2005) The Female Inheritance Movement in Hong Kong. *Current Anthropology*, **46**, pp. 387–409.

Nandy, A. (1983) *The Intimate Enemy: Loss and Recovery of Self Under Colonialism*. Delhi: Oxford University Press.

Nandy, A. (2014) Memory Work. Working paper, unpublished, presented at Shih Hsin University, Taipei, 18 July.

Ng, K.C. (2000) Kuk fights for right to tall storeys. *South China Morning Post*, 26 March.

Ng, K.C. (2015) Rural leaders amassing war chest for Hong Kong villagers jailed in homes scam. *South China Morning Post*, 27 December.

Nissim, R. (2012) *Land Administration and Practice in Hong Kong*. Hong Kong: Hong Kong University Press.

Rosaldo, R. (1989) Imperialist nostalgia. *Representations*, **26**, pp. 107–122.

Roy, A. (2004) Nostalgia of the modern, in AlSayyad, N. (ed.) *The End of Tradition?* London: Routledge, pp. 63–86.

SCMP (*South China Morning Post*) (2015) Editorial: Rights and wrongs: Hong Kong's small-house policy for indigenous villagers is outdated and unfair. *SCMP*, 14 December.

Sit, V. (2011) *A History of the Heung Yee Kuk N.T.* Hong Kong: Hong Kong Baptist University.

Sparke, M. (2004) Nature and tradition at the border: landscaping the end of the nation state, in AlSayyad, N. (ed.) *The End of Tradition?* London: Routledge, pp. 87–115.

Upton, D. (2001) 'Authentic' anxieties, in AlSayyad, N. (ed.) *Consuming Tradition, Manufacturing Heritage: Global Norms and Urban Forms in the Age of Tourism*. London: Routledge, pp. 298–306.

Wang, W. (2014) Voices from the vegetable garden: grass-roots planning and the design of Choy Yuen ecological village, in Kee, T. et al. (eds.) *We Own the City: Enabling Community Practice in Architecture and Planning*, Amsterdam: Trancity*Valiz, pp. 96–103.

Watson, J.L. (2004) Virtual kinship, real estate, and diaspora formation: the man lineage revisited. *The Journal of Asian Studies*, **63**, pp. 893–910.

Watson, J.L. and Watson, R.S. (2004) *Village Life in Hong Kong: Politics, Gender, and Ritual in the New Territories*. Hong Kong: Chinese Hong Kong University Press.

Yau, E. (2014) Call for incentives to help farmers stay on the land and boost Hong Kong's self-sufficiency. *South China Morning Post*, 18 July.

Yiu, C.Y. (2015) The History of the Relocation of Tsuen Wan Village. Working paper.

Yu, C. (2013) *Saving the Garden for the Past and the Future*. Hong Kong: The V-Artivists.

Chapter 5

Their Voice or Mine? Debating People's Agency in the Construction of Adivasi Architectural Histories

Gauri Bharat

It was 9 o'clock in the morning, and the main street in the village of Bhagabandh, in Jharkhand state, was alive with excitement. People were milling around a display of photographs and architectural drawings I had produced and installed of their village and houses. The event was part of my research on conceptions of space and place among the Santals, an indigenous community in eastern India.[1] Part of the larger, heterogeneous Adivasi population (the indigenous people of South Asia), Santals are locally renowned for the precision and craftsmanship of their domestic architecture, and through my research I hoped to construct an architectural history of Santal built environments by examining how their sense of place had transformed since the mid-nineteenth century.

As an architect-researcher, my work focused on Santal dwellings and settlements as both sites and processes. I thereby framed architectural transformations as gestures representing Santal relationships with their social, material, and historical worlds. Yet, apart from exploring built forms and everyday practices from a professional viewpoint, I was also interested in how Santal villagers, themselves, perceived and valued their built environment.[2] The display in the street would provide an opportunity for the villagers to participate in my research by engaging with and commenting on architectural representations of their environment. In total, the display included nearly forty images of the village and its surroundings: of institutions such as the central street, the sacred grove,

Figure 5.1. Villagers gathered around the display on the street. (*Photo*: Gauri Bharat)

and the village school; of important everyday places such as paddy fields, grazing pastures, and water bodies; and of village dwellings and interior spaces. These sites and objects represented key aspects of Santal everyday life, including places of living, livelihood, and worship. Gathered around the images, the villagers excitedly identified and pointed to familiar places and objects (figure 5.1).

At this juncture, my plan was to ask the villagers to identify their favourite photographs. In particular, I wanted them to select five images that represented the most significant aspects of their built environment. The villagers' responses were interesting, but more importantly, they were completely unexpected because the ones they chose largely ignored the structures I had come to study (figure 5.2).

Nearly unanimously, the first image the villagers chose was of the *jahira*. This sacred grove is found in every Santal village and is the abode of important spirits.[3] Collective rituals and feasts take place at this site, and participation in them is an important marker of community membership. The villagers suggested that the *jahira* was equivalent to a Hindu temple, and therefore the most important place in the village. The second image chosen also had ritual significance. It was of the *manjhithan*, a shrine dedicated to ancestral village headmen. Santal communities are governed by a council

Figure 5.2. Images selected by villagers from the display. (*Photos*: Gauri Bharat)

of five, led by a *manjhi*, or headman.[4] The position is hereditary, and a *manjhi* typically traces his ancestry to the village's founders. The *manjhithan*, which commemorates the headman's ancestors, is important therefore because it keeps the entire village under its protective influence.[5] Santals believe they cohabit their world with spirits, including various deities and deceased ancestors. Ritual practices at sites such as the *manjhithan* are aimed at worshipping and appeasing these spirits to ensure a peaceful and uneventful life.

The nature of Santal religion was thus paramount in singling out the first two important places. The *jahira* was a place of synchronic continuities between the human and spirit worlds, while the *manjhithan* was one of diachronic continuities between the spirits of ancestors and the people themselves.

The next image chosen, however, was that of the village school. This was puzzling because schools are set up in rural areas by the state and vary considerably in size and quality of education provided. In some villages, school buildings may sit empty and derelict, used only occasionally by children for play. Many Adivasi communities, however, see such buildings as an important icon of progress, irrespective of their actual qualities as places for education. And in cases where they are properly functioning, residents may further value them simply for their cleanliness and neatness of appearance. In contrast to ritual sites, therefore, the village school registers a different trajectory of significance that stems from a desire to be seen as modern and developing. In this case, the villagers felt the school was important because it was a sign they were availing themselves of education, which was viewed as a symbol of societal progress.

Apart from these images of institutions, I was further surprised when the villagers next identified photographs of cattle and of natural features such as fields and local water bodies. Cows, according to the villagers, are a very important part of Santal life. Santals do not keep cows for milk or meat. Indeed, they do not have a culture of consuming milk or milk products at all; nor do they slaughter cattle for food.[6] Rather, Santal families rear cows as a form of currency for gift exchanges during weddings or for payment of fines for certain transgressions. Cows are considered as symbols of wealth and security and provide a basis for social transactions. In a slightly different vein, water bodies, such as a village pond or local river, are considered important because they contain a resource that sustains Santal life.

The final category of images chosen were photographs of greenery around the village, such as fields ready for harvest or nearby trees. The villagers told me they chose these because they were 'beautiful sights' – the most photogenic places in the village and its vicinity. They were considered better than manmade environments. As I later learned, this preference for the natural environment is not restricted to Santals, but is common to many Adivasi communities in the region and may be rooted in memories of a forest-dwelling past.[7] This past is reiterated in Santal folklore and mythic imagination, and in narratives of broader Adivasi political identity, *jal, jangal, jameen* (water, forest, land) have been articulated as central to Adivasi life.[8] These multivalent associations clearly led to these images being included among those chosen to represent important places in the village environment.

Listening to the various responses to the display, it became increasingly clear that the villagers were choosing to represent everyday life and culture in terms of ritual locations, important institutions and social practices, and aesthetically pleasing views of the natural environment. What was conspicuously missing from these choices – with the exception of the school building – were built forms. This was odd considering that Santal houses are remarkably well crafted and well decorated, and that the cycles of annual decoration and weekly maintenance using mud and cow-dung plaster are important tasks performed by Santal women (figure 5.3). This skill at domestic decoration is widely recognized as characteristic of Santals. Thus, its absence from a self-representation of Santal environments was

Figure 5.3. Decorated Santal houses in Singhbhum. (*Photo*: Gauri Bharat)

surprising and indeed distressing. I had come to explore Santal relationships to the environment through architectural forms, but the Santal villagers did not consider this relationship to be of primary importance to their life and culture. I began to doubt my choice to make dwellings the focus of my research. Had I picked the wrong sites to study?

Constructing a Santal Architectural History

Though the Santal villagers did not identify their dwellings as an important part of their environment, changes in domestic architecture do offer some important insights into how the lives and experiences of Santal communities have changed over the past two centuries. The region of my case study, Singhbhum, is home to nearly forty different Adivasi communities, including the Santals. But it is also one of India's most important sites for various mining and metallurgical industries. Since the mid-nineteenth century, the area has undergone massive change, having been transformed from a thickly forested landscape to one of paddy cultivation and heavy industry. These large-scale environmental and economic transformations were prompted by non-Adivasi people, who migrated into the region precisely because of its forest and mineral resources (Bandopadhyay, 1999).

Against this backdrop of transformation, the region's Adivasi inhabitants, correspondingly, shifted gradually from living in the forest to becoming settled agriculturists and industrial labourers. As a result, it is difficult today to categorize Adivasi communities as composed exclusively of hunters, gatherers, or agriculturists.[9] Most groups, including the Santals, vacillate between these modes of living, and the meshing of Adivasi worlds with agricultural and industrial development has resulted in a landscape that reflects complex social, economic, and historical factors. My work constructing a Santal architectural history thus required locating Santal dwellings within this meta-narrative of change.

Present-day Santal dwellings are of three types: the *orak*, the *ath-chala*, and the courtyard house.[10] Of these, the *orak* is the smallest, typically formed of a single volume sheltered by a pitched roof with an open yard at the back. Small households, such as widows or elderly couples living alone, are usually the only ones who build and occupy such structures.[11] In contrast, the *ath-chala* is a larger type, comprising two concentric orthogonal volumes with hipped roofs. But it is the courtyard house that is the most common type today. It comprises a set of volumes, the number and complexity of which vary greatly. The volumes may be connected to each other or remain discrete, and they may have been built over a period of time rather than all at once; but together they define an open interior space. All three dwelling types are orthogonal in layout and include an entrance space, a cooking area, a cattle shelter, a grain store, and a *bhitar* (an interior space where the family may worship). All three typically also open onto a yard, which serves as a space for socializing, and are built using cob-wall construction with pitched wooden roofs.

Interestingly, apart from these present-day house types, a fourth type became discernable in conversations with villagers. However, it was not possible to document this dwelling form since examples of it no longer exist. Nevertheless, elderly Santal villagers clearly recollected this type as a small shack-like dwelling known as a *kumbaha*, built out of wood and leaves. The *kumbaha*, together with the *orak*, *ath-chala*, and courtyard house, comprise the present morphological range of development in known Santal domestic architecture (figure 5.4).

To study the relationship between these dwelling types I first had to locate them in temporal relation to one another. By analyzing their similarities and differences in terms of configuration, domestic functions, and materials, I could construct a trajectory of dwelling transformation in the region. I was able to analyze the *orak*, *ath-chala*, and courtyard house on the basis of documentation and observation. And I managed to arrive

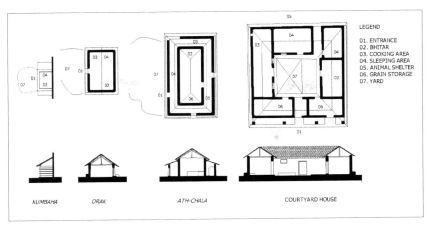

Figure 5.4. Diagram of different Santal dwelling types. (*Diagram*: Gauri Bharat)

at the architectural features of the *kumbaha* by conjecture based on oral narratives. However, creating a temporal sequence was difficult because most houses in Santal villages today appear to be composites of the *orak*, *ath-chala*, and courtyard types. Thus, for instance, an *ath-chala* and a few other spaces may together form a courtyard house. Also, since most houses had been continuously occupied and modified using similar materials and techniques, there was no architectural record or evidence to distinguish old and new construction. In these circumstances, the only cues for identifying the older houses, or parts of houses, were the oral accounts of villagers. For instance, only when villagers pointed to an example of an *ath-chala* as the oldest type of house did it become evident that the *ath-chala* was a complete, older dwelling to which other spaces had been added.[12] Villagers also stated that *ath-chala*-type dwellings were no longer made today since their relatively large size required more time, labour, and materials to build. What became clear as a result was that the *ath-chala* was an older type of dwelling, and that at some point it had given way to the courtyard house as the dominant type.

In order to ascertain the time period during which the shift from *ath-chala* to courtyard houses took place, I compared records of the villages that contained both types. Not all villages in the region had *ath-chala* houses; indeed, of the three villages I studied, two had *ath-chala* houses, while the third had only courtyard houses. Probing into village histories, it emerged that the villages with *ath-chala* houses had existed as long ago as the mid-nineteenth century, while the village with only courtyard houses had been established at the beginning of the twentieth century.[13] This suggested that the practice of building *ath-chala* houses may have been prevalent in the late nineteenth century, but that it had become less popular by the early twentieth century – which would explain why such houses were not found in villages established later.

Around the same time (at the turn of the twentieth century), P.O. Bodding (1940) noted that Santal ways of building were transforming. From wooden structures, built using a series of poles and panels made of branches, Santal families were beginning to use mud in the form of cob-style construction. Bodding further suggested that this was likely to become the dominant way of building in the years to come. Although Bodding did not use the term *kumbaha*, his description of older dwelling forms matches what elderly Santals remember as the type they know by that name today. Putting these inferences together, it became clear that the *ath-chala* and *kumbaha* were both common types at the turn of the twentieth century, but that they gave way to the mud *orak* and to the courtyard houses seen today.

Establishing the broad sequence of transformation allowed me to turn my attention to shifts in spatial configuration and construction materials. The general activities that take place within Santal dwellings – such as cooking, sleeping, grain storage, shelter for cattle, and worship in the *bhitar* – were found across all four dwelling types but with various degrees of spatial differentiation. In the older *kumbaha* and *ath-chala* all these functions took place within the single or continuous volume of the house, while in the courtyard type different spaces are designated for each activity. The dwelling interior was thus transformed from a single, multiuse space to include multiple rooms designated for different domestic functions.

Concurrent with the development of differentiated spaces was the emergence of a central courtyard. Both the older *kumbaha* and the *ath-chala* types are single volume units with open yards in the front and back, where the front yard serves as a space for socializing and the back yard is used as a vegetable garden. Present-day courtyard houses, as the name suggests, feature a central space in addition to the front and back yards. Here, the front yard and internal courtyard are both used as sites of socializing, though the latter has relatively more restricted access. For instance, people familiar to the family, such as other villagers, have unrestricted access to the courtyard, while strangers are allowed in the front yard only. The internal courtyard is thus an intermediate site for socializing that only developed in recent Santal dwellings and blurs the clear inside-outside dichotomy of earlier dwellings. Overall, Santal dwellings have transformed from being single-volume structures during the nineteenth century, with a clear distinction between interior and exterior space, to more elaborate layouts in the twentieth century that feature differentiated spaces and a more complex interior syntax.

Another aspect of dwelling transformation was a shift in building materials. The older *kumbaha,* according to villagers' descriptions, were built using panels of wooden members or branches that were thatched with leaves (figure 5.5). As people remained settled in the same place for longer periods of time, these *kumbaha* structures came to be plastered in mud, and eventually transformed into the mud houses that one sees today. Of course, the shift was not just of materials, but also of ecologies of procurement and practice, of building knowledge, and, broadly, of the sense of dwelling as becoming more permanent. Considered together with the changes in configuration, it is clear that in the gradual move from *kumbaha* to *athchala, orak,* and courtyard house, Santal domestic architecture became more internally differentiated, complex, and permanent.

By juxtaposing these architectural developments against the broader social, environmental, and political changes taking place in Singhbhum,

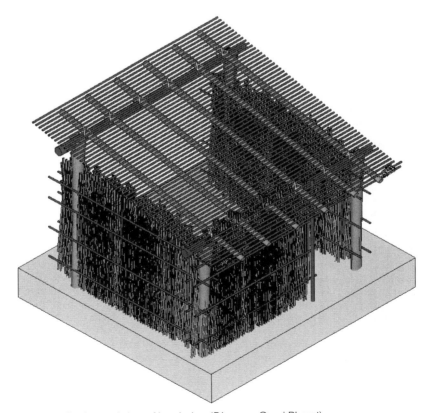

Figure 5.5. Conjectural view of kumbaha. (*Diagram*: Gauri Bharat)

some key correlations became evident. The period when Santal dwellings began to undergo the transformation that led to the mud courtyard houses popular today, the mid-nineteenth and early twentieth century, corresponds to a time of considerable social and environmental change in Singhbhum. Indeed, this was when the lives of Adivasi communities such as the Santals underwent major transformation as a result of the migration of nontribal people into the region. It was at this time that land and other natural resources came under the control of these new nontribal landowners or the colonial government.[14] And it was at this time that native Adivasi communities were being extensively dispossessed of their old habitats and mobile ways of living, and gradually resettled in villages across the region.[15]

The transformation of Santal dwellings into complex and permanent structures corresponds to this change in mode of living. As Santal societies became sedantarized, their dwellings became larger and more internally differentiated. During this time, the villagers' access to common resources such as forests was reduced, and wood became scarce as a building material. As a result of being settled in particular sites, families now also had access to mud for construction from their own backyards.[16] The emergence of a more complex pattern of interior spaces and the development of intermediate privacy thresholds may also be linked to these social and political transformations in Singhbhum. Santal families were no longer living in vast forested landscapes, but in sedentary village communities in frequent contact with disruptive and exploitative outsiders. Santal domestic architecture responded by becoming more introverted and internally differentiated.

In sum, shifts in social, economic, political, and environmental conditions in Singhbhum all contributed to the transformation of Santal houses in the region. Conversely, a study of architectural transformation provides insights into the texture of Santal everyday life and relationships with the environment in the late nineteenth and early twentieth centuries.

Differences and Dialogue

As discussed above, the history of how Santal dwellings have changed is clearly an important register of shifts in Santal relationships with the social, political, and natural worlds. Yet, as the responses to my display of images suggested, Santal villagers do not necessarily consider the dwelling as a site that represents their particular lives and culture. They picked other sites and described other registers of significance. This signalled a clear divergence between the architectural-historical gaze and the 'lived' perspectives of the inhabitants themselves. Both points of view were concerned with the same subject (architecture as a gesture of people's relationship to their environment), but they were centred on different sites and structures of signification. The disjuncture between the two voices would need to be critically examined to establish the possibility of 'dialogue' between them.

In order to understand the nature of the villagers' self-representation, it proved useful for me to explore the ontology of the display event itself. In the display, the villagers were encountering images from their everyday environments that were selected and framed for them. When encountering the images, the first reaction of most villagers was to try to orient themselves; they asked where certain photographs were taken, looked for familiar faces, and were excited to find them. A common response was that the photographs made their everyday surroundings look beautiful – and, interestingly, that they made the village look much nicer than they had previously imagined. These responses suggested that the act of framing images and the event of the display had removed the sites and objects from the mundane orbit of everyday experience and presented them afresh. This was an important realization, since it highlighted how the villagers' choices were not made from the near infinity of places and objects that made up their everyday environment, but were responses to my selection of images. In the display, I had 'constructed' the village based on my experiences during fieldwork. Had I carried out fieldwork during a different time of the year, such as at the peak of the agricultural season, some of the images might have been different. The village as constructed through the images would have been different as well. The 'village' in the display was thus a phenomenologically constructed entity rather than a representation of an objective totality that lay beyond experiences. And when people were making choices about which images were representative of their environment, the encounter was unavoidably mediated by how I had experienced and constructed it. The point here is not to diminish the validity of the villagers' self-representation but to clarify its subjectivity in relation to the research project and the display encounter.

Another aspect of the display event was the nature of choice and evaluation that the villagers' were exercising. In a similar case, audience responses to an exhibition about a tsunami disaster in Papua New Guinea, Moutu (2007) suggested that photos of the event did not merely represent people's experiences, but added another layer to their memories. This was the case with my display at the Santal village as well. At least temporarily, the display event removed sites and objects from the continuum of people's experiences and framed them as something to consider. I was adding another dimension to the villagers' own experiences. In fact, I was imposing an alien conception and evaluation on their built environment. When else would the villagers have considered the significance of a pig farm vis-à-vis the sacred grove of worship or the fishing net? These elements typically belong to different arenas of village life, and questions of their relative value never arise. People's choices from the display thus could not be seen as objectively revealing what was important in the built environment. Rather, they needed to be thought of as windows that opened new horizons of association and meaning between people, objects, and places.

The subjectivity of the villagers' choices notwithstanding, in choosing the images that best represented themselves to others, they were constructing narratives that defined their community – both as similar to and different from others. For instance, places of worship were singled out from the display as a distinguishing marker of a Santal community, while the school became an indicator of the desire to belong to a more universal developed world. Their choices were also underlined by social or aesthetic considerations – as in the case of cattle or natural features such as forests and fields. In these cases, it was not the uniqueness of the object or place that made it important; it was the villagers' way of seeing cattle as social currency, or finding the natural world more beautiful than the manmade. If these choices may be considered as an expression of heritage, then the villagers' ideas pertaining to the built environment as heritage operated in spaces of overlap: between the tangible and the intangible, between the indigenous and the non-indigenous, and between the past, the present, and the future.

The display event certainly therefore problematized the core premise of my study (the centrality of architectural forms in Santal perceptions of the environment). However, this may be seen as a bias in most architectural research into lived environments. Architectural researchers typically work with 'hard', 'factual', and 'visual' data. The materiality of the built environment as an archive leads us to privilege 'objectivity' over 'personal responses' (Kellett, 2011, p. 341). Consequently, architectural analyses and interpretation of fieldwork data tend to consider the material in absolute terms, and thereby deny the possibility of other points of view. The historical narrative of the Santal built environment drew from this disciplinary norm and focused almost entirely on the past and on physical forms as indices of social and environmental change. From an outsider/researcher's point of view, aspects of Santal built environments could thus become 'ethnographic' by the act of detaching them from their original cultural contexts and 're-contextualizing' them into a narrative of architectural history.[17]

Through this process built forms could become representative of an abstract totality of the lives and experiences of the community itself. For the Santal villagers, however, the environments were lifeworlds. Specific elements and images – even when isolated in the display – did not constitute an abstract whole, but remained located within a meshwork of continuity between them and their environment that linked their past, present, and future lives. Both points of view (the villagers' and mine) were negotiating being-in-the-world, but the 'existential immediacies' that we each considered were different (Csordas, 1994). I was looking for shifts in practices and built forms that suggested broader changes in people's relationship with their environment, while the villagers identified sites that marked their continuities with their ancestors (i.e. the past), their sources of sustenance in the present, and their aspirations for the future. Rather than placing these two voices in opposition to each other (as I initially did), the different imaginaries conceived through the project needed to be brought to bear upon and enrich each other.

The dialogue between the two voices eventually took place in various ways. The first and more obvious interaction was between the villagers and myself during the course of the research project. The villagers were not only informants, but, on account of various participatory fieldwork methods (such as the village display), they became participants and evaluators of research findings. For instance, after the primary fieldwork was completed and I began my analysis and writing, I returned to the field repeatedly to discuss the arguments and findings. In some cases, the villagers concurred with my findings, while in others they offered their own explanations for historical change or other developments. These conversations helped clarify and add nuance to the various correlations that I was attempting to establish between Santal built environment and its various contexts. Over time, however, the process of dialogue with the villagers went beyond being a methodological choice, and turned into an ethical commitment where the voices of inhabitants became an intrinsic part of the narrative about their own community, their built environment, and its past.

On the other side of the relationship, the villagers' engagement with the architectural narrative during our various interactions suggested that it was received in complex and unanticipated ways. Recurring comments during the display, such as 'making the built environment seem more beautiful than they had previously imagined', hinted that the process was helping the villagers fill perceived gaps in their own histories. Though the villagers were aware of building practices in the past, encountering a narrative of architectural history proved revelatory to them. The correlation between dwelling and the broader changes in Singhbhum also articulated connections between individual Santals, their everyday lives, and popular dominant histories of the region. In other words, for the villagers, the encounter with an architectural history about their built environment created a new understanding of their own past.

This effect was also not restricted to the villages where the research was carried out, but resonated with wider Santal institutions and society. Cultural institutions and private individuals were both interested in this narrative; at various times people mentioned that it was an opportunity for Santals to learn about their own past beyond the romantic constructions of tribal histories or narratives of rebellion. And the narrative I constructed of transformation of Santal domestic architecture is being incorporated and reproduced in popular publications, with the intention of disseminating it to a wider Santal audience.[18] The architectural history obviously resonated within Santal audiences and, in its own way, complemented the efforts made by these individuals and institutions to articulate a contemporary Santal identity.

The Potential of Dialogue in Architectural Research

The process of reflecting on and analyzing the differences between villagers' perceptions of their environment and the architect-researcher's point of view suggests the simple yet critical idea that historical narratives of architecture need not be singular. By challenging the authoritative gaze of the architectural historian and recognizing the voices of indigenous inhabitants, themselves, it is possible to explore different readings of built environments as multivalent sites of meaning, cultural memory, and social identity. This becomes possible, however, when the narratives are not just *about* these societies but *from within* their subject position as well. That this subject position is distinct from an architect's point of view became amply clear where people's choice of representative sites straddled past, present, and future imaginations and pointed to things such as cattle and flora, which I had completely missed with my own architectural gaze. In short, though architectural discourses about indigenous environments may address issues of tradition and meaning, those who write them cannot assume to represent the subjectivity of the inhabitants themselves. Rather, by recognizing the role of inhabitants as informants and participants in the research process, and clearly locating their voices within architectural histories, it will become possible to produce more nuanced and multivalent narratives.

It is also useful to take note of the processes of fieldwork as an inherent dialogue. As I have tried to point out here, it was only through a process of dialogue that I was able to glean important information and assessments of my research ideas and findings. At the same time, in the course of fieldwork interactions, the villagers encountered a narrative about their past, of which they were only nominally aware. While the former was responsible for the recursive method and reflexive approach to indigenous architectural histories, the latter opened up the possibility of academic discourse as a mnemonic device for shaping social identities. This stemmed partly from the fact that discourses on Adivasi everyday life are few, and narratives that are relevant and accessible to Santal (and other Adivasi) villagers are even fewer. Given this condition of subalternity, the process of writing a history – even an architectural one – became a process for constructing self-identity.[19]

Notes

1. Santals have been studied extensively in anthropology, though architectural scholarship about the community is limited. See, for instance, Archer (1974), Bodding (2001 [1916]), Datta-Majumder (1955), and Troisi (1979).
2. To this end, I employed a number of participatory fieldwork methods such as guided photography, drawings of dwellings and settlements by village children, and the public display of the architectural documentation discussed in this chapter.
3. The Santal pantheon comprises a number of spirits. The most important ones worshipped by the entire village are located in the *jahira*, while clan and household spirits are believed to reside in the *bhitar* of individual dwellings. Santals also worship a number of other location-specific spirits such as water, field, or boundary spirits and practice-specific spirits such as those connected to hunting. For more on Santal religion, see Troisi (1979).
4. The *manjhi* and his council are the social and political leaders of a Santal community, though decisions on most matters are made by discussion and consensus among all adult male members of a village. For more on governance among Santals, see Carrin-Bouez (1991). For a detailed discussion of the role of the *manjhi* in Santal society, see Somers (1977).
5. There are instances where villagers have found the *manjhi* to be an unsatisfactory leader and have elected a different *manjhi* – i.e. an individual not belonging to the lineage of the founding fathers. In such cases, the *manjhithan* commemorates a different lineage – i.e. of the newly elected *manjhi*.
6. Many Santal villagers pointed out to me that Santals do not 'consume' cattle in the same way that other herding or beef-eating communities do. This underscored the proposition that Santals value cattle differently.
7. Compared to ritual locations reflecting a particularly Santal sense of place, the natural environment is part of a wider Adivasi aesthetic and cultural orientation. This may be seen in the domestic murals of the various Adivasi communities in the region. See Rycroft (1996).

8. For more on Adivasi identity and its relationship to the environment, see Corbridge *et al*. (2004) and Damodaran (2006).
9. For more on shifting livelihoods and its impact on Santal village communities, see Shah (2006).
10. The Santal term for a house is *orak*, which is also used to describe rooms. For clarity of discussion, I employ these terms to describe morphologically different dwelling types. In the villages, however, with the exception of the *ath-chala*, Santals refer to all dwellings as *orak*.
11. In Santal societies, the nuclear family, comprising a married couple and their unmarried children, is typically considered a basic social unit. When resources (such as land, money, and materials) permit, a married couple will build their own separate dwelling, or at least demarcate a part of the extended family's dwelling as their own space. In the case of small families, spatial requirements are few, and a single volume may suffice.
12. Until this point, in terms of morphology, the *ath-chala* had only appeared to me to be a variation in roof – i.e. a part of the house with a hipped roof rather than a complete dwelling.
13. These villages were recorded in survey maps produced by the colonial government from 1859 onwards. Subsequent maps and land reports form an important archive, recording the presence and emergence of villages in this region over time. See, for example, Survey of India (1891).
14. For more on the Adivasi history of this time, see Bandopadhyay (1999).
15. For narratives of conflict and dispossession of Adivasis, see Areeparampil (1995).
16. This conjecture was based on field observations indicating that families constructing houses typically dug mud from their own backyards. Villagers also mentioned that other sources of mud, such as from village ponds and river beds, were reserved for special uses, such as plastering – and in any case were not sufficient to meet the village's collective need.
17. Kreps (2012) has suggested that the ethnographic gaze allows specific objects/images to stand in for abstract totalities. She discussed the similar case of the Museum Balanga in Kalimantan, Indonesia, where the collection of objects representing Dayak culture were 'seen as ordinary by the staff and local people'. This 'quotidian perception' influenced the way the museum staff handled and managed the collection, and led to the perception among locals that the museum was not a place to visit.
18. For instance, articles about the transformation of Santal dwellings were requested and published in local sites (www.livelystories.com) and journals (in particular, *BAHA* magazine – a monthly publication about Adivasi culture and fashion).
19. For a discussion of the subaltern nature of Adivasi histories, see Chakrabarty (1998).

References

Archer, W.G. (1974) *The Hill of Flutes: Love, Life and Poetry in Tribal India: A Portrait of the Santals*. Pittsburgh, PA: University of Pittsburgh Press.

Areeparampil, M. (c.1995) *Tribals of Jharkhand: Victims of Development*. New Delhi: Indian Social Institute.

Bandopadhyay, M. (1999) Demographic consequences of non-tribal incursion in Chotanagpur region in the colonial period (1850–1950). *Social Change*, **29**, pp. 10–46.

Bodding, P.O. (1940) *How the Santals Live*. Bengal: Royal Asiatic Society.

Bodding, P.O. (2001 [1916]) *Traditions and Institutions of the Santals*. New Delhi: Gyan Publishing House.
Carrin-Bouez, M. (1991) Inner Frontiers: Santal Responses to Acculturation. Working paper, Department of Social Science and Development, Chr. Michelsen Institute, Bergen.
Chakrabarty, D. (1998) Minority histories, subaltern pasts. *Postcolonial Studies*, **1**, pp. 15–29.
Corbridge, S., Jewitt, S. and Kumar, S. (2004) *Jharkhand: Environment, Development, Ethnicity*. New Delhi: Oxford University Press.
Csordas, T.J. (1994) Introduction: the body as representation and being-in-the-world, in Csordas, T.J. (ed.) *Embodiment and Experience: The Existential Ground of Culture and Self*. Cambridge: Cambridge University Press, pp. 1–24.
Damodaran, V. (2006) Politics of marginality and the construction of indigeneity in Chotanagpur. *Postcolonial Studies: Culture, Politics, Economy*, **9**(2), pp. 179–196.
Datta-Majumder, N. (1955) *The Santal: A Study in Culture Change*. Delhi: Department of Anthropology, Government of India.
Kellett, P. (2011) Living in the field: ethnographic experience of place. *Architecture Research Quarterly*, **15**(4), pp. 341–346.
Kreps, C.F. (2012) Museum Balanga as a site of cultural hybridization, in Dudley, S.H. (ed.) *Museum Objects: Experiencing the Properties of Things*. London: Routledge, pp. 280–88.
Moutu, A. (2007) Collecting as a way of being, in Henare, A., Holbraad, M. and Wastell, S. (eds.) *Thinking through Things: Theorising Artefacts Ethnographically*. London: Routledge, pp. 93–112.
Rycroft, D. (1996) Born from the soil: the indigenous mural aesthetic of Kheroals in Jharkhand, Eastern India. *South Asian Studies*, **12**, pp. 67–81.
Shah, A. (2006) The labour of love – seasonal migration from Jharkhand to the brick kilns of other states in India. *Contributions to Indian Sociology*, **40**(1), pp. 91–118.
Somers, G. (1977) *The Dynamics of Santal Traditions in a Peasant Society*. New Delhi: Abhinav Publications.
Survey of India (1891) District Singhbhum ([Surveyed by] Captain J.E. Gastrell and G.C. De Pree, Seasons 1859–65). Singhbhum, Bihar (District) – Maps. Calcutta: Survey of India Offices.
Troisi, J. (1979) *Tribal Religion: Religious Beliefs and Practices among the Santals*. Columbia, MO: South Asia Books.

Acknowledgements

The author would like to thank Dr Dan Rycroft and Professor John Mack from the University of East Anglia, Norwich, for encouraging the reflexive turn in thinking and for their comments on the chapter.

Chapter 6

Malaysianization, Malayization, Islamization: The Politics of Tradition in Greater Kuala Lumpur

Tim Bunnell

When I was a child growing up in a predominantly Chinese city in Malaysia, it seemed as though we were always trying to catch up with the West, represented first by Britain and later by the United States. Although Malaya gained independence from the British in 1957 (and became Malaysia in 1962), British-type education and the mass media constructed our worlds as failed replicas of the modern West. This colonial effect of trying to learn from and imitate the global center has been a preoccupation of post-colonial elites seeking to articulate a destiny that is a mixed set of Western and Asian interests. Now a resident in the United States, my annual visits to South-east Asia intensify my awareness that an alternative vision of the future is being articulated, an increasingly autonomous definition of modernity that is differentiated from that in the West.

Aihwa Ong (1996, p. 60)

An interrogation of tradition is not possible without an equal engagement with the concept of modernity. Tradition and modernity are two sides of the same coin...

Nezar AlSayyad (2014, p. 43)

The predominantly Chinese city that Aihwa Ong hails from is Georgetown on the island of Penang. As a historical port city, once plugged into the circuits of British colonial trade, Georgetown was not only somewhere that was exposed to Euro-American conceptions of modernity and progress but also served as a point of departure for people keen to experience modern 'elsewheres'. Among them were men who worked as seafarers. Until well into the second half of the twentieth century young Malay men used the key ports of British Malaya – Malacca and Singapore as well as Penang – to obtain seafaring employment and, in turn, as an opportunity to see wider worlds. In particular, the aspiration was to visit *Eropah* – a toponym that literally translates as Europe, but which for young seafarers meant the Western world where *orang puteh* (white people) lived. Drawing on recently completed research on Malay seafarers who settled in the city of Liverpool in the United Kingdom (Bunnell, 2016), but also connecting back to scholarly interests in urban Malaysia (Bunnell, 2004), this chapter considers the experiences of a small group of men who made post-seafaring return journeys to Malaysia. These men found that the Malaysian capital city of Kuala Lumpur and its wider urban region had in some ways 'caught up' with, and even 'overtaken', *Eropah*. However, like Aihwa Ong, the returning men also encountered entirely different articulations of modernity. With these came new (and in some cases utterly unrecognizable) forms of tradition and indigeneity. It is in this sense that Nezar AlSayyad (2014) has reminded us that tradition and modernity are dialectically related.

This chapter comprises three main sections. The first elaborates on why and how young Malay men left the Malay world region (or *alam Melayu*) in the middle decades of the twentieth century and ended up in Liverpool. The second considers material and discursive transformations that took place both in Liverpool and 'back' in Southeast Asia during the decades when the men concerned were 'away'. In broad terms, while post-imperial Liverpool and its wider urban region experienced profound commercial demise, post-colonial Malaysia and Singapore experienced a correspondingly miraculous economic rise. The third and main section of the chapter concerns three historical processes of transformation that served to (re)shape the greater Kuala Lumpur that was experienced by returning ex-seamen. These are, in turn, what I refer to as 'Malaysianization', 'Malayization', and 'Islamization'.

The Modern Is Out There: Leaving *Alam Melayu*

For young men in British Malaya after the Second World War, seafaring was the quickest route to *Eropah* and, thereby, to becoming modern. Among the ex-seafarers whom I interviewed in Liverpool in 2004, was a man known as 'JJ'. JJ served on Japanese ships with Malay crews during the war, and when it ended, found himself stranded in Rabaul, New Guinea. On his eventual return to Singapore, JJ began to train as a wireless operator while most of his Malay friends continued to work at sea. JJ recalled his experience some months later:

I met some of my friends from New Guinea – Rabaul. You know, seamen. All in flashy gear [i.e. fashionable, modern apparel], and all that like, you know. I say, 'Hey! Where you guys been, man?' He says, 'What are you doing here?' I said, 'I'm learning to be a wireless operator.' 'Ah', he says, 'I've been to America, Australia, all over the world, man.' Yeah … all my mates, like you know, all the flashy gear. 'Ah', I say, 'so that's where you got them.' 'Yeah! I got it from New York, man', and all that like, you know? So my heart started to beat, I said, 'Oh, blimey. What the hell am I doing here?'[1]

Living and training in Singapore after the war, JJ already imagined himself as being further along the pathway to modernity than he had been as a child growing up in the small Malayan town of Seremban. Although he might have been able to eventually acquire the kinds of 'flashy gear' that his friends obtained in New York (thus able to fashion himself as a modern young man), JJ was not content to remain in what Dipesh Chakrabarty (2000, p. 9) has referred to as the 'waiting room of history'. When JJ's seafaring friends came to set sail again, an opportunity arose to join them, and JJ left the wireless operator training and Singapore behind. JJ and his friends travelled far beyond the *alam Melayu* (Malay world region in Southeast Asia) as seafarers, visiting many port towns and cities in *Eropah*, including New York.

JJ, eventually, became one of scores of Malay ex-seamen who settled in ports on the other side of the North Atlantic (Cardiff, Glasgow, London, as well as Liverpool). Why did they settle in British port towns and cities, rather than New York City, given popular imagination of the latter as the leading edge of global modernity after the Second World War? In part, this was because Malay seafarers (or at least those who had been born in the Straits Settlements of Malacca, Penang and Singapore) were officially British subjects – a status that made living and obtaining (legal) onshore employment in Britain much easier than in the United States. Additionally, in Liverpool (in particular) the onshore effects of a postwar rebound in British shipping, as well as wider economic diversification efforts, meant an abundance of onshore jobs. Add to this ambitious municipal urban renewal plans for '21st-Century Liverpool' (Murden, 2006), and it is not difficult to understand how Malay ex-seamen came to form hopeful and optimistic feelings of brighter times to come. Although Liverpool had long looked to New York for lessons in high-rise modernity (Milne, 2006), young Malay men experienced Liverpool in the 1950s as both a modern destination and as a hearth of modern futurity.

Liverpool-based seafarers' (or, in a growing proportion of cases, ex-seafarers') sense of themselves and their place in the world as 'modern' was, of course, sustained in opposition to imagining the Malay world that they left behind as 'traditional'. Whether constructed through what Ong (1996) has termed a 'British-type education', or (more likely) simply through selective memories of their own lives growing up, they imagined British Malaya (territories that during the 1950s and 1960s became the separate independent nation-states of Malaysia and Singapore) in terms of slow-paced *kampung* (village) life, social and sexual conservatism, primitive housing, and antiquated transportation. In an album of photographs from the 1950s taken for the shipping firm with which many Liverpool-based men obtained their first seafaring employment (the Singapore-headquartered Straits Steamship Company), traditional bullock carts feature prominently in shots of 'typical' or 'picturesque' Malayan landscapes.[2] And while the same album also includes photographs of modern buildings and infrastructure in British Malaya, it is revealing that these are almost all images of British rule and/or commerce. Not only does the album reflect the images of 'traditional' Malaya that existed in the heads of ordinary people, but also, to the (limited) extent that the Malaya of the 1950s is depicted as a modern Southeast Asia, these images were associated exclusively with investment from a modern West.

The Modern Is (Still) Elsewhere

Western-centred imaginings of the geography of modernity were to undergo profound reworking during subsequent decades. And, in part, it was the transformation of Liverpool itself that did much to unsettle Liverpool-based Malay men's imaginings of *Eropah* as modern versus Southeast Asia as traditional or 'backward'. From the 1970s, Liverpool and the surrounding Merseyside region of northwest England were hard hit by wider trends of deindustrialization in the UK and shifting patterns of trade (Lane, 1997). Grand visions of, and plans for, the future were not only unrealized but consigned to an economic 'Golden Age' (Murden, 2006), which was (re)imagined as well as truly past. In their place arose powerful images of industrial abandonment and social unrest. Employment in Liverpool fell by 20 per cent between 1966 and 1978, and then by a further 18 per cent in the subsequent 3 years alone (Meegan, 2003, p. 58). Then, 1981 saw high-profile race riots in the Toxteth area of the city, imprinting images of Liverpool as a radicalized 'city of conflict' as well as of local economic devastation (Meegan, 2003, p. 58). And in 1989 the wider Merseyside region received 'Objective Two' status as a 'declining industrial region' within the European Union (Boland *et al.*, 1995). By 1993 this changed to 'Objective One' designation, meaning that Merseyside was officially calculated to be lagging behind other regions of Europe and in need of structural-adjustment funds.

Shifting imagined geographies of development also had to do with changes in Southeast Asia. So spectacular was Singapore's economic growth from the 1970s that by the 1990s the city-state's per-capita gross domestic product (GDP) exceeded that of Britain. Among JJ's generation of men, Singapore, as the main commodity and trans-shipment port of British Malaya, had always been perceived as more modern than the neighbouring peninsula. However, during the final decades of the twentieth century other territories of the former British Malaya (that had become the nation-state of Malaysia) also came to be mapped into powerful narratives of an (East) Asian 'economic miracle' (World Bank, 1993) and the imminent commercial eclipse of the West. Not surprisingly, many Liverpool-based Malay men left the city during this period. They either went elsewhere in the UK – especially to the southeast of England, which benefitted from the same changing national spatial division of labour that had left Liverpool 'marooned on the wrong side of the country' (Lane, 1997, p. 23), or they returned to Southeast Asia.

The lives of these Liverpool-anchored Malay men may be examined in the light of influential work by James Ferguson (1999) on 'expectations of modernity' – albeit with an important twist. From the 1970s, the city of Liverpool, like the East African copper belt that is the focus of Ferguson's study, certainly experienced 'a demotion in the worldwide ranking of things' (1999, p. 12). And for Liverpool-based Malay ex-seamen, as much as for men connected to the mining industry boom in Zambia, this wider loss of standing translated into diminished senses of self-worth. However, for the men who form the focus of this study of Malay Liverpool, the concomitant economic 'rise' of their homelands in Southeast Asia is an important point of differentiation from the lives of rural-to-urban migrant Zambians as considered by Ferguson. Thus, the twist on Ferguson is that while Malays' expectations of modernity were unfulfilled at the site of migrant destination (Liverpool), modern futures appeared to have relocated to their territories of origin – to what had become the postcolonial nation-states of Malaysia and Singapore.

In previous iterations of my Malay-Liverpool work, I likened ex-seafarers' return visits to Malaysia and Singapore to going back to the future: men going back 'home' to forms of urban modernity and development that they had once expected to find 'away' (in *Eropah*). This idea of going 'back to the future' works at the macro level of shifting geographies of economic growth and uneven development. Malay men returning to Singapore or Malaysia after many decades away certainly found ample evidence that the locus of global industrial and urban development had shifted eastwards. But they also found countries that were about more than a future that they had once hoped and expected to find elsewhere. In interviews with Liverpool-based men who had made return trips to Malaysia, I had expected the most widely cited evidence of modern transformation to be the cityscape or skyline of the nation's capital city, Kuala Lumpur. In fact, the most frequently referenced signifier of modern transformation was much more mundane and concerned the toilet or bathroom facilities in relatives' houses (Bunnell, 2016). No doubt there are multiple explanations that could be offered as to why this was the case. This chapter, however, argues that at least part of the reason has to do with the shifting ways in which the dialectic of tradition and modernity has played out in Malaya over the past half a century or so, and the ways in which this is manifested in the built environment of Kuala Lumpur and Singapore (and their wider urban regions). Spectacular as this transformation has undoubtedly been, the resultant urban landscape did not conform to ex-seafarers' historical expectations of modernity in terms of a linear pathway of transformation away from the 'traditional' pasts that they left behind in the middle decades of the twentieth century. 'Back-to-the-future' modernization was discernible in domestic bathroom changes, but transformation of the built environment variously departed from and exceeded prior expectations in the form of new articulations of modernity and tradition.

Tradition/Modernity in Greater Kuala Lumpur: Three (Geo)Historical Processes

To characterize and explain this excess, in what follows I analyze three sets of processes manifested in the built environment of greater Kuala Lumpur during the last half century. Each of them involves different dialectical configurations of tradition and modernity. They are dealt with here in broadly chronological terms, although one has not so much been replaced by as folded into the next. All three sets of processes, in different ways, raise important questions of 'Whose tradition?' and involve consideration of the politics of tradition and indigeneity.

Malay(si)anization – From the 1950s

The first set of processes may be referred to as 'Malaysianization'. In the widest political or geopolitical sense, this refers to the making of the independent nation-state of the Federation of Malaya in 1957 (prior to official use of the toponym Malaysia, and so initially Malayanization) and its subsequent expansion and renaming as 'Malaysia'. As the capital of the new federation, Kuala Lumpur immediately came to play an important role in the political and cultural aspects of Malaysian nation-building (McGee, 1963). But processes of Malaysianization were also, in many ways, the making of Kuala Lumpur. It was through political independence and Singapore's separation from Malaysia in 1965 that Kuala Lumpur assumed centrality to national development – in much of the territory that was formerly British Malaya – and in the postcolonial quest for modernization.

Kuala Lumpur had functioned as the administrative centre of the Federated Malay States from the end of the nineteenth century. As a result, the settlement featured India-inspired Mahometan- or Indo-Saracen-style government offices (King, 2008), which, according to one British visitor in 1913, 'would be considered handsome in any city in the world' (Powell, 1913). Despite the presence of such 'modern' buildings that so impressed F.E. Powell, even prior to independence in 1957, Kuala Lumpur remained essentially a provincial town overshadowed by Singapore (Gullick, 1983, p. 166). Many of the Malay seafaring men whose mobilities were traced from the middle decades of the twentieth century had not even visited Kuala Lumpur until they went 'back' to (what had become) Malaysia from Britain in later life (Bunnell, 2016). One of the few men who had visited in his pre-seafaring days was Fadzil Mohamed. Fadzil worked in Kuala Lumpur as a 'peon' (servant boy) for a British family immediately after the Second World War and his recollections were of Kuala Lumpur having been mostly 'jungle' in the 1940s![3]

It was only in the build-up to *Merdeka* (national independence) during the subsequent decade that Kuala Lumpur emerged from the shadow of Singapore. Kuala Lumpur-centred nation-building was manifested in a range of modern urban developments that have been carefully documented by Chee Kien Lai (2007). The first project that Lai examined in his *Building Merdeka* is Merdeka Stadium, which was completed in and for independence in 1957. Subsequent national infrastructure projects included the University of Malaya campus at Pantai Valley (in 1958) and a new international airport at Subang (not actually in Kuala Lumpur proper), which opened in 1965 (Lai, 2007). Such postcolonial national development meant not only that the political map of the region had changed (with Singapore and Malaysia forming separate, independent nation-states), but also that Kuala Lumpur came to assume imaginative and material centrality to Malaysia. This implied geographies of development that contrasted sharply with the Straits Settlements-centred mental maps held in seafarers' heads when they had first left British Malaya in preceding decades. Even those Liverpool-based men who had returned to Southeast Asia as seafarers tended to call in at Singapore, which remained the largest and busiest port in the region, rather than Kuala Lumpur. In contrast, men who made return visits to Penang or Malacca – or, anywhere in the former British Malaya other than Singapore – in post-seafaring life stages came through airports built to serve the Malaysian capital. Until the 1990s, when a new Kuala Lumpur International Airport was opened, this meant Sultan Abdul Aziz Shah Airport at Subang.

While the economic geography of national and wider regional development may have changed dramatically, Subang Airport and other architectural and infrastructural transformations during the immediate post-independence period were very much in line with the modern (and modernizing) imaginings of the men in the study. This was the 'modern' of international or Western-style, urban development. Its constitutive outside was the nonurban, the rural locus of tradition. To the extent that 'tradition' found visible expression or found a place in Kuala Lumpur-centred nation-building during this period it was in the style and contents of the national museum (Lai, 2007). What kind of 'tradition' was this? And 'Whose tradition' was it? It was the traditional 'other' of modernization theory which underlays the developmental imaginings of Western and Western-trained local experts involved in the (literal) process of nation-building in Malaysia; it was also the traditional other of young Malay men who left British Malaya with aspirations to realize themselves as 'modern', in the image of *Eropah*.

Malayization – From 1969

The second set of processes, 'Malayization', began from 1969. This was the year when Malaysia experienced what was, and remains, its most serious intercommunal violence, mostly in and around Kuala Lumpur. This is not the occasion for in-depth examination of the causes for the events that have been cast in official memory as the 'riots' of 13 May 1969. 'May 13' is conventionally and officially said to have arisen from Malay dissatisfaction with their social, political and, especially, economic position, given the apparently continued ethnic Chinese-Malaysian domination of the economy more than a decade after independence (see Comber, 1983). However, work over the past decade, drawing upon previously classified archival material, has suggested that the translation of that dissatisfaction into interethnic urban violence involved more orchestration than has been acknowledged in official accounts, as part of efforts to deepen Malay political supremacy (*ketuanan Melayu*) (see Kua, 2007). What is not in doubt is the wider political economic effect of May 13. The riots were followed by state policies to promote specifically Malay economic development and to raise the proportion of the national economy that was in Malay hands, especially through the so-called New Economic Policy that began in 1971 (Gomez and Jomo, 1997). Less well-known is that the New Economic Policy was accompanied by a national cultural policy (in the early 1970s), the first principle of which was that 'the national culture of Malaysia must be based on the cultures of the people indigenous to the region' (Tan, 1992, p. 283), specifically, ethnic Malays and other so-called *bumiputera* (mostly of East Malaysia territories of Sabah and Sarawak on the island of Borneo).

In this context of heightened Malay political supremacy, it is no surprise or coincidence that the 1970s bore witness to the beginning of a 'Malayization' of the national capital. This could be understood through a variety of registers, from the demographic – encouragement of Malay urbanization and rural-urban migration (Ong, 1987) – to the symbolic expression of Malay-ness in the material fabric of the city, and a corresponding 'roll back' of non-Malay cultural symbols in urban public space (Loo, 2013, p. 3). Two of the best-known examples of the latter are Bank Bumiputera and Menara Maybank, both of which incorporate ostensibly Malay cultural designs, aesthetics, and/or symbolism. The Bank Bumiputera building that was completed in 1980 includes a five-storey banking chamber on stilts with what architect Ross King describes as 'a vast "traditional" Malay-style roof' (King, 2008, p. 105). Menara Maybank, meanwhile, is 'based on the form of a Malay *keris* or traditional ceremonial dagger' (p. 107).

Explanation of the emergence of such buildings clearly necessitates consideration of more than just the ethnic politics of Malaysia. The international rise of regionalist architecture during the same period was another important, and interwoven, historic trend. An official book on '80 years of architecture in Malaysia' categorized the 1970s as follows: 'architects began to search for a national identity by looking at traditional architecture and cultural heritage' (Lim and Tay, 2000, p. 111). Overwhelmingly, it was specifically Malay cultural heritage and 'traditional' elements that were deployed, in a postcolonial, 'plural society' context where Malay elites desired a national capital that reflected and exuded Malay political dominance.

Drawing attention to such cultural or aesthetic politics is not to suggest that individual architects or other design professionals involved in Malayizing the urban landscape starting in the 1970s were (or are) necessarily Malay chauvinists. The point is city builders were working in the Malay-centred political context of what planning scholars have referred to as 'ethnocracy' (Yiftachel and Ghanem, 2004). Also, while the use of 'Malay' symbols in such a political context could be seen or 'read' as signs of Malay-centeredness, this is not necessarily or inevitably the case. Indeed, there is evidence of some designers having sought to use 'traditional' elements in much more inclusive ways. One such example is Lim Jee Yuan's book *The Malay House* (1987), which highlighted the sense of community that this traditional form supports and its supposedly harmonious relationship with the environment. In his brilliant analysis of Lim's work, the anthropologist Joel Kahn noted how in the text of *The Malay House* the reader is 'asked to learn from traditional architecture certain things which can be made relevant to the modern scene' (Kahn, 1992, p. 175), and that while 'at one level architecturally anti-modern, the argument in the text is paradoxically modernist' (p. 176). Specifically, Malay traditional elements are deployed by Lim as part of a search for a set of principles for sustainable and more-than-Malay national community building.

In terms of the Malay ex-seafarers in my study, it is inconsequential whether the proliferation of supposedly indigenous Malay forms in the city are attributed to exclusivist Malay nationalism or to more inclusive Malaysian nationalism, or to international architectural regionalism (critical or otherwise). What is significant is the very presence and often-oversized visibility of ostensibly Malay traditional forms in the landscape of the national capital and in other major towns and cities of postcolonial Malaysia. These are very different from the visual expectations of urban modernity or modernizing 'catch up' held by men who left the *alam Melayu* long before 1969.

Islamization – From the 1980s

The third and final set of processes are associated not merely with the proliferation of 'traditional' design elements in the built environment, but also with attempts to articulate the kind of alternative vision of modernity referred to by Aihwa Ong in the epigram to this chapter – the role of Islam in 'an increasingly autonomous definition of modernity that is differentiated from that in the West' (Ong, 1996, p. 60). This, again, implies norms and forms of modernity that are very different from those held in the heads of Malay men who sailed westwards from the *alam Melayu* in the 1950s. But Islamization was also about more than intranational politics of indigeneity.

Taking a brief chronological step back, it is possible to trace a renewal of interest in 'Islamic' aesthetics in the built environment in Malaysia to the national cultural policy. The third of the official principles outlined in that policy was that 'Islam will be an important element in the national culture' (Tan, 1992, p. 283). In this sense, Islamic design references might be cast as simply a subset of elements of Malayization from the 1970s. But it is important to note that the politics of Islam became about more than expressing 'Malayness' as part of interethnic rivalry. The 1980s saw the rise to prominence of intra-Malay political contest as the ruling Malay party, the United Malays National Organization (UMNO), was challenged by the Pan-Malaysian Islamic Party (PAS). Its response was to try to proclaim its own Islamic credentials in what amounted to efforts to out-Islamize the Islamic party, in order to retain or win back the Malay vote. Indeed, Mahathir Mohamad, who became prime minister in 1981, announced an official Islamization policy; and insofar as this increased the prominence of specifically Islamic aspects of Malay 'tradition' in public and quasi-public architecture, Islamization *was* an outgrowth of the earlier period of Malayization.

The focus for Islamization I wish to focus on here, however, extends beyond the position of Malays and 'Malayness' in Malaysia, and even beyond attempts by UMNO to 'out-traditionalize' PAS. There are important international dimensions to Islamic resurgence going back to the 1970s (Mutalib, 1993). The rise of PAS as an electoral force and opponent to UMNO might be understood at least partly in this light. Prime Minister Mahathir's own thinking was also shaped, at least partly, in relation to wider geopolitical transformation and discourse (Schottman, 2011). Writing in the late 1990s, Malaysian anthropologist A.B. Shamsul distinguished 'modernist' and 'fundamentalist' factions of *dakwah* (Islamic resurgence) in Malaysia (Shamsul, 1999). Mahathir was cast as the archetypal modernist. His was not a concern to draw upon Islam as a repository of traditional symbolism in order to localize or regionalize an essentially Western modernity (in the way that Malay-centred regionalist architecture in Malaysia had arguably attempted). Rather, Mahathir saw and presented himself as more consciously turning away from the West and as formulating an alternative vision of modernity, including (but not only) in relation to international Islamic revivalism (Mahathir, 1986). That said, for all of his non-Western and even anti-Western rhetoric, Mahathir's (and

UMNO's) vision of modernist Islam continued to be one 'attuned to the needs of global capital and the development agenda' (Noor, 2005, p. 223).

Some of the contradictions of Mahathir's modernist Islam, in a multiethnic and multi-religious country, are materialized in his most high-profile effort to market Kuala Lumpur and Malaysia to the world – the Petronas Twin Towers. On the one hand, the architect Ross King has pointed to aspects of the design of the towers that speak to the ethno-religious traditions of Chinese and Indian Malaysians. Here the Petronas Towers are cast as alluding to a multicultural Malaysia rather than in terms of Malay-centred Islamization (King, 2008). In contrast, the anthropologist Julian Lee (2014, p. 80) has suggested that:

While these allusions may seem apparent to King, it is not at all clear that these allusions are intended. Whether on a tour of the Twin Towers' sky bridge, in official literature or elsewhere, I have not seen any suggestion of the accommodation of non-Muslim/non-Malay traditions have been [sic] declaratively expressed.

For Lee, the towers are unambiguously 'an instantiation of an Islamic modernity' (p. 79), in a country where Malay and Muslim are increasingly conflated to the point of being almost synonymous (see also Martinez, 2004). Here, the politics of multiple and overlapping conceptions of modernity and tradition – as in many other times and places – defy a singular or settled authoritative interpretation. Both King's and Lee's readings of the Petronas Towers are plausible. Perhaps it is even possible for both to be 'correct', just as it is possible that the Petronas Towers are about both global capital and Islamic modernity.

It is when one looks at the tradition that forms the 'reverse side of the coin' (AlSayyad, 2014) – in this case, the other side of grand visions of Islamic modernity – that one can most clearly see Islamization as more than Malayization. Traditional Islamic references in Malaysia are increasingly drawn, not so much from within the *alam Melayu*, but rather from 'great' Islamic civilizations in other regions of the world – especially the Middle East. And what the geographer Sarah Moser (2012) has termed 'Fantasy Middle Eastern' architecture is manifested most spectacularly in Malaysia's federal government administrative centre, Putrajaya, a purpose-built city located 30 kilometres south of the federal territory of Kuala Lumpur (but very much part of the greater Kuala Lumpur region). When I studied plans for Putrajaya and the initial stages of its construction in the 1990s among the impacts I examined were those concerning the lives of the Tamil (i.e. Tamil Malaysian) plantation workers who were being evicted – and whose temples were being demolished – to make way for a city of mostly Malay-Muslim civil servants (Bunnell, 2002; Bunnell et al., 2010). Yet to cast this as a case of symbolic as well as demographic Malayization is an oversimplification. Ethnic Malay-Muslim scholars have commented to me that they cannot relate meaningfully to the symbolism of Putrajaya. If this is Malay(sian) national architecture, they have said, then they feel as marginal to it as Chinese Malaysians. This raises, once again, questions central to the current volume: Whose tradition? And, tradition in whose name?

Examination of key texts on Islam and architecture in contemporary Malaysia raises several further key questions about much-more-than-Malay forms of Islamization (Mohamed Tajuddin, 2005; King, 2008; Moser, 2012). First, to what extent is the downplay of explicitly Malay references (compared to some of the examples considered above in relation to the Malayization of the built environment of Kuala Lumpur from the 1970s) about fostering a form of national identity that is more inclusive, cosmopolitan, and less Malay-centric? Second, is the growing preference for non-Malay Islamic references evidence of fundamentalist strands of Islamic resurgence, which wish to do away with syncretic Malay-world Islamic traditions in favour of 'purer' forms found elsewhere? And, third, is the growing propensity to reference great Islamic civilizations and Golden Ages bound up with efforts to find suitably great traditions upon which to construct grand visions of global Islamic modernity? Other scholars, including those cited above, are better placed to answer these questions. As a partial response to the third question, though, it is worth reiterating Ross King's argument (originally made by Frederic Jameson): 'utopian desire is always nostalgic for an imagined, perfected past' (King, 2008, p. 259). The Malaysian architect Mohamed Tajuddin (2005), meanwhile, has boldly suggested that Putrajaya's foreign Islamic design references are evidence of a Malay(sian) inferiority complex in relation to the great Islamic civilizations, especially in the Middle East.

It is ironic that the hierarchy of value (of cultures, civilizations and traditions) diagnosed by Mohamed Tajuddin is reminiscent of that once held by British colonial administrators. For example, the colonial government offices in Kuala Lumpur mentioned earlier in this chapter, took the form of Mahometan-style designs imported from British India as 'high' Islamic culture for the Malay Peninsula (King, 2008). A very important historical difference, however, is that the city of Putrajaya is the product of a government which (at least at times) explicitly claims to be Islamic. So, to return once again to the Malay ex-seafarers, the material manifestation of Islamization in late-twentieth and earlier-twenty-first-century Malaysia has been difficult for them to fit into their mental schemes of progress, as these are based upon the distinctly secular, modernist vision of the late-colonial and early-post-independence period.

Navigating the Currents of Globalization

This chapter has sketched three broadly chronological periods of transformation for Kuala Lumpur (and its wider urban region) during the decades when the Malay seafarers in my study were away in Liverpool. Each of those periods of transformation involved different dialectical configurations of modernity and tradition. The first, the period of independence architecture and national infrastructure development (called Malaysianization), is the one most in line with the systems of evaluation of those young Malay seafarers who headed west in search of a secular, modern *Eropah*. The second period (Malayization) saw the proliferation of traditional Malay elements in the built environment of the Malaysian national capital partly through a search for a national identity that was visibly differentiated from international/Western style, but also as a result of the enflamed ethno-cultural politics of identity and indigeneity in postcolonial Malaysia after 1969. The third period (Islamization) drew on Islamic elements from beyond the Malay world as part of efforts to identify suitably great civilizational traditions upon which a global Islamic modernity may be constructed. While the initial period of Malaysianization was in line with the expectations of modernity of young Malay seamen in the middle decades of the twentieth century, the second and third periods were bound up with urban transformations that they found difficult to fit into their late-colonial images of development and progress.

Novel (re)configurations of tradition-modernity partly account for why Malay ex-seafarers rarely cited the skyline of the national capital (or the grand Islamic edifices of Putrajaya) as evidence of progress. As noted, men such as Fadzil Mohamed, returning to (what had become) Malaysia after many decades, tended instead to locate evidence of modern development in much more mundane, domestic transformations. In interview after interview with elderly ex-seafarers in Liverpool, it was the shift from *jamban* (open latrines) to *tandas* (modern bathrooms) that was used to encapsulate half a century of modern progress. This 'excremental transition' (Bunnell, 2016, p. 144) is much more easily accommodated in mid-twentieth-century imaginings of modernization than the neotraditionalist design styles or Islamic visions of modernity that have been articulated through the urban landscapes of Malaysia's national capital region. Of course, there are other possible explanations for why domestic transitions made such an impression on men returning home after decades away. One could be that Liverpool-based men already knew about the spectacular transformation of urban landscapes and skylines in Malaysia before they made return journeys. Images of the skyline of Kuala Lumpur, often focusing on the Petronas Towers and other urban megaprojects made their way to diasporic Malays through postcards, Malaysian tourist promotion imagery, television coverage of the 1998 Commonwealth Games, and even through the Hollywood movie *Entrapment* – among many other channels (Bunnell, 2013). This, in turn, serves as a reminder that Malay men who moved to Britain during the 1950s or 1960s are not some cultural relic of late-colonial British Malaya, entirely cut off from the politics of indigeneity or Islamic revivalism in Malaysia. Perhaps the point is that relational re-imaginings of Malaysia from a distance are much more likely to have been based on visible, public expressions of modernity-tradition than on mundane transformations in the private sphere. At the same time, the 'excremental transition' that returning ex-seamen observed is one apparently unaffected by emergent iterations of the modernity-tradition dialectic that are visible in the skyline of the national capital.

Notes

1. Interview, Liverpool, 23 September 2004.
2. Untitled and undated album of photographs taken by R.K. Tyers, staff of Straits Steamship Co. Ltd., Singapore, in the Ocean Archive held at the Merseyside Maritime Museum, Liverpool (OA/947).
3. Notes from conversation, Liverpool, 24 May 2008.

References

AlSayyad, N. (2014) *Traditions: The 'Real', the Hyper, and the Virtual in the Built Environment*. London: Routledge.
Boland, P., Mannin, M. and Wallace, J. (1995) Merseyside – implications of Objective 1 and the Government Office. *Regional Studies*, **29**(7), pp. 698–705.
Bunnell, T. (2002) Multimedia utopia? A geographical critique of high-tech development in Malaysia. *Antipode*, **34**(2), pp. 265–295.
Bunnell, T. (2004) *Malaysia, Modernity and the Multimedia Super Corridor: A Critical Geography of Intelligent Landscapes*. London: RoutledgeCurzon.
Bunnell, T. (2013) Encountering Kuala Lumpur through the 'travel' of UMPs, in del Cerro Santamaría, G. (ed.) *Urban Megaprojects: A Worldwide View*. Bingley: Emerald Group Publishing Limited, pp. 61–79.
Bunnell, T. (2016) *From World City to the World in One City: Liverpool through Malay Lives*. Chichester: Wiley.
Bunnell, T., Nagarajan, S. and Willford, A. (2010) From the margins to centre stage:

Indian demonstration effects and Malaysia's political landscape. *Urban Studies*, **47**(6), pp. 1257–1278.
Chakrabarty, D. (2000) *Provincializing Europe*. Princeton, NJ: Princeton University Press.
Comber, L. (1983) *13 May 1969: A Historical Survey of Sino-Malay Relations*. Singapore: Graham Brash.
Ferguson, J. (1999) *Expectations of Modernity: Myths and Meanings of Urban Life on the Zambian Copperbelt*. Berkeley, CA: University of California Press.
Gomez, E.T. and Jomo, K.S. (1997) *Malaysia's Political Economy: Politics, Patronage and Profits*. Cambridge: Cambridge University Press.
Gullick, J.M. (1983) *The Story of Kuala Lumpur, 1857–1939*. Singapore: Eastern Universities Press.
Kahn, J.S. (1992) Class, ethnicity and diversity: some remarks on Malay culture in Malaysia, in Kahn, J.S. and Loh, F. (eds.) *Fragmented Vision: Culture and Politics in Contemporary Malaysia*. Sydney: Allen and Unwin, pp. 158–78.
King, R. (2008) *Kuala Lumpur and Putrajaya: Negotiating Urban Space in Malaysia*. Singapore: NUS Press.
Kua, K.S. (2007) *May 13: Declassified Documents on the Malaysian Riots of 1969*. Petaling Jaya: Suaram Komunikasi.
Lai, C.K. (2007) *Building Merdeka: Independence Architecture in Kuala Lumpur, 1957–1966*. Kuala Lumpur: Galeri Petronas.
Lane, T. (1997) *Liverpool: City of the Sea*. Liverpool: Liverpool University Press.
Lee, J.C.H. (2014) Citizenship and the city: visions and revisions of Malaysia, in Yeoh, S.G. (ed.) *The Other Kuala Lumpur: Living in the Shadows of a Globalising Southeast Asian City*. London: Routledge, pp. 72–91.
Lim, J.Y. (1987) *The Malay House: Rediscovering Malaysia's Indigenous Shelter System*. Pinang: Institut Masyarakat.
Lim, T.N. and Tay, L. (2000) *80 Years of Architecture in Malaysia*. Kuala Lumpur: Pertubuhan Akitek Malaysia.
Loo, Y.M. (2013) *Architecture and Urban Form in Kuala Lumpur: Race and Chinese Spaces in a Postcolonial City*. Farnham: Ashgate.
McGee, T.G. (1963) The cultural role of cities: a case study of Kuala Lumpur. *Journal of Tropical Geography*, **17**, pp. 178–196.
Mahathir, M. (1986) *The Challenge*. Petaling Jaya: Pelanduk Publications.
Martinez, P. (2004) Perhaps he deserved better: the disjuncture between vision and reality in Mahathir's Islam, in Welsh, B. (ed.) *Reflections: The Mahathir Years*. Washington, DC: Johns Hopkins University Southeast Asia Studies Program, pp. 28–39.
Meegan, R. (2003) Urban regeneration, politics and social cohesion: the Liverpool case, in Munck, R. (ed.) *Reinventing the City? Liverpool in Comparative Perspective*. Liverpool: Liverpool University Press, pp. 53–79.
Milne, G.J. (2006) Maritime Liverpool, in Belchem, J. (ed.) *Liverpool 800: Culture, Character and History*. Liverpool: Liverpool University Press, pp. 257–310.
Mohamad Tajuddin, M.R. (2005) *Malaysian Architecture: Crisis Within*. Kuala Lumpur: Utusan Publications.
Moser, S. (2012) Circulating visions of 'high Islam': the adoption of fantasy Middle Eastern architecture in constructing Malaysian national identity. *Urban Studies*, **49**(13), pp. 2913–2936.
Murden, J. (2006) City of change and challenge: Liverpool since 1945, in Belchem, J. (ed.) *Liverpool 800: Culture, Character and History*. Liverpool: Liverpool University Press, pp. 393–485.
Mutalib, H. (1993) *Islam in Malaysia: From Revivalism to Islamic State*. Singapore: Singapore University Press.

Noor, F.A. (2005) *From Majapahit to Putrajaya: Searching for another Malaysia*. Kuala Lumpur: Silverfish Books.

Ong, A. (1987) *Spirits of Resistance and Capitalist Discipline*. Albany, NY: SUNY Press.

Ong, A. (1996) Anthropology, China and modernities: the geopolitics of cultural knowledge, in Moore, H. (ed.) *The Future of Anthropological Knowledge*. London: Routledge.

Powell, F.E. (1913) *With Eastern Merchandise: A Landsman's Log on Board a Cargo Boat*. London: Thomas Murby and Co.

Schottman, S. (2011) The Pillars of 'Mahathir's Islam': Mahathir Mohamad on being-Muslim in the modern world. *Asian Studies Review*, **35**(3), pp. 355–372.

Shamsul, A.B. (1999) From *Orang Kaya Baru* to *Melayu Baru*: cultural construction of the Malay 'new rich', in Pinches, M. (ed.) *Culture and Privilege in Capitalist Asia*. London: Routledge, pp. 86–110.

Tan, S.B. (1992) Counterpoints in the performing arts of Malaysia, in Kahn, J.S. and Loh, F. (eds.) *Fragmented Vision: Culture and Politics in Contemporary Malaysia*. Sydney: Allen and Unwin, pp. 282–305.

World Bank (1993) *The East Asian Miracle: Economic Growth and Public Policy*. New York: Oxford University Press.

Yiftachel, O. and Ghanem, A. (2004) Understanding 'ethnocratic' regimes: the politics of seizing contested territories. *Political Geography*, **23**, pp. 647–676.

Part III

Colonialism: Whose Architecture?

Chapter 7

How the Past and the Future Have Influenced the Design of Guam's Government House

Marvin Brown

Guam's Government House, in its various iterations, is a visual narrative of what different individuals with different political and cultural agendas have chosen to present as the public face of a long-colonized land. Each party in the conception, design, and redesign of the governor's residence has, throughout the building's brief but architecturally tumultuous history, cast one eye back to a particular historic past and the other forward to a distinctive vision of the future. A progressive American naval officer and modernist Vienna-born architect, a conventional Pacific Northwest American governor and his equally conventional wife, and a martyred Chamorro native son all turned to different but legitimate histories and traditions for inspiration. Each attempted to mould the governor's residence into a representation of his or her own vision of the island's past, present, and future.

This chapter considers how this varied group of individuals who participated in the design of Government House used selective views of the island's past and its traditions to address perceived present needs and to project their broad visions into the future. It also considers how a building that at first blush seems to represent the architecture of a land's two principal colonial occupiers can transform those styles into the symbols of a modern and (semi-) independent place.

Architectural forms and styles are inherently ambiguous as cultural signifiers, open to appropriation and imitation for many purposes. The chapter concludes by considering what enables a work of architecture to embody a tradition of a people, and what empowers architecture to provide a new sense of identity in a colonial and postcolonial world.

Guam's History and Architecture

Guam is a 212-square-mile (549 km^2) island in the northern Pacific — about 1,500 miles (2,415 km) east of the Philippines. It anchors the southern end of the Northern Marianas archipelago. With the landfall of Ferdinand Magellan in 1521, Guam became the first inhabited Pacific Ocean island to be encountered by Europeans. And in 1565 the Spanish laid claim to it because of its strategic position on their newly established Manila galleon trade route from Acapulco to Manila. At first, they only provisioned their ships on Guam, but with the founding of its first Catholic mission in 1668, they permanently settled there (Rogers, 1995, p. 1).[1]

Spain's colonization profoundly affected the native Chamorro – as was the case with Spanish subjugation of other native peoples in the Pacific. As Ronald Stade (1998, p. 2) noted:

From being a center in the Micronesian archipelago of the Chamorros, the Mariana Islands had been removed to the outskirts of a global empire. The Chamorro village of Hagåtña became the provincial town of Agaña … Oceania's first European style city.

The Spanish ruled Guam for more than three centuries. With intent and without – through war, displacement, and disease – the Spanish reign decimated Guam's native Chamorro population and destroyed its ocean-going culture. Centuries of proselytizing and, in many cases, *de facto* governance by Jesuits and Franciscans also subsumed native religious practices and installed Catholicism as the island's religion. Remarkably, though, the native language of Guam and other islands in the Northern Marianas survived (Wuerch and Ballendorf, 1994, pp. 40–44). Thus 'Chamorro' today names both the language and the people of Guam. However, the Chamorro retained their identity not only through holding on to much of their language (which now contains many words of Spanish origin), but by putting their own stamp on Catholic practices. In particular, this meant retaining a tradition of public feasting, or *fi'estas*, by merging it with Catholic saints' days. The practice still exerts influence over island life, and it even informed the design of Government House (Wuerch and Ballendorf, 1994, pp. 40–44).

What Chamorro architecture looked like prior to the arrival of the

Spanish is unclear. Large, tapered, upright megaliths with cup-shaped capitals, known as *latte*, survive on Guam and elsewhere in the Northern Marianas. However, the appearance of the structures that stood upon the *lattes*, which were arranged in two parallel rows, is not known. Most likely, these structures rested on a broad platform placed atop the stones and had high gabled roofs (Cunningham, 1992; Hunter-Anderson, 2016) (figures 7.1*a* and 7.1*b*).

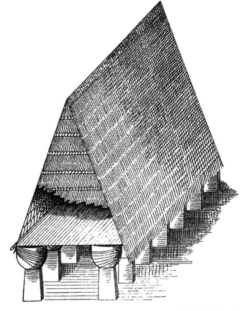

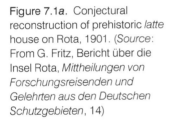

Figure 7.1a. Conjectural reconstruction of prehistoric *latte* house on Rota, 1901. (*Source*: From G. Fritz, Bericht über die Insel Rota, *Mittheilungen von Forschungsreisenden und Gelehrten aus den Deutschen Schutzgebieten*, 14)

Figure 7.1b. Traditional houses in Umatac village, 1937. (*Source*: Don Farrell collection, courtesy of *Guampedia*)

During more than 330 years of Spanish occupation, most Chamorro lived in houses that probably resembled these structures. The dwellings were rectangular, with thatch, reed, or board walls and steeply pitched, thatched, gabled roofs. Early- and mid-twentieth-century photographs depict such houses lifted off the ground on wooden posts, rather than *latte* (it was only after super typhoon Karen in 1962 that concrete and tin houses became the norm) (Cunningham, 1992 and 2016; de Freycinet, 2003). The traditional houses were also not limited to the space contained within their walls, but extended to exterior spaces where many domestic Chamorro activities took place (Hunter-Anderson and Moore, 2006, pp. 11–14).

The Spanish occupiers, meanwhile, erected Spanish-style structures amidst the island's indigenous architecture. Among these were churches and bridges, which they scattered across the island, and dwellings and prominent structures built in the capital city of Agaña (now called Hagåtña). Particularly prominent was the complex of buildings at Plaza de Espana, erected in 1669 as the colonial seat of government. Portions of the plaza's arched walls still stand (de Freycinet, 2003; Driver and Hezel, 2004) (figure 7.2).

In 1898, by terms of the treaty that ended the Spanish-American War, Guam became a US territory, and America installed itself as the new colonial ruler. The island's size, location, and harbours captivated the

Figure 7.2. Plaza de Espana, 2010. (*Photo*: CC Abasaa)

second colonizers as much as they had the first. And American interest only grew with the advent of the airplane, as Guam's high, level landforms were well suited to the construction of airfields. The Americans continued to use the governor's residence, which the Spanish had established at the Plaza de Espana. But during the entire period when the US Navy governed the island – between 1898 and 1948 (excluding World War II) – the Americans, in contrast to the Spanish, showed little interest in putting their stamp on the island's public architecture (Platt, 1975). By the early twentieth century, some Chamorro had also adopted Spanish Colonial-style dwellings, with thick, plastered walls and red-tiled, hipped roofs.[2] By this time, Chamorro houses had evolved 'in response to the physical realities of Guam's climate and other geographic conditions as well as to prevailing social and demographic factors' (Hunter-Anderson and Moore, 2006, p. 14). There was thus no single house form or type by mid-century that one could identify simply as Chamorro.

In December 1941 – within hours of the bombing of Pearl Harbor – Japan shelled and seized Guam, dramatically changing life for the Chamorro. A fierce US bombardment and bloody landing in July 1944 subsequently reclaimed the island from the brutal regime of the Japanese. But the settlements and economy of the island had been decimated (Marsh, 2014; Martinez, 1991; Higuchi, 2014). Confronted with a largely homeless population, the Navy supported construction of new houses and villages that used the steeply pitched, thatched-roof form. It also erected Quonset huts and other temporary metal buildings across the island, which became the most visible architectural evidence of American occupation.[3] A less ephemeral effect on Guam's architecture was the American application of 'Western block' development, comprised of houses, built within delineated property lines, that edged against roads and were connected to electric, telephone, and water lines (Hunter-Anderson and Moore, 2006, pp. 13–15).

Postwar reconstruction provided the immediate context for the design of Guam's new Government House. At the time, an architect could have looked back to traditional Chamorro buildings and sought precedent in *latte*-type columns, steeply pitched gable roofs, and natural materials. Or, he or she could have turned to a long history of Spanish design – which might have carried the baggage of Spanish domination. Or, he or she could have picked and chosen from both precedents. However, an architect might also have considered a style or form new to Guam – perhaps based on classical American designs, American planning, or the ideas of modernism. A thoughtful design would have considered what these choices had to say about Guam's past, how they might address its present needs, and how they might be viewed by the Chamorro and by non-natives in the future. The principals involved in the design of the residence did just that.

Carlton Skinner's Vision of a Firm Foundation for Government House

Five figures, individually or in pairs, played primary roles in the design and current appearance of Government House: Governor Carlton Skinner; architect Richard Neutra; Governor Ford Elvidge and his wife, Anita; and Governor Ricardo Bordallo (Murphy, 2014).[4]

In 1949 US President Harry Truman appointed former Navy Lieutenant Carlton Skinner (1913–2004) as Guam's first civilian governor. Skinner had solid progressive credentials. In 1943 he had lobbied for and been given command of the first integrated ship in the US Navy, the *Sea Cloud* (Tanenbaum, 2004; Rogers, 1995, p. 221; Skinner, undated).[5] And despite continuous friction with naval authorities, who still coveted control of the island, he became a key figure in establishing a measure of self-rule on Guam under the terms of the Organic Act. Historians have admired Skinner's cooperation with the new Guam legislature, his appointment of Chamorros to high-level government positions, and, in general, his vision for the island. He is today remembered for his deep concern for Guam and its native inhabitants (Tanenbaum, 2004; Rogers, 1995, p. 221). According to one history of the island, 'The aggressive and intelligent leadership which [Skinner] provided during a confused transitional period established the government on a firm and solid foundation' (Carano and Sanchez, 1965, p. 370).

Skinner's appreciation of Guam came with application – on arriving, he made a concerted effort to visit, inspect, and participate in the celebrations of each of the island's twenty-one villages and sub-villages (Skinner, 1997, pp. 27–28). And he carefully thought out all aspects of the new governor's residence (required by the physical destruction from the war) – from its name, to its location, to its architect. He decided to call it 'Government House', rather than the previous Spanish name, *palacio* (*palayso* in Chamorro). He wished to wipe that part of the colonial slate clean. He chose for its location the site of a former officers' club that was already in US government hands and therefore would not require condemnation. 'Land condemnation', he wrote, 'was of course, a thing that I tried very hard to avoid because taking of private land by the Navy, Army and Air Force, or condemnation even though legal, proper and necessary, had caused great difficulty to Chamorro families and the Chamorro social system which was very strongly linked to the land.' He also considered the accessibility of the site to roads, its view of the capital (Hagåtña) and the Pacific, its ability to catch cooling ocean breezes, and even the presence of a swimming pool built for the former club (Skinner, undated).

When Carlton Skinner looked back at the past and out at the present, he saw the Chamorro people soldiering on in the face of cold, unreconstructed colonialism. To counter this, he attempted to build Government House on a firm foundation, literally and symbolically. He wanted the residence erected in a fair fashion, sensitive to traditional landownership, so it would not become a contested site even before its first square foot of concrete was poured (Skinner, 1997; Carano and Sanchez, 1965, p. 370; Wuerch and Ballendorf, 1994, pp.106–107; Rogers, 1995, p. 221).[6] Out of respect for the island and its citizens, he wanted it to be easily accessible and comfortable. And he wanted it to be up-to-date and modern, which greatly influenced his choice of architect. Overall, he wanted a building that would, in the present and the future, symbolize respect, honour, dignity, equality, and progress. Skinner had spearheaded the effort to make blacks and whites equal on the *Sea Cloud*. Should he not do the same for the Chamorro and their American masters on Guam? Even before it was built, therefore, Government House was intentionally freighted with symbolism.

Richard Neutra's Design of Government House

Carlton Skinner's concerns and goals were apparent in his selection of the architectural and planning firm Neutra & Alexander. He understood they were a progressive partnership and chose them to design, in addition to Government House, various other public buildings and facilities, as well as to create a master plan for the entire island. He pushed forward with his plans for the governor's residence even with the belief, which proved to be true, that he would never occupy it (Skinner, 1952).

Austrian-born Richard Neutra (1892–1970) had attended architecture school in Vienna, where he had been immersed in modernism. In 1923 he emigrated to the United States and briefly worked in Frank Lloyd Wright's studio before moving to Los Angeles. By 1929 he had risen to the top of his field in Southern California. Indeed, in 1932, when the Museum of Modern Art put on its seminal international exhibition of modern architecture, the museum's director, Alfred Barr, identified Neutra as second only to Wright among American architects in terms of international reputation (Lamprecht, 2000, p. 19). Moving into the 1940s and 1950s,

Neutra's commissions extended across the country and throughout the world. He is today acknowledged as one of the principal figures in the history of modernist design (Boesinger, 1959; Lamprecht, 2000; Neutra, 1989, pp. 158–72).[7]

Neutra's partner, the architect Robert Alexander (1907–1993), was a prominent figure in Southern California urban planning who, in 1948, was named president of the Los Angeles Planning Board (Hines, 2006, p. 224). Although he is not addressed further here, he was as central to Skinner's hiring of Neutra & Alexander as was his more famous partner. Skinner hoped that a proper, modern plan – one that encompassed the 'physical development of the island, including roads, villages, subdivisions, port and harbor development, types of public buildings and others' – would bring much needed services and advances to Guam (Skinner, 1952).

Before embarking on any design work, in 1952 Richard Neutra spent a week on Guam. In his typically methodical fashion, he observed and took notes on activities at the governor's temporary residence for an entire 24-hour period. He also travelled the island to see how Chamorro life was lived, and he absorbed the central Chamorro tradition of 'frequent fiestas with free food and warm hospitality' (Rogers, 1995, p. 104).

Neutra designed the new residence to be welcoming and open, with three principal components: a family quarter, an expansive open area for public functions, and a large service area. He understood the importance of communal gatherings to the Chamorro and accordingly designed a central public area with a shielding overhang and a wide expanse of walls without doors, which opened into a deep outdoor courtyard facing the ocean. The purpose of this indoor/outdoor public area was to facilitate gatherings and provide natural cooling. As he wrote at the time: 'The character of openness rather than seclusion is chosen. This is an informal building group rather than a forbidding palace…' (Neutra, *c*. 1952) (figure 7.3).

With all Skinner's and Neutra's talk of names and symbolism and sensitivity to the traditions of Guam, the new Government House was without question a nontraditional, modern dwelling. It was a long, one-storey, flat-roofed building with a projecting bedroom wing at one corner and a projecting garage at another, elements that gave it a pinwheel-shaped footprint typical of Neutra designs. Approaching the house from its entry drive, one saw the slightly elevated residential quarters at the left and, at the right, walls with fixed concrete louvres shielding the service area and garage. Straight ahead, widely spaced columns, horizontal bands of windows, and paired entry doors punctuated a long concrete wall. The entry led into a large reception hall to the right and, straight ahead, to the grounds and a

Figure 7.3. Rear (north) elevation of Government House, 1953. (*Source*: UCLA Library Special Collections)

view of the sea. The residential quarters to the left were cut off from the building's public spaces. The rear elevation, like the front, had both long rows of windows and, at the residential quarters, walls with louvres.

When Carlton Skinner looked back on Guam's history, he saw a legacy of colonialism that he hoped to redress. What did Richard Neutra see and how did he choose to respond? Neutra did not focus on the island's architectural traditions; his design included no *latte* stones or raised platforms, no high-pitched gables, no thatch or reed or other natural materials, nor any Spanish arches. The building itself was in many ways the antithesis of the island's traditions. Hugging the ground, flat-roofed, and made of concrete, steel, and glass, it was brashly modern; indeed, its closest precedent on Guam might have been the ubiquitous, prefabricated, metal Quonset hut. Neutra did see, though, the past and present tradition of public gathering and celebration, which he reflected in his use of public space within and without the structure. As he explained, he chose the 'character of openness' rather than that of the 'forbidding palace'. Subsequent use of the building has borne out the insightfulness of this perception.

Later in his life, Neutra's Guam experience informed his essay 'Bioreal Benchmarks for the Third World'. In it, he stressed the importance of harmony between man and nature in architectural design, and he identified the different requirements in the design of buildings for the mild-tropical climate of Puerto Rico and the tempestuous weather of Guam (Neutra, 1989, p. 168).[8] He also displayed an understanding of the importance of tradition and the difficulties faced by societies confronting colonialism and modernization:

> [O]ur job as architects and planners is to lead these 'condemned' people into the technological civilization – which they very evidently desire to be part of – through patient teaching and attentive partnership. At the same time, we must respect the integrity of older cultural values and social customs.
>
> Equally important is the need to plant new development in the physiographic character of a given country, region, or locale – giving expressive rein to its *spiritus loci*. This educative process is reciprocal, and should be planned for as an integral phase of design and development. This is especially important in countries that are just emerging from a colonial past, as many of them are experiencing a turbulent transition to political and economic autonomy. (Neutra, 1989, p. 161)

Like Carlton Skinner, Richard Neutra was keenly aware of the effects of the colonizers on the colonized.

Ford and Anita Elvidge's Un-Design of Government House

The construction of Government House had begun in November 1952. It ended fourteen months later with its design incomplete and Carlton Skinner and Richard Neutra removed from the project. These abrupt changes introduce the next two actors in the story of the residence: Governor Ford Elvidge and his wife, Anita.

A liberal Democrat, Skinner rightly anticipated that he would not occupy the new Government House, and with the election of a Republican president, Dwight Eisenhower, Ford Elvidge (1892–1980) replaced him in early 1953. A Seattle attorney, Elvidge was seen by conservatives as an antidote to Skinner. He and the US Department of Interior quickly called into question all of Neutra & Alexander's efforts on Guam, from Government House, to new schools, to the island-wide master plan.[9] An in-place pool, a planned guest house, and open porches at Government House failed to survive review by the Interior Department, Governor Elvidge, and, in particular, Anita Elvidge (1895–1981) (Elvidge, 1972, p. 79).

During the design phase of the Government House project, Neutra had sketched his thoughts on the open nature of much of the public realm of the house and how it would be sealed during storms. As he wrote:

The entire social unit was really a porch protected against driving rain by overhangs and by outer porches... Prefab taifun [sic] panels for storm enclosure stored in under story of guesthouse, were to be inserted in detailed stops in all openings upon taifun [sic] alarm. Screening was assumed in all openings, except in social section[s]. (Neutra, c. 1952)

In short, he believed that in Oceania, 'boarding or prefab panels quickly locked in place with thumbscrews is often more effective than sliding or folding enclosures requiring expensive and easily rusted hardware' (Boesinger, 1959, p. 224).

Anita Elvidge, in her self-published account of the family's tenancy on Guam, offered an explanation of why her husband did not carry forward these and other parts of Neutra's design for the house and the island. She wrote that the new governor, a champion of 'conservative spending', recognized the programme as 'too grandiose and extravagant'. She found the swimming pool 'very glamorous and picturesque', but 'took a firm stand and ordered it filled'. She further noted that the couple found the 240 square feet (22.3 m²) of reception room and dining area 'all wide open to insects, wind and rain' and, therefore, unacceptable. To remedy these problems, they ordered (expensive) large plate-glass windows and doors to seal in the space and gutters and downspouts to deal with heavy rains (Elvidge, 1972, pp. 80–81). Without apparent intent, they thus expunged the one Chamorro characteristic of the house.

Not surprisingly, Neutra & Alexander were offended by the actions of Governor Elvidge and vigorously supported his predecessor's vision. In unpublished memoirs, Alexander remembered Carlton Skinner as 'an energetic young idealist with powerful dreams of reconstructing not only the physical ruins of civilian Guam, but also the social and economic condition of the Guamanians' (Hines, 2006, p. 231). Elvidge, on the other hand, had 'no use for governmental planning, a communist concept, and no sense of aesthetics or even fair play'. As Alexander recalled, Elvidge's view was that 'Anyone hired by that idealistic dreamer, Skinner, must be all bad' (Hines, 2006, p. 231).

Whether the open plan would have worked at Government House cannot be determined. Neutra himself, while imagining the pleasure of eating barbequed meat and drinking 'a lot of gimlets' in the open house or on its terraces, also wondered whether flying beetles and other insects would be a problem (Lamprecht, 2000). However, the decision of the Elvidges to largely enclose all its spaces – made before the common use of central air conditioning – guaranteed that the communal heart of the building would remain almost unusably hot for decades.

When the Elvidges looked back at Guam's history they saw, like Skinner, the rearing head of colonialism. But unlike Skinner, they viewed this colonialism as a beneficial and even necessary force. No frills, no waste of America's precious resources – this was the message they sought to project into the future with their changes to Government House. Their changes were also a comment on the present to their contemporaries. Anita Elvidge had nothing but contempt for Neutra's designs; in her estimation he lacked the architectural ability or common sense to understand the need to plan for typhoon winds and the everyday occurrence of insects and rain. With relief, the Elvidges left Guam in 1956, and Government House changed little over the next 20 years.

Whether the Elvidges and Carlton Skinner had any direct exchanges concerning their view of the Chamorro and colonial governance has not been determined. Skinner, however, indirectly addressed the attitude of the Elvidges, as expressed in Anita Elvidge's account of their time on Guam.[10] As he wrote in *Foreign Affairs* in 1963:

There is an obnoxious, insulting and inaccurate phrase, which has in the past been used to justify neglect of economic, social and political advancement. It is 'happy native people'. Administrators in many cases imposed a do-nothing program, ostensibly so that the 'happy native people' would not change. This is more properly known as the 'zoo' theory of colonial administration… It ignored the practical condition that once a land is entered by trade, traffic, exploration or naval or military bases, change is inevitable; the question is what kind and to what end… (Skinner, 1963, p. 143)

Ricky Bordallo's Reimagined Chamorro-Spanish-Accented Government House

In 1975 the next important individual in the architectural history of Government House, Ricardo 'Ricky' Bordallo (1927–1990), was elected governor of Guam. A life-long resident of Hagåtña, he became the island's second native-born Chamorro to be directly elected governor, and the first to be re-elected. Bordallo had been educated in Guam public schools and at the University of San Francisco. And he was an outspoken populist who was steeped from birth in Chamorro rights and island politics (Skinner, 1997: p. 28).[11] His two terms as governor, 1975 to 1978 and 1983 to 1986,

Figure 7.4. Ricardo 'Ricky' Bordallo and supporters during his unsuccessful bid for governor in 1970. (*Source*: *Guam U.S.A. Magazine*, courtesy of *Guampedia*)

were dominated by the twin themes of capital development and Chamorro self-rule (Wuerch and Ballendorf, 1994, p. 8; Rogers, 1995, pp. 252, 254–256, 271–289; Quinata and Murphy, 2014) (figure 7.4).

In early 1975, following his first inauguration, Bordallo made numerous cosmetic changes to Government House. As a pamphlet released in association with the building's festive reopening stated: 'Furnishings reminding us of the past have been added. Government House now reflects the heritage of the people of Guam. It is a modern building with Chamorro-Spanish accents' (Johnston and Gould, 1975). However, the following year super typhoon Pamela slammed into Guam and heavily damaged innumerable structures, including Government House. This gave Governor Bordallo the opportunity to dramatically alter the residence and many other island resources. To do so, he secured $367 million from Washington for typhoon reconstruction, capital improvement projects, and government-of-Guam investments. He applied some million dollars of this to Government House (Quinata and Murphy, 2014; Rogers, 1995).

Bordallo's changes to the residence included converting the family wing to offices and guest space and placing a second storey, for family

Figure 7.5. Front (south) and side elevations of Government House, 2002. (*Photo*: Marvin Brown)

quarters, over much of the structure. More cosmetically, he added stucco walls and arcades of Spanish Colonial-style arches to the first floor and arched windows and balustrades of turned posts to the second. He also canted a fringe of red tiles around the edges of the house's flat roof, giving it the appearance of a hipped-roof, Spanish Colonial dwelling. Finally, he relocated two prehistoric *latte* to a spot near the main entrance. Government House remains to the present, at least outwardly, the house that Ricky Bordallo built (figure 7.5).

What is one to make of Ricky Bordallo's Spanish Colonial reworking of Government House? If Bordallo wanted to draw on an 'authentic' past for his redesign of the structure, why did he not choose the two most recognizable elements of native architecture – the *latte* and the steeply pitched roof? Conversely, why did he choose the most recognizable piece of colonial architecture on Guam – the Plaza de Espana's walls – as at least a partial model for its design?

To begin to understand Governor Bordallo's decisions, it is important to consider the appearance of other major, public structures he erected during his two terms. One of these was the reworking and conversion of the Adelup School, which was also designed in 1952 by Neutra, into a government complex (Hines, 2006; Quinata and Murphy, 2014). Incorporated into that design are two large, courtyard structures with raised platforms and steeply pitched roofs – a clear reference to the traditional

Figure 7.6. *Latte* motif at Won Pat Airport, c. 1982. (*Source*: Public domain)

Chamorro dwelling. Another building project, Won Pat International Airport, similarly employed *latte*-stone motifs (some heavily stylized as interior columns).[12] But for every *latte* motif used at a Bordallo-era government, civic, or transportation project it seems there was a balustrade, an arch, a swath of stucco, or a roof of red clay tiles at another. One need look no further than to one of his most prominent projects: the grandly arched, Spanish Colonial, Umatac Bridge (Babauta, 2015) (figure 7.6).[13]

Again, what does one make of the symbolic meaning of Ricky Bordallo's redesigned Government House? Does it have 'Chamorro-Spanish accents'? Is it Chamorro at all? What traditions did it consider? What pasts did it perceive? What futures did it imagine?

Scholarly writings based in postcolonialism and decolonialization studies of Euro-American colonies and former colonies – and places such as Guam that occupy a region somewhere between – offer arguments that can be applied to accept or condemn Bordallo's embrace of Spanish Colonial-style architecture. The reasoning behind two studies of modernism and the Spanish Colonial in Puerto Rico may also be particularly apt for Guam. Both islands were long-time Spanish possessions handed over to America in 1898 and have the official political status today of unincorporated territories (US General Accounting Office, 1997; Underwood, 2014).

One of the studies, by Luz Marie Rodriguez, found San Juan's modernist Caribe Hilton (1949), designed by the Puerto Rican firm Toro Ferrer y Torregrosa, performed as a version of North American architecture, even though in some ways it was tailored for the tropics (Rodriguez, 2013, p. 177). She also considered a 2011 statement by Puerto Rico's then-governor, Luis Fortuña – which viewed the island's long-time Spanish and American colonial rulers as parent figures – to be a 'rather nostalgic approximation [that] permanently ties Puerto Rico to representations of the subaltern' (Rodriguez, 2013, p. 171). In the other study, John Hertz (in deciphering a Puerto Rican architectural progression that was the reverse of that embodied in Government House) called for retaining San Juan's locally designed, modernist Hotel La Concha. He argued that the proposed (and ultimately dismissed) replacement of the hotel with a Spanish Colonial-style complex would have been inauthentic. According to Hertz (2002, p. 226): 'The [proposed Spanish] architecture – which to the casual, uneducated eye appears to be a more authentic expression of Puerto Rican culture – turns out to be the imported architecture of colonialism, whereas the [modernist] design that appears to be 'foreign' is an authentic expression by local practitioners of an appropriate architecture that expresses a specific place and time in the struggle with modernity on the island'.

While the arguments made in these studies might be used to condemn Bordallo's architectural decisions, one might alternatively consider Bordallo's decisions through the nuanced views of Abidin Kusno regarding Indonesia's postcolonial architecture, or Johan Lagae, Luce Beeckmans and Sofie Boonen with regard to the shared colonial heritage of the Democratic Republic of the Congo (the former Belgian Congo). Rooted in decolonization studies, these assessments allow one to begin to understand Bordallo's choices at Government House. According to Kusno (2013, p. 16), 'Decolonization can be understood as both a rupture and a continuation of the existing power relations. It entails the appropriation of symbols and the investment of meanings into the architecture of the colonial era'. In terms of Indonesia's architecture and urban design, he has further observed that: 'the past returns, in an active form, in the present' (Kusno, 2000, p. 5; see also Appadurai (1995)). Lagae *et al.* have viewed the process of decolonizing former colonial space with similar depth. As they argued, 'The current physical landscape in the Democratic Republic of the Congo can be read as a territorial palimpsest [*sic*] which testifies to a continuing process of layering uses and meaning, a process that occurred during colonial times but is still ongoing today' (Lagae *et al.*, 2010).

At Government House, as well as at Won Pat Airport, Umatac Bridge, and the former Adelup School, Ricky Bordallo reclaimed Chamorro (and appropriated colonial and modernist) architectural symbols. Through these actions, he invested them with new meaning. Bordallo's choices clearly represent the absorption of Spanish Colonial architecture into modern Chamorro architecture. Any notion that Government House cannot be connected to the Chamorro experience because it freely used Spanish Colonial-style elements is shortsighted at best. When Bordallo redesigned the residence, the Chamorro had been living with, and in many instances living in, Spanish Colonial-style buildings for well over 300 years. Is that not sufficient time for them to have taken that style as their own? And the Government House that Bordallo built was certainly more recognizable and comfortable to the Chamorro than the modernist dwelling raised by Carlton Skinner and Richard Neutra, in spite of Neutra's claims of traditional influence in the design.[14]

Were Ricky Bordallo's choices at Government House inauthentic and, therefore, wrong? Perhaps. But they cannot be dismissed, if only because Bordallo was as far from a neocolonialist as one can get.[15] One need only consider his tragic death to perceive the depth of his feelings for his island and his people. In 1987 ex-Governor Bordallo was convicted of charges of witness tampering and obstruction of justice, and in 1989 he was sentenced to a 4-year prison term to be served in California. On the afternoon of 31 January 1990, at one of the island's major intersections, unwilling to serve a sentence he claimed was politically motivated, Ricky Bordallo bid farewell to Guam on his own terms. Robert Rogers, in his history of the island, recounted Bordallo's final act:

With his back to the rear of the statue [of seventeenth-century Chamorro leader Quipuha] and to the Americanized postmodern world beyond, Bordallo placed about him hand-lettered placards that he had made. The signs called for justice and a halt to the deculturation of the Chamorro people. He draped a Guam flag around his shoulders in a final symbolic gesture. Then he removed a loaded .38-caliber pistol from his leather jacket. (Rogers, 1995, p. 289)

With a single shot to the head, he ended his life.

The residence of the governor of Guam, as re-envisioned by Bordallo, remains symbolic of the rejection of colonialism through a bold or – in perhaps even more compelling fashion – commonplace and commonsense revision of the colonial past. On the heights overlooking the island's capital city, Government House declares that its Spanish Colonial architecture – as well as that found throughout Guam – need not be viewed as a symbol of colonial oppression. Rather, it declares that such architecture can stand as a symbol of resoluteness and determination. It calls out: 'We're still here. Where are you?' It also declares that a modernist building erected by outsiders can represent a peoples' stride towards the future, rather than the conceit, however well intended, of yet another colonial dominator.

Whether Ricky Bordallo's actions had a lasting effect on Guam's architecture and identity over the past 40 years is a subject that remains to be studied. A review of architect-designed buildings erected on Guam since 1976 reveals, on the surface, a number that blend modernist, Spanish Colonial, and Chamorro elements – but not their deeper meaning.[16] And yet, there are parallels. According to Joy Giguere, the Egyptian Revival style in American memorialization was transformed from the foreign exotic in 1790 to 'characteristically American' by the late 1930s. During that time (less than half the span of years Guam has been a colony), she concluded, 'The Egyptian Revival *as* revival dissolved and what was left was simply the American style' (Giguere, 2014, p. 222). The future will reveal whether the reclaiming, appropriating, and layering of Guam's architecture, spurred by Ricky Bordallo, will dissolve into a style 'simply' characteristic of Guam.

Notes

1. Along with Rogers (1995), other notable general resources on Guam's history are Carano and Sanchez (1965), Wuerch and Ballendorf (1994), and individual articles in the scholarly, peer-reviewed, electronic publication *Guampedia: The Encyclopedia of Guam* (hereafter *Guampedia*), which can be accessed online at http://guampedia.com/. In addition, O.H.K. Spate (1979) has explicated the Spanish role in the Pacific after Magellan.
2. See, for example, the photographs of Spanish-influenced residences at Jillette Leon-Guerrero, 'Hagåtña', and Jack B. Jones, 'Agana Houses Thematic Resources' and 'Agana Historic District', National Register of Historic Places Inventory – Nomination Forms, 1980.
3. See, for example, photographs of post-World War II traditional dwellings erected by the US military in the town of Agat at Leo Baubauta, 'Agat (Hagåt)', *Guampedia*; and Nicholas Yamashita Quinata, 'Quonset Huts', *Guampedia*.
4. Madeleine Bordallo (born 1933), Governor Bordallo's wife, certainly also played a role, not identified or explored here, in the redesign of Government House. An important political figure in her own right, she was Guam's first non-native, elected lieutenant governor, and since 2002 she has been Guam's nonvoting delegate to the US House of Representatives.
5. Skinner imbibed internationalist views from his father, Macy M. Skinner, a professor and 'spreader of the gospel of international comity', according to the Harvard College, *Fiftieth Anniversary Report, 1894–1944* (Norwood, MA: Plimpton Press, 1944). He was politic in explaining his desire to integrate the Coast Guard and the other service branches. In an undated account titled 'U.S.S. Sea Cloud, IX-99, Racial Integration for Naval Efficiency' (which may be found on the Coast Guard's website at http://www.uscg.mil/history/articles/Carlton_Skinner.asp), he referred to a search for 'military and naval effectiveness'. This mirrored his testimony before The President's Committee on Equality of Treatment and Opportunity in the Armed

6. Services on 25 April 1949 (which may also be found on the Coast Guard's website at https://www.uscg.mil/history/docs/personnel/1949_SkinnerCarlton_Testimony.pdf). Skinner's efforts were never publicized, which he later regretted according to his *Boston Globe* obituary (Tanenbaum, 2004).
6. For additional background on traditional landownership, see Phillips (1996).
7. Books about and writings by Neutra are numerous. Works consulted here included Boesinger (1959), which contains plans, elevations, and photographs of Government House and other actual and planned Neutra & Alexander projects on Guam; Lamprecht (2000), which includes an entry on 'Governor's House'; and Neutra (1989).
8. Although Neutra stressed the different climatic and geographic conditions of the two islands, he 'pursued a theme' for his design of schools on Guam that he had developed in his Puerto Rican school commissions.
9. Governor Elvidge letter of 17 September 1953, to William C. Strand, Director of the Office of Territories of the Department of the Interior; Strand letter of 1 October 1953, to Governor Elvidge; and response letter of Governor Elvidge to Strand of 17 October 1953. Copies of the three letters, all of which involve the contractual relationship of Neutra & Alexander, are located in the Government House vertical file at Nieves M. Flores Memorial Library, Hagåtña.
10. As Anita Elvidge (1972, p. 24) wrote: 'the Island servants really were children – to direct, to treat for their aches and pains, to mother, and best of all, to laugh with and enjoy.'
11. B.J. Bordallo, the governor's father, was a prominent nationalist who, as president of Guam's House of Council, accompanied Carlton Skinner on his 1949 survey of Guam's villages.
12. His other projects included a public market, an open meeting hall, a marina, and a sewage-treatment plant in Hagåtña; a public beach next to the Hilton hotel; and multiple youth centres and bridges (Rogers, 1995, p. 256). Bordallo also reportedly 'took a direct hand in the aesthetic design of the terminal' (Sanchez, 1987, p. 389).
13. The architects of Government House and Governor Bordallo's other public projects have not been determined, but it is clear that he was the driving force behind their symbolic content.
14. According to Dell Upton (1993, p. 12): 'It is easy to argue that a certain landscape is intended to incorporate given cultural values, but it is very difficult to claim that the users see this or that they are persuaded by the artifact's claims.'
15. Bordallo had his opponents, but they did not question his commitment to his people. According to Rogers (1995, p. 19): 'Ricky Bordallo was seen as a charismatic champion of Chamorro rights by his supporters, and as a volatile, romantic dreamer by his opponents.'
16. See, for example, the design by Taniguchi Ruth Makio Architects for Ironwood Heights at http://www.traguam.com, and the designs by Architects Laguana for the University of Guam's College of Arts & Sciences, Santa Teresita Church, and Bank of Guam at http://architectslaguana.com.

References

Appadurai, A. (1995) Playing with modernity: the decolonization of Indian cricket, in Breckenridge, C.A. (ed.), *Consuming Modernity: Public Culture in a South Asian World*. Minneapolis, MN: University of Minnesota Press, pp. 23–48.

Babauta, L. (2015) Umatac (Humåtak). *Guampedia*, 29 April. Available at: http://www.guampedia.com/umatac-humatak/.

Boesinger, W. (ed.) (1959) *Richard Neutra, 1959–60: Buildings and Projects*. Zurich: Editions Girsberger.

Carano, P. and Sanchez, P. (1965) *A Complete History of Guam*. North Clarendon, VT: Charles E. Tuttle Company.

Cunningham, L.J. (1992) *Ancient Chamorro Society*. Honolulu: Bess Press.

Cunningham, L.J. (2016) Pole and thatched homes. *Guampedia*, 16 June. Available at: http://www.guampedia.com/pole-and-thatched-homes/.

de Freycinet, L.C.D. (2003) *An Account of the Corvette l'Uraine's Sojourn at the Mariana Islands, 1819*. Northern Mariana Islands: CNMI Division of Historic Preservation.

Driver, M.G. and Hezel, F.X. (2004) *El Palacio: The Spanish Palace in Agaña, 1668–1898*. Guam: Richard F. Taitano Micronesian Area Research Center, University of Guam.

Elvidge, A. (1972) *Guam Interlude*. Privately printed.

Giguere, J.M. (2014) *Characteristically American: Memorial Architecture, National Identity, and the Egyptian Revival*. Knoxville, TX: University of Tennessee Press.

Hertz, J. (2002) Authenticity, colonialism, and the struggle with modernity. *Journal of Architectural Education*, **55**(4), pp. 220–227.

Higuchi, W. (2014) Impact of Japanese military occupation of Guam. *Guampedia*, 6 July. Available at: http://www.guampedia.com/impact-of-japanese-military-occupation-of-guam/.

Hines, T. (2006) *Richard Neutra and the Search for Modern Architecture*. New York: Rizzoli.

Hunter-Anderson, R.L. (2016) Latte. *Guampedia*, 15 June. Available at: http://www.guampedia.com/latte/.

Hunter-Anderson, R. and Moore, D.R. (2006) *A Study of Eight Post-World War II Resettlement Villages on Guam*. Micronesian Archaeological Research Services, Division of Historic Resources.

Johnston, E. [sic] and Gould, E.S. (1975) Welcome to Government House, Agana, Guam. *Star Press*. Nieves M. Flores Memorial Library, Hagåtña, Guam.

Kusno, A. (2000) *Behind the Postcolonial: Architecture, Urban Space, and Political Cultures in Indonesia*. London: Routledge.

Kusno, A. (2013) *After the New Order: Space, Politics, and Jakarta*. Honolulu: University of Hawaii Press.

Lagae, J., Beeckmans, L. and Boonen, S. (2010). Decolonizing spaces: a (visual) essay on strategies of appropriation, transformation and negotiation of the colonial built environment in postcolonial Congo. *Hagar*, **9**(2), pp. 53–90, 193–194.

Lamprecht, B. (2000) *Richard Neutra: Complete Works*. Cologne: Taschen.

Marsh, K.G. (2014) US Naval era governors: contributions and controversies. *Guampedia*, 3 July. Available at: http://www.guampedia.com/us-naval-era-governors-contributions-and-controversies/.

Martinez Jr., A. (1991) Japanese Defense Fortifications on Guam. National Register of Historic Places Multiple Properties Documentation Form.

Murphy, S.J. (2014) Madeleine Zeien Bordallo. *Guampedia*, 8 July. Available at: http://www.guampedia.com/madeleine-z-bordallo/.

Neutra, R. (c. 1952) 'Government House for the People of Guam' and 'Palacyo – Government house of Guam, Explanation of enclosures'. Descriptions of intended architectural program for Guam's Government House, with renderings. Copies located in the Alexander Papers at the Micronesian Area Research Center, University of Guam; originals in the Alexander Papers, Cornell University Library, Ithaca, NY.

Neutra, R. (1989) Bioreal benchmarks for the Third World, in Marlin, W. (ed.) *Nature Near: Late Essays of Richard Neutra*. Santa Barbara, CA: Capra Press.

Phillips, M.F. (1996) Land, in *Issues in Guam's Political Development: The Chamorro*

Perspective. Agaña: The Political Status Education Coordinating Committee, pp. 2–15.

Platt, D.P. (1975) Spanish-American War. *Guampedia*.

Quinata, N.Y. and Murphy, S.J. (2014) Governor Ricardo J. Bordallo. *Guampedia*, 6 July. Available at: http://www.guampedia.com/governor-ricardo-j-bordallo/.

Rodriguez, L.M. (2013) To be for (an) *other*: the Caribe Hilton or ambivalence as presence in a United States colony, in Bandyopadhyay, S. and Montiel, G.G. (eds.) *The Territories of Identity: Architecture in the Age of Evolving Globalization*. London: Routledge, pp. 169–179.

Rogers, R.F. (1995) *Destiny's Landfall: A History of Guam*. Honolulu: University of Hawaii Press.

Sanchez, P.C. (1987) *Guahan Guam: The History of Our Island*. Agana: Sanchez Publishing House.

Skinner, C. (1952). Letter of May 15, responding to an inquiry by James P. Davis of the Office of Territories of the Department of the Interior concerning the Guam efforts of Neutra & Alexander. The letter is located in the Government House vertical file at Nieves M. Flores Memorial Library, Hagåtña, Guam.

Skinner, C. (1963) Self-government in the South Pacific. *Foreign Affairs*, **42**(1), pp.137–147.

Skinner, C. (1997) *After Three Centuries: Representative Democracy and Civilian Government for Guam*. San Francisco, CA: Macduff Press.

Skinner, C. (undated) Origins of Guam's Government House. Manuscript attached to a letter of 27 June 1975, from Skinner to Guam first lady Madeleine Bordallo. Located in the Government House vertical file at the Micronesian Area Research Center (MARC), University of Guam.

Spate, O.H.K. (1979) *The Spanish Lake*. Minneapolis, MN: University of Minnesota Press.

Stade, R. (1998) *Pacific Passages: World Culture and Local Politics in Guam*. Stockholm: Stockholm Studies in Social Anthropology, Stockholm University.

Tanenbaum, J. (2004) Carlton Skinner; helped integrate Coast Guard. *Boston Globe*, 7 July. Available at: http://archive.boston.com/news/globe/obituaries/articles/2004/07/07/carlton_skinner_helped_integrate_coast_guard/.

Underwood, R. (2014) Guam's political status. *Guampedia*, 6 July. Available at: http://www.guampedia.com/guams-political-status/.

Upton, D. (1993) The tradition or change. *Traditional Dwellings and Settlements Review*, **5**(1), pp. 9–15.

US General Accounting Office (1997) *Report to the Chairman, Committee on Resources, House of Representatives, U.S. Insular Areas, Application of the U.S. Constitution*. Washington DC: US Government Printing Office.

Wuerch, L. and Ballendorf, D.A. (1994) *Historical Dictionary of Guam and Micronesia*. Lanham, MD: Scarecrow Press.

Chapter 8

The Missing 'Brazilianness' of Nineteenth-Century Brazilian Art and Architecture

Pedro Paulo Palazzo and Ana Amélia de Paula Moura

Despite their ideological opposition, Brazilian modernists and traditionalists in the early twentieth century had one stance in common: both agreed that the country's art and architecture had, since the second half of the previous century, lacked national character and adaptation to Brazil's climate and social conditions. This postulate was partly refuted in Portuguese-language scholarship since the 1960s, which exposed the persistence of colonial-era patterns in the hinterland – and, in a few cases, in urban settings. Yet, in the drive to rehabilitate nineteenth-century Brazilian art and architecture, the actual discourses by which it came to be ostracized have themselves been suppressed from scholarship.

This chapter examines a few of the landmark narratives on the issue of national character published between 1880 and 1940. The authors of these works are the academic art critic Gonzaga Duque, the engineer and neocolonial advocate Ricardo Severo, the physician José Marianno Filho, the Beaux-Arts architect Adolfo Morales de los Ríos Filho, the writer Monteiro Lobato, and the modernist architect Lucio Costa. Writings by these figures provided a variety of views of Brazilian character and the purported lack thereof in the art and architecture of the generations that preceded them. Yet, as the chapter will show, the aesthetic movements they were affiliated with were actually less relevant to how each addressed this matter than their understanding of the nature of artistic endeavour and the building professions. And this, in turn, had much to do with their own social, racial, and regional backgrounds.

The late nineteenth and early twentieth centuries saw the decline of colonial and imperial plantation elites from northeast Brazil and the rise to power of coffee-growing and cattle-ranching oligarchies from the southeast, followed by the rise of industrial capitalism. Urban growth and renewal displayed eclectic styles of architecture, at least until the 1910s when the moralistic traditional or neocolonial movement began to set the tone for architectural debate.

Assessing National Character

The Brazilian cultural establishment, in the early twentieth century, took a keen interest in the matter of national character in art and architecture. This interest can be traced to two concurrent influences: the nation-building debates spearheaded by the Brazilian Historical and Geographic Institute (IHGB), beginning in the 1840s, and the nationalistic themes of European romanticism. A landmark in the first instance was the publication, in 1854, of Francisco Adolfo de Varnhagen's *História Geral do Brasil* (*General History of Brazil*), which defined the Brazilian nation as the junction of three races: the white Portuguese, black African, and Amerindian. Nationalistic romanticism, meanwhile, had its most acclaimed expression in the literary movement known as Indianism, which was later picked up in painting, as in Rodolfo Amoedo's (1857–1941) series of Indianist works from the 1880s. But in historiography as well as literature and art, Indianism portrayed the South American native more as an allegorical icon than a true actor in the formation of the Brazilian nation. Agency, and especially intellectual agency, was still a concept reserved for the white ruling elite of ancestral Portuguese descent, while black Africans were regarded as mere menial labour without any role in the making of Brazilian culture. This view of native people was evident in Amoedo's masterpiece, *The Last Tamoyo* (1883), in which the Indian's death, historically placed in 1567, is symbolic of the onset of European rule (figure 8.1).

Around the same time, the young art critic Luiz Gonzaga Duque Estrada (1863–1911) worried, paradoxically, about the disappearance of national character in art. In the book that provided a synthesis of his early thinking, *A Arte Brasileira* (*Brazilian Art*) (1888), he gave a pessimistic account of his subject matter:

The novels, history, and poetry of this country had no influence whatsoever in these works, which remained impervious to the dawn of national thought ...

Figure 8.1. Rodolfo Amoedo, *The Last Tamoyo*, 1883.

One concludes, then, that this art is missing native features and originality, primordial qualities for the founding of a School.

The defining feature of our art is cosmopolitanism, and a nation, to have a School, needs, foremost, a national art. (Gonzaga Duque Estrada, 1995, pp. 258–59)

As a critic, Gonzaga Duque was not the least impressed by earlier art. Even the monumental architecture of the colonial period (1530–1808), which so captivated later writers, was to him 'a flagrant evidence of bad taste and lack of intelligence' (Gonzaga Duque Estrada, 1995, p. 74). To their credit, he conceded, painters such as Manoel da Cunha (1737–1809) had, at least, a sort of crafty authenticity about them (Gonzaga Duque Estrada, 1995, p. 81). But national character was not to be extracted from the achievements of previous eras, as was the view among European romantics; it was something yet to be produced out of the maturing of late-nineteenth-century artists. Neither was it to be found in any specific style, but in the choice of proper subject matter, chiefly Indians (Gonzaga Duque Estrada, 1995, p. 185).

Later on, however, in 1909, an aging Gonzaga Duque would soften his views and commend Amoedo for having outgrown Indianism, 'vanquished by the assimilating force of a superior environment' (Gonzaga Duque Estrada, 1929, p. 13). That 'superior environment', of course, was European academic culture, in the form of classical nudes and mythological scenes. And in his last survey of Brazilian art, the opening speech at the 1908 Salon in Rio de Janeiro, he summarized a triumphal picture of national art:

> The characteristic art, truly Brazilian, shall appear from this admirable nature, from this golden light, from this popular soul made of the Indian's nostalgia, the animal infallibility of the African, and the lyrical soul of the uprooted, seafaring Portuguese. (Gonzaga Duque Estrada, 1929, p. 255)

Thus, by this time, Gonzaga Duque no longer saw European influence as harming the expression of national character. On the contrary, it would provide the necessary professional expertise and cultural environment in which national character would gradually emerge. The colonial heritage, of Portuguese and Catholic extraction, was the mythical ancestor of contemporary national character. It was a 'historical document' of utmost importance, one to which ritual deference was owed. Yet it was also one that should exert minimal influence on contemporary conceptions of national art (Gonzaga Duque Estrada, 1929, p. 247). This positive, yet condescending, notion of colonial art would be picked up a few years later by the first Brazilian traditionalists as a means of reconciling tradition with modernization.

Tradition and Decay

The years leading from the restructuring of the federal debt in 1902 to the national exposition of 1908 witnessed a build-up of momentum for pairs of conflicting urges: cosmopolitanism and the expression of national character; exaltation of modernity and industrialization and the taste for exuberant tropical nature; political centralization and regionalism (Pereira, 2011). In keeping with the romantic nationalist drive that first established the debate on national character, Brazil was seen as having started off under the yoke of Portuguese culture, but then slowly differentiating herself under the influence of climate and land. To this way of thinking, a national character in art and architecture was an optimistic prospect rather than something already achieved at any point in the past or present. This placement of national character in the future was a boon, in the first quarter of the twentieth century, for authors and movements claiming to construct Brazilianness. And where Gonzaga Duque forecast a natural, unconscious development of a Brazilian art school, other writers laid out actual programmes to create this national style.

Around the time of Gonzaga Duque's passing in Rio, a sharp critical and literary scene was also emerging in São Paulo. One of the most prolific writers, addressing the issue of national character both explicitly and implicitly in this milieu, was José Bento Monteiro Lobato (1882–1948). His debut work of fiction, *Urupês* (1918), was an attack on the agrarian society that had once dominated national politics, and that he viewed as socially and culturally decrepit. The closing chapter of *Urupês* featured an unforgiving criticism of the literary infatuation with this old-fashioned culture. Monteiro Lobato was, like many of his fellow intellectuals from São Paulo, an outspoken enthusiast of material progress and industrialization. The juxtaposition of unrelated anecdotes from remote towns was a literary device used at the time to create contrast with the conventional and uneventful ways of life typically portrayed in literature. On the one hand, it exacerbated the naturalistic tendency towards depicting individual scenes; yet, on the other, it refused to condone the idealized image of country folk as authentic representatives of the national character (Silva, 2013, p. 303). Indeed, in the 1910s, the icon of rural culture was the *caipira*, Brazil's version of a country bumpkin sunk into endemic poverty, who had recently replaced the Indian as a favourite literary character (Monteiro Lobato, 1944, pp. 208–209)

Monteiro Lobato's criticism of the inert social and material underdevelopment of small inland towns in *Cidades Mortas* (*Dead Cities*) (1919) was, however, more complex than such images might make it appear. The pretentious self-sufficiency of the establishment in the aptly named fictional city of Oblivion, for instance, alluded to a sort of timeless decrepitude, rather than mere underdevelopment.[1] People in Oblivion died of boredom, not material want (Monteiro Lobato, 1919, p. 5). And the dead towns contained: 'impressions of a dead youth that vegetated in the stagnation of the dead cities. There is also some modern stuff. But both modern and old are worth the same – nothing' (Monteiro Lobato, 1919, epigram).

This sense of hopelessness, of something that would have been yet did not bear fruit, struck a strong chord with Monteiro Lobato's contemporaries, as it clearly alluded to the material and moral decadence of once-thriving urban centres in the depleted coffee-growing regions in upstate São Paulo (Silva, 2013, p. 299). Thus, according to Monteiro Lobato (1919, p. 8):

There, everything was, nothing is. No verbs are conjugated in the present tense. Everything is preterit.

A group of dying cities drag on a decrepit living, spent weeping in today's pettiness the nostalgic greatness of yore.

Monteiro Lobato rejected the romantic and naturalistic ideal of glorifying a national (or even regional) character, embodied in traditional society. His fiction – and his political activism – were thus at odds with rural oligarchies of colonial Portuguese descent. These oligarchies had, up to this time, claimed to be the true makers of high culture and had been prominently portrayed as nation-builders in Indianist literature and art. Yet, in contrast, Monteiro Lobato represented the aspirations of emerging urban industrialists who rejected the lingering dominance of this decadent rural elite. This rivalry was all the more evident in the cosmopolitan, eclectic architecture favoured within São Paulo city, as opposed to the persistence of Neoclassicism upstate.

Nevertheless, *Cidades Mortas* evidenced a different sort of nostalgia, harking back to Gonzaga Duque's early writing. The idea here was that some process of national character-building had been underway, crude but authentic, but that it had been stifled before reaching cultural maturity. This was thus a construction of a mythical 'time outside time' (Eliade, 1966). And, built on the sense of eternal decay from an acme that never was, it set the stage for the elaboration of a highly malleable image of lost Brazilianness. Crucial to this narrative of mythical loss (of something that never existed) was the implicitly perceived gap retaining a tenuous link to chronological continuity (Silva, 2012, p. 293). It would have been clear to Monteiro Lobato's readers that decay in the region of the dead cities set in around the 1860s, and had begun to be felt more strongly after the 1880s, when the early coffee-growing lands were becoming depleted and fledgling industries were being set up with the arrival of the railway in São Paulo city.

Reconstructing Brazilianness

Monteiro Lobato saw in material and cultural modernization the only means of escape from this eternal decay. To him, the heyday of the coffee-growing urban society was little more than an abstract backdrop for criticizing the backwardness of traditional elites. Meanwhile, in São Paulo, the Portuguese engineer, archaeologist, and republican activist Ricardo Severo was promoting similar ideas about a stifled development of national character followed by a period of decay and the need to reassert the greatness of Brazilian identity. Severo's position can be seen to coincide with the development, in the early twentieth century, of traditionalist movements throughout the Americas. Rooted in the European romantic nationalism of the mid-nineteenth century, traditionalist architecture reached the United States, where the Mission Style provided a template for Hispanic revivals elsewhere. It then spread southwards, influencing South America around the centennial of independence of many of its countries (Amaral, 1994, p. 12).

In 1914, Severo gave a highly influential lecture at the Artistic Culture Society in São Paulo, titled 'Traditional Art in Brazil: The House and the Temple'. The text of this talk circulated widely, after being reworked with additions (Severo, 1917). Severo shared Gonzaga Duque's late view that local culture had not yet developed sufficient strength to establish a national artistic character. However, unlike the art critic, he would not wait patiently for a national school to emerge spontaneously. He outlined, instead, a programme to give Brazilian architecture a distinctive character right away. As Azevedo (1994, p. 249) has pointed out, Severo argued that the forms and plans implanted in the Americas by Portuguese colonists, chiefly derived from both Roman and Moorish sources, were to be the basis for the establishment of a national-traditional art in Brazil.

> The Portuguese always gave a particular mark to the architecture he imported, and this phenomenon, noted by the most illustrious historians of Portuguese art, shows up in colonial Brazil as well, where the Baroque, said to be Jesuitic, took on expressions of modest simplicity, but with a noteworthy local mark. (Severo, 1917, p. 402)

Severo made a point of showing how colonial houses and churches, such as the parish church of the Rosary in Santos, displayed exactly that sort of plainness (figure 8.2). '[B]eing appropriated into the local setting and in their aspect of characteristic originality', this would constitute 'what is or may come to be Traditional Architecture [his capitals]' in Brazil. And he proceeded to decry the arrival of fresh immigrants at that time – 'deft stuccoists come from Italy and Portugal' who brought a 'façadist' habit of making up 'incomprehensible styles that shocked mostly by their disconnection with the local setting and its destination' (Severo, 1917, p. 415). The solution, he asserted, was to reclaim an authentic national tradition, consisting of the adaptation of old Portuguese styles (which even his fellow countrymen had abandoned) as transformed by the influence of local climate and geography.

Indeed, as a recent Portuguese immigrant, Severo was at odds with two groups who sought to establish their own narratives of architectural tradition. One was the aforementioned rural oligarchies against which

Figure 8.2. Our Lady of the Rosary parish church, Santos (dedicated 1754, demolished 1908). (*Photo*: Militão Augusto de Azevedo, 1865)

Monteiro Lobato rose; the other was a diverse class of skilled immigrants of various nationalities, among whom were several architects and their patrons, who introduced eclecticism to Brazil's major cities. Severo, therefore, set out to uphold traditional Portuguese architecture, which he had studied at length in his youth, against both the sophisticated cultural tradition of the rural Brazilian elites (who had departed from their Portuguese roots to embrace French neoclassicism), and from the eclectic architecture of European immigrants, which was unrelated to local history and climate.

The argument constructed by Severo then rested on the ideal of a national character consisting in a timeless, natural Portuguese adaptation to the South American *genius loci*. This had been suppressed by unfortunate eclectic influence in the second half of the nineteenth century. This was the same idea of a cycle of timeless authenticity followed by a historical gap fostering decadence which would be represented 2 years later in Monteiro Lobato's 'dead cities'. Yet where the fiction writer had a much more negative view of rural society, the Portuguese engineer was careful not to romanticize old houses, especially inasmuch as they were the abodes of the landed elite, who had also been partly responsible for the recent degeneration. He made his case for material and even aesthetic progress, if only tempered by traditional adaptation to the site:

Traditional Architecture does not mean, then, literal reproduction of traditional things, of archaeological fossils, of rammed earth or cob houses, of little adobe churches, of alleys between shacks three fathoms deep, with door and louvered window, or of the gloomy houses in the city centres of yore, without hygiene or aesthetic appeal.

Traditional art is the stylization of earlier artistic forms that constitute at some point in time the local environment, the moral character of a people, the hallmark of its civilization; it is the product of a rhythmic evolution of successive cycles of art and style... (Severo, 1917, pp. 423–424)

Modernity and Preservation

Severo wrote, spoke, and designed in São Paulo – a city that, between the late eighteenth century and the 1860s, had been almost as 'dead', economically and architecturally, as Monteiro Lobato's fictional cities. Little of any significance had been built there between the reconstruction of the emblematic Jesuit College, in 1700, and the opening of the railways, in 1867–1871 (Lemos, 1987, p. 72). Rio de Janeiro, in contrast, was in the 1910s the nation's capital, twice as large as São Paulo, with a much more diverse architectural heritage. Moreover, it had undergone a continuous process of urban infill and extension throughout the nineteenth century, with a self-conscious interest in up-to-date architecture, crowned by the large-scale renewal of its core, starting in 1902. The differences between traditionalist discourse in São Paulo and Rio are therefore not surprising.

In the capital, José Marianno Carneiro da Cunha Filho (1881–1946), a hygienist physician and amateur architect, was the chief advocate of the traditionalist movement, to which he gave the name 'neocolonial' (Kessel, 2008, p. 132). Marianno was also instrumental in rousing public support for monumental buildings to be designed in the neocolonial style, in addition to having sponsored, with his personal wealth, a number of architectural competitions biased toward the same style. José Marianno Filho's family belonged to the old northeast landed elite, having owned plantations there since the colonial period. It was also a highly cultured family; during the mid-twentieth century alone, it had contributed three members to the forty-seat Brazilian Academy of Letters (among them Marianno's own brother, the poet Olegário Marianno.)

Because the colonial architecture of Rio had been heavily affected by later development, traditionalists in the capital had to look elsewhere for documentation. Former gold-mining towns such as Ouro Preto and Diamantina – now both World Heritage sites – were, conversely, their ideal image of a traditional urban culture, supposedly frozen in time up to the day twentieth-century critics 'rediscovered' them (figure 8.3).[2]

Figure 8.3. Panoramic view of Ouro Preto. (*Photo*: Pedro Paulo Palazzo, 2010)

The picture Marianno drew in 1943 of this inland architectural tradition was one that gave all the laurels to his own colonial forebears at the expense of every other group in modern Brazil. Specifically, there was no place in it for South American Indians, nor for influences from Portuguese architecture after the end of the colonial period. And, although the sociologist Gilberto Freyre (1900–1987) had published, 10 years earlier, *The Masters and the Slaves* (a dense account of Africans' ubiquitous role in shaping Brazilian culture), they, too, were absent from Marianno's narrative. His lone hero was the weathered Portuguese explorer, barely stepping out of the Middle Ages and of Arab domination to exert his no-nonsense creativity on a virtually virgin new world:

The Portuguese colonist, old friend of the sun, brought to the Brazilian land the centuries-old experience of his race, drawn out of the contact with the oriental civilizations, and learned above all from the Moorish experience. Thus, in confronting the Brazilian architectural problem, the Portuguese colonist had not the slightest hesitation… During the first two centuries of national life [the sixteenth and seventeenth centuries], Portuguese architecture was imperceptibly adjusting itself to the Brazilian way of life… The absence of classical elements, together with the lack of a properly skilled workforce, led the people to improvise new practices and processes, unknown in Portugal. (Marianno Filho, 1943, p. 10)[3]

Marianno's national tradition, even more so than Severo's, hinged on the notion of the self-sufficiency of the Portuguese colonist *vis-à-vis* the other ethnic groups that made up Brazilian society – as well as of more recent Portuguese immigrants. For him, 'the preference of man for the architecture of his homeland' had an emotional source, based on domestic reminiscence and unconscious references. He therefore deplored the newly arrived Portuguese immigrants who, 'instead of proceeding like the Italians, British, or Germans, who favour the styles of their own nations … seek intently to hide or mask their own' (Marianno Filho, 1943, p. 32). This hiding of the national style, in 1943, could be applied both to the immigrants' eclecticism and to the characterless and 'stateless styles' of modern architecture, championed by several young Brazilian architects. Marianno bemoaned the modernist mentality, which, in seeking to abolish the principle of decor, reduced 'the art of building to the science of making housing', requiring mere efficiency and economy (Marianno Filho, 1943, p. 15).

This dispute had consequences for the new preservationist mindset that was taking shape in Brazil at the time. This view regarded historic preservation as the same as the antiquarian conservation of 'archaeological fossils'. And it emphasized instead that a living tradition had no need for physical vestiges of the past, only for its documented knowledge. However, documentation proved selective. And even Severo gave in to the contemporary taste for modern plans and massing (Mello, 2007, p. 178). Thus, late in life, probably after seeing many of his 'documents' disappear beneath the march of progress, Severo commissioned the painter José Wasth Rodrigues (1891–1957) to make a comprehensive study composed almost entirely of details. This was published in instalments, but only after Severo's death (Rodrigues, 1975).

For his part, Marianno, who was not a regularly practising architect (and thus took no notice of the public's architectural taste) wanted the documentation of traditional architecture to yield different results – but with the same disregard for physical conservation:

> I do not care for the plastic qualities of traditional Brazilian architecture, because what I seek in it is far above these qualities… Less of an artist than a sociologist myself, I consider architecture to be the social instrument of nationality. I do not care for artistic virtues, the charm of lines, or the splendour of details, by means of which the architectural styles are expressed. What I seek are the organic qualities, the healthy virtues, the structural fundamentals, from which stem the perfect accord of architectural feeling with the nation's soul. (Marianno Filho, 1943, p. 64)

For both Severo's and Marianno's purpose, the perennial preservation of old buildings was inconsequential; the knowledge extracted from their documentation was all that was needed to revive tradition. Severo thus celebrated the reconstruction of the São Paulo Law School by the firm Ramos de Azevedo in 1930–1934, which replaced a seventeenth-century rammed-earth monastery with a neocolonial concrete building (figure 8.4). Modern materials and technologies were welcomed in this endeavour to forge a new Brazilian architecture that was to remain abstractly grounded in deeper principles, respecting its ancestral 'Roman spirit, characterized by the constant proportion of its compositional elements, and by its rectangular geometric projection' (Marianno Filho, 1943, p. 124).

Figure 8.4. *Left*: The Franciscan monastery dedicated in 1654. (*Photo*: Militão Augusto de Azevedo, 1862) *Right*: São Paulo Law School, which replaced the monastery. (*Photo*: Pedro Paulo Palazzo, 2007)

This ideal of material progress rooted in social conservatism was echoed in the writings of the young architect Lucio Marçal Ferreira Ribeiro Lima Costa (1902–1998). Lucio Costa is nowadays best known for the modernist design of Brasilia (1957), but during the 1920s he was a neocolonial practitioner under Marianno's wing. In 1929, he argued against the example of the exceptional monumental buildings of Brazilian Rococo. Following the views of his patron, Costa held that it was instead the simple architecture of anonymous master builders that embodied the functional, technical, and aesthetic homogeneity of Brazilianness (Puppi, 1998, p. 22). After Costa's conversion to modernism, he authored an article in 1937 describing what he held to be the natural development of traditional

Brazilian architecture. True to his roots, he was speaking of residential architecture, built by masons and carpenters, which remained impervious to:

> ... the unforeseen development of bad architecture teaching – giving future architects a whole, confused 'technical-decorative' education, with no link whatsoever with life, and not explaining them the why of each element, nor the deep reasons that conditioned, in each period, the appearance of common features, that is, of a style... (Costa, 2007c, p. 93)

Because Costa did not focus his narrative on learned architecture, as late as 1910 he was able to circumvent the problem of 'bad teaching' and argue for the survival of an authentic traditional architecture. He could thereby synchronize its decay precisely with the onset of the traditional architecture movement (to which he had previously belonged) and which he later condemned. This opposition notwithstanding, all elements of the post-romantic nationalist narrative were represented in his text: an original period of authentic national character followed by another of pretentious decay; the possibility of overcoming that decay by promoting a certain architectural movement; and the defence of technical modernization and aesthetic advance while remaining anchored in that authentic national tradition. A few years later, though, Lucio Costa drifted from the broad sociological picture of national character to a romantic view, which favoured individual artistic intent (Costa, 2007b, p. 113) and personal genius (Costa, 2007a, p. 125), both embodied in his friend, Oscar Niemeyer (1907–2012).

Although Costa put forward the thesis of a chain of authentic architecture broken only by the neocolonial movement, his practice as a preservation official effectively upheld Marianno's view that proper Brazilian architectural tradition did not reach far beyond 1800. In practice, though, dating often relied on conventional wisdom about local history as well as *a priori* assumptions about pre-nineteenth-century styles, since historical documentation was still sparse (Pinheiro, 2012, p. 25). Proof of this uncertainty was that typological studies of colonial buildings published in the SPHAN (National Historic and Artistic Heritage) journal during the 1930s and 1940s (one of which was penned by Lucio Costa himself) were unable to ascribe even so little as rough date ranges to buildings or styles.

This view, both partisan and clouded, entailed questionable choices even for those buildings meant to be preserved. A number of supposed neoclassical or eclectic accretions to historic churches were thus carelessly replaced with modern re-creations of that original 'simplicity' heralded by

Figure 8.5. Chapel of Padre Faria, Ouro Preto, c. 1740. *Above*: Anonymous photograph published in Diogo de Vasconcello's *A arte em Ouro-Preto*, before 1934. *Below*: The church as restored in 1936–1937 by Epaminondas de Macedo. (*Photo*: Pedro Paulo Palazzo, 2007)

the neocolonial architects (Pinheiro, 2012, p. 238). One example was the Chapel of Padre Faria in Ouro Preto (1936–1937) (figure 8.5). Meanwhile, in São Paulo, campaniles were stripped of their spires and entire wings in farmhouses were removed, in an infatuation with the ideal of volumetric simplicity promoted by Marianno and Costa (Mayumi, 2008, p. 61). As part of this programme, elements that seemed to prefigure modern architecture were particularly favoured, while the chronological uncertainty of the vestiges was ideologically interpreted as timeless wisdom:

Colonial constructive devices, such as buildings on stilts, trellised louvers, and cob on wooden frames, were associated with pilotis, brise-soleils, and reinforced concrete. For modernist architects, the resemblance between their own architecture and the colonial one was not one of appearance or effect, as was the case in Neocolonial buildings, but one of structure. (Fonseca, 2005, p. 188)

Tradition and the Professional Architect

The onset of the Modern Movement in Brazilian architecture thus entailed a power struggle between the proponents of the neocolonial movement and their younger rivals. Both camps deployed the same narrative about the development of national character in order to promote opposing views of architectural style and space, and both derided their rivals as being so beneath them as to make 'non-architecture'. In the meantime, a single, dissonant chord struck the debate in Rio: Adolfo Morales de los Ríos Filho's book *Grandjean de Montigny e a evolução da arte brasileira* (*Grandjean de Montigny and the Evolution of Brazilian Art*) (1941). In this work, Morales de los Ríos (1887–1973), then director of the National Fine Arts School, celebrated the school's founder and the first French architect to have worked in Brazil, Auguste Henri Victor Grandjean de Montigny (1776–1850). The book harked back to Gonzaga Duque's positive view in his later years of European influence on Brazilian art:

Yes, it dignified Brazilian art, fighting the neglect and ignorance of a fledgling society ... and contributing to the foundation of an art school, where it would have been difficult to create it using existing [local] resources. (Morales de los Rios Filho, 1941, p. 157)

Morales de los Ríos had a personal axe to grind as well. The Beaux-Arts method had been under critical fire for well over two decades, first from the traditionalists, then from the modernists. Morales himself, the son of a Spanish eclectic architect, was the embodiment of the non-Portuguese, noncolonial practitioner that Severo, Marianno, and Costa collectively decried. The National Fine Arts School was somewhat open, nevertheless, to the teaching of neocolonial architecture in the 1920s, although it was but one of several eclectic styles used and mixed by students and teachers. Moreover, urban renewal in Rio, stepped up since 1920, was threatening the nineteenth-century eclectic heritage just as much as it had disfigured the monuments of the colonial period.

Morales de los Ríos's arguments, however, were of a different nature from those of the neocolonial and modernist groups. Unlike these, he was directly implicated in the education of a class of elite artists, expected to succeed in both public and private commissions. Thus, he defended not only the historical roots of his school, but also the diversity and adaptability of architects in a time of rapidly changing tastes among the public – particularly at a moment when support for neocolonial-styled public buildings had all but disappeared. Also, the fascist government led by Getúlio Vargas (1930–1945) no longer sought the example of the other American republics, preferring that of Italy, in politics as well as in art and culture. Public architecture in the Vargas regime oscillated between the stripped classicism, then popular in most European countries, and modernism, which was half-heartedly supported by fascist Italy at the same time. As for the fickle bourgeois of São Paulo, they moved on to favour aestheticist variations of Art Deco, Italian rationalism, and whitewashed modernism.

In opposition to this, both Ricardo Severo and José Marianno Filho had advocated a sort of sociological collectivism in the architectural profession. Severo, a republican activist who, at first, moved to Brazil to avoid political persecution in late-monarchical Portugal, expected architecture and architects to play a role in the forging of a modern – meaning nationalist – state, conscious and proud of its ethnic origins (Mello, 2007, p. 29). Severo sought to balance his archaeological interests, which led him to favour a structuralist cohesion of sorts between a centuries-old culture and its present developments, and his practice as an architect, where he ultimately gave in to public expectations of wholly modernized, eclectic plans and picturesque massing. Nevertheless, he was successful in fostering public taste for such traditional Brazilian elements as seventeenth-century *alpendres* (deep and wide colonnaded porches) and generous roof overhangs. These features went on to become favourites of Brazilian single-family houses throughout the twentieth century.

As for Marianno, a scion of the landed elite from the Brazilian northeast, architecture was a dilettante passion as much as a political cause. Free from the need to make a living out of the trade, he had little interest in matters of professional cohesion and the construction industry. Conversely, with his disposable income, he was able to fund documentation projects, as well as publicity stunts in the form of design competitions. He was also a regular contributor to the press throughout the 1930s. As state support for neocolonial architecture waned during that decade, his criticism of the Modern Movement increasingly resorted to the sort of political slander expected to appeal to the heads of the fascist government. 'Architectural Judaism' and 'Communist architecture' were expressions used in his later writings (Marianno Filho, 1943, p. 41). And he compounded these with attacks on artistic 'freemasonry' that were appealing to a conservative, Catholic public.

Because of his early years in the neocolonial movement, and in reaction to Marianno's criticism of Modern architecture, Lucio Costa, too, resorted to an ethnic narrative about the roots of national artistic character. Thanks to a few years spent in France during his youth, he had come into contact with the architectural and political aspects of racial discourses. Moreover, as soon as he became a heritage official, he was free from the concern of day-to-day professional practice.

Figure 8.6. Oscar Niemeyer, Grand Hotel Ouro Preto, 1939–1944. (*Photo*: Pedro Paulo Palazzo, 2007)

Costa at first supported Marianno's narrative of a collective, anonymous architecture – even through his first decade as a leader of the Modern Movement in Brazil. And this led him to shun, initially, the few known masters of Brazilian art in the colonial period. But by 1945 his writings focused chiefly on self-conscious artistic intent and the importance of individual genius for the development of style. A hinge moment in his views probably occurred around 1939, when he supported Oscar Niemeyer's attempt to insert a modernist hotel at the heart of the historic district in Ouro Preto (figure 8.6). Costa then moved away from the ethnological understanding of architectural coherence, to argue that an architectural work of art 'shall not resent the proximity to other works of art' (quoted in Comas, 2010). Throughout the remainder of his long writing career, he strove to reconcile both views, as the discourses on the artistic originality of the Modern Movement became hegemonic. The unchallenged ethos of national genius that Costa helped construct for Niemeyer remains to this day a favourite topic of debate on the nature of professional practice in Brazilian architecture.

Against the 'Weakness' of Brazilian Culture

Despite their differences, Gonzaga Duque, Monteiro Lobato, Ricardo Severo, José Marianno Filho, and Lucio Costa constructed and upheld a long-lived teleological history of Brazilian art. It was fuelled by a nationalistic spirit, raised against what they considered to be weaknesses in Brazilian culture. The starting point of this narrative was invariably a timeless period of formation of the national identity, followed by a clearly circumscribed period of decay. The starting point did not need to be an exemplary or admirable stage. The essential point was that it provided fundamentals of national identity that could be later reworked and improved: Portuguese language and way of life, adaptation to climate and geography, simplicity, and rationality. Yet the contribution of South American Indians and enslaved Africans was entirely disregarded, despite growing evidence of their fundamental role in shaping Brazilian culture.

Disagreements among these authors revolved mostly around which social group claimed the authority to define national character and, therefore, whose tradition was to be held up as the true architectural image of Brazil. Gonzaga Duque, at the dawn of the twentieth century, wanted the artists themselves to take the lead; in this, he was followed three decades later by Adolfo Morales de los Ríos Filho. Although Monteiro Lobato did not promote any architectural style, he outspokenly condemned the decrepit tradition of old-fashioned rural society. It was this very rural tradition, of colonial origins, that was, on the other hand, José Marianno Filho's model of Brazilianness, to be resurrected by means of architecture. Ricardo Severo claimed a middle ground between the latter two authors, disparaging the architectural decadence in contemporary Brazil while upholding the authority of Portuguese tradition as represented in the rustic colonial architecture of São Paulo. Lucio Costa, a former neocolonial practitioner converted to modernism, emphasized the practicality of colonial builders and the simplicity of their forms – so much so that several later historians of Brazilian architecture, acting perhaps out of moral reverence for their predecessor, ascribed this quality of simplicity even to the most ornate of colonial monuments (Campello, 2001).

This shunning of nineteenth-century art had strong consequences for Brazilian architectural historiography. The colonial period had been little known until the documentation efforts of the traditionalists, but vernacular architecture of the nineteenth century remained poorly studied throughout most of the twentieth century. While the high art of the same period survived, several important buildings were allowed to be destroyed because they did not fit into the continuous march of national character through history.

Nevertheless, research on nineteenth-century art and architecture has flourished in Brazil over the past two decades, and the writings of Monteiro

Lobato, Severo, and Marianno have been reappraised as important historical documents. Incidentally, this has led to an unfortunate reaction, one which has portrayed the period between 1930 and 1990 as a dark valley in Brazilian architectural historiography (Puppi, 1998). Meanwhile, the contributions of Gonzaga Duque and Morales de los Ríos Filho to the study of Brazilian art have yet to receive major scholarly attention, probably because they do not fit into the broad teleological theses that have been the favoured subjects of recent historical revisions.

Notes

1. The name 'Oblivion' appears in English in the original.
2. These and other inland settlements from the mid-eighteenth century were, of course, later found not to have been 'frozen' at all after the end of the gold rush, nor to have been representative of colonial architecture as a whole. Furthermore, they retained a living, literate culture that preserved narratives from local history, which went largely ignored in the capital.
3. The acknowledgment of a 'Moorish' background was popular with the hygienist community at the time, due to the belief that the Arabs had introduced urban sanitation to medieval Europe.

References

Amaral, A.A. (1994) *Arquitectura neocolonial: América Latina, Caribe, Estados Unidos*. São Paulo: Memorial: Fondo de Cultura Económica.

Azevedo, R.M. de (1994) Las ideas de Ricardo Severo y la relación con el academicismo, in Amaral, A.A. (ed.) *Arquitectura neocolonial: América Latina, Caribe, Estados Unidos*. São Paulo: Memorial: Fondo de Cultura Económica, pp. 249–258.

Campello, G. de O. (2001) *O brilho da simplicidade: dois estudos sobre arquitetura religiosa no Brasil colonial*. Rio de Janeiro: Casa da Palavra: Departamento Nacional do Livro.

Comas, C.E.D. (2010) O passado mora ao lado: Lúcio Costa e o projeto do Grand Hotel de Ouro Preto, 1938/40. *Arquitextos*, **122**(00). Available at: http://www.vitruvius.com.br/revistas/read/arquitextos/11.122/3486.

Costa, L. (2007a) Carta-depoimento, in *Sôbre arquitetura*. Porto Alegre: Editora UniRitter, pp. 119–128.

Costa, L. (2007b) Considerações sôbre o ensino da arquitetura, in *Sôbre arquitetura*. Porto Alegre: Editora UniRitter, pp. 111–117.

Costa, L. (2007c) Documentação necessária, in *Sôbre arquitetura*. Porto Alegre: Editora UniRitter, pp. 86–94.

Eliade, M. (1966) *Aspects du mythe*. Paris: Gallimard.

Fonseca, M.C.L. (2005) *O patrimônio em processo: trajetória da política federal de preservação no Brasil*, 2nd ed. Rio de Janeiro: Editora UFRJ: MinC–IPHAN.

Gonzaga Duque Estrada, L. (1929) *Contemporaneos: pintores e esculptores*. Benedicto de Souza.

Gonzaga Duque Estrada, L. (1995) *A arte brasileira*, T. Chiarelli (ed.). Campinas: Mercado de Letras.

Kessel, C. (2008) *Arquitetura neocolonial no Brasil: entre o pastiche e a modernidade*. Rio de Janeiro: Universidade Estácio de Sá, Curso de Arquitetura e Urbanismo: Jauá Editora.
Lemos, C.A. (1987) Ecletismo em São Paulo, in Fabris, A. (ed.) *Ecletismo na arquitetura brasileira*. São Paulo: Nobel/Edusp, pp. 69–103.
Marianno Filho, J. (1943) À *margem do problema arquitetônico nacional*. Rio de Janeiro: Mendes Junior.
Mayumi, L. (2008) *Taipa, canela-preta e concreto: estudo sobre o restauro de casas bandeiristas*. São Paulo: Romano Guerra.
Mello, J. (2007) *Ricardo Severo: da arqueologia portuguesa à arquitetura brasileira*. São Paulo: Annablume.
Monteiro Lobato, J.B. (1919) *Cidades mortas: contos e impressões*. São Paulo: Revista do Brasil.
Monteiro Lobato, J.B.M. (1944) *Urupês*, 2nd ed. São Paulo: Martins.
Morales de los Rios Filho, A. (1941) *Grandjean de Montigny e a evolução da arte brasileira*. Rio de Janeiro: A Noite.
Pereira, M. da S. (ed.) (2011) *1908 um Brasil em exposição*. Rio de Janeiro: Casa 12.
Pinheiro, M.L.B. (2012) *Neocolonial, modernismo e preservação do patrimônio no debate cultural dos anos 1920 no Brasil*. São Paulo: EdUSP.
Puppi, M. (1998) *Por uma história não moderna da arquitetura brasileira: questões de historiografia*. Campinas: Pontes: Unicamp.
Rodrigues, J.W. (1975) *Documentário arquitetônico: relativo à antiga construção civil no Brasil*. São Paulo: Livraria Martins Editora.
Severo, R. (1917) A arte tradicional no Brasil. *Revista do Brasil*, **2**(4), pp. 394–424.
Silva, L.M. da (2012) Cidades Mortas: o declínio da 'civilização cafeeira' no Vale do Paraíba segundo a elite agrária decadente. *Idéias*, **1**(4). Available at: http://www.ifch.unicamp.br/ojs/index.php/ideias/article/view/867.
Silva, M.V. da (2013) A modernidade em Monteiro Lobato: Cidades Mortas e o retrato de um Brasil decadente no início do século XX. *Revista Virtual de Letras*, **5**(1), pp. 293–308. Available at: http://www.revlet.com.br/artigos/188.pdf.

Chapter 9

Empire in the City: Politicizing Urban Memorials of Colonialism in Portugal and Mozambique

Tiago Castela

This chapter examines how mid-twentieth-century urban memorials to colonialism, mostly evoking the late-nineteenth-century European occupation of southern Africa, have been managed since the political independence of former Portuguese colonies in 1975.[1] In particular, it explores how state management of these visual and sculptural representations located in urban spaces – which I propose to understand as integral to urban planning[2] – was differently articulated following the formation of new, postcolonial political orders in Mozambique and Portugal. The chapter further attempts to show how contemporary modes of valuing built heritage have retained aspects of a colonial rationality of rule, both in formerly occupied territories and in erstwhile imperial capitals. Thus, in independent Mozambique, colonial traditions of emplacing representations of state formation were rearticulated in new urban plans after independence, even as colonial urban memorials were displaced and reframed to celebrate a new tradition of anticolonial struggle. Meanwhile, in Portugal, there seems to have been little political reflection since the simultaneous end of empire and the beginning of political democratization about the authorship of urban memorials to colonialism, or on the persistent role of a colonial tradition of memorialization in the formation of national subjectivities.[3]

The main sections of the chapter address three issues: the construction of a Portuguese tradition of domination in late-colonial Mozambique;

the project of a postcolonial spatial pedagogy during the early period following independence there; and the continuing, fragmentary presence in contemporary Portugal of a pedagogy of inequality. The term 'pedagogy' is here employed because the designers and patrons of official memorials (or of their reframings) explicitly envisioned them as a means to instruct citizens. In addition, in the case of Portugal, it can be evinced from discourse by both officials and citizens that these intended teachings are still valued and effective today – at least as elements of a supposedly inoffensive heritage.

The chapter opens by focusing on the history of the central Fortaleza (Fortress) in Mozambique's capital, Maputo – a 1940s museum where a collection of colonial sculptures was assembled after political independence. These monumental sculptures of Portuguese colonial heroes had been removed from urban foci in Lourenço Marques (the colonial name for the city) after the September 1974 ceasefire agreement between Portugal and FRELIMO, the Mozambican Liberation Front. The second section of the chapter then suggests that this collection can be understood today as a persistence of the postcolonial spatial pedagogy deployed by the Mozambican state in the decade following independence, which was aimed explicitly towards a decolonization of urbanity. The third section subsequently foregrounds the numerous mid-twentieth-century representations evoking the European occupation of southern Africa extant in present-day urban spaces in Portugal – notably in the capital of Lisbon, but also in Porto, the country's second largest city. These representations, which often depict African bodies as unequal, can be found in such exhibition spaces as Lisbon's Tropical Garden and Coimbra's 'Portugal of the Little Ones' [4]; in institutional spaces such as the former headquarters of the Bank of the Atlantic in Porto; and in spaces of consumption, both privileged and ordinary. The chapter's conclusion defends the idea that serious democratic deliberation will be needed finally to disarticulate memorials of colonialism from a legacy reflecting the supposed technocratic government of subjectivities.

Overall, the chapter will suggest that memorials can contribute to the spatial violence of unequal urban division – two concepts that emerged from a larger project of ethnographically informed historical research on urban planning in late-colonial Mozambique. The history of urban planning in late European colonialism (for example, in Mozambique or in South Africa in the third quarter of the twentieth century) supports a concept of unequal urban division, understood as the conditions for city life established by a dual planning regime. In practice, this relied on the application of two different sets of techniques for spatial management, in order to foster the development of cities in which one part was defined as 'peripheral' to the other.

The larger project on which the chapter is based aimed to understand how planning was suffused with the aspirations not only of the state and the professionals it employed, but also of the unequal citizens of the so-called peripheries. And it sought to understand this history in relation to the circuits of knowledge through which prospective imaginations were formed in cities such as Maputo, Beira, and Quelimane. Such circuits linked the primate southern African city, Johannesburg, with Maputo, created to serve as a harbour for the inland mining region and a gateway for labourers. In addition, circuits of knowledge connected Maputo, Beira, and Quelimane with Lisbon, the political capital of the Portuguese empire. Within this network, late-colonial experts articulated their own role in the spatial violence of unequal urban division by increasingly valuing so-called peripheries that were supposedly 'indigenous' as a developmental space of emergence that purportedly contrasted culturally with a normative urbanity.

'Spatial violence' is defined here as the endangering of actual modes of urban life by urban planning practices. Such practices usually invoke normative dichotomies whose contingent formation is elided; for example, in the opposition between legality and illegality, urbanity and non-urbanity, or normality and abnormality. This can correspond to a selective exercise of state power, often benefitting privileged citizens. Examples of spatial violence in contemporary Maputo include various known states of fragility, experienced by citizens due to the danger of eviction or partial privation of possession, expectancy for the formalization of the use of land, or the very persistence of the opposition between *cidade* (city) and *bairros* (neighbourhoods).

Of course, spatial violence is not an experience exclusive to colonial or postcolonial urbanism, nor of planning by Portuguese-speaking state apparatuses. However, as the chapter will argue, the spatial violence of unequal urban division is inherent to representations of bodies as unequal in extant memorials from the colonial era in Lisbon and Porto. And it was inherent to representations of occupation in colonial Lourenço Marques, such as the 1940s Fortaleza.

Constructing a Tradition of Colonial Domination

The Maputo Fortaleza is a museum built in the mid-1940s on the site of a former Portuguese military enclosure. The effort was led by the Portuguese architect Joaquim Areal Silva, who at the time worked for Portugal's Direcção dos Monumentos Nacionais (DMN) (Directorate for National Monuments), a division of the Direcção-Geral de Edifícios e Monumentos Nacionais (DGEMN) (Directorate-General for National Buildings and Monuments) (Corvaja, 2003, p. 36). The DGEMN was created in 1929, during the military dictatorship of 1926 to 1932, which preceded and prepared the way for the Salazar and Caetano dictatorships that ended in 1974. The preamble to the executive decree that created this department stated that its main objective was to foster 'unity of orientation' regarding public buildings in Portugal and its colonies.[5]

The work of Monumentos Nacionais (as the Directorate is usually called in professional discourse in Portugal) included sites like the former enclosure in the Mozambican colonial capital of Lourenço Marques. 'Unity of orientation' was here imagined according to a frame of technical government that denied the possibility of properly political decisions.[6] Through the creation and consolidation of institutions such as Monumentos Nacionais, architects would be trained as technocrats able to manage public buildings, conceived within the situated practice of corporatism as crucial nodes for the reformation of the city as a socially harmonious space (Castela, 2011, pp. 42–45).[7] This conception of architectural expertise emerged partly through the collaboration of the Paris urbanism school with the Portuguese state during the early Salazar dictatorship (Castela, 2011, p. 42).[8] Through a non-political management of buildings such as the enclosure, Portuguese architects like Silva, who have been largely forgotten today, contributed to the hegemony of a nationalist history through the reinvention of the built environment, thus participating in the work of governing subjectivities both in Portugal and its colonies.

Before travelling to Mozambique in 1945, Silva had served as head of a regional section of DMN from 1940 onward (Brito, 2013, p. 86, note 66). During that time he had gained experience through his involvement in a project to rebuild the erstwhile palace of the Dukes of Bragança in the northern Portuguese city of Guimarães.[9] He was thus already involved in the formation of an authoritarian and colonial state apparatus invested in developing a unified notion of architectural practice. This sought, among other things, to restore spaces seen as commemorating the history of the Portuguese aristocracy, recast as monuments of a national community characterized by social harmony between the classes. Guimarães had been designated in journalistic and other publications as the 'cradle of the nation' from the 1930s onwards. The palace Silva worked on had been abandoned in the early 1600s, but repurposed as army barracks from the early 1800s onwards. As the author of the design noted, however, by 1942, 'nothing else remains than walls blackened by the centuries that lent that austere air of respectable ancientness' (Azevedo, 1942, p. 8).

In Lourenço Marques, there were also few remains of the fortress enclosure. But Areal Silva faced a different question: how could the design suggest a solidity of Portuguese occupation in southern Mozambique that had no historical foundation? Although the trading enclosure of Lourenço Marques had originally been built in 1781, the Portuguese garrison there had exerted no control over the polities in the area until the late nineteenth century (Castela, 2010, p. 79). Instead, the settlement had had to pay tribute, and had sometimes been attacked – as when the Zulu monarch Dingane ordered his soldiers to attack it and execute its governor, Ribeiro, in 1833 (Liesegang, 1969). In his design, Silva thus arguably decided to invoke an ideal Portuguese bastioned fortress 'of the sea against the land', like those built along the Moroccan and Indian coasts from the sixteenth-century onward as part of the formation of Portugal's first empire.[10] He was certainly also inspired by his visit to Mozambique Island in northern Mozambique in 1945, and by the report he prepared on the São Sebastião fortress there (Simão Gonçalves, 2011, p. 57, note 391). In a text on the project for the Fortaleza, he noted that the *'reconstitution'* was a 'simple work, but one that demands a careful and constant observation so that we can create the character of the building that we intend to represent, avoiding phantasies in the design or in the execution' (Areal Silva, 1945, p. 44, emphasis added).

Besides conjuring centuries of Portuguese occupation of the KaMpfumo polity surrounding the settlement, the building of the Fortaleza created a space of unchanging memoriality at the symbolic centre of mid-twentieth-century Lourenço Marques. In terms of urban prospective, this was an operation analogous to what was envisioned by coeval master plans in Portugal. For example, within the frame of an anti-Communist discourse, the 1948 master plan for Coimbra, prepared by a French architect of Polish origin, Étienne de Gröer, imagined the management of the formerly walled city as a museum space surrounded by residential extensions strictly segregated according to income (de Gröer, 1948).[11] In Lourenço Marques, increasingly segregated according to 'race', the museum at the Fortaleza would also contribute to the broader colonial discourse of the time, which Jyoti Hosagrahar (1992, p. 86) has described as 'establishing the superiority of a small European minority [through] the theatrical display of power'. The rebuilding of the Fortaleza was undoubtedly also directed toward South Africans of European origin or descent, notably from the Rand (present-day Gauteng), who visited southern Mozambique every year. Silva's design thus may also be seen as heralding architectural strategies deployed more recently in 'heritage sites that have a legitimate claim to an authentic past ... developed for touristic purposes', such as Colonial Williamsburg in the United States (AlSayyad, 2014, p. 135). In all these ways, the Fortaleza project contributed to the broader project of constructing tradition to justify a southern African region dominated by a minority of settlers of European descent.

The Reframing of Colonial Memorials

Today, the Fortaleza belongs to the foremost public university of Mozambique, University Eduardo Mondlane, named after the US-educated anthropologist who was the first leader of the country's liberation movement. The space is practised in the everyday under conditions created as a result of a renovation project started in 1999. The design team was led by a US-educated Mozambican architect of Portuguese origin, José Forjaz, who founded the university's School of Architecture and Physical Planning. At the time of this project, the monumental sculptures recalling the military subjection of southern Mozambique were already collected at the Fortress, having been removed from their pedestals at the two main urban foci of Lourenço Marques in 1975.

The largest sculpture is the equestrian statue of Mouzinho de Albuquerque, the Portuguese army officer who had captured the monarch Ngungunyane in 1895. Ngungunyane was the sovereign of the Northern Nguni state of Gaza, during the conquest by the Portuguese army of what is today southern Mozambique (figure 9.1). Sixty-two years after Dingane's attack, the Gaza campaign turned Albuquerque into 'the most famous colonial combatant of modern times' in Portugal (Wheeler, 1980, p. 295). Nevertheless, armed resistance continued throughout the occupied territory of present-day Mozambique until the 1920s – particularly in the north. Indeed, only 40 years had passed since the end of these hostilities and the beginning of the independence war in 1964. The beginning of four decades of occupation without widespread armed resistance in Mozambique coincided with the early Salazar dictatorship, during which 'Mouzinho was adopted as a military patron saint, the secular saint of the regime' (Wheeler, 1980, p. 295).

The equestrian statue was created by the Portuguese sculptor José

Figure 9.1. The equestrian statue of Albuquerque at the Fortaleza in 2014. (*Photo*: Tiago Castela)

Simões de Almeida, following a 1936 public competition.[12] It was part of a larger monument inaugurated in 1940 at a square named after Albuquerque (today Independence Square). This entire monument was demolished in early 1975, during the transitional government that ruled Mozambique between the ceasefire agreement signed on 7 September 1974, and the declaration of independence on 25 June 1975. Other Portuguese statues continued to be removed throughout Mozambique after independence – for example, at Mozambique Island.[13]

The collection at the Fortaleza also includes a statue of António Enes, who, as Portugal's high commissioner in Mozambique, organized the military campaign led by Albuquerque (figure 9.2). This statue was removed from the southern section of the city's main square, adjacent to the Fortaleza, where it had been installed in 1910 by Alfredo Freire de Andrade, the governor-general of Mozambique from 1906 to 1910.[14] The collection further includes panels that were part of the 1940 monument to Albuquerque, including one that depicts the capture of Ngungunyane at Chaimite (figure 9.3).

The garden inside the Fortaleza is one of the few places downtown where citizens of Maputo can sit in the shade away from the constant noise of car traffic without being forced to consume food or drink. Most

Figure 9.2. The statue of Enes at the Fortaleza in 2014. (*Photo*: Tiago Castela)

Figure 9.3. Tourists taking a photograph in front of a panel representing the capture of the monarch Ngungunyane in 2014. (*Photo*: Tiago Castela)

are reasonably unconcerned with the demonumentalized representations. The same was probably true, however, of their predecessors encountering the monuments in the late colonial period. Thus, in April 1970, according to the municipal councillor Leonardo Samissone Bucucha, one of the very few black Mozambicans involved in municipal government at the time:

We have observed the mistreatment of the lawns of monuments. Of the [monument] to the Combatants of the Great War, located at Mac-Mahon Square, and of the statue of António Enes, where stevedores, shoeshiners, and polishers sometimes do laundry. They lay dirty rags, they step on the grass, without any consideration for the significance of the place and of the monuments. I would ask your excellency to ensure that the Municipal Police passes by those squares.[15]

Today, it is mostly visitors who do not practice the space everyday – both students in small groups or foreign tourists – who are attentive to the representations. In particular, they are drawn to the panels, which serve well as a background for photographs. I suggest that such subjects are practicing the space under conditions that articulate the persistence of a postcolonial spatial pedagogy deployed by the Mozambican state in the decade after political independence.

This 'postcolonial spatial pedagogy' was an assemblage encompassing the curtailing of the market in urban space, participatory interventions in the so-called peripheries, and the management of the built legacies of colonialism. Soon after independence, urban space started to be framed in statements of officials and journalistic accounts as a political question, not a technical one – notably with the nationalization of all rental housing in Mozambique in July 1976. Heralding nationalization, the cover of the 15 February 1976 issue of the magazine *Tempo* proclaimed the need to 'Liquidate Racism, Allow the People to Take the City, Organize Democracy within the City'. The edition included the transcript of a speech by President Machel at the Airport Roundabout on 3 February (thereafter known as the Day of Mozambican Heroes). The words on the cover reiterated the 'three objectives' emphasized by the president at the very end of his speech:

The State from now on will take care of rental housing buildings, of the abandoned houses, of the houses whose owners fled from Mozambique. The State will negotiate, will establish the rules of occupation. There is no invasion. Now there is no invasion of the buildings. The State will provide, from today, soldiers for security… Our comrades fell precisely for this. We respect the house where each one lives. Renting, no. It will be the State. Building to live is a right. To exploit, no.¹⁶

The following year, after curtailing the market in urban space, the state started to experiment with participation techniques in urban areas that had been defined as peripheral during colonial occupation. An exploratory urban planning project in the Maxaquene neighbourhood of northern Maputo, in particular, focused on a process of collaboration between spatial professionals and citizens. Instead of prioritizing design and visual order, it encouraged regular discussions with residents and sought to foster new institutions of local government, such as so-called 'dynamization groups' and block committees. In addition, the project introduced a simplified system for building licensing, and included the creation of blocks in collaboration with residents, to make the future construction of public infrastructure easier (Pinsky, 1983; Saevfors, 1986).

By the end of the 1970s, the project of using space as a pedagogical tool for the formation of a postcolonial subjectivity (encompassing both the celebration of past struggles and a challenge to the persistence of the rationality of colonialism) became more explicit. This was when – beyond the housing question – the state began to face the need to manage the built heritage of colonial occupation. State resolution #4 of the Permanent Committee of the Popular Assembly envisioned a committee at each Provincial Assembly to identify and inventory the extant 'historical places':

With the victory of the National Liberation Struggle directed by FRELIMO [the Front for the Liberation of Mozambique] the Mozambican People is engaged in this high moment of its history, in the construction of the socialist society. It is thus important to conserve, as a symbol of the tenacity and determination of our People, as a memory of humiliation and foreign domination and as a source of inspiration and teaching for the coming generations all the historical vestiges of the creativity and struggle of the Mozambican People, *as well as those of the foreign colonial presence in Mozambique*.¹⁷

However, monumentality itself was not eschewed; indeed, colonial traditions of emplacing representations of state formation in the city were deliberately rearticulated. And, by 1985, the government demanded the creation of an annex to the first master plan for Maputo as the capital of a politically independent state. According to that annex, 'Monumental Plan: Paths and Significant Areas of the City' (Secretaria de Estado do Planeamento Físico, 1985, p. 1), prepared by the State Secretariat of Physical Planning:

The colonial city developed formally, with grand avenues, gardens, squares, and monumental buildings ... thus, the central city represents a great urban investment that must be protected and maintained. With the transformation of Maputo in the capital city of the country, its international role grows, and we verify the lack of accommodation for the organisms of the State and national equipments. Thus the monumental and architectural structure of the city needs not only conservation but also reinforcement and augmentation.

The annex included the characterization of downtown Maputo as '*a zone of historical importance*' where 'architecture and landscape should be maintained and conserved' (Secretaria de Estado do Planeamento Físico, 1985, p. 2, emphasis in the original). Arguably, this prescription encompassed the Fortaleza, which was located adjacent to the main downtown square.

Today, students and tourists at the Fortaleza are particularly attentive to evocations of monarch Ngungunyane. Tourists seem to prefer to diffuse images of humiliation and struggle through photographs taken in front of the panel representing the imprisonment of the monarch by Albuquerque. In contrast, students proclaim victory over the colonial regime next to the sculpted coffin holding the remains of the monarch, symbolically returned to Mozambique during the visit of President Machel to Portugal in 1983 (figure 9.4). Such is 'the unruly fortune of colonial constructs' (Jacobs,

Figure 9.4. The sculpted coffin symbolically holding the remains of monarch Ngungunyane in 2014. (*Photo*: Tiago Castela)

1996, p. 163). Nevertheless, this flexible diffusion of images seems only to have been made possible through the conditions created as the legacy of the late-1970s project of postcolonial spatial pedagogy.

An Unchallenged Pedagogy in Democratic Portugal

In contrast to this reframing of heritage, political democratization in Portugal did not entail critical reflection or challenge to another kind of spatial pedagogy: the constant reinforcement of a sense of inequality through urban memorials of colonialism. Fragments of this persistent pedagogy include two state exhibition spaces that seem to suggest that the role of expertise in colonialism remains largely unexamined as a properly political question. They also include one space of finance and one space of consumption that continue to diffuse a violent aesthetic of inequality.

In the roundabout called Empire Square at the centre of the privileged neighbourhood of Foz in western Porto (Portugal's second largest city) stands a monument that initially marked the entrance of the 1934 Colonial Exhibition at Porto's Crystal Palace gardens (figure 9.5). The monument was rebuilt at its present location in 1984 during the administration of the

Figure 9.5. The 'Monument to the Portuguese Colonizing Effort' at Porto's Empire Square in 2013. (*Photo*: Tiago Castela)

mayor Paulo Valada, who led a liberal-conservative coalition. As were many of his contemporaries, Valada had once been a settler, having worked as a civil engineer and a contractor in Mozambique from 1950 to 1958, and later in Angola. At the time, many Mozambican construction workers laboured under the *xibalo* system – i.e. as forced labourers (Penvenne, 1994). However, evocations of their bodies are entirely absent from the monument's representation of the 'Portuguese colonial effort'. Instead, it celebrates (once again from the mid-1980s onwards) the various male expertises crucial for colonization, as well as female reproductiveness.[18] Even though very few citizens walk close enough to it to appreciate its content, this evocation of the Colonial Exhibition is valued as evidence of an important event in the city's twentieth-century history. For example, in 2009, the Foz ward council contested plans by the subway company to move the monument from its central position in the roundabout.[19] In addition, rebuilding the monument was seen as an important detail of Valada's work as mayor, from 1982 to 1985. Thus, in the section of the webpage of the University of Porto devoted to 'illustrious' alumni, this decision is foregrounded in the biographical note on Valada.[20]

The director of the 1934 exhibition, Henrique Galvão, explicitly conceived the temporarily transformed gardens, including the monument, as a teaching space (Ferraz de Matos, 2006, p. 190). Galvão was particularly concerned with the 'colonial education of children'. As he wrote in the exhibition's newspaper, *Ultramar* (Overseas): 'We do not assign today in the education of the child a role to colonial education – so necessary to achieving the highest of objectives faced by the Portuguese Nation' (Galvão, 1934, p. 1). In the preface to a book on the exhibition, Valada (who was 10 years old when he visited it in 1934) himself seems to suggest that Galvão's pedagogy of inequality was effective. In it he conflated an uncritical remembrance of the pedagogy with a 'Love of the Homeland':

The Colonial Exhibition had an emotional component, so delicate that children of those times, like Ercílio and myself, still recall today young Rosita and little Augustinho [young Guineans being exhibited], and the long rosary of striking figures like the Landins Soldiers and the Fathers of the Missions. Everything remained in our memory. (Valada, 2003, p. 7)

In contrast to this monument in Porto, some of the unequal representations of African bodies in Lisbon's Tropical Garden (a research garden used in 1940 for the 'Colonial and Ethnographic Section' of the Exhibition of the Portuguese World) were never dismantled (figure 9.6). As

Figure 9.6. Lisbon's Tropical Garden in 2013. (*Photo*: Tiago Castela)

the Exhibition Guide noted, such representations were based on colonial research undertaken by Porto's Institute of Anthropology:

AVENUE OF COLONIAL ETHNOGRAPHY: Exhibited through sculptural reproductions, the most characteristic heads of races and tribes of the Portuguese Colonial Empire based in photographic documentation of the Porto Institute of Anthropology. (*Guia da Exposição do Mundo Português*, 1940)

The Institute, founded in 1912 as part of the (then) new University of Porto, was led by the biological anthropologist Mendes Correia. Correia organized the First National Congress of Colonial Anthropology in Porto in 1934 as part of that year's exhibition, and was also the unelected mayor of Porto from 1936 to 1942. As one Portuguese anthropologist has noted, the institute was crucial for the 'launching of a nationwide programme of anthropological research focusing on the colonies and their "indigenous" populations' (Santos, 2012, p. S42, note 20). The Salazar dictatorship:

...set out to build a Third Empire in Africa. Anthropologists did not oppose this enterprise and were called on to produce useful 'colonial knowledge'. Physical anthropologists ... played a salient role in this process. By and large, their work offered 'scientific' support to the regime's colonial rhetoric. (Santos, 2012, p. S34)

For the present-day visitors of the garden, this exhibition and its teachings – notably regarding the expertise of colonialism – seem to persist.[21]

This persistence can also be noted in urban representations of African bodies as unequal bodies in privately owned spaces of finance and consumption. One example is the 1951 ceramic mural evoking the colonization of Brazil in the lobby of the Palácio Atlântico (Atlantic Palace) in Porto. This building was originally the head office of the private bank, Banco Português do Atlântico (BPA), led by Arthur Cupertino de Miranda, the son of privileged farmers from the northern town of Famalicão. BPA had had business in Brazil since the early 1930s, due to the large contingent of Portuguese emigrants – mostly from northern Portugal – there (Banco Português do Atlântico, 1993, p. 11). At the time of the opening, the BPA head office was the tallest building in the city, and there was certainly the expectation that the mural would be seen by many workers, clients, and passersby (Banco Português do Atlântico, 1993, p. 14). Indeed, the mural stands behind the main door, and is clearly visible from the busy square (figure 9.7).

Evidently, at the time, the mural could also have suggested the bank's perspective on the continuing colonization of Africa – and on projects for future expansion. It is thus instructive to note that the first BPA logotype, from the creation of the public limited company in 1942 onward, included the motto 'Por Um Portugal Maior' (For a Larger Portugal). And even

Figure 9.7. Detail of the ceramic mural at the Palácio Atlântico in 2014. (*Photo*: Tiago Castela)

though, at the time of the mural's creation, BPA had not yet started to develop branches in Angola and South Africa, the affiliated Banco Comercial de Angola was founded soon after, in 1956. The Bank of Lisbon and South Africa was later founded in 1965 (Banco Português do Atlântico, 1993, pp. 16, 19).

The content of the mural is further instructive of this colonial programme. In it, the sculptor Jorge Barradas was arguably evoking his brief settler experience. In 1930, Barradas had sojourned on the African island of São Tomé, where, according to one critic, 'his art, of a baroque tendency, found ample correspondence in the tropical landscape' (Galeria São Mamede, 1972). On the right side of the mural, Barradas depicted a young white peasant turning his head as he walks towards the left of the viewer, bidding farewell to a woman and a boy, possibly his wife and child, who stand barefoot outside their dwelling. The latter is represented as a whitewashed house, with traits that evoke southern Portuguese vernacular architecture, and it seems to be late summer, as another peasant couple is busy gathering grapes for winemaking. Meanwhile, on the left side of the mural (seemingly after crossing the Atlantic, as a sailing ship is visible at the top of the composition), a beardless young white man faces two bearded white gentlemen. All are finely dressed and stand amidst lush green foliage. At the centre of the composition on this side, what seems to be a Native American female figure lies in a reclined position, looking towards the beardless man. Behind the white men, can be discerned the only two human bodies that are not fully visible in the whole of the mural: two black men, who seem to be carriers, wearing loincloths. The one on the right is possibly kneeling, behind the beardless man. The mural thus evokes the idea of colonization as a mode of social elevation for Portuguese peasants: in the space of the colony where activity is represented as male, the peasant male becomes a white gentleman, who is served by black carriers.

Other representations of African bodies as unequal can be found today in spaces of consumption in downtown Porto and in Lisbon. One example is the colourful painted sign above the Casa Oriental (Oriental House) grocery store, located close to the entrance of the main landmark of Porto, the eighteenth-century Clérigos Tower. This painted sign is seen, at least at a glance, by most of the tourists that visit the city. It depicts a standing black man, wearing only short white pants, holding a tray with a cup of coffee. In the background, the viewer can see a series of idealized round huts, surrounded by a lush forest. The loin-clothed black man is serving a white, bearded male wearing a white sun helmet, a light brown jacket, a long-sleeved white shirt, white pants, and black boots. The last detail is important because the man's booted right foot seems to stomp on the black man's naked right foot.

This painted sign is clearly valued by the current owners of the grocery store. Not only was it recently restored, but a photograph of the sign is displayed at the top of the store's webpage. The text there also explicitly links the history of the store to early-twentieth-century empire, framing the sign as integral to the heritage valued by tourists visiting the city:

> The Oriental House was founded in 1910 … and in its beginnings products from the Oriental and African colonies were sold. Coffee, chocolate, and teas … are still foregrounded in the façade of this famous grocery store, in the representation of a scene of Colonial Africa, an attraction to all the tourists that visit Porto. (Home, www.casaoriental.pt/base.asp)

Authorship of Built Traditions, Democratic Government, and Memorials of Colonialism

While in postcolonial Mozambique sculptural representations – formerly celebrating domination – have been redeployed by the state as a means of fostering autonomy, in contemporary Portugal, political democratization has not entailed a challenge to the persistence of a colonial rationality of government, which operated partly through a pedagogical aesthetic of racial inequality. Instead, the violence of the spatial division inherent in the representation of African bodies as unequal has been neglected in relation to a sustained and hegemonic discourse of Portuguese imperial reason founded upon a developmental valuation of cultural difference (Castela, 2010).

Recalling Mozambique's postcolonial spatial pedagogy can help historians of the built environment mitigate the conditions that engender experiences of spatial violence. These experiences include the violence inherent in the persistence of subjectivity formation through unchallenged memorials of colonialism and their aesthetics of inequality. However, expert knowledge of the city (a domain that encompasses urban planning, but is not limited to it) tends to define the opposition that undergirds the experience of spatial violence as technical and even ahistorical (not political and contingent). It is crucial that scholars and citizens work collectively towards forms of planning knowledge that are not inimical to democratic urban government. Deliberation on how to acknowledge the violence of memorials of colonialism should be properly political, to render a decolonization of contemporary urban planning in Portugal and elsewhere in Europe. This can best be accomplished through the politicization of urban memorials of colonialism, possibly fostering urban design and planning strategies that are more aware of the authorship of the colonial legacy in cities.

Notes

1. Portugal's participation in the European occupation of Africa is often characterized as the third Portuguese empire. It followed the establishment of Portugal's sixteenth-century commercial empire in the Indian Ocean, administered from Goa (which was annexed by India in 1961), and the settlement of present-day Brazil, which became politically independent in the 1820s under the rule of Portuguese King Pedro IV. The political independence of the five Portuguese colonies in Africa was achieved after three long independence wars, started after the retreat of other European states from neighbouring colonies on the continent. These wars began in 1961, in Angola, immediately following the independence of the neighbouring Belgian Congo; in 1963, in Guinea-Bissau; and in 1964, in Mozambique, following the independence of neighbouring Tanzania.
2. I propose to understand the management of memorials as part of urban planning for two reasons. First, while memorials are today largely excluded from professional conceptions of what an urban plan should be in both Portugal and Mozambique, official memorials were historically often explicitly included in state plans, such as in the 1985 Structure Plan for Maputo. Second, the very exclusion of the management of extant memorials from contemporary urban plans is a productive planning decision.
3. Unlike the situation in the United Kingdom or France, the end of empire in Portugal was closely associated with the beginning of formal democracy. One reason was the geopolitics of Portugal's two largest colonies, Angola and Mozambique, within the frame of the Cold War. While claiming to the United Nations that Portugal did not have a colonial empire but was instead a pluri-continental state, the Salazar and Caetano dictatorships entered an alliance with South Africa and Rhodesia to maintain the dominance of minority European settlers in southern Africa. For a study of the secret Alcora pact, see Meneses and Martins (2013). The period of the Salazar and Caetano dictatorships was ended by a military coup in April 1974 – the 'Carnation Revolution'. The objective of the coup was to swiftly create the conditions for democratization in Portugal, as well as for the independence of all seven Portuguese colonies in Africa and Asia – including also the island territories of Cape Verde, São Tomé, East Timor, and Macao, where there were no ongoing armed conflicts. In Mozambique, a ceasefire was reached in September 1974, and independence was formally declared in June 1975. Meanwhile, in Portugal the first election by universal suffrage was held in April 1975, and the first democratic constitution was approved one year later.
4. For an anthropological critique of 'Portugal of the Little Ones', a theme park containing scaled-down versions of Portuguese houses and monuments, see Mota Santos (2014).
5. Decree 16,791 of April 30, 1929.
6. The term 'properly political' evokes the work of the French philosopher Jacques

206 Whose Tradition?

    Rancière on democracy *vis-à-vis* government based on titles to govern, such as science. Rancière (2006 [2005], p.76) noted that 'political practices ... are always practices of dividing the people...'.
7. For a classic discussion of corporatist theory, see Panitch (1977).
8. For an anthropology of the provenance of spatial technocracy in France, see Rabinow (1989).
9. Building began in 1937 and continued until 1959, following a design by the Portuguese architect Rogério de Azevedo, who led the regional section of DMN from 1936 to 1940, before Silva.
10. The expression 'of the sea against the land' is borrowed from the work on Portuguese coastal fortresses in Morocco and Gujarat of the architectural historian João Barros Matos (2012).
11. The value of a purportedly unchanged historical centre for the new city was heralded by another professional of the Paris Institute, Henri Sellier: 'The old city played a historical, touristic role as well as keeping the character, the specificity of the city's culture, alive' (Rabinow, 1989, p. 341).
12. The first committee for the creation of a monument began work in 1916 under the direction of the Portuguese governor-general. See chapter 4 in Verheij (2011).
13 In a travelogue published in the professional journal *PLAN* in late 1975, the South African architect Joe Noero lamented: 'Once ashore on Mocambique [sic] island, one cannot believe that one is in Africa. The architecture is totally European ... Now that Frelimo has taken control one can only hope that the buildings will be maintained in the same condition. *Already one can see evidence of their dislike for past Colonial rule. All the statues have been stripped from the historical buildings and squares*, and street names, named after Portuguese heroes have been changed' (Noero, 1975, p. 7, emphasis added).
14. Authorship of the statue has been attributed to Portuguese sculptor António Teixeira Lopes (Verheij, 2011, p. 31).
15. The quote is from the minutes of the Municipal Chamber of Lourenço Marques from 15 April 1970. Samissone Bucucha was a *vereador* (alderperson), representing the black 'suburbs'. Born in the village of Bucucha in the Homoíne district of Inhambane province, Bucucha became the first radio announcer doing a regular Sunday programme in the xiRonga language for Rádio Moçambique. The broadcast, which began in 1957, was sponsored by the local store of the Dutch company Zuid-Afrikaansch Handelshuis, where he worked (Loforte, 2007). By 1970, when Bucucha was one of the very few black municipal councillors in Mozambique, he had been promoted to store manager, and had become a member of Acção Nacional Popular (Popular National Action), the single party during the late dictatorship (Casamento [Wedding]. *Tempo*, **9**, 1970, p. 26). In 1973, Bucucha had acquired the store, and accepted a grant from the Foreign Leader exchange programme of the US Department of State.
16. Dia dos Heróis Moçambicanos: Presidente Samora Anuncia Importantes Medidas Revolucionárias (Day of Mozambican Heroes: President Samora Announces Important Revolutionary Measures), *Tempo*, **280**, 1976, p. 27.
17. Resolution #4/79 of the Permanent Committee of the Popular Assembly, May 3, 1979, emphasis added. In 1988, a new law determined 'the legal protection of material and immaterial goods of Mozambican cultural heritage' (Law #10/88, 22 December 1988). An initial draft was prepared with the support of a UNESCO consultant (Warburton, 1986).
18. Before the opening of the exhibition on 16 June, the monument was conceived as

'a homage to the sacrificed of Portuguese colonization'. The original figures were conceived by the 'artist' Ponce de Castro, an army officer, and created by the local sculptor and instructor Sousa Caldas. O Missionário (The Missionary), *Ultramar*, **4**, 1934, p. 4.
19. Metro do Porto quer tirar monumento do meio da rotunda da Praça do Império (Porto Metro intends to remove monument from the centre of the Empire Square roundabout), *Público*, 14 March 2009.
20. Antigos Estudantes Ilustres da Universidade do Porto: Paulo Vallada (Illustrious Alumni of the University of Porto: Paulo Vallada). Available at: http://sigarra.up.pt/up/pt/web_base.gera_pagina?P_pagina=1000687.
21. Lisbon's more recent exhibitionary space, EXPO '98, demonstrated 'the continued importance of ... seductive and nostalgic scriptings of imperial adventure'. It 'offered a sanitized and unbloodied history of imperial adventure' (Power, 2002, pp.146, 142).

References

AlSayyad, N. (2014) *The 'Real', the Hyper, and the Virtual: Traditions in the Built Environment*. London: Routledge.
Areal Silva, J. (1945) A Praça de Nossa Senhora da Conceição em Lourenço Marques e o Projecto da sua Reconstituição [The Fortress of Our Lady of the Conception in Lourenço Marques and the project for its reconstitution]. *Moçambique: Documentário Trimestral*, **43**, pp. 23–44.
Azevedo, R. (1942) *O Paço dos Duques de Guimarães: Preâmbulo à Memória do Projecto de Restauro* [The Palace of the Dukes of Guimarães: Preamble to the Memory of the Restoration Project]. Porto: Livraria de Fernando Machado.
Banco Português do Atlântico (1993) *O Banco Português do Atlântico: Esboço Histórico* [The Portuguese Bank of the Atlantic: Historical Sketch]. Porto: Banco Português do Atlântico.
Barros Matos, J. (2012) Do Mar contra Terra: Mazagão, Ceuta, e Diu, Primeiras Fortalezas Abaluartadas da Expansão Portuguesa [Of the Sea against the Land: Mazagão, Ceuta, and Diu, the First Bastioned Fortresses of the Portuguese Expansion]. PhD dissertation, University of Seville.
Brito, M.M. (2013) Paço dos Duques de Bragança em Guimarães: Alguns Vetores de Leitura [Palace of the Dukes of Bragança in Guimarães: some vectors for a reading]. *Monumentos*, **33**, pp. 74–87.
Castela, T. (2010) Imperial Garden: Planning Practices and the Utopia of Luso-Tropicalism in Portugal/Mozambique, 1945–1975. Traditional Dwellings and Settlements Working Paper Series, 238. Berkeley, CA: International Association for the Study of Traditional Environments, pp.75–98.
Castela, T. (2011) A Liberal Space: A History of the Illegalized Working-Class Extensions of Lisbon. PhD dissertation, University of California, Berkeley.
Corvaja, L. (2003) *Maputo: Desenho e Arquitectura* [Maputo: Design and Architecture]. Maputo: Edições FAPF.
de Gröer, É. (1948) *Anteprojecto de Urbanização, Embelezamento, e Extensão da Cidade de Coimbra* [Pre-design for the Urbanization, Beautification, and Extension of the City of Coimbra]. Coimbra: Coimbra Editora.
Ferraz de Matos, P. (2006) *As Côres do Império: Representações Raciais no Império Colonial Português* [The Colours of Empire: Racial Representations in the Portuguese Colonial Empire]. Lisbon: Imprensa de Ciências Sociais.

Galeria São Mamede (1972) *Jorge Barradas: Cerâmicas* [Jorge Barradas: Ceramics]. Lisbon: Edições Galerias São Mamede.
Galvão, H. (1934) As Crianças e as Colónias [The children and the colonies]. *Ultramar*, **4**, p. 1.
Guia da Exposição do Mundo Português [Guide of the Exhibition of the Portuguese World]. Lisbon, 1940.
Hosagrahar, J. (1992) City as durbar: theater and power in Imperial Delhi, in AlSayyad, N. (ed.) *Forms of Dominance: On the Architecture and Urbanism of the Colonial Enterprise*. Aldershot: Avebury.
Jacobs, J.M. (1996) *Edge of Empire: Postcolonialism and the City*. London: Routledge.
Loforte, L. (2007) *Rádio Moçambique: Memórias de um Doce Calvário* [Radio Mozambique: Memories of a Sweet Calvary]. Maputo: CIEDIMA.
Liesegang, G. (1969) Dingane's attack on Lourenço Marques in 1833. *Journal of African History*, **10**(4), pp. 565–579.
Meneses, M.P. and Sena Martins, B. (eds.) (2013) *As Guerras de Libertação e os Sonhos Coloniais: Alianças Secretas, Mapas Imaginados* [The Liberation Wars and Colonial Dreams: Secret Alliances, Imagined Maps]. Coimbra: Edições Almedina.
Mota Santos, P. (2014) The imagined nation: the mystery of the endurance of the colonial imaginary in postcolonial times, in Salazar, N. and Graburn, N. (eds.) *Tourism Imaginaries: Anthropological Approaches*. Oxford: Berghahn Books, pp. 194–219.
Noero, J. (1975) Of islands and winds of change. *PLAN*, September, pp. 3–13.
Panitch, L. (1977) The development of corporatism in liberal democracies. *Comparative Political Studies*, **10**(1), pp. 61–90.
Penvenne, J. (1994) *African Workers and Colonial Racism: Mozambican Strategies and Struggles in Lourenço Marques, 1877–1962*. Portsmouth, NH: Heinemann.
Pinsky, B. (1983) *Territorial Dilemmas: Urban Planning and Housing in Independent Mozambique*. Copenhagen: WUS.
Power, M. (2002) Exploding the myth of Portugal's 'maritime destiny': a Postcolonial voyage through EXPO '98, in Blunt, A. and McEwan, C. (eds.) *Postcolonial Geographies*. London: Continuum, pp.132–151.
Rabinow, P. (1989) *French Modern: Norms and Forms of the Social Environment*. Chicago, IL: University of Chicago Press.
Rancière, J. (2006 [2005]) *Hatred of Democracy*. London: Verso.
Saevfors, I. (1986) *Maxaquene: A Comprehensive Account of the First Urban Upgrading Experience in Mozambique*. New York: UNESCO.
Santos, G. (2012) The birth of physical anthropology in late imperial Portugal. *Current Anthropology*, **53**(S5), pp. S33–S45.
Secretaria de Estado do Planeamento Físico (1985) Anexo II [Annex #2], in *Cidade de Maputo: Plano de Estrutura* [City of Maputo: Structure Plan]. Maputo: Secretaria de Estado do Planeamento Físico.
Simão Gonçalves, N. (2011) O Projecto para a Fortaleza da Ilha de Moçambique atribuído a Miguel de Arruda [The Design of the Fortress of Mozambique Island attributed to Miguel de Arruda]. Masters thesis, University of Coimbra.
Valada, P. (2003) Prefácio [Preface], in Azevedo, E., *Porto 1934: A Grande Exposição* [Porto 1934: The Great Exhibition]. Porto: Ercílio de Azevedo, p. 7.
Verheij, G. (2011) Monumentalidade e Espaço Público em Lourenço Marques nas Décadas de 1930 e 1940: Dois Casos de Estudo [Monumentality and Public Space in Lourenço Marques in the 1930s and 1940s: Two Case Studies]. Masters thesis, New University of Lisbon.
Warburton, H. (1986) *National Legislation for the Protection of the Cultural Heritage*. Paris: UNESCO.

Wheeler, D. (1980) Joaquim Mouzinho de Albuquerque (1855–1902) e a política do colonialismo [Joaquim Mouzinho de Albuquerque (1855–1902) and the politics of colonialism]. *Análise Social*, **16**, pp. 295–318.

Acknowledgements

The research on which this chapter is based is part of a project titled 'Urban Aspirations in Colonial/Postcolonial Mozambique: Governing the Unequal Division of Cities, 1945–2010', undertaken at the Centre for Social Studies of the University of Coimbra, Portugal, for the Portuguese Foundation for Science and Technology (FCT). The reference codes attributed by FCT are EXPL/ATP-EUR/1552/2012 and FCOMP-01-0124-FEDER-027615. I am particularly indebted to two colleagues from the University of Porto: Fátima Vieira for encouraging me to pursue my interest in urban memorials of colonialism; and Ricardo Cardoso for his remarks on an advanced draft. I also thank the editors for their helpful comments. Translations from original Portuguese sources are by the author.

Part IV

Time:
Whose Identity?

Chapter 10

Whose Neighbourhood? Identity Politics, Community Organizing, and Historic Preservation in St. Louis

Susanne Cowan

In 1990, 15 years after the neighbourhood of Soulard in St. Louis had been designated a historic district, the *St. Louis Globe Democrat* printed two columns debating the pros and cons of stricter enforcement of the district's historic preservation code. In one, Fred M. Andres, the chairman of the code committee of the Soulard Restoration Group, argued that in order to preserve heritage and protect homeowner investment, Soulard needed a code that would be more effective at preventing 'slap-dash "improvements"' to historic structures (Andres, 1990). In the other, Bob Brandhorst and Joyce Sonn, spokespeople for the Soulard Neighborhood Improvement Association, argued for maintaining the existing, more flexible preservation code, noting that stricter aesthetic rules based on matters of taste would pose a financial hardship for poor residents (Brandhorst and Sonn, 1990). The two opinions reflected ongoing controversies over neighbourhood identity that had developed during the process of gentrification in Soulard.

The two neighbourhood associations had formed in the 1970s, representing increasingly divergent positions with regard to the development of the district. The Soulard Restoration Group (SRG) reflected a nostalgic, bourgeois vision of re-inhabiting a multiethnic nineteenth-century urban village, and its members championed a purist preservation programme celebrating the neighbourhood's 'French'-style row houses. In contrast, the Soulard Neighborhood Improvement Association (SNIA) saw itself as preserving working-class culture and economic practices by protecting the interests of the neighbourhood's remaining ethnic immigrant population and more recent rural migrants. As the City of St. Louis had developed historic-district guidelines for Soulard in the 1970s, and debated how to implement them in the 1980s and 1990s, these two neighbourhood groups had fought to assert their respective visions of the aesthetic and social character of the neighbourhood. Growing investment and increased property values had then exacerbated the differences between them as the neighbourhood struggled to deal with the impacts of gentrification and the displacement of its low-income population.

The battle over preservation codes in Soulard eventually became a struggle over who could assert influence over urban policies – a contest invoking what Henri Lefebvre (1996, pp. 147–159) called 'the right to the city'. In this conflict, community organizing became a tool for contesting class-based place identities and the cultural meaning of the built environment. Examining which voices were amplified or silenced in narratives of local history and in preservation codes today highlights whose traditions and history were ultimately conserved. By cloaking aesthetics in history, middle-class homeowners could tame the unwieldy urban environment into a familiar and controlled landscape for consumption. Meanwhile, their actions invisibly excluded and dislocated the inconvenient social practices and material culture of longtime working-class residents – diminishing, but not entirely eliminating, the diverse social community they claimed to have returned to the city to experience. In the process, historic preservation, often touted in St. Louis as a populist tool for economic development, also provided a hegemonic device for asserting class values and tastes.

A wide body of literature has examined the ways tradition and heritage have been used to propagate the interests of particular social groups in response to the perceived threat of change. Scholars such as Nezar AlSayyad and members of the International Association of the Study of Traditional Environments (IASTE) have shown that tradition is rarely value neutral; instead, local heritage is often packaged or even 'manufactured' for consumption by tourists or real estate investors (AlSayyad, 2001, p. 9). J.S. and N.G. Duncan have further shown that the process of protecting historic buildings and landscapes may not only be a strategic economic practice but also a means to assert class identity in the landscape. As they have argued, the 'seemingly innocent ... desire to protect local history' can serve as a 'subtle but highly effective' means of 'exclusion' (Duncan and Duncan, 2004, p. 4). Thus, preferences for certain traditional architectural forms can provide a tool for what Pierre Bourdieu (1984 [1979]) has called 'social positioning', allowing people with the social capital to define taste to impose a 'dominant aesthetics' through 'symbolic violence' and the repression of working-class material culture. In this process, the idea of tradition may not only provide a rationale to legitimize taste but also be used to evoke nostalgia, romanticizing (and thus concealing) the class-based nature of aesthetics. David Lowenthal (1999, pp. 8, 40) has thus argued that idealized visions of the past reflect 'less the memory of what was, than what was once possible' or a hope for what may be, and thus serve as a 'reaffirmation and validation' of the new. And Eric Hobsbawm and Terrance Ranger (1983, p. 2) have noted that attempts to borrow, revive, or create 'invented traditions' usually seek to shape new modes of behaviour for the novel conditions of the present by drawing on the authority of the social and aesthetic order of the past. This literature has shown that appeals to tradition rarely involve a neutral past to be restored. Rather, the trope of tradition may be mobilized by social groups for particular ideological and pragmatic purposes, particularly during processes of social change. In the case of Soulard, it is possible, using taste and nostalgia as lenses of understanding, to see how preservationists 'manufactured heritage' and 'invented traditions', and how their conflicting narratives of place eventually shaped whose voices were empowered in local development debates.

This chapter will examine how selective narratives of local history established a hierarchy among groups claiming to represent the will of the community in preservation policies. In Soulard, where four different socioeconomic subgroups existed in a single, predominantly white neighbourhood, appeals to history served to define who had a rightful claim to local citizenship. Narratives about the resurrection of the area's former ethnic, immigrant identity empowered middle-class 'hippy' and 'yuppie' newcomers, who claimed to be the rightful heirs of a nineteenth-century patrimony.[1] However, by romanticizing Soulard's historical social diversity, these two groups empowered the few remaining immigrants, as a 'deserving' poor, while disenfranchising more recently arrived rural southerners. The way these community groups defined their local history, through tropes of ethnicity and class, had lasting effects on the extent to which historic-district policies reflected inclusiveness in defining whose neighbourhood it would be.

Organizing the Neighbourhood

By the 1970s, the 'back-to-the-city' movement in the United States and a rising interest in historic preservation had resulted in an influx of new residents to older inner-city residential neighbourhoods. Here, they found cheap homes to buy and renovate in areas with high vacancy rates, allowing them to develop equity by capitalizing on what Neil Smith (1979) called 'the rent gap' in devalued areas. However, this move to the inner city in St. Louis was geographically uneven. A legacy of redlining, slum clearance, and public housing had led to a racial divide, in which north St. Louis became increasingly black, and south St. Louis remained primarily white. Thus gentrification centred on the Near Southside, where a new generation of homebuyers were able to move into an area with historic homes, neighbourhood shops, and parks, allowing them to consume the cultural amenities of the city, as described by David Ley (1980).

Soulard, an isolated pocket south of the central business district, in particular, attracted a slow but steady influx of new, middle-class residents despite its modest houses and formerly working-class character (figure 10.1). As the 'oldest intact residential area in St. Louis' (whose houses

Figure 10.1. Just south of the Central Business District (lower right side), Soulard was isolated from the rest of the Near Southside by highways and an industrial district. (*Source*: Community Development Commission (1975), Soulard Restoration Plan, p. 19, by courtesy of Missouri History Museum, St. Louis)

Figure 10.2. By the 1970s hundreds of structures in Soulard were abandoned and decaying. The buildings depicted here were demolished by the Boy's Club (visible in the background on the right) for their new sports fields, despite a lawsuit by the Soulard Restoration Group. (*Source*: Bob Moore, *St. Louis Globe Democrat*, 5 December 1977, by courtesy of the St. Louis Mercantile Library)

had an average construction date of 1889), it offered a plethora of house types, of various sizes and architectural styles (Rowley, 1977, p. 32). In the nineteenth century, Soulard had been known as a stepping-off place for immigrants and was one of the most densely populated and diverse neighbourhoods of any city in the world. However, for many decades in the early twentieth century, Soulard had also been the poorest white area of St. Louis, characterized by decrepit structures, depopulation, and crime. As it started to decline, it faced problems with absentee landlordism and lack of building maintenance, which further degraded its aging housing stock. Indeed, only 19 per cent of buildings in the area were classified as structurally sound in 1960 (Cohn, 1978, p. 15) (figure 10.2). And between 1960 and 1970, the neighbourhood lost more than 43 percent of its population, with one-third of the remaining residents classified as living below the poverty line (City of St. Louis, 1970). Over time, the area also gained a reputation as the city's 'most transient area' and a 'second-class place' (Schoenberg, 1974, p. 9). In order to revitalize the neighbourhood physically and socially, its new residents thus had to struggle not only to reverse decades of neglect, but to counteract negative perceptions by redefining its historical narrative.

Beginning in the late 1960s Soulard began to see evidence of this new trend, as newcomers bought and restored houses and formed new neighbourhood groups. The first phase of community organizing revolved around trying to prevent further depopulation and decline. In 1969 a handful of newcomers formed the Soulard Neighborhood Improvement Association (SNIA) to try to bring a new sense of stability. Sometimes called a 'spirit morale group', it fought demolitions, boarded-up vacant homes, and hosted events to attract outsiders (Schoenberg, 1974, p. 9) (figure 10.3). The SNIA also successfully established the area as a National Historic District in 1972 (Toft, 1988). However, its members' aim was to do more than protect the physical fabric; they also sought to preserve Soulard's working-class social structure. Thus, the SNIA, and its partner organization, Youth Education and Health in Soulard (YEHS), provided philanthropic services to children and the elderly through twenty different social programmes, including ones aimed at promoting cottage industry and craft enterprises to help existing residents supplement their incomes (Brandhorst, 1976; Bry, 1978). Yet, while the SNIA tried to engage with existing residents, most of its leaders were newcomers born into the middle class, who had chosen to adopt a hippy lifestyle. It was thus also criticized for its paternalistic approach – 'doing for' the area's remaining ethnic immigrants and more recently arrived rural southern whites in a way that

Figure 10.3. Early restorationists engaged in sweat equity, rebuilding their own homes and helping their neighbours. (*Source*: Bob Moore, *St. Louis Globe Democrat*, 24 August 1977, by courtesy of the St. Louis Mercantile Library)

was 'not representative' and could not facilitate a 'true taking of control' by the poor (Hurwitz, 1975, pp. 46–48, 284).

In 1974, as SNIA's successes brought population growth and a new concern for historic preservation, another group formed in the neighbourhood from about thirty families who had recently purchased and begun rehabilitating houses there. The Soulard Restoration Group (SRG) reflected the interests of a changing demographic of homebuyers – more yuppie than hippie. The SRG has often claimed to represent 'all sorts of people', including 'skilled professional people' and 'blue collar workers' (Rowley, 1978, pp. 41–42). However, most of the early SRG members were artists, public employees, young professionals, and small business owners. They typified what David Ley (1980) has called 'the new middle class'. The new residents, often from outside the city, wanted to throw off the constraints of suburbia, frequently critiquing wealthy suburbs like Clayton and Ladue (SRG, 1977c, p. 12; Hurwitz, 1975, pp. 49–50). They saw themselves as urban homesteaders, who, with 'pioneer spirit', would tame the wilds of the city (Anonymous, 1979). Yet, despite their claim to want to live in a diverse community, few longtime ethnic or poor southern white residents were members of the SRG. Instead, the group actively marketed the area to potential new homebuyers from outside the neighbourhood, who would share their value for historic homes and their objective to create community (Rowley, 1977, p. 7).

Together, these two groups successfully reversed the trend of decay in the neighbourhood, taking two different approaches – one stressing social and the other economic recovery. While the SNIA was praised for its social outreach and community service, some considered it to be ineffective in addressing the policy hurdles needed to reverse a legacy of redlining and to increase real estate investment in the area. Their efforts were balanced by the formation of the SRG, which led the charge in 'real estate and housing matters' (Schoenberg 1974, p. 16). However, the two groups – each playing an essential role in the neighbourhood – expressed ambivalence, and even open hostility, towards the other. It was a conflict that would grow as their approaches to revitalization further diverged over time.

Narrating the Neighbourhood's Ethnic History

Despite the division between the two organizations, they shared a romanticized view of the neighbourhood's ethnic heritage. Their interest in its diverse history of inhabitation also coincided with a changing attitude in the United States towards ethnicity. Formerly, immigrant groups had been disparaged as foreign others, outside of American culture; however, by the 1960s, after the assimilation of nineteenth- and early-twentieth-century European immigrants into the suburban middle class, many younger Americans began to embrace the ethnic identities their parents and grandparents had discarded. Rejecting the 'melting-pot' ideal and the conformity of 1950s American culture, they turned to 'ethnic reverie' as a means to reclaim identity and assert difference (Jacobson, 2009, pp. 2–4). Changing ideas about race in the face of the Civil Rights Movement also opened up a new interpretation of whiteness, one that accepted and mobilized ethnic identity as a means to assert reactionary political power (Stepick et al., 2011, p. 876; Bush, 2011, p. 25). Thus, family heritage gained new popularity, and scholars and lay people alike brought new attention to the ethnic histories of urban neighbourhoods (Smith, 1983, pp. xxvii, 94; Sagert, 2007, p.136; International Council on Monuments and Sites, 1997, p. 192). And in St. Louis, this 'upsurge in interest in Ethnic Studies' was reflected in the rise of events such as the Ethnic Heritage Studies Colloquium organized by the Social Science Institute at Washington University (Corzine et al., 1975, p. 52).

In Soulard, both the SRG and SNIA employed historical narratives to romanticize the neighbourhood's ethnic past. Many new middle-class residents were attracted to the social diversity of Soulard, where the variety of nationalities 'provided much of the city's color and flavor' (Anonymous, 1979; Anonymous, 1992). German brewers, bricklayers, and carpenters had first settled in Soulard in the 1830s, establishing the local industry and building traditions. And between 1875 and 1914 the neighbourhood grew to include a dozen distinct Eastern European and Mediterranean ethnic groups, causing an adjacent area to be called Bohemian Hill (Corzine et al., 1975, p. 29). Stereotypes prevalent in St. Louis in the 1970s praised these immigrants as 'self-respecting' and 'law-abiding', in particular lauding the original Germans as 'thrifty and industrious' (Anonymous, 1973; Corzine et al., 1975, p. 35). Sociological narratives from the 1970s further emphasized the 'solidarity' of the old ethnic communities, which had established their own churches, schools, banks, and other 'valuable welfare organizations' (Corzine et al., 1975, p. 33). Meanwhile, neighbourhood organizers like Brandhorst equated the formerly 'healthy fabric' of the neighbourhood with these institutions, which 'held the place together' (Schoenberg, 1974, p. 55). Overall, newcomers looked at these nineteenth-century community groups as an inspiration for their own neighbourhood organizing. Indeed, they saw their groups as continuing the past collectivism of the area, rather than creating a new social structure.

Both the SRG and SNIA imagined that the revitalization of the neighbourhood would involve a 'homecoming' of the ethnic population, which would be 'one of the best nutrients for developing a stable community' (SRG, 1978a, pp. 9–10; Corzine et al., 1975, p. 55). However, most of the new residents were not the prodigal children or grandchildren of prewar immigrant families, but rather whites without a clear claim to ethnic identity. Sociologists who studied the area argued that 'ethnic enclaves no longer exist in Soulard', except for a few older residents and parish churches (Schoenberg, 1974, p. 8; Corzine et al., 1975, p. 36). Nonetheless, both the SRG and SNIA embraced the supposed ethnic identity of the neighbourhood. As newcomers, they also utilized ethnic heritage as a jumping-off place for their social-organizing efforts. Thus, students and faculty at local universities worked with local churches and community associations to host ethnic festivals and architectural tours (Toft, 1975). In the early 1970s SNIA events featured the Little Wall Annis Polka Band, goulash, and bratwurst, and even gave a nod to rural southern whites with a fish fry. Such events tried to revive the dying traditions of ethnic identity in the area and tie a new community of homesteaders to longtime neighbourhood residents and institutions.

The SRG's events also emphasized the ethnic character of the neighbourhood, but the SRG sometimes sidelined its Eastern European identity in favour of an imagined French history. Their narratives resuscitated the idea of Soulard as 'Frenchtown' by emphasizing wealthy Francophone settlers, like Antoine Pierre Soulard. Inspired by the pseudo-French character of the neighbourhood's mansard roofs, the SRG looked to other French-style settlements, such as New Orleans, as a model 'elixir' for developing the 'special quality' of the neighbourhood (SRG, 1978b, p. 12). In 1978 neighbourhood organizers inaugurated Mardi Gras as a new local tradition. And complete with a parade, jazz bands, and competitive cook-offs, the event soon came to replace other ethnic festivals. By the 1990s the Soulard Mardi Gras was drawing 250,000 celebrants, equivalent to more than half the entire population of the city (Sutin, 1995). As a result, the area gained a reputation for rowdy nightlife, which was ironically apropos since Soulard also means 'drunken' in French. This invented tradition promoted Soulard as a landscape of consumption for a new affluent urban lifestyle and regional tourism. The lack of real ties between the SRG's ethnically unidentified white members and the area's historic ethnic communities allowed the SRG to further curate which traditions and heritage would best help them promote their vision for Soulard's future, rather than being tied to more accurate but less marketable depictions of its history.

This attempt to revitalize ethnic culture selectively derived, in part, from the idealized meaning that newcomers assigned to historic architecture as a representation of cultural diversity and social harmony among the classes. The Soulard Restoration Plan of 1975 attributed the 'distinctive European character' of the neighbourhood's row-house 'streetscape' to the 'German and Bohemian heritage' imported from the 'old country' (Community Development Commission, 1975a, p. 1; 1975b, pp. 8, 21). The SRG (1977b, p. 4) further romanticized the neighbourhood as a place where their 'ancestors learned to be Americans'. From the SNIA perspective, Brandhorst and Sonn (1990) portrayed Soulard as a 'melting pot' of diverse 'people living side by side'. And the SRG (1977b, p. 2) noted that, throughout its history, the neighbourhood's assorted residents had 'each made their own unique contribution' to its eclectic architecture; and it praised the buildings for their 'dignity', 'solidness', and 'attention to detail'. Observers admired local oddities as symbols of working-class ingenuity, like the lopsided 'flounder' houses built by low-income owners to appear unfinished so as to avoid taxation (Raiche, 1972). And Clark Rowley (1978, pp. 32–42), from the SRG, described the diverse scales, typologies, and styles of building as the physical manifestations of an urbane culture that allowed social cohesion among people from different backgrounds. The newcomers thus expressed nostalgia for a lost diversity, which they hoped could be revived through an influx of new middle-class residents who would re-establish the lost upper tiers of the local class spectrum.

In local histories from the 1970s, the deterioration of the neighbourhood's social and physical character was attributed to the loss of its ethnic population. They dated the beginning of this decline to the Immigration Act of 1924, which greatly restricted immigration to the US, and to the postwar pressures for assimilation of ethnic groups (Corzine and Dabrowski, 1975, p. 5). While these local historical narratives lamented that ethnic individuals and communities had chosen to migrate to the suburbs, they emphasized that this population was responding to national and local factors. And they noted that many ethnic residents were either pulled away by Federal Housing Administration (FHA) policies that favoured new development, or else were pushed out by building projects such as construction of the 3rd Street Interregional Expressway or by urban renewal in the form of the Darst Webbe public housing project, which largely displaced the Czech community of Bohemian Hill (Corzine et al., 1975, pp. 36–37). These histories thus naturalized the dispersion and assimilation of 'upwardly mobile' ethnic and religious minorities, rather than holding them responsible for the decline of the area as representatives of 'white flight' (Corzine et al., 1975, p. 42).

Quite the opposite, it was those who stayed, not those who left, who were most often blamed for the fall of the neighbourhood. The 1970s histories often vilified poor rural southerners, making them the scapegoats of Soulard's urban decline. Much of this population had moved into the area between 1950 and 1960, fleeing a 6-year drought in the Ozark farmlands (Schoenberg, 1974, p. 9). For them, Soulard was one of the cheapest all-white areas in the region close to potential jobs. Thus, unlike the later arrivals, these new residents saw the neighbourhood as a means to an end, and did not seek to become emotionally or socially invested in it. Disparagingly called 'hillbillies' and 'hoosiers', they were seen as unfit for urban living due to their rural habits and aesthetics, dearth of community organizations, and lack of long-term commitment to the neighbourhood (Hurwitz, 1975, p. 18).[2]

The new middle-class residents often blamed the poor southern whites for the physical degradation of the neighbourhood. Journalists and restorationists further reproached these 'established residents' as an impediment to revitalization, criticizing them for not taking more care or pride in the neighbourhood and for 'waiting to be helped' rather than taking initiative (Shinkle, 1972, p. 31). In terms of the cityscape, 'hoosiers' were associated with a disparaged material culture of chain-link fences, peeling paint, rusting cars, and large trucks. For example, comments printed in a faux advice column, 'Dear Abner', in the SRG's *Soulard Restorationist* newsletter, included complaints about the neighbours' pink and white awnings and an eighteen-wheeler truck parked on a lawn. The columnist responded by calling the offenders 'shady characters', who should 'hit the road, Jack' (SRG, 1979a; 1979b). Such evidence of lowbrow taste was seen as a crime against the neighbourhood, which desperately needed to be curtailed.

These historical narratives about ethnicity created a hierarchy within the nearly all-white Near Southside, dividing the community into four distinct groups – yuppies, hippies, 'hoosiers', and ethnic immigrants – each with varying rights to shape the local identity. In these narratives, community historians covertly alluded to discourses about the 'deserving poor', implying distinctions between the productive low-income ethnic communities and the 'undeserving poor' of apathetic rural southern whites (Mink and O'Connor, 2004, p. 226). This moral distinction, based on stereotypes of ethnic difference, led middle-class residents in Soulard, like others across the country, to develop discriminatory attitudes and promote unequal welfare policies toward the 'undeserving' (Bullock, 2008, p. 60). Such a moral distinction also came to personify the divide between an idyllic past and a troubled present. By contrast, the future was imagined as a time of rebirth, led by historic-preservationist heroes who would re-establish middle-class economies, organize community institutions, and save the neighbourhood's built fabric. The reality of revitalization was more complicated.

Dislocation of the Poor and Affordable Housing

In the late 1970s efforts to preserve the historic character of the district and the renewed availability of loans led to rising property values and increased tension over affordable housing in Soulard. In 1977 rents in the neighbourhood varied from $30 to $275 a month – with those at the lower end gradually disappearing, to the detriment of elderly tenants on fixed incomes (Anonymous, 1977b). By 1979, hundreds of new residents had moved to the area, and 350 out of its 1,100 structures had been renovated (Anonymous, 1979). These renovations and home purchases led to the dislocation of poor residents, who were priced out of higher-rent units or displaced by new homesteading owner-occupants.

From early in the process of Soulard's revitalization, some observers had worried about the displacement of longtime residents. At the Urban Neighborhoods Colloquium in St. Louis in 1974, Bob Brandhorst had joined social scientists in expressing concern that the 'mixed-income personality' of the neighbourhood was 'seriously threatened', and that the 'needs of the poor' would be 'sacrificed to the middle-class demand for security' (Schoenberg, 1974, pp. 12, 17, 58). The 1975 Soulard Restoration Plan also anticipated this dislocation, arguing that opportunities should be made available for low-income residents to remain in the neighbourhood by reporting displaced tenants and coordinating their move with the city's Centralized Relocation Agency (Community Development Commission, 1975b, p. 33).

By the late 1970s reports of dislocation also circulated in local newspapers. These articles noted 'sky-high prices squeezing buyers out' of the housing market, and argued that class differences were 'harmful to many established residents' who felt 'threatened' (Cohn, 1978, p. 15). In one particularly influential incident, Karen J. Mondale (a niece of then-US Vice President Walter Mondale), reported meeting several elderly tenants who had 'come up crying' because they were going to be evicted when their landlord sold their multiunit home (Anonymous, 1977b).

She convinced the middle-class homebuyers to back out of the purchase before escrow, and bought the home herself. After she renovated it, she allowed the tenants to stay using Section 8 rent subsidies. Concerned by the inaction of the SNIA and the SRG, she also began to advocate that all concerned citizens 'adopt' poor elderly neighbours and buy their homes as rental properties so they could remain as tenants (Anonymous, 1977a).

At first, the SRG acknowledged the concern with dislocation. In 1977 the group supported an infusion of federal money and loans for low-income homebuyers to help address the problem. It also organized a survey to determine 'the extent of displacement', and study 'alternative forms of housing' to decide what approaches it should advocate (SRG, 1978c, pp. 1–2). Nonetheless, the group argued that despite concern for the 'social costs of the back to the cities movement, we cannot allow our fear of success to frighten us off' (SRG, 1977a, p. 9). And while arguing that resources should be invested in the city – for the poor and the middle class alike – it insisted that the important mission of urban revitalization should not be sacrificed in the name of preventing dislocation.

As the tensions around dislocation increased in Soulard, some restorationists began to deny that displacement was even occurring. Because of its high vacancy rates, some SRG members treated the neighbourhood as a 'frontier', a social *tabula rasa* (SRG, 1977c, p. 9). Doubting accusations that new homebuyers were displacing the poor, they called for proof that displacement was even occurring (Young, 1979c, p. 7). One member wrote an op-ed article that derided the concerns, claiming that the only inhabitants being displaced were pigeons. As a parody, it called for the formation of a Pigeons for Equitable Housing Society (PEHS), and for government-subsidized rental roosts to address the 'hoards of middle-class restorationists [who] have moved in … without regard to the welfare of the pigeons' (SRG, 1979c, p. 6). While this article did not represent the sentiments of all restorationists, it showed the defensive posture that some within the SRG were taking towards accusations they were creating 'yuppie enclaves' (Anonymous, 1990a).

The rise of public awareness of the dislocation led to new controversies about how to address the affordability of housing in the neighbourhood. By the 1980s St. Louis city government was focused both on facilitating rental housing subsidies and building low-income infill housing in Soulard. SRG residents, however, argued that the neighbourhood was bearing too much of the city's affordable-housing burden, and that the supply of subsidized units should 'not exceed [the] demand' of displaced neighbourhood residents – thus attracting poor people from outside the

Figure 10.4. Proposed infill housing projects for Soulard used traditional row-house typologies, but were criticized for only using brick on the front façades. (*Source*: *St. Louis Globe Democrat*, April 1982, by courtesy of the St. Louis Mercantile Library)

area, whom they did not trust to share their values (Young, 1979a, pp. 9–10; Anonymous, 1980a). And, while the SRG grudgingly accepted affordable-housing projects which used federal Section 8 funding to rehabilitate historic structures, they were much more critical of new infill construction. In particular, it was argued that even when the massing and scale of infill townhouses was similar to traditional typologies, the aesthetic features and materials were often 'inconsistent' with the historic homes. Many such structures only had brick veneer on the front façade, and would use materials, like vinyl siding, prohibited by the codes for historic structures, elsewhere (Young, 1979b, p. 4) (figure 10.4).

Despite the SRG's resistance, the SNIA promoted the construction both of new Section 235 owner-occupied town homes and Section 8 family apartments in Soulard. They argued that this federally subsidized housing would allow rehabilitation to continue, while ensuring that displaced residents could find affordable units nearby. This debate about the quantity and quality of affordable and infill housing exhibited the two groups fundamentally different approaches to urban revitalization.

Enforcing Aesthetic Norms

These debates over the aesthetics of infill housing signified a shift towards stricter enforcement of historic codes in the early 1980s. The original Soulard Restoration Plan, passed by the city in 1975 with input from the community, had reflected a compromise between the SRG aesthetic values and the pleas by SNIA for flexibility. It specifically tried to 'unify' the 'varying interests' of the neighbourhood into 'a single planning unit to achieve a compromise acceptable to all' (Community Development Commission, 1975b, p. 32). Early discussions of the plan had highlighted concern that overly strict codes might make normal maintenance prohibitively expensive for owners and landlords, pricing poorer longtime residents out of the neighbourhood (Anonymous, 1976). The push for less restrictive codes reflected an attempt to prevent rental increases, evictions, or residents being forced to sell homes they could no longer afford to repair.

While the SNIA advocated more open-ended historic guidelines, the SRG wanted strict codes that would protect the historic character of buildings. And with some caveats, the 1975 Soulard Restoration Plan did reflect the SRG's aesthetic concerns. The code protected existing architectural details such as mansard roofs and dormer windows, and promoted the use of 'compatible' materials. It also prohibited 'imitation, artificial or simulated materials', such as aluminium or plastic siding or awnings (Community Development Commission, 1975a). Nonetheless, the plan was rather vague in its wording, often using nonbinding language such as 'not recommended' to discourage materials like chain-link fencing (figure 10.5). Meanwhile, code requirements for the height, setbacks, and

Figure 10.5. The 1975 Soulard Restoration Plan prohibited aluminium or plastic siding or awnings, and discouraged chain-link and wire-fabric fences (on the right) in favour of traditional materials like canvas and wrought iron (on the left).
(Source: Community Development Commission (1975), Soulard Restoration Plan, p. 30, by courtesy of Missouri History Museum, St. Louis)

façades of new infill buildings were tied to the character of nearby buildings on a block, rather than to a consistent standard, which allowed for some interpretation during enforcement. Overall, the plan reflected the idea that standards would protect the neighbourhood against 'garish' additions or 'lack of sensitivity', on the principle that it would be 'bad taste to mar the historical character' (Community Development Commission, 1975*b*, p. 33).

While the SRG did not focus strongly on code enforcement in the 1970s, by the 1980s the group expressed a vigorous interest in requiring building permits and penalizing violations (Anonymous, 1980*a*). As a wider group of homebuyers started moving to the area, tensions increased over matters of taste – with some clinging to antiquarianism and others embracing a more contemporary style (figure 10.6). The head of the SRG at the time, Peter Sortino, complained that even an expensive rehabilitation project often 'looks horrible'. Hoping building permits could reign in unruly rehabilitations, the SRG (1981) pressured their members to 'set

Figure 10.6. Some members of the Soulard Restoration Group were antiquarians, who decorated their homes in the Victorian style. (*Source*: *St. Louis Globe Democrat*, 26 September 1986, by courtesy of the St. Louis Mercantile Library)

an example' and get approval for even small repairs to their homes. One of the most public controversies over these aesthetic codes involved the Boy's Club, the local branch of a national non-profit organization, which provided afterschool recreation for 3,000 youths from around the area. In 1980 the SRG threatened legal proceedings to try to force the Boy's Club to remove a new $20,000 twelve-foot-high barbed-wire and chain-link 'safety' fence from around its sports fields. The SRG called it an 'eyesore' conjuring the image of 'a jail' (Anonymous, 1980b). The city eventually ruled that the barbed-wire had to be removed, but that the chain link could stay. This incident was characteristic of the SRG's increasingly vigilant approach to enforcing code violations – even against community groups.

By 1990 the SRG was pushing for a revision of the preservation code to clarify and strengthen its aesthetic guidelines for the neighbourhood. A spokesman, Fred Andres, defended these changes as necessary to address problems with long wait times to get permits, arbitrary committee rulings, and uncertainty about what would be accepted (Anonymous, 1990b). Over the past 15 years the codes for the various preservation districts in St. Louis had reflected 'subtle differences' in how strict and 'purist' to make their rehabilitation codes (Toft, 1977). Ideologically, the SRG's new proposals aimed to increase the purity of their approach, with the aim of restoring architectural structures to the style that might have been present at the neighbourhood's height. Andres (1990) argued that in order to 'preserve the heritage of our ... grandparents ... for our grandchildren', there was a need for codes with 'unambiguous language'. He further argued that current code enforcement was based on 'arbitrary judgments' that 'confuse homeowners'. Thus the 1975 codes 'must be replaced by ... fair, evenly imposed' guidelines for renovation. Using provocative language, he tried to persuade the public of the need for stricter codes by arguing that poorly constructed renovations 'brutalize once-handsome facades' with 'bricked-up doorways and aluminum awnings'. In these statements he tried to stake out the moral high ground by claiming to protect the rights of buildings and the interest of future generations, while ignoring the rights of the poor living in the neighbourhood in his own time.

In the face of these revision proposals, controversy arose over who should have the right to shape the codes. While a city agency, the Heritage and Design Committee, was responsible for evaluating code violations, the residents themselves also played a large role in enforcement. The Soulard Restoration Plan had tried to establish a citizen committee that would represent 'all neighborhood interests' using a 'dynamic' framework for shaping future development (Community Development Commission,

1975b, pp. 27, 32). And while the SRG did not necessarily represent the interests of the whole neighbourhood, they eventually came to assume this role. Robert Brandhorst and Joyce Sonn, from the SNIA, however, called the new code the 'tyranny of the minority'. And they insisted that the SRG 'who represent less than 100 of the 2,100 Soulard households', should not be able to 'force their aesthetic preferences on their neighborhood' just because they have more political pull in city hall. This debate led to the formation of the Soulard Committee for a Fair Historic Code, which conducted a survey showing that most residents believed 'they should be able to vote on any proposed changes' (Brandhorst and Sonn, 1990).

This concern about who had the power to make decisions regarding the code reflected a perceived middle-class bias within the SRG, whose members often seemed unaware and unsympathetic towards the needs of lower-income residents. In particular, the SRG seemed deaf to concerns of financial hardship. For example, replacing a roof with the recommended shingles cost $5,000 more than the prohibited roll roofing that many poorer residents typically would have preferred to use. SNIA organizers, by contrast, feared low-income residents would be 'driven out' by the new codes recommended by the SRG, because their requirements for expensive 'traditional' building materials increased the cost of home repairs. Brandhorst and Sonn (1990) thus argued that the code should remain vague and flexible in order to 'to fit everyone's pocketbooks and taste'.

One of the main underlying debates concerned whether preservation should only seek to protect homes from demolition or whether it should also regulate a class-based sense of taste. Brandhorst and the SNIA had originally supported historic preservation codes in the 1970s to save buildings from destruction. Their goal was to allow local renters to remain in their homes – protected from eviction and demolition orders by the city or negligent absentee landlords. However, Brandhorst and Sonn argued that the Heritage and Urban Design Commission, under the influence of the SRG, had overreached its authority not only by regulating demolitions and major renovations, but by requiring permits for ordinary maintenance and repair. They criticized the implementation of the codes for 'nit-picking' about paint colours and minor details. So, too, they balked at the hypocrisy of restricting the use of cheaper, modern materials by poor residents, while allowing more affluent homeowners to build trendy wooden decks that were 'no more historic than chain link fences'. This type of double standard showed that the new stricter code was less about protection of historic buildings than about class identity and 'matters of taste'. Thus, while the preservation purists at the SRG wanted to safeguard the original aesthetics of the building, they argued that the 'litmus test' for approving a new code should be whether it is necessary to protect the existence of the buildings and streetscapes (Brandhorst and Sonn, 1990).

Debate also arose as to whether dictating historic forms with preservation guidelines ran counter to the spontaneous diversity and affordability that had shaped the historic character of the neighbourhood. Brandhorst and Sonn emphasized that the neighbourhood, though 'visually harmonious', originally developed 'without architectural plans, building codes or design standards'. The materials chosen – brick, wrought iron, and wood – were chosen not only for aesthetics, but also because of 'their affordability and availability'. Brick, produced locally, was more affordable than stone, but more durable than wood, ensuring that 'structures were built to last' (Rowley, 1978, p. 32). Based on this logic, Brandhorst and Sonn argued that modern, economical materials should also be allowed. Rather than violating the history of the neighbourhood, they argued that roll roofing, chain-link fencing, and metal and fibreglass awnings and tool sheds represented the material culture of the place – a continuation of the tradition that had been developed by residents in the postwar period. This more open interpretation of historic preservation, which emphasized the social and cultural rather than aesthetic definition of conservation, aimed to 'preserve Soulard's melting-pot culture', not merely the built environment of 'its unique row house architecture' (Brandhorst and Sonn, 1990).

The Power to Define

Despite the SNIA's resistance, the SRG did successfully strengthen the Historic District Code, putting greater restrictions on the use of non-historic materials in repairs, renovations, and infill development. However, the SNIA was able to push through several low-income infill projects in the 1980s, which helped maintain the diverse character of the neighbourhood. In the end, the neighbourhood did indeed gentrify, but only partially, remaining somewhat integrated by class, ethnicity, and now (to some extent) by race. This diversity can be attributed at least in part to the SNIA and to the city's emphasis on building affordable housing, but it was also probably affected by the cooler real estate market endemic to shrinking cities like St. Louis.

Throughout the process of historic preservation and gentrification, the neighbourhood underwent a struggle to define a new identity that could address both its past and envisioned future. Both the SNIA and the SRG used historical narratives and identity politics to shape the way they approached urban revitalization. However, they did so with different methods, shaped by two divergent value systems – one focused on what Marxist scholars would call capitalist 'exchange value', and the other on communitarian 'use value' (Marx, 1936, p. 45; Logan and Molotch, 1987, p. 20). The Soulard Restoration Group (SRG) defined the neighbourhood through its physical appearance, particularly as this pertained to the preservation of what they saw as its traditional French-style row houses. This group of formerly suburban, middle-class professionals applied the familiar subdivision logic of codes, covenants, and restrictions (CCRs) – here in the form of a historic district code – to try to enforce a standardized vision of beauty and taste to promote real estate sales. By defining what aspects of history and the built environment were worth preserving, they created a landscape of exclusion, from which they tried to eradicate the inconvenient social practices and material culture of longtime working-class residents. Its members justified these exclusionary aesthetics, which cleansed the neighbourhood into a respectable product for consumption, in the name of exchange value: tax revenue and property values. However, this financial incentive was often cloaked in more sentimental concerns such as nostalgia for the past and the dignity of quaint historic buildings.

The incomplete success of the SRG in enforcing historic codes has contributed to the continuing diverse class character of the neighbourhood today. The countering force of the SNIA, which defined the neighbourhood socially and through 'use value', has also helped celebrate and maintain the diversity of the people and place, including its ethnic heritage and working-class culture. It attempted to realize what has been termed 'social preservation' through symbolic preservation of local culture, such as festivals and artwork; political action, including organizing protests; and private investments in individuals and property that were part of the existing community (Brown-Saracino, 2010, p. 104). Nevertheless, the pride of local middle-class residents today, who claim the diversity of the neighbourhood as a type of cultural capital, masks decades of class conflict in Soulard. These have concerned whose neighbourhood it really was, and who had the power to define how and for whom its history would be preserved.

Notes

1. For the purpose of this chapter, a 'hippy' may be understood as a person whose unorthodox lifestyle is premised on challenging accepted standards of economic value. A 'yuppie', derived from the phrase 'young urban professional', may be understood as one who seeks to challenge cultural orthodoxy, by eschewing the

normative suburban lifestyle, but who retains concern for accepted economic values.
2. In St. Louis the term 'hoosier' is used to mean 'white trash'. The term dates back to the 1930s when Indianans worked as scabs during a strike of St. Louis workers. It has become a generalized term for denigrating low-income whites who migrate to St. Louis from rural areas.

References

AlSayyad, N. (2001) *Consuming Tradition, Manufacturing Heritage: Global Norms and Urban Forms in the Age of Tourism*. London: Routledge.
Andres, F. (1990) Guidelines would protect historic area. *St. Louis Globe Democrat*, 7 June.
Anonymous (1973) City's old world neighborhood. *St. Louis Post Dispatch*, 25 November.
Anonymous (1974) Soulard Sunday a real bell-ringer. *St. Louis Globe Democrat*, 13 July.
Anonymous (1976) Making things work in Soulard. *St. Louis Post Dispatch*, 11 January.
Anonymous (1977a) Mondale's niece saves elderly persons from eviction. *St. Louis Globe Democrat*, 1 September.
Anonymous (1977b) Soulard's rise is displacing low income renters, group says. *St. Louis Post Dispatch*, 19 September.
Anonymous (1979) Soulard's modern face lift. *St. Louis Globe Democrat*, 11 May.
Anonymous (1980a) Limit of subsidized housing sought in Soulard. *St. Louis Globe Democrat*, 4 June.
Anonymous (1980b) Soulard group, Boys Club, battle over 12-foot fence. *St. Louis Globe Democrat*, 1 April.
Anonymous (1990a) Soulard battles over housing codes. *St. Louis Globe Democrat*, 7 June.
Anonymous (1990b) Soulard needs new code, says some residents. *St. Louis Globe Democrat*, 1 February.
Anonymous (1992) The soul of Soulard. *St. Louis Globe Democrat*, 24 September.
Bourdieu, P. (1984 [1979]) *Distinction: A Social Critique of the Judgment of Taste*, translator R. Nice. Cambridge, MA: Harvard University Press.
Brandhorst, R.J. (1976) *Pilot Study to Determine the Feasibility of Developing a Cottage Industry Program in the Soulard Historic District*. St. Louis, MO: Youth, Education, and Health in Soulard, Inc.
Brandhorst, R. and Sonn, J. (1990) Tyranny of the minority. *St. Louis Globe Democrat*, 7 June.
Brown-Saracino, J. (2010) *A Neighborhood that Never Changes: Gentrification, Social Preservation, and the Search for Authenticity*. Chicago, IL: University of Chicago Press.
Bry, C. (1978) Senior citizens crochet their way to Soulard. *St. Louis Globe Democrat*, 3 August.
Bullock, H.E. (2008) Justifying inequality: a social psychological analysis of beliefs about poverty and the poor, in Lin, A.C. and Harris, D.R. (eds.) *The Colors of Poverty: Why Racial and Ethnic Disparities Persist*. New York, NY: Russell Sage, pp. 52–75.
Bush, M.E.L. (2011) *Everyday Forms of Whiteness: Understanding Race in a 'Post-Racial' World*. Lanham, MD: Rowman & Littlefield.
City of St. Louis (1970) *Program Area 16*. St. Louis: City of St. Louis.
Cohn, L. (1978) Soulard historic district: the new must exist with the old. *Subject to Change*, 26 October.

Community Development Commission (1975a) *Development Plan for the Soulard Historic District*. St. Louis, MO: Community Development Commission.
Community Development Commission (1975b) *Soulard Restoration Plan*. St. Louis, MO: Community Development Commission.
Corzine, J. and Dabrowski, I. (1975) *The Ethnic Factor and Neighborhood Stability in St. Louis: The Czechs in Soulard and South St. Louis*. St. Louis, MO: Washington University.
Corzine, J. *et al.* (1975) Soulard, in *Ethnic Heritage Studies Colloquium*. St. Louis, MO: Social Science Institute, Washington University, 10 May, pp. 29–58.
Duncan, J.S. and Duncan, N.G. (2004) *Landscapes of Privilege: The Politics of the Aesthetic in an American Suburb*. New York: Routledge.
Hobsbawm, E. and Ranger, T. (eds.) (1983) *The Invention of Tradition*. Cambridge: Cambridge University Press.
Hurwitz, J.G. (1975) The Politics of Participatory Planning in Soulard. Masters thesis, Washington University, St. Louis, MO.
International Council on Monuments and Sites (1997) *The American Mosaic: Preserving a Nation's Heritage*. Detroit, MI: Wayne State University Press.
Jacobson, M.F. (2009) *Roots Too: White Ethnic Revival in Post-Civil Rights America*. Cambridge, MA: Harvard University Press.
Lefebvre, H. (1996) *Writings on Cities*. Oxford: Blackwell.
Ley, D. (1980) Liberal ideology and the postindustrial city. *Annals of the Association of American Geographers*, **70**, pp. 238–258.
Logan, J.R. and Molotch, H.L. (1987) *Urban Fortunes: The Political Economy of Place*. Berkeley, CA: University of California Press.
Lowenthal, D. (1999) *The Past is a Foreign Country*. Cambridge: Cambridge University Press.
Marx, K. (1936) *Capital: A Critique of Political Economy*. New York: The Modern Library.
Miller, Z.L. and Tucker, B. (1998) *Changing Plans for America's Inner Cities: Cincinnati's Over the Rhine Neighborhood*. Columbus, OH: Ohio State University Press.
Mink, G. and O'Connor, A. (2004) *Poverty in The United States: An Encyclopedia of History, Politics, and Policy*. Santa Barbara, CA: ABC-CLIO.
Raiche, S.J. (1972) *Soulard Neighborhood District National Registrar of Historic Places Inventory Nomination Form*. St. Louis, MO.
Rowley, C. (1977) Selling Soulard. *Soulard Restorationist*, **2**(9), pp. 6–9.
Rowley, C. (1978) Soulard, in *Progress in Historic Preservation*. St. Louis: East-West Gateway Coordinating Council St. Louis (Illinois-Missouri) Metropolitan Area, pp. 32–42.
Sagert, K.B. (2007) *The 1970s*. Westport, CT: Greenwood.
Schoenberg, S. (ed.) (1974) *Urban Neighborhoods Colloquium*. St. Louis, MO: Washington University.
Shinkle, F. (1972) A tale of two city neighborhoods. *Pictures, St. Louis Post Dispatch*, 16 April.
Smith, J.C. (1983) *Ethnic Genealogy: A Research Guide*. Westport, CT: Greenwood.
Smith, N. (1979) Toward a theory of gentrification: a back to the city movement by capital not people. *Journal of the American Planners Association*, **45**, pp. 538–548.
SRG (Soulard Restoration Group) (1977a) Back to the city. *Soulard Restorationist*, **2**(3), p. 9.
SRG (1977b) *If You Crossed the Mississippi in 1860, Where Would You Settle?* (pamphlet). St. Louis, MO: Soulard Restoration Group.
SRG (1977c) Who is interested in Soulard? *Soulard Restorationist*, **2**(7), p. 12.

SRG (1978a) Coming home. *Soulard Restorationist*, **3**(4), pp. 9–10.
SRG (1978b) New Orleans, an elixir. *Soulard Restorationist*, **3**(3), p. 12.
SRG (1978c) Update on Section 8 and the SRG proposal. *Soulard Restorationist*, **3**(5), pp. 1–2.
SRG (1979a) Dear Abner. *Soulard Restorationist*, **4**(1), p. 7.
SRG (1979b) Dear Abner. *Soulard Restorationist*, **4**(7), p. 12.
SRG (1979c) Housing needed for displaced pigeons. *Soulard Restorationist*, **4**(6), p. 6.
SRG (1981) Warning to all SRG members. *Soulard Restorationist*, **10**(13).
St. Louis Landmarks Association (1973) *Landmarks Association Letter*, **8**(3).
Stepick, A. *et al*. (2011) Becoming American, in *Handbook of Identity Theory and Research*. New York: Springer, pp. 867–894.
Sutin, P. (1995) Mardi Gras neighbors survive crowds. *Globe Democrat*, 27 February.
Toft, C.H. (1975) *Soulard: The Ethnic Heritage of an Urban Neighborhood*. St, Louis, MO: Social Science Institute, Washington University.
Toft, C.H. (1977) Letter to Charlene Prost, 28 December. St. Louis, MO: Missouri History Museum Collections, Charlene Prost, B.12. F.7.
Toft, C.H. (1988) *St. Louis Landmarks and Historic Districts*. St. Louis, MO: Landmarks Association of St. Louis, Inc.
Young, P. (1979a) Notes form the brick house. *Soulard Restorationist*, **4**(3), pp. 9–10.
Young, P. (1979b) Notes form the brick house. *Soulard Restorationist*, **4**(4), p. 4.
Young, P. (1979c) Notes form the brick house. *Soulard Restorationist*, **4**(6), p. 7.

Chapter 11

Cosmopolitan Architects and Discourses of Tradition and Modernity in Post-Independence Africa

Jennifer Gaugler

> *Upon Europe's 'discovery' of lands and cultures in Asia and Africa, historiography essentialized and froze their architectural character, even as cultural upheavals transformed the landscapes.*
>
> Hosagrahar, 2005, p. 4

In colonizing Africa, Europeans set up a binary of the 'modern' (which they claimed as their own) and the 'traditional' (which they assigned to others). In theory, this binary was based on a directional notion of progress, with the traditional as the origin and the modern as the endpoint. Following this model, early colonial policies took an approach of assimilation, in which the traditions of the 'natives' were to be broken down in the interest of 'modernization' and 'civilization'. However, when the colonial grip started to loosen between the First and Second World Wars, administrations shifted their strategy towards preserving traditions in order to pacify native populations, freeze them in a state of subjugation, and thereby attempt to quell resistance. As a result, many African traditions were assigned a status entirely outside the trajectory of progress. Europeans essentially declared their colonized territories to be primitive, changeless places where time was frozen; and they thus denied residents of these colonies any claim to history or the capacity to become modern without European help.

A similar approach has characterized conventional architecture histories, in which the dissemination of modernism is typically framed as a diasporic movement with Western origins. Most architecture historians (inadvertently or otherwise) seem to echo the colonizer's belief that 'traditional' societies could only mimic, adopt, or adapt forms of modernism. Little attention has been paid particularly to African 'indigenous modernities' – meaning the ways native African architects *originated* their own ideas of modernity.[1] Instead, most analyses of sub-Saharan African architecture focus on colonial and Tropical Modernist designs produced by European expatriates or on the assimilation of European ideas by local African architects. This typical view of modernism as a one-way trajectory from Europe to Africa has long ignored the ways that modernism was appropriated for local objectives by African architects and used in ways unforeseen by Europeans.

During the post-independence period on the African continent, there were scattered sparks of an emerging African architecture that did not regard modernism as an imposed condition, but as a dialogue. For certain native African architects, Western modernism could, in a sense, be grafted onto local culture. Rooted initially in one place, it could then be planted in a new one, free to grow as needed and become something different. These architects claimed *both* tradition and modernity as their medium. They did not necessarily think in terms of 'African' tradition or 'Western' modernity, because in borrowing traditions from around the world, they conceptualized their own notion of modernity founded on global engagement.

This chapter illustrates this complex negotiation by examining the work of Demas Nwoko, Anthony Bosco Almeida, and Beda Amuli. Even though these African architects lived on opposite sides of the continent (Nwoko in Nigeria, and Almeida and Amuli in Tanzania), they all worked in the context of recent independence movements and engaged in important postcolonial identity discourses in nations that sought to position themselves in a global context. These identity discourses were not yet articulated as legibly in sub-Saharan Africa as in northern Africa or South Africa, so there was more room for exploration. Furthermore, these architects were true cosmopolitans, all three having been exposed to international education and travel that shaped their later work. Their resulting ability to pick and choose from different references, as well as generate new and original ideas, begs the questions 'Whose tradition?' and 'Whose modernity?'

The Evolution of African Modernism

In Africa, 'modernism' as a particular cultural movement and architectural style was imposed by external forces. These originated with European colonialism, but continued after independence first with the Cold War struggle over the so-called 'Third World', and then with IMF- and World Bank-driven programmes of foreign aid and structural readjustment. Throughout these eras, Africa was a particularly important site for Western modernism, because modernism was enlisted to accomplish major goals: to erase signs of indigenous culture, commercialize popular tastes, and facilitate social and economic control.

However, it would be false to assume that the concept of modernity has no roots on the African continent. For example, the architect and researcher Antoni Folkers (2013) has made a compelling argument that ideas of modernity were expressed in the buildings of some precolonial African rulers, such as the lightweight steel and cast-iron structures of the palace built in the late 1880s by the Ethiopian emperor Menelik II. In addition, although modernism was originally a colonial project, the late 1950s and early 1960s brought major change to the continent in the form of political independence. With nationhood, new African governments took over the project of modernism in an effort to define identities, unify disparate ethnic groups, and assert their equity and competitiveness on a global stage. During this era, national identities were often tenuously defined; nonetheless, many governments commissioned architecture to symbolize the stability they sought to establish. Indeed, the architectural historian Nnamdi Elleh (2002, p. 9) has suggested that 'architecture [was] employed as a tool for fudging postcolonial national identity in many newly independent African states'.

The nature of architectural practice itself also changed. In post-independence Africa, Johan Lagae (2011, p.1) has written, 'building and planning evolved from design professions at the service of a colonial agenda to more global practices of consultancy within a framework of emerging international developmentalism … with new agents coming to the fore'. And while their numbers were still low in the early post-independence period, some of these new agents were indigenous African architects. How did they become involved in the project of modernity?

Among Africans immediately following the end of the colonial era, a growing sense of cultural nationalism developed into two competing views on the arts and architecture. One advocated that traditional buildings should be referenced as precedents for a new African architecture, while the other argued that, to move towards the future, traditional buildings should be left behind as remnants of the past (Elleh, 2002, p. 17). Across Africa – a battleground of Cold War politics and aid programmes from 1950 to 1970 – the First and Second Worlds also competed to promote their respective ideologies. As a result, some African architects divested their work of anything that could be labelled as 'African' in order to align themselves more closely with the side they perceived to embody the future.

However, other post-independence African architects confronted these imported ideals and emerged with a distinctly African form of modernism. For them, 'modern' did not mean simply mimicking Western or Soviet models, but rather an attempt at *global* engagement without losing relevance to local context. They thus declared that the project of being modern could be as much African as it was European. These architects have largely been ignored by 'global' architecture histories, even though they engaged deeply with the world beyond Africa, typically having very cosmopolitan career trajectories.

A photograph from the *Jewish Floridian* newspaper in 1960, for example, showed the Tanzanian architect Beda Amuli studying at the Technion in Israel, an institution supported in part by Jewish donors from the United States (figure 11.1). It provides evidence today that Amuli was part of an international network – a condition that would not have been unusual at the time, because there were few architecture programmes in the nations of sub-Saharan Africa. Without options in their home countries during the early decades following independence, aspiring African architects almost always went abroad for (at least part of) their training. Their places of study included India for Anthony Bosco Almeida, Paris and Japan for Demas Nwoko, and Israel for Beda Amuli. Of course, foreign study was often made feasible by their elite social and economic status. For example, Nwoko was born into a royal lineage, his grandfather having been a village founder and his father the head of a town (Godwin and Hopwood, 2008, p. 15). Likewise, Almeida's family owned a trading firm and coconut plantation (ArchiAfrika, 2008).

It is likewise important to note that these architects' cosmopolitanism was not necessarily dependent on physical mobility. Benedict Anderson, in his influential *Imagined Communities* (1991), argued that print capitalism – made possible by the invention of the printing press and the development of capitalist markets – contributed directly to the rise of nationalism, as nation-states became 'imagined communities' through the wide circulation of ideas in a common language. And extending Anderson's concept of the imagined community to an imperial context, Partha Mitter (2009, p.

Figure 11.1. This photograph from a 1960 edition of the *Jewish Floridian* newspaper is evidence that African architects were part of international networks of funding, education, and influence. (*Source: Jewish Floridian*)

25) has suggested the notion of the 'virtual cosmopolis' to describe 'the transmission of knowledge between center and periphery [that] took place through an imagined community' in the era of colonialism. Through printed text and drawings, the 'virtual cosmopolitan' in the colonies was able to engage with ideas that came from the metropole without ever going there. For example, before Nwoko enrolled in art school as a young man (and before he had the opportunity to travel to France or Japan), he was able to order technical publications from the United Kingdom with which to study the load-bearing masonry of Christopher Wren, the stonework of Gothic cathedrals, and the Renaissance-era St. Paul's Cathedral (Godwin and Hopwood, 2008, p. 15). Thus, even when they could not travel abroad, these architects had the means to engage actively with cultural ideas from other parts of the world. Mitter (2009, p. 26) thus argued that, 'the reception of Western ideas in the peripheries, and in colonized countries in particular, was an active process that centered on the agency of the colonized'.

Critical Regionalism in the African Context

Their cosmopolitan trajectories made these architects particularly sensitive to the negotiation between the local and the global – and, more specifically, to how architecture can preserve local identity in a globally connected world. Their work can thus be considered to have been a form of 'regionalism' – an approach to design seeking to mediate between global and local architectural languages.

In 1955, just before many African nations gained their independence, the French philosopher Paul Ricœur wrote an essay titled 'Universal Civilization and National Cultures'. In it he described the challenges involved in reconciling the local and the universal:

> Thus we come to the crucial problem confronting nations just rising from underdevelopment. In order to get on the road toward modernization, is it necessary to jettison the old cultural past which has been the raison d'être of a nation?... Whence the paradox: on the one hand, it [the nation] has to root itself in the soil of its past, forge a national spirit, and unfurl this spiritual and cultural revendication before the colonialist's personality. But in order to take part in modern civilization, it is necessary at the same time to take part in scientific, technical, and political rationality, something which very often requires the pure and simple abandon of a whole cultural past. It is a fact: every culture cannot sustain and absorb the shock of modern civilization. There is the paradox: how to become modern and to return to sources; how to revive an old, dormant civilization and take part in universal civilization...

The architectural critic and historian Kenneth Frampton quoted this passage in his *Modern Architecture: A Critical History* (2007, p. 314). He went on to suggest that within the field of architecture, 'critical regionalism' might provide a solution to the predicament, posed by Ricœur, of 'how to become modern and to return to sources'.

The term critical regionalism was first introduced by the architects Liane Lefaivre and Alexander Tzonis in 1981. For them, it embodied a call for designers to think critically about how to welcome exchange with global influences while valuing the uniqueness of the region and the worth of its physical, social, and cultural resources (Tzonis and Lefaivre, 1981). Frampton expanded upon this concept in a 1983 essay, 'Towards a Critical Regionalism: Six Points for an Architecture of Resistance' (Frampton and Foster, 1983). As discussed in his essay, regionalist architecture engages with modernism, but is also tied to geographical and cultural context. It thus strives to counter the placelessness and ahistoricism of the International Style, but it also rejects the whimsical or superficial ornamentation characteristic of postmodernism. Frampton later argued that while 'opposed to the sentimental simulation of local vernacular', critical regionalist work may 'insert reinterpreted vernacular elements as disjunctive episodes within the whole' (Frampton, 2007). Frampton, however, largely illustrated these positions with examples from such European architects as Jørn Utzon and Alvar Aalto.

Both during and after colonialism, Africa was a laboratory for regionalist architectural explorations. For example, European architects experimented with importing modernism – but with modifications to make it more climatically appropriate. This led to the birth of a style known as Tropical Modernism, as practiced by Maxwell Fry and Jane Drew, Otto Koenigsberger, and other Western architects. However, African architects were also exploring regionalism in a variety of other ways. The relatively unknown history of African modernist architecture shows that, although the concept of critical regionalism may be best known through the work of Westerners, its basic tenets are by no means exclusively theirs. For example, the theory of 'natural synthesis' developed by the Zaria Art Society in Nigeria in 1960 proposed a similar approach *two decades* before the term 'critical regionalism' was coined by Tzonis and Lefaivre. After Nigeria won its independence, the group's manifesto called for an art that neither fell back on old ways nor imitated European art, but that thoughtfully engaged with tradition while incorporating practices suitable for a new society:

The artist is essentially an individual working within a particular social background and guided by the philosophy of life of his society. I do not agree with those who advocate international art philosophy; I disagree with those who live in Africa and ape European artists. Future generations of Africans will scorn their efforts. Our new society calls for a synthesis of old and new, of functional art and art for its own sake. (Okeke, 1960)

The manifesto also specifically rejected the machinistic element of Western modernism, and it called attention to the unprecedented circumstances of a new post-independence social order:

Western art today is generally in confusion. Most of the artists have failed to realize the artists' mission to mankind. Their art has ceased to be human. The machine, symbol of science, material wealth and of the space age has since been enthroned. What form of feelings, human feelings, can void space inspire in a machine artist? It is equally futile copying our old art heritages, for they stand for our old order. Culture lives by change. Today's social problems are different from yesterday's, and we shall be doing grave disservice to Africa and mankind by living in our fathers' achievements. For this is like living in an entirely alien cultural background. (Okeke, 1960)

The Zaria Art Society developed its theory of 'natural synthesis' according to these principles, suggesting that modernism could combine the native or indigenous with the imported or borrowed (Okeke-Agulu and Udechukwu, 2012, p. 1).

In the decades that followed, work produced by Demas Nwoko, Anthony Bosco Almeida, and Beda Amuli arguably provided an answer to Ricœur's paradox of 'how to become modern and to return to sources', offering a more culturally sensitive synthesis of the local and the imported than the bulk of work by Europeans. These native Africans were responding to the core values of their societies – using new technology but at the same time respecting cultural heritage. Their approach combined the native and imported in a way that allowed for growth and modernization, and it related back to traditional culture, but without relying on imitation or kitsch. This leads to a key question: what distinguished the work of these African architects from their Western contemporaries?

Practising African Modernism

In his 1963 book *New Architecture in Africa*, the art historian Udo Kultermann suggested that the work of African architects was shaped by 'limited means', an 'intimate knowledge of the terrain and of the climatic conditions', as well as by a familiarity with certain 'social requirements'. As a result of these factors, their work was distinguished by 'an imaginatively free conception of spatial design, a style which presents each individual construction as a plastic entity, and an emphasis on the importance of colour for the general effect created by an architectural unit' (Kultermann, 1963, p. 8). Three particular qualities in the work of Nwoko, Almeida, and Amuli – materiality, expressionism, and discontinuity – can be used to extend Kultermann's analysis. These factors helped mould a dialectic between native and imported, local and global, tradition and modernity.

In an edited *festschrift* (celebration) of the work of Nwoko, the Nigerian scholar David Aradeon (2012, p. 37) argued that 'in the architecture of our built environment, construction material is the popularly recognized code for tradition'. This was particularly true in sub-Saharan Africa, where the contrast between traditional and imported materials may be great. However, all three architects profiled here performed material translations that allowed the transubstantiation of traditional building methods into new 'modern' (i.e. Western) ones. Arguably, this strategy implies recognition that new materials could be more durable, less expensive, or more climatically appropriate. However, material translation also provided them with a means to bridge between the native and the imported. It was a way to acknowledge the inevitable adoption of the foreign, but to resist a complete takeover, and to preserve local forms and aesthetics.

Of the three architects, Demas Nwoko explored materiality in a particularly thoughtful way with respect to tradition. Born in the village of Idumuje Ugboko in Nigeria in 1935, he aspired to become an architect as a young man, but found that architectural training in Nigeria was more akin to a course in technical draftsmanship, stunting the medium's expressive capacity. Feeling that he would be better informed by exploring other spatial arts, he then switched to the art department of the Nigerian College of Arts, Science, and Technology (Godwin and Hopwood, 2008, p. 15). Near the completion of his schooling, Nwoko was awarded a scholarship from the French Embassy in 1961 to spend twelve months in Paris, where he studied theatre, stage design, and fresco painting. In the world of theatre production, Nwoko found an ideal vehicle for combining traditional elements of African culture with contemporary design innovations. On his return from Paris in 1962, he took a position as a lecturer in the School of Drama at the University of Ibadan in Nigeria, where he taught theatre arts until 1978.

Although he worked in theatre, sculpture, painting, and publishing, Nwoko still found himself drawn to building. And in 1964 he received grants to travel to both the United States and Japan, where he was interested to find that the woodwork of Japanese architecture displayed an 'affinity with traditional African architecture' (Godwin and Hopwood, 2008, p. 15). In 1967 he began work on the design of a New Culture Studios arts centre in Ibadan, and he subsequently went on to produce designs for a range of buildings including monasteries, cultural centres, theatres, and residences. He was never formally registered as an architect, but moved fluidly throughout his career between different disciplines.

At the time Nwoko was graduating from university and beginning his career, Nigeria was going through major political upheaval. The country gained its independence from Britain on 1 October 1960, after an independence struggle that had profoundly influenced the mindset and artistic production of Nwoko and his colleagues. At the Nigerian College, Nwoko had been a founding member of the Zaria Art Society, which developed the theory of 'natural synthesis'; this was a concept he would continue to develop throughout his career. As he wrote in *The*

Impoverished Generation (1992, p. 30), 'No longer under covert pressure to adopt foreign cultures ... we are under obligation to look inward. But that means searching for independent and unique values in our culture to hinge our personality on to achieve a distinct identity in the world community'. Nwoko's architecture represents transformation or evolution by the combination of the local/traditional with the global/modern – but always the essence of identity is preserved.

Nwoko's design for the Akenzua Cultural Center (Arts Theater) in Benin City, Nigeria, provides an early expression of an African modernism that was moving away from a two-way conversation with Europe to a broader engagement with global references. According to Nnimmo Bassey (2012, p. 171) the design sought to create 'a model African Playhouse'. Nwoko first built a mini-theatre at his New Culture Studio to see whether he could re-create the acoustics of an ancient Greek theatre without the use of elaborate acoustic panelling and engineering. Then, after this test was successful, he began work on the Akenzua Cultural Center in 1973. Ultimately, his design used both classical Greek and Japanese motifs to create a new kind of design language. As mentioned, its layout was based in part on the acoustic achievements of theatres on the Acropolis at Athens. But its front façade features a pair of stacked roofs, with the upper one having slightly upturned corners that recalled a Japanese temple (examples of which Nwoko would have seen on his trip to Japan) (Bassey, 2012, pp. 170, 174). However, the cultural centre is also situated opposite the *oba's* (king's) palace on the city's central square, and from this position it engages in a dialogue with Nigeria's past through its materiality. Specifically, its horizontally grooved, red-brown sandcrete blocks, with recessed cement joints, echoed the fluted walls of the *oba's* palace, thus reflecting Nigerian heritage.

Another of Nwoko's designs provides even more compelling evidence of this effort to translate local aesthetic sense into modern forms and materials. In his design for the Miss Pearce Chapel (begun in 1987, never completed), he made clear allusion to the traditional Igbo architecture of Nigeria, but with the use of new materials such as concrete and corrugated metal (figures 11.2 and 11.3). The chapel's high roof and geometrically patterned concrete reference the steeply pitched roofs and elaborate wood door carvings of traditional Igbo houses. However, the spatial proportions of the chapel and its cruciform plan are also reminiscent of churches from the Italian Renaissance (Godwin and Hopwood, 2008: p.78). Nwoko's addition of crossed arches in the chapel is also an allusion to the *baldachin*, the canopy over the altar in a European cathedral.

Figure 11.2. Demas Nwoko's Miss Pearce Chapel deftly negotiates between references to traditional Igbo houses and to European ecclesiastic architecture. (*Source*: Godwin and Hopwood, 2008; *photo*: Kelechi Amadi-Obi)

Figure 11.3. Traditional Igbo houses had large, steeply pitched roofs and elaborate wood carving. These features are reflected – but materially translated – in the Miss Pearce Chapel. (*Photo*: Edward Rowland Chadwick, *c*. 1927–1943)

The Miss Pearce Chapel is one of the clearest examples of Nwoko's deft negotiation between traditional Nigerian building and the architectural styles of other cultures (in this case, European Christianity). While the materials used are quite different from those of the traditional Igbo house, there are parallels between the heaviness of the chapel's concrete and the house's clay/mud walls, and between the lightness of the chapel's grooved metal sheets and the house's thatched roof. Through the negotiation of materiality Nwoko made reference both to the traditions of his own Nigerian culture and to the European culture of his Catholic clients, combining them into something entirely new.

Although working on the other side of the African continent, the Tanzanian architect Anthony Bosco Almeida developed a similar attitude towards the combination of the traditional and the modern. Almeida wrote that a purely traditionalist approach could only be relevant if nothing had changed between the previous generation and the current one (Almeida, 2005, p. 127). However, he also did not believe in unthinkingly adopting Western modernism. Almeida considered his 'Eleventh Commandment' (which he attributed to the Chinese 'Studio Buddha') to be: 'Except to an ignoramus or intellectualist, nothing imitative can equal that which is imitated. Instead of imitating effects, search for the principles that made them original and own your own effects' (Almeida, 2005, p. 127; Sharp, 2005, p. 78). In this regard, Folkers (2010, p. 251) commented that 'Almeida represents an architecture adapted to the local climate and the natural environment, without losing faith in the universally valid principles of the modern movement'.

Almeida was born in Tanzania (then the British colony of Tanganyika) in 1921 to parents from Goa, a state on the West coast of India. As a young man, he travelled to Bombay, India, to attend architecture school from 1941 to 1947. There he studied the work of Frank Lloyd Wright, Mies van der Rohe, Le Corbusier, and Louis Kahn, as well as the 'regional characteristics of Goa and Indian cultures' (Sharp, 2005, p. 76). In 1948 he became an associate of the Royal Institute of British Architects and returned home to Tanzania (which was still a colony), where he opened his own architectural practice in 1950 (Burssens, 2005).

When Tanganyika achieved independence in 1961 (and subsequently united with Zanzibar to form the new nation of Tanzania), Julius Nyerere became the first prime minister of the new socialist government. As opposed to classical socialism, Nyerere believed in sharing economic resources in a 'traditional' African way, and called for the preservation of the 'traditional African values' of a classless society. According to Pieter Burssens (2005, p.

120), Almeida began to design architecture that was 'in accordance with the socialist ideology of Nyerere: low-rise, modest, stripped [of] any fringes, designed economically to function but not to impose'. In conjunction with Almeida's own self-professed frugality and admiration for modernism, this led to numerous simple yet elegant designs. While working with a modernist palette of horizontal slabs and clear structural expression, Almeida used devices like overhangs and screens to create shaded porches and breezeways that were suitable for a tropical climate.

The Central Library in Dar es Salaam, designed in 1968, was an opportunity for Almeida to create a building that reflected the socialist ethos of Tanzania at the time (figure 11.4). Almeida wrote of the project that, 'being the first Library of its kind for Tanzania, whose people had now begun to enjoy education and its benefits, [I] wanted the building to appear to call the people to come in' (Burssens, 2005, p. 122). For this reason, Almeida designed a non-imposing structure built at a modest, human scale. The building has two storeys, but due to strong horizontal bands that project from the façade, it reads more as an elevated single-storey structure. The screen is one feature that revealed Almeida's multiple, varied influences: it was inspired in part by Le Corbusier's *brises-soileil* but also by architects in India who used sun-shading devices for climate control and to create patterns of light and shadow (Sharp, 2005). In addition, the curved

Figure 11.4. Anthony Almeida designed the Central Library to suit both the local climate and contemporary political circumstances, but the building also references a variety of architects and projects from regions around the world. (*Photo*: Joep Mol, architect)

pattern painted on infill panels along the base of the building might have been at home in Oscar Niemeyer's work in Brasilia.[2] Thus the design of the Central Library was both local and global. It was optimally designed for the climate of Dar es Salaam and was influenced by the specific political circumstances of Tanzania's immediate post-independence period, but it also made reference to a variety of architects and projects from regions around the world. In it Almeida adapted a myriad of influences to create a building that was both of the world but also uniquely its own.

In 1975 Almeida was commissioned to design an interdenominational Joint Christian Chapel for the University of Dar es Salaam (Sharp, 2005, p. 77). The plan of the church is relatively simple, with a central chapel flanked by two side chapels. But the building is remarkably sculptural, with tall, thin windows and vertical projections that provide an expressive verticality, and a cantilevered concrete roof that pulls the whole composition together. Its deep overhang shades the main space from the sun, but clerestory openings allow indirect light to enter the sanctuary and warm air to rise and escape. And the almost mystical effect of the roof levitating above the walls is even more pronounced on the inside than on the exterior (figure 11.5). Although the exterior of the chapel is white, coloured glass windows tint its interior with warm shades of pink, blue, and yellow.

Like many of Nwoko's projects, Almeida's Joint Christian Chapel is a highly expressionist work.[3] Although the 'floating' roof and deep

Figure 11.5. The roof of Anthony Almeida's Joint Christian Chapel seems to float above the walls, evoking a divine power. (*Photo*: Francesca Snelling)

overhang are climactically appropriate, these elements also seem to evoke a divine power. Indeed, the roof seems to hover over the church and to 'embrace' the side chapels – expressing a protective benevolence toward the congregation inside. This kind of stylistic, abstract representation of a spiritual subject is a hallmark of traditional African art.[4] With the design of this building, Almeida negotiated between Western geometric rationality and African expressionist spirituality, creating a building that is both suited to its particular context, and yet at the same time otherworldly.

Beda Amuli also used expressionism to bring the essence of traditional spaces or cultural practices into modernist structures, using experiential qualities rather than superficial imagery. Amuli was born in 1938 in colonial Tanganyika, and was the first native African from there to study architecture at the Royal Technical College of East Africa in Nairobi, Kenya. In his second year, Amuli won a scholarship to the Technion Institute of Technology in Israel, and when he enrolled in a full-time programme in 1960 he became its first African student. He was also selected for an exchange programme that sent him to Utrecht, Holland, in the summer after his third year. After completing his degree, Amuli was hired by Zevet International Architects of Tel Aviv, and sent back to Tanzania to supervise construction of the Kilimanjaro Hotel. He oversaw several other projects over the next few years, before starting his own private practice in 1969 (Kanywanyi, 2011).

The effect of exposure to Western modernism is clearly present in Amuli's design of the Kariakoo Market, built in 1974 in Dar es Salaam (figure 11.6).[5] Western modernists were often motivated by functionalism; here, the hyperbolic-parabola roof funnels of the Kariakoo Market are both pragmatic and functional because they collect rainwater for storage in underground tanks. The building is also well suited for the local climate, as its openness allows for air circulation.[6] However, this design is much more than a matter of 'form follows function'. The roof funnels also symbolically recall the trees under which markets were traditionally held, thus resonating with a deeply embedded cultural memory (Kanywanyi, 2011). Amuli's design combines a modernist design sensibility and form (through the use of exposed concrete, the unadorned planes of the rectangular base, and a large uninterrupted interior open space) with local climatic suitability and allusions to African culture and everyday life. Traditional ways are thus not reproduced, but echoed in their substance. Yet the building is unquestionably modern, and even iconic. If architectural historiography were less Eurocentric, perhaps this visually striking building would be better known on the world stage.

Figure 11.6. Beda Amuli's Kariakoo Market combines a modernist design sensibility with local climatic suitability and allusions to African culture and everyday life. (*Photo*: Joep Mol, architect)

In addition to material exploration and an expressionist character, the third distinguishing feature of the architecture described above is that it is characterized by – and even embraces – the unfamiliar or the unexpected, and sometimes even the incoherent, discontinuous, or chaotic. Jyoti Hosagrahar (2005, p. 6) coined the term 'indigenous modernities' to describe strategies that 'negotiate the uniqueness of a region and its history with the "universals" of science, reason, and liberation'. She suggested that indigenous modernities are defined by duality, discontinuity, ambivalence, and even chaos:

Indigenous modernities are expressed in built forms prompting ambivalent readings and reactions. As socially constructed identities, buildings and spaces cannot be labeled as inherently 'modern' or 'traditional' on the basis of their visual characteristics at a moment in time… In the tumult of cultural change, customary spatial practices and social institutions are in flux. The spatial experiences of *indigenous modernities* are marked by the presence of formal contradictions and the absence of coherence. For those who expect unity, and those who imagine 'modern' and 'traditional' to be complete, visually identifiable features of a built form, *indigenous modernities* are disturbing in their discontinuity and incompleteness… In the altered context familiar forms acquire new uses and meanings and strange elements are incorporated into familiar arrangements. (Hosagrahar, 2005, pp. 7–8)

In the context of post-independence African architecture, this discontinuity reflected both the flux of cultural change and the necessary coping strategy of creating a new third space. In Demas Nwoko's design for the Akenzua Cultural Center the juxtaposition of influences in the front façade, combining elements of a Greek temple and a Japanese pagoda, may seem incongruent and strange. From the exterior, Almeida's Joint Christian Chapel is not even visually recognizable as a church. And the giant funnels atop Amuli's Kariakoo Market seem almost preposterously oversized. But it was through such unfamiliar and almost jarring incoherence that *new* forms of indigenous modernity could be found. These architects sought not to mimic other works, but to push the boundaries of architecture into a new, third way. If their architecture was less than fully coherent or harmonious, it was a reflection of the tumult of their societies and the struggle to originate new forms of modernity. If architecture was to have the power to inspire new discourses of identity, it could not be mundane.

What Went Wrong?

In 1969, scarcely 10 years after the start of Africa's wave of independence, Udo Kultermann expressed his disappointment at the dissipation of the high hopes for African architecture he had held at the beginning of the decade:

Without undue pessimism it can be said that after the great advances of the early sixties, political development is regressive. The same holds true for architecture, which is linked inseparably to social and political conditions. Only scattered results have materialized after the high hopes and expectations of the early sixties which we can now examine much more soberly. (Kultermann, 1969, p. 12)

Any survey of architecture in Africa over the last few decades reveals that things have continued along the same lines described by Kultermann in 1969. Today, African cities contain a *mélange* of generic, vaguely Western-style glassy towers and residential developments composed of cookie-cutter houses with little or no relation to local modes of dwelling. What went wrong? Kultermann (1969) attributed the disappointing results to two main causes: regressive political developments and misguided attempts by Europeans to work with African traditions they did not fully understand. However, he made these observations less than a decade after many African nations achieved their independence, and the passage of nearly half a century has allowed identification of some additional causes.

Postcolonial African governments have commissioned many buildings since this time that seek to convey an image of themselves as modern nations ready to engage with the world's economic powers. And in order to attract foreign investment and compete in the international markets, they have sought to develop global cities which are connected to financial markets, outfitted with modern infrastructure, and stocked with generic, imported styles of architecture. The tall, glassy buildings in African downtowns are thus built to attract both capital and immigration (particularly of foreign experts and professionals) by declaring parity with the West.[7] In part, the obsession with modernity could also be a rejection of stereotypes from the not-so-distant past. The desire to import trendy architecture and 'keep up with the times' is thus likely a reaction to being treated as 'timeless' and ahistorical during the colonial era. Above all, African governments wish to assert that their nations are part of the same temporality as 'First World' societies. Thus, despite the appeal of early regionalist work, a desire to be viewed as culturally equal and contemporary has usually translated into architecture that mimics Western styles with minimal attention to local climate or culture.

Furthermore, such architecture can be read as the outcome of the attitude that design can be used to shape not only cities but citizens. This harks back to the colonial era, when modernist European models of housing were imposed on cities in the hopes that, in adapting to new forms of *physical dwelling*, colonized peoples would also Westernize their *ways of living*. In post-independence Africa, African governments seem to have followed the same strategy of importing external models to mould populations into suitable residents. This strategy has involved both positive and negative actions, including the creation of large Western-style housing developments and the demolition of slums and shantytowns. In this regard, Gavin Shatkin (2011) has argued that the private nature of integrated urban mega-projects has allowed governments to avoid debates on the cultural appropriateness of modernism by presenting these models as responses to market demand.

The role of the architect in society must also be subject to scrutiny. It has not only been *styles* of architecture that have been imported to Africa, but the very idea of the architecture profession. According to Aradeon (2012, p. 26), one of the challenges with contemporary architecture practice in Africa is that the architect is an unfamiliar player in the customary relationship between client and builder. And when clients and builders feel it is their prerogative to revise an architect's design, its integrity can be lost. One could also argue that architecture as a profession has been devalued in many

African societies, as STEM (science, technology, engineering, mathematics) fields increase in value due to their importance in industrialization. Thus, as the historian Ikem Stanley Okoye has pointed out, in the period immediately following independence in Nigeria, architecture was valued as an artistic and intellectual pursuit. It is now seen more as a technocratic practice, largely irrelevant to social and cultural debates (Okoye, 2012, pp. 40–41).

A Forgotten Legacy

For all of the above reasons, the promise of the post-independence era of African architecture has unfortunately been squandered. A number of notable African architects have continued to produce innovative work, including Oluwole Olumuyiwa, A. Ifeanyi Ekwueme, Kersey D. Moddie, Pierre Goudiaby Atepa, Max Faladé, and Francis Kéré. However, many city master plans and much of the new architecture on the continent (particularly government and commercial buildings) are non-contextual and non-innovative imitations of what has been done in other places, because this is what is sought by the governments, planners, and development agencies to show 'progress'. This has resulted in cityscapes of generic concrete and glass curtain-wall high-rises, even though this type of architecture necessitates the importation of expensive materials and results in higher embodied and ongoing energy costs.

The true success of the early post-independence African architects was in their participation in a global dialogue. They recognized that it was impossible to return back to tradition, as circumstances had fundamentally and irrevocably changed. However, they aspired to do more than simply mimic imported modernist styles. They used their cosmopolitan education and travel abroad as a springboard for participation in a global design culture, in which they could draw on discourses of tradition and modernity from around the world. Their strategy was neither regression nor imitation, but evolution. To this end, they pursued a synthesis of 'native' and 'imported' that went beyond the superficial, and was more than just 'a *pastiche* exterior imposed on interior spaces from another tradition' (Aradeon, 2012, p. 24). Through this synthesis, they pushed modernism beyond the expression of 'universal' principles to a new hybrid of the local and global. As the Senegalese architect Pierre Goudiaby Atepa has said about his work, 'I don't want to bring Africa into modernity, but rather to use modernity with what is profoundly African in order to create a kind of symbiosis, or *metissage*, in architecture' (quoted in Morollo, 2013).

Of course, this was happening at the time not only in Africa but in other parts of the globe as well. Alvar Aalto was exploring how to combine the modern, global, and machine-made with the traditional, Finnish, and hand-made. And, in Japan, Kenzo Tange was exploring the parallels between concrete frames and traditional timber construction. Le Corbusier attempted to translate 'basic Indian typologies for dealing with climate, rhetoric and space in his buildings in Ahmedabad and Chandigarh in the 1950s' (Curtis, 1986, p. 26). Charles and Ray Eames's Case Study House #8 also demonstrated a shift in modernism, as the spare interior of the very simple and rational home was filled with crafts from around the world. A new kind of modernism emerged at the time that was not homogenous and universal but diverse and accepting of an aggregate of influences from different parts of the world (Castillo, 2014). Thus, modernism in the post-independence period was *not* simply a Eurocentric diaspora – a linear flow from the West into the 'Third World'. It was a multifaceted conversation in which influence flowed in multiple directions.

At a time when much of the architecture in sub-Saharan Africa is imported or imitative rather than innovative, the projects described here provide examples of how modernity can be embraced without the loss of traditional identity. In the words of Nezar AlSayyad (2014, p. 10), these examples show how tradition can 'incorporate change in order to sustain itself through space and time'. Placing value on tradition does not prevent it from being *transformed*, as it was in the work of Nwoko, Almeida, and Amuli. By considering tradition and modernity not as a binary but as a dialectic, these cosmopolitan architects developed unique and locally situated modes of thinking, designing, and building.

Notes

1. The concept of 'indigenous modernities', which will be returned to later in the chapter, was introduced by Jyoti Hosagrahar (2005).
2. Greg Castillo, personal conversation, 13 October 2014.
3. Expressionism was a loose movement in art and architecture that peaked in Central Europe in the years after World War I, and was characterized by the celebration of architecture as both an artistic expression of human subjectivity and a means to achieve social utopia; it was also distinguished by the use of nature as an inspiration. However, the term 'expressionism' can also refer more generally to an emphasis on the symbolic or stylistic expression of inner experience, often to produce an emotional effect, as opposed to naturalism or the depiction of objective reality.
4. Indeed, Western modernist artists studied traditional African sculptures for their 'sophisticated approach to the abstraction of the human figure' and the 'spiritual aspect of the composition' (Murrell, 2000).

5. The word Kariakoo is thought to be a corruption of the British 'Carrier Corps', an institution that was based there in the colonial era.
6. Unfortunately, the ground level has subsequently been blocked by market stands.
7. It should be noted, however, that the cities that are mimicked today are as likely to be Asian as Western; for example, Kigali, Rwanda, is aspirationally called the 'Singapore of Africa' by both politicians and developers (Caryl, 2015; Chu, 2009).

References

Almeida, A. (2005) To be or not to be, traditionalist or modernist, nationalist or internationalist, that is the question, in *ArchiAfrika Conference Proceedings: Modern Architecture in East Africa around Independence*. Dar es Salaam, Tanzania, pp. 127–128. Available at: http://archnet.org/publications/4920.

AlSayyad, N. (2014) *Traditions: The 'Real', the Hyper, and the Virtual in the Built Environment*. London: Routledge.

Anderson, B. (1991 [1983]) *Imagined Communities: Reflections on the Origin and Spread of Nationalism*. London: Verso.

Aradeon, D. (2012) Nigerian architecture: tradition and change, in Okeke-Agulu, C. and Udechukwu, O. (eds.) *Ezumeezu: Essays on Nigerian Art and Architecture – A Festschrift in Honour of Demas Nwoko*. Glassboro, NJ: Goldline and Jacobs Publishing, pp. 23–28.

ArchiAfrika (www.archiafrika.org) (2008) Anthony Almeida. 3 April. Available at: http://www.zoominfo.com/p/Anthony-Almeida/385430317.

Bassey, N. (2012) Demas Nwoko's architecture, in Okeke-Agulu, C. and Udechukwu, O. (eds.) *Ezumeezu: Essays on Nigerian Art and Architecture – A Festschrift in Honour of Demas Nwoko*. Glassboro, NJ: Goldline and Jacobs Publishing, pp. 165–178.

Burssens, P. (2005) The (non) political position of the architecture of Anthony B. Almeida between 1948 and 1975, in *ArchiAfrika Conference Proceedings*, Dar es Salaam, Tanzania. Available at: http://archnet.org/publications/4919.

Caryl, C. (2015) Africa's Singapore Dream. Democracy Lab Blog on the Foreign Policy Website, 2 April. Available at: http://foreignpolicy.com/2015/04/02/africas-singapore-dream-rwanda-kagame-lee-kuan-yew/.

Castillo, G. (2014) Lecture Notes. University of California, Berkeley, 30 September.

Chu, J. (2009) Rwanda rising: A new model of economic development. *Fast Company*, 1 April. Available at: http://www.fastcompany.com/1208900/rwanda-rising-new-model-economic-development.

Curtis, W.J.R. (1986) Towards an authentic regionalism, in Khan, H.-U. (ed.) *Mimar 19: Architecture in Development*. Singapore: Concept Media Ltd.

Elleh, N. (2002) *Architecture and Power in Africa*. Westport, CT: Praeger.

Folkers, A. (2010) *Modern Architecture in Africa*. Amsterdam: Sun.

Folkers, A. (2013) Early modern African architecture: the House of Wonders Revisited. *Docomomo Journal*, **48**(March), pp. 20–29.

Frampton, K. (2007) *Modern Architecture: A Critical History*, 4th ed. London: Thames & Hudson.

Frampton, K. and Foster, H. (1983) Towards a critical regionalism: six points for an architecture of resistance, in Foster, H. (ed.) *Postmodern Culture*. London: Pluto Press, pp.16–30.

Godwin, J. and Hopwood, G. (2008) *The Architecture of Demas Nwoko*. Lagos: Farafina Books.

Hosagrahar, J. (2005) *Indigenous Modernities: Negotiating Architecture and Urbanism: Negotiating Architecture, Urbanism, and Colonialism in Delhi.* London: Routledge.

Kanywanyi, K.S. (2011) Beda Amuli: the story of the boy from Tanganyika who went to Israel to study architecture. *ANZA Magazine.*

Kultermann, U. (1963) *New Architecture in Africa.* New York: Universe Books.

Kultermann, U. (1969) *New Directions in African Architecture*, J. Maass translator. New York: George Braziller.

Lagae, J. (2011) Kultermann and after: on the historiography of 1950s and 1960s architecture in Africa, in Avermaete, T. and Lagae, J. (eds.) *OASE 82: L'Afrique, C'est Chic: Architecture and Planning in Africa, 1950–1970.* Rotterdam: nai010 Publishers, pp. 5–24.

Mitter, P. (2009) Frameworks for considering cultural exchange: the case of India and America, in Mills, C., Glazer, L. and Goerlitz, A.A. (eds.) *East-West Interchanges in American Art: A Long and Tumultuous Relationship.* Washington, DC: Smithsonian Institution Scholarly Press. Available at: http://dx.doi.org/10.5479/si.9781935623083.20.

Morollo, M.K. (2013) The rise of African architecture. *Selamta Magazine* (September). Available at: http://www.selamtamagazine.com/stories/rise-african-architecture.

Murrell, D. (2000) African influences in modern art, in *Hellbrunn Timeline of Art History.* New York: The Metropolitan Museum of Art. Available at: http://www.metmuseum.org/toah/hd/aima/hd_aima.htm.

Nwoko, D. (1992) *The Impoverished Generation.* Ibadan: New Culture Studios.

Okeke, U. (1960) Natural Synthesis. Manifesto. Zaria Art Society, Nigeria. Available at: http://www.csus.edu/indiv/o/obriene/art116/Readings/final%20Okeke%20Natural%20Synthesis%20Manifesto%201960.doc.

Okeke-Agulu, C. and Udechukwu, O. (2012) Introduction, in Okeke-Agulu, C. and Udechukwu, O. (eds.) *Ezumeezu: Essays on Nigerian Art and Architecture – A Festschrift in Honour of Demas Nwoko.* Glassboro, NJ: Goldline and Jacobs Publishing, pp. 1–7.

Okoye, I.S. (2012) Nigerian architecture on the wrong road, or, Learning from Demas Nwoko, in Okeke-Agulu, C. and Udechukwu, O. (eds.) *Ezumeezu: Essays on Nigerian Art and Architecture – A Festschrift in Honour of Demas Nwoko.* Glassboro, NJ: Goldline and Jacobs Publishing.

Ricœur, P. (1965 [1955]) Universal civilization and national cultures, in Kelbley, C.A. (ed.) *History and Truth.* Evanston, IL: Northwestern University Press.

Sharp, D. (2005) The message of modern architecture in East Africa: the work of Anthony Almeida in Tanzania. *Docomomo Journal*, **32**.

Shatkin, G. (2011) Planning privatopolis: representation and contestation in the development of urban integrated mega-projects, in Roy, A. and Ong, A. (eds.) *Worlding Cities: Asian Experiments and the Art of Being Global.* Chichester: Wiley-Blackwell, pp. 77–97.

Tzonis, A. and Lefaivre, L. (1981) The grid and the pathway, in *Architecture in Greece*, **15**. Athens: Orestis B. Doumanis.

Chapter 12

New Traditions of Placemaking in West-Central Africa

Mark Gillem and Lyndsey Deaton

> *Postmodern (or multinational) space is not merely a cultural ideology or fantasy, but has genuine historical (and socio-economic) reality as a third great original expansion of capitalism around the globe.*
>
> Fredric Jameson (1984)

In 2014, when the rector of the Université Omar Bongo in Libreville, Gabon, publicly announced plans to open a Confucius Institute on campus – a project funded by the Gabonese government – the response was one of clear displeasure. As measured by the boos and hisses from the assembly of 1,200 students, faculty and staff, why was this investment in Chinese culture so alarming?[1] Among numerous answers, one explanation, offered by a faculty member, stood out: the Gabonese were tired of fostering Chinese largesse, because such 'partnerships' only came at the cost of access to Gabon's natural resources, from raw wood to light, sweet crude oil.

The situation in Gabon is by no means unique. Africa covers 11.67 million square miles (30.23 million square kilometres) and is projected to have roughly 25 per cent of the world's population by 2050 (Sautman and Hairong, 2007, p. 78). Given the continent's size, it should come as no surprise that vast tracts of African land are rich in natural resources – including diamonds, oil, gold, and rare-earth minerals. However, many nations in Africa are struck by a 'resource curse', in the form of a 'minority of the population that enjoys close ties to political, military and economic power' (Garcia-Rodriguez *et al.*, 2015, p. 164). This elite typically appropriates most of the revenue from resource exploitation while neglecting the development of the lower socioeconomic tiers. In the past, local leaders joined with Western colonial powers to profit from the continent's resources. But within the last 50 years, these powers have ceded the landscape to nationalist projects, and these have sought assistance from a new 'colonial' presence – China. In exchange for access to Africa's abundant resources, Chinese enterprises are today building infrastructure to support new levels of resource extraction and erecting buildings to flatter visions of national grandeur.

In light of this shift, this chapter investigates how tradition, modernity, and power are under construction in one part of the continent – west-central Africa. It first explores the concept of neocolonialism associated with the rise of Chinese influence and its reliance on a familiar model of foreign resource exploitation (in this case, largely oil). It then discusses how this model of foreign-sponsored development has created significant problems that illuminate the power disparity between investors and debtors. Among these are rampant corruption, opaque development processes, imagined prosperity, and a failure to build local capacity. The chapter then turns to an examination of the recent architectural payoff from Chinese resource exploitation in Angola, Gabon, and the Republic of Congo. In this new geopolitical equation, it asks: whose traditions will prevail?

Chinese-African Development: A Neocolonial Model

Nations have no permanent friends or allies, they only have permanent interests.[2]
Lord Palmerston

The emerging new colonial power in west-central Africa is clearly China. As Martyn Davies, a former director of the Centre for Chinese Studies at Stellenbosch University in South Africa, observed, 'China's move into Africa is displacing traditional Anglo-French and U.S. interests' (Zafar, 2007, p. 103). Similarly, Elizabeth Economy, the director for Asia Studies at the Council on Foreign Relations, noted in a speech to the World Economic Forum in 2006: 'All over Africa today you will see Chinese construction firms building railroads, highways, telecoms, enormous dams, even presidential palaces' (Naidu and Mbazima, 2008, p. 748). Largely at issue in these investments is access by China to Africa's oil.

China is a relatively new player in the international oil game. Yet, according to the World Bank researcher Ali Zafar (2007, p. 118), it has been investing 'billions of dollars in the promising African oil market, which has long been dominated by U.S. and European petroleum interests'. As

Chinese energy demand exceeds domestic supply, African countries with little infrastructure and a nonchalant attitude towards human rights are regarded as perfect partners for Chinese energy corporations. African crude today accounts for around 25 per cent of China's oil imports. Angola, for example, is 'currently Africa's second largest oil producer after Nigeria, and is China's top supplier, providing more than 400,000 barrels per day, or close to 15 percent of China's oil imports' (Zafar, 2007, p. 119).

China has gained influence in west-central Africa partly by funding construction projects and providing other forms of assistance. To build connections and trustworthiness, Chinese construction companies first swoop in to build and improve local facilities. But these trust-gaining exercises are largely designed to gain access to the area's high-quality oil reserves.

Several factors underlie China's drive to exploit foreign energy markets and resources. On the one hand, Chinese leaders would like to diversify the country's sources of supply and move away from burning domestic coal. But purchasing oil on the open market exposes China to global price fluctuations; and by investing in oil-rich countries without the technological or financial ability to build their own drilling and processing facilities, China hopes to avoid some of this risk. The high quality of the oil itself is also important. But so is the fact that countries in west-central Africa do not belong to the Organization of Petroleum Exporting Countries (OPEC) – meaning they do not have to follow export and production restrictions (Naidu and Mbazima, 2008, p. 753).

In pursuit of African oil (and other resources), China's version of colonialism is a bit different from that which historically emerged in the West. Western powers pursued both socio-political and economic objectives in their colonial possessions. Thus, a 'civilizing mission' frequently attended their drive for profit from the continent's mines and oilfields. But Chinese leaders seem to care less about the governing systems of host nations, provided they assure Chinese enterprises relatively unrestricted access to resources. As John Bing, a professor of anthropology and political science at Heidelberg University, and Stephen Ceccoli, a professor of international affairs at Rhodes College, have argued (Bing and Ceccoli, 2013, p. 122), the exclusive focus on economic gain thus highlights how 'the end of formal colonization in the 1950s and 1960s did not substantially change these economic realities'. They have further pointed out that revenues generated by the export of raw materials today support only very narrow purposes – primarily funding infrastructure to facilitate further exports and supporting the power of existing political elites.

Where the older Western model of colonial development came with socio-political strings attached, this neocolonial model is largely silent on issues of democracy, transparency, graft, workers rights, and environmental protection. But, according to Bing and Ceccoli (2013, p. 121), this model is actually more attractive to African rulers, who 'seek to resist outside pressures to ameliorate dangerous working conditions and negative environmental impact'. Chinese intervention through an oil-for-infrastructure approach thus supports the local desire for access to capital, technology, and engineering expertise without moral or political conditions. Meanwhile, on the other side of the equation, African natural resources fill a strategic need within China's developing, energy-intensive, industrial economy. Indeed, according to Sophal Ear, an associate professor of diplomacy and world affairs at Occidental College, and Sigrido Burgos, a consultant in development, political economy, and foreign affairs, 'Africa has emerged as one of the centerpieces of China's overseas energy strategy' (Burgos and Ear, 2012, p. 352).

Sanusha Naidu, a research specialist at the South African Regional Poverty Network, and Daisy Mbazima Lando, an economist from Stellenbosch University, have argued that the Chinese-African development model is actually supported by five guiding principles: mutual respect for territorial integrity; equality and mutual benefit; non-interference in each other's internal affairs; nonaggression; and peaceful coexistence (Naidu and Mbazima, 2008, p.,751; see also Power, 2012, p. 994). They further believe these principles have 'found resonance in the developing world given its experience of being manipulated' by earlier colonial powers.

For African leaders, such a relationship represents a move away from the judgmental attitude of the West and its forays into regime change. With China, these leaders can continue to conduct business as usual and not worry about external threats. Sahr Johnny, a former Sierra Leone ambassador to Beijing, put it plainly: 'We like Chinese investment because we have one meeting, we discuss what they want to do and then they just do it ... there are no benchmarks or preconditions' (Zafar, 2007, p. 103). And, as Burgos and Ear (2012, p. 353) have written, 'China does not seem to regard political instability, ethnic schisms, or social discords in some African countries as an obstacle to its far-reaching ambitions'.

On the other hand, China's policy of non-intervention may be partly responsible for delaying reforms that might lead to greater accountability and openness in many African countries (Zafar, 2007, p. 106). After all, why should unscrupulous leaders who benefit from Chinese investment seek to change their approach to governing?

The Problems of Unequal Exchange

Chinese firms that are both state and privately owned use their advanced skills and equipment to extract resources for use in China. Payment, meanwhile, often takes the form of physical development in the host nation – from roads and bridges to hotels and stadiums. Implicit in this relationship are a number of problems.

In return for its largely unquestioned support of local elites, China demands heavy concessions from its African partners. For example, according to Lucy Corkin, a research associate at the School of Oriental and African Studies (2012, p. 476), the China EXIM Bank, which finances the bulk of China's overseas projects (and whose purpose is to stimulate demand for Chinese goods and services), generally requires that Chinese firms be awarded all infrastructure contracts. This means that Chinese firms provide local design and construction services largely without the active collaboration of host-nation entities. Indeed, until recently, in Africa the funding for such projects rarely even passed through local agents. Chinese bankers would send funds directly to their Chinese construction colleagues, bypassing potentially graft-ridden local institutions (Bing and Ceccoli, 2013, p. 116).

The EXIM bank typically further mandates that a large percentage of contract procurements (i.e. materials, equipment, supplies, etc.) originate in China (Power, 2012, p. 996). To appease local leaders, the EXIM bank may allow a small percentage of contract value to be allocated to local firms. However, if this set-aside threatens project scheduling, Chinese firms may ignore it (Corkin, 2012, p. 476). Indeed, given the limited skills of local workers and the outdated equipment owned by local firms, this condition is more typically the reality. Additionally, on many projects, Chinese funds pay not only for Chinese design and planning but also for skilled Chinese construction workers. If there are supply and quality problems in a host nation, they may even pay for such materials as cement, gravel, and charcoal to be imported from China (Corkin, 2012, p. 478). Repayment for these inputs is, after all, guaranteed by income from the host nation's resources – be they oil, minerals, diamonds, or even agricultural products.

As Zafar (2007, p. 125) has noted, China's role in African development thus has 'mixed blessings'. China has used its trade surplus with the West to embark on a programme of direct investment in Africa, which has led to accelerated economic growth, improved infrastructure, and increased investment in areas at the margins of global finance. China has also been able to provide access to low-cost consumer goods (e.g. motorcycles, electronics, and t-shirts). But this has come at a steep cost for host countries – from environmental degradation to alleged human-rights violations. Moreover, since much of the intellectual work is done by Chinese investors, developers, and builders, the neocolonial model of Chinese-African development does little to boost local 'capacity for planning and administering development or to maintain the new infrastructure' (Power, 2012, p. 1011). As a result, 'local people remain passive in the process of implementing development projects. They do not get the opportunity to be involved in the project and build their leadership skills' (Bado, 2012, p. 37).

As Burgos and Ear (2012, p. 365) have therefore argued, some African governments have become increasingly uncomfortable with this new type of 'disguised colonization'. As the former South African President Thabo Mbeki claimed: 'The potential danger, in terms of the relationship that could be construed between China and the African continent, would indeed be a replication of that colonial relationship' (Bing and Ceccoli, 2013, p. 107). With its oil-for-infrastructure focus and rules privileging Chinese companies, China's African development model thus warrants considerable wariness – despite the assurances of former Chinese Premier Wen Jiabao's that the 'China-Africa relationship is truly a model of equality and friendship for the international community' (Bing and Ceccoli, 2013, p. 107).

While the relationship may not be as equal as Chinese leaders claim, Leni Wild of the Overseas Development Institute and David Mepham of Human Rights Watch have argued: 'The question is less *does* Africa gain or lose from China, but rather, which Africans might gain or lose, in which countries or sectors, and in which circumstances' (Bing and Ceccoli, 2013, p. 110). In west-central Africa, the present reality is that the ruling elites tend to gain the most because they are the ones leveraging the 'resource curse'. They realize that outside help is needed to extract profits from their countries' resources, and the outside investor with the most tolerance for their often-murky political systems is China. However, their limited track record with profitable development demands concessions, and for most west-central African countries this translates into the oil-for-infrastructure equation.

As Justin Podur, an associate professor of environmental studies at York University, has pointed out (2014, p. 56), multiple frames of view can be at work in the same story. On the one hand, a development narrative may justify interventions-cum-investments in part based on the 'eternal chaos and ethnic conflict' that still plagues most west-central African nations. According to this view, China may be seen as a benevolent suitor lending a helping hand. On the other hand, an anticolonial narrative may highlight ongoing experiences of 'interference and plunder' at the hands of 'neocolonial' powers. The forced duality of these perspectives, however, may also conceal a more complex scale of experiences between host nations, Chinese investors, and construction firms.

Architecture and Visual Capitalism

While the oil-for-infrastructure model is clearly a neocolonial one, it is not without benefits for the nations of the region. Key among these may be the new urban spaces being created by these countries' ruling elites.

In postcolonial Africa, as in many parts of the globe, traditional patterns of development are evaporating under the heat of modernity. In west-central African cities, dirt lanes, metal shacks, and tangles of overhead wires are today being replaced by showpieces of capitalism and images of prosperity. Sparkling waterfront developments, instant high-rise cities, and aggressive redevelopment master plans embody the hope of leap-frogging into a globalized world. Thus, Corbusian-inspired layouts – with isolated, single-use towers floating in undefined open spaces – are touted as representations of modernity. Similarly, New Urbanist neighbourhood plans are hailed for organizing the chaotic mix of uses that long challenged the colonial desire for order. In their drive to be recognized as players in the global capitalist economy, the elites of west-central Africa are enlisting the services of international design and construction firms to provide the image of modernity, no matter how contradictory the underlying design principles.

Such development represents in part a search for new traditions and a new beginning – trading a perceived backward local heritage for the glass façades, metal trim, and orderly spaces of such new hubs of international commerce as Shenzhen, Dubai, and Singapore. But the demand for a new scale and materiality is also distancing new built environments in the region from locally derived vernacular knowledge and craft – encouraging instead the embrace of seemingly efficient but ultimately unsustainable foreign packaged designs.

How is it possible for an outsider to confront this destructive modality when the very residents most exploited by it welcome it? A principal criticism from an academic perspective is that these new trends promote an imported imaginary of prosperity and wealth through an aesthetic of consumption. Yet this view is largely absent from contemporary design discourse in the region.

Such a critique has, however, appeared with regard to other forms of cultural expression. In her article 'Aesthetics of Acquisition' (2015), Florence Bernault, a professor of west and equatorial African history and contemporary Africa at the University of Wisconsin-Madison, examined the transactional nature of daily life in Gabon through three popular local spectacles: the televised and nationally acclaimed Miss Gabon Beauty Pageant; a TV commercial ('Donations aux Populations') in which politicians donate to marginalized citizens; and the gyrating bodies of female sex workers in the mirrored bars and clubs of Libreville. As she wrote, 'Such visual parades are rooted in colonial performance and borrow from global repertoires of individual success and consumerism. They also mobilize key norms in the reproduction of power and gender relations' (Bernault, 2015, p. 753).

An aesthetics of architectural acquisition may also be seen to underlie the design and construction of new urban environments in the region. According to Bernault (2015, p. 755), physical and symbolic 'things' are part of a capitalist visual economy, and have commoditized exhibition value. To extend her argument, elements of the built environment can be seen to trade on the same desire for image value as Gabon's 'young female prostitutes and urban fashionistas' (Bernault, 2015, p. 759). This line of reasoning builds off the view within African studies that 'often blames the crumbling of older moral norms on the rise of predatory consumerism, and focuses on how visual capitalism introduces massive possibilities for transforming images and people into commodities' (Bernault, 2015, p. 758). After all, buildings have at least one thing in common with Libreville's sex workers and the bikini-clad women striding down the runway in hopes of winning the Miss Gabon pageant: they are, in part, designed to be scrutinized and acquired visually.

Yet, while urban forms may be valued as spectacle, buildings must also serve a functional purpose. And it is here that an imaginary of globalized modernity relies on promoting the supposed presence and interests of a wealthy new middle class over any sense of shared economic reality or African identity. According to the author, editor, and professor Mike Davis and Daniel Monk, director of the Peace Studies Program at Colgate University, in such places, the *nouveau riche* occupy 'bright archipelagos of utopian luxury … fantasy Californias … dreamworlds of neoliberalism' (Power, 2012, p. 1005). A prime example is the bayside Marginal district in Luanda, Angola's capital, which Marcus Power, a professor of geography at Durham University (2012, p. 1005), has described as being transformed from a sleepy, low-rise colonial waterfront into a 'skyline of shining steel

Figure 12.1. Development along Baia de Luanda Marginal (Luanda, c. 2003). (*Source*: Pintoroux Architects. (http://pintoroux.wix.com/pintoroux#!__page-2/stackercoverflowalbum1=2))

and glass' indicative of Angola's new image as 'a country of the future' (figure 12.1). It is an image designed to project effortless modernity, technological competence, and profitable capitalism.

A Building Boom with Limited Benefits

Among the planned developments that are rapidly re-creating cities in the region with the help of foreign firms are government complexes, high-end housing, mega-malls, and commercial centres. However, these cities are also expanding to accommodate vast unplanned areas. And despite the appearance of shiny new areas for the elite, the majority of the urban population is still housed in squatter settlements and other informal districts with limited access to electricity, running water, and sewerage.

For the old colonial powers, unplanned growth at the fringe was a necessary aspect of urban development (Rodrigues and Tavares, 2012, p. 690). But in the current neocolonial development model such areas are often simply viewed as lying in the way of progress. The 'attractive pull of city life' is seen to require extension of cities beyond older colonial lines (Rodrigues and Tavares, 2012, p. 696). And such extension requires the removal of informal settlements and their residents, who rarely have the political and economic resources to mount an effective opposition (Power,

2012, p. 998). As a result, according to Patience Kabamba, an assistant professor of international studies at Marymount Manhattan College, 'certain groups have been able to take advantage of both the absence of the nation-state and the presence of (resources) to modernize and institute new forms of order and development' (Kabamba, 2012, p. 670).

Of course, the realization that modernity presents a radical threat to history and tradition is not new (Berman, 1982). Indeed, the very experience of modernity was planted in the region by the Western colonial powers. And it was according to such notions as rational city form and capitalist modernity, developed by figures such as Le Corbusier, that the social and urban fabric of indigenous civilizations was originally swept aside (Çelik, 1992, p. 74). However, in the mid-twentieth century, the ideological justification for colonial holdings and the seizure of natural resources became increasingly less tenable. And over the next half century, legal control over occupied regions was gradually relinquished to new nation-states – with varying degrees of geographic legitimacy.

In many cases, however, independence from colonial rule did not spread access to power beyond a limited and self-serving 'nationalist' elite. For example, Omar Bongo ruled Gabon as president for four decades before his death in 2009, and his son has continued in the same capacity for nearly another. In Angola, José Eduardo dos Santos has held the presidency continuously since 1979. And in the Republic of Congo, President Denis Sassou Nguesso has held power for two extended periods (1979 to 1991, and 1997 to the present). If he makes it to the end of his current mandate in 2023, he will have led that country for nearly 40 years.

Without question, independence has allowed all three men (as well as their close associates) to enrich themselves and their families. But through the high-profile building campaigns they have pursued, they have largely pursued ideas and images originally sold to them by their former colonizers. Meanwhile, the vast majority of the citizenry reside in poverty and squalor, hidden behind glamorous new boulevards and gleaming high-rises largely paid for and built by Chinese companies in exchange for the region's oil.

Angola's New Image

Perhaps no country in west-central Africa has benefitted more from the largesse of Chinese investors than Angola. In a land rich in resources, from oil to diamonds, most Angolans barely survive, while a small minority accumulates most of the benefits. Barry Munslow, a professor at the Humanitarian and Conflict Response Institute, has noted that in a land rich in resources, from oil to diamonds, most Angolans barely survive, while a small minority accumulates most of the benefits (Munslow, 1999, p. 551). 'Internal conflict, economic policy failure, and corruption', he has argued, are largely to blame for this inherently unsustainable condition.

The paradox is clearly revealed in urban planning for Luanda. Following a quarter century of civil war, rural-to-urban migration has created an overwhelming problem of population concentration. The colonial city was originally designed for 500,000 people, but it now supports approximately 5.3 million (Power, 2012, p. 1002; UN Data, 2016). As a result, those seeking refuge there from poverty, terrorism, and unemployment face 'a lack of access to water and proper housing' (Power, 2012, p. 1002). Faced with this problem, the Angolan government's plans call for a decanting of population into hugely expensive peripheral megaprojects. Such programmed developments, however, appear as empty shells compared to actual, thriving urban environments.

Since the disastrous civil war (fought largely by proxies for the Cold War powers), which ended in 2002, its economy has grown almost ten-fold. The capital, Luanda, in particular, has experienced a development boom, with 'roads, highways, airports, railways, office buildings, hotels, shopping centers, hospitals, universities, and apartment blocks [that] rise up out of green jungle bushes' (Burgos and Ear, 2012, pp. 356–357). Much of this development has been financed by open-ended, multibillion-dollar lines of credit guaranteed by Chinese purchases of Angolan oil. The result is that Angola is today regarded as having one of the most 'successful' economies on the continent (Power, 2012, p. 995).

To move beyond the deep-seated animosities that fuelled the war, a narrative was created as part of a government-sponsored advertising campaign entitled 'Angola: Do you recognize this nation?'. The campaign envisioned a country thriving under the forces of 'modernization, development, progress, and democratization' (Power, 2012, pp. 998–999). Such a bold promise, however, necessitated large-scale action, and this required outside investors with the ability to transform imagery into reality. Angola's long-term plans thus privilege mega-projects over small-scale solutions, with the result that luxury shopping malls and sports complexes are rapidly replacing 'the "dirty" or "disorderly" informal spaces that preceded them' (Power, 2012, p. 999).

Those in charge of the country's makeover are today selling 'high-technology contemporary architectural styles and designs ... as key symbols and statements of Angola's wider transformation' (Power, 2012, p. 1004). According to one promotional website (RMB Westport, 2016), in Luanda (as in Nigeria, Ghana, and elsewhere), 'you'll spot a modern shopping mall with high-grade finishes, an A-grade office block or industrial park from RMB Westport'. As the subsidiary of South Africa's largest bank, however, RMB Westport must answer to shareholders who demand profits beyond what the needs and context of local communities might otherwise justify. To provide these, its strategy has been to sell access to the image of a youthful, multicultural, Western-oriented middle class through consumerism. Yet, the physical spaces it creates largely reproduce urban designs the West now deems to have been failures. And this is nowhere more apparent than in its Muxima Shopping Center (a subject of the website above), whose peripheral location and vast expanses of parking exclude access to anyone without a car (figure 12.2).

Figure 12.2. Rendering of Muxima Shopping Centre and surrounding parking lot Luanda. (*Source*: http://www.muximashopping.co.ao/)

Moreover, Luanda's makeover relies in part on the labour of the urban underclass that occupies the city's *musseques* (slums). Residents of these neighbourhoods, who represent perhaps four million of Luanda's six million inhabitants, live without access to clean water or electricity (Garcia-Rodriguez *et al.*, 2015, p. 172). To address this problem, the government drafted plans for new satellite housing areas, including Sassa Bengo, Caxito, and Barra do Dande – to be built by 2030. Predictably, the contracts for these have largely gone to outsiders, foremost among them Pan-China Construction, Ltd (Power, 2012, p. 1004).

To date, however, the government's experience with such projects (known colloquially as *centralidades*) has not been good. In 2008 it began construction of a new satellite city to provide hundreds of middle-class housing units. The new city, Kilamba Kiaxi, was financed through a partnership with Chinese state-owned enterprise CITIC (Power, 2012, p. 1008). But to clear the land for it, the government employed a legal principle largely similar to that used to justify the seizure of land by Portugal, Angola's former colonizer: 'the state is the owner and manager of all Angolan land' (Burgos and Ear, 2012, p. 564). Furthermore, Kilamba Kiaxi has faced numerous other challenges, such as high initial rents (which left the site abandoned from 2012 to 2013), limited public services, and a lack of connection to surrounding areas. Indeed, at one point it became an international news sensation as the 'ghost town' of Angola (Benazeraf and Alves, 2014, p. 3) (figure 12.3). According to the architect Alain Cain (2014, p. 564), a specialist in planning, microfinance, and urban development living in Angola, such projects are 'expensive mistakes that [have] diverted investment from potentially more sustainable economic and social projects', leaving the nation with a burden of debt and the challenge of maintenance.

David Harvey (2008, p. 30) has pointed to the social costs of such developments: 'In China (and Angola), since previous occupants of land lack private property rights, the state can simply move them by fiat, offering

Figure 12.3. High-rise towers compose the "ghost town' of Angola (Kilamba City, c. 2012). (*Source*: http://www.chinaafricarealstory.com/2014/04/chinese-built-angolan-ghost-town-wakes.html)

a minor cash payment to help them on their way before turning the land over to developers at a large profit'. However, in Angola, Cain (2014, p. 564) has written, instead of investing in in-situ upgrades or strategic slum-prevention projects, Chinese and other international investors have offered quick-fix solutions, touting an image of Luanda as a new 'world-class African metropolis'.

Without a national style to draw from, the aesthetics of such projects have also had to be imported by foreign design firms. This now includes the growing international discourse on sustainability. One example is the design for a new campus for Universidade Agostinho Neto, Angola's largest public university. A team from the American firm Perkins + Will described its style as 'human-centered Modernism', which they claimed was appropriate to its site on Luanda's partially developed urban periphery (Melvin, 2012). And, according to one review (Ngare, 2015), the combined effect of democratic planning and passive-energy systems, resolved in high-tech ways using modern industrial materials, created the image of a contemporary, progressive institution.

However, other aspects of the design show how its foreign designers misread the context. On the one hand, they modified the typical quad system of Western universities, using the buildings to shade outdoor spaces, increase natural ventilation, and create microclimates (Melvin, 2015). With computer-generated models, they also fine-tuned the buildings' distinctively angled roofs to serve as airfoils (Melvin, 2012). And they developed a modular construction system they hoped would provide economy of scale, lend a democratic ambience, and respond to the socialist views of both the government and campus educators (Ngare, 2015). However, the design concept was based on abstract economic, architectural, and climactic concerns rather than existing building types and architectural styles (Ngare, 2015). As a result, its barren plazas, widely spaced buildings, and glaring concrete promenades today make one wonder if 'human-centered Modernism' was the right choice for such a tropical site (figure 12.4).

Such high-profile developments also ignore the reality, mentioned above, that 80 per cent of Luanda's population still resides in *musseques*. While Luanda's 'new suburbs and condominiums', 'old urban centre', and 'industrial zone' all have adequate basic services, the city's poorer, heavily populated areas remain largely unserviced (World Bank Development Workshop, 2012, p. 7). Indeed, by concentrating new development, and thus new infrastructure, in peripheral bands, projects like Universidade Agostinho Neto only perpetuate these patterns. As shown most recently

Figure 12.4. Rendering of Universidade Agostinho Neto (Luanda, c. 2011). (*Source*: http://www.architectural-review.com/today/perkinswills-university-campus-in-luanda-angola/8629302.fullarticle)

through an interactive website by the University of Iowa's Colin Gordon (2016), such *de facto* economic segregation (which usually instigates racial and cultural segregation) ultimately leads to urban decline.

Quest for Prestige in Gabon

While Luanda is the city in the region that has been most affected by neocolonial development patterns, the stark difference between rich and poor is perhaps nowhere more evident than in Libreville, Gabon's capital. Here, older patterns of French-colonial development underlie the developing neocolonial landscape. Wide boulevards, including the aptly named Boulevard Triomphal, are lined with an odd consortium of modern and postmodern designs: fluted façades erupt into the skyline; trees jut from elevated balconies; and ungainly cantilevers shade a pedestrian realm devoid of pedestrians. Largely concealed from view behind these structures and away from the imposing grand avenues, meanwhile, are the congested dirt alleyways of informal settlements lined with makeshift shelters built from the debris of modernism.

These slums are home to a growing migrant underclass who have moved to Gabon to seek prosperity. They drive taxis wildly through the congested streets, clean hotel rooms reserved by the well-connected, cook outdoors along deteriorating back streets, and help build modernist apparitions for the wealthy along the city's waterfront. On the one hand, the relative stability guaranteed by the forceful hand of the Bongo family has attracted migrants to Libreville from across the region. But there is also a growing sense that Gabon's stability may not last. As oil prices have recently dropped, so has the government's ability to pacify the public through graft and (more legitimate) public investment. Violent clashes between supporters and opponents of the government of Ali Bongo accompanied the 2016 presidential campaign.

The Bongo clan, in power collectively for nearly five decades, has long used architectural monuments to emphasize their personal connection to national prestige. The legislative assembly building is the Palais Omar Bongo; the flagship university is Université Omar Bongo; and the primary athletic facility is Gymnase Omnisport Omar Bongo (Nossiter, 2009. p. 1). Any loss of revenue would jeopardize its ability to continue this strategic campaign of 'public' building. Nevertheless, three projects facilitated by Gabon's ANGT (Agence Nationale des Grands Travaux) show the scope and direction of the Bongo clan's current ambitions.

Outside of Libreville, in the Angondjé district, ANGT planners are currently working with the international engineering firm Bechtel to build the massive new Cité de la Démocratie. According to one Bechtel report, this development will include a '1,000-person conference center, a 500-person banquet hall, an amphitheater, diplomatic villas, government buildings, a golf course, and a public education animal park highlighting the wildlife and plants of Gabon' (Kimball, 2013, p. 27). Ultimately, plans also call for the area to accommodate 120,000 residents in a series of districts designed with help from the UK-based Prince's Foundation using the form-based New Urbanist Smart Code and its rather cumbersome logic of 'transects'.[3]

Critics, however, have pointed to several problems with this satellite development, including the need to convince future residents that the distance to Libreville will not be prohibitive. An intense campaign has thus been mounted to sell the project by highlighting the hope that 'the vast new urban center … [will] embody the ideal city, to be the model of an urban policy based on a social and functional diversity which [will] spread to the rest of the country' (Esteban, 2014). Given its distance to jobs and commerce in Libreville, however, the same report concluded that

> … the new city will also need to be an example of functional diversity, as opposed to a city-dormitory. Habitat areas should therefore include shops, kindergartens, parks and offices, while being served by a good network of roads and paths… 'It is necessary that people can live and work in Angondjé without the need to visit the downtown every day', said Virginia Mozogo Akele, director of communication of ANGT. (Esteban, 2014)

Without this hoped-for mix, despite the best of New Urbanist intentions, the development will exacerbate the negative effects of sprawl, including traffic congestion, environmental degradation, and excess resource consumption.

The centrepiece of the new district is the Stade d'Angondjé, built by a Chinese developer for the 2012 Africa Cup football competition. Radiating out from it, the circular, 200-hectare Cité de la Démocratie is ultimately planned to include both mixed-use, mid-rise urban centres and low-rise, low-density suburban areas. The development thus attempts to reprise the spectacle of such icons of New Urbanism as Seaside and Celebration, Florida. And like these insular American developments, which have both appeared in feature films, the entire project is designed to sell an image of safety and security, as an enclave apart from the perils of actual urbanity, with graceful tree-lined avenues, walkable streets, and attractive architecture (figure 12.5).

Figure 12.5. Angondje New Town Master Plan illustration (Libreville, c. 2012). (*Source:* http://opticosdesign.com/opticos-works-with-the-princes-foundation-in-gabon-africa/)

At the outset of planning for this vast new peripheral development, the construction of the Stade d'Angondjé was used to clear the area of existing informal settlements. Elsewhere in this volume, Anne-Marie Broudehoux describes how the staging of high-profile sporting events is a common tactic used by elites to relocate the working poor and create space for more profitable development. However, the image of modernity that results

Figure 12.6. Rendering of Stade d'Angondje (Libreville, c. 2012). (*Source*: http://gabon review.com/can2012/comment-se-rend-t-on-au-stade/)

is often a disappointment. Indeed, under the guise of Sino-Gabonese friendship, the existing residents of the Angondjé area were displaced to create a work of placeless architecture surrounded by massive parking lots, ambiguous manicured spaces, and characterless modern buildings (figure 12.6).

The second example of contemporary planning and design in Gabon is the proposed $450 million redevelopment of Libreville's waterfront into a tourist destination, high-end residential setting, and symbol of the country's modernization. According to a government website, the 4 hectares of the city's existing Port Mole will be transformed as part of this 44.3-hectare 'forward-looking complex' (Emerging Gabon, 2012). The site will include a 'conference centre with a capacity of 10,000, two skyscrapers, a museum-cultural centre, shopping malls with restaurants and boutiques, as well as beach, sports fields and a marina' (Emerging Gabon, 2012). But the plan also includes expensive elements with little functional purpose such as a towering ocean-fountain, an extravagant boardwalk, and life-sized elephant sculptures (figure 12.7).

In his exploration of lowbrow aesthetics, Daniel Harris, author of *Cute, Quaint, Hungry, and Romantic* (2001), showed how a symbology of the 'cute', 'quaint', and 'romantic' may be used to leverage acceptance of a new aesthetic of consumerism. But in this case the projected image of extravagant wealth is not supported by local incomes. And, aside from

Figure 12.7. Rendering of Boardwalk (Libreville, c. 2014). (*Source:* http://www.osskama.org/developpement/le-gabon-emergent-en-action-libreville-se-veut-capitale-du-futur/)

some additional government employment, the tangential benefits of such a megaproject (e.g. new jobs, stimulus through material procurement, and increased demand for white-collar workers) will likely also be missing because the project has been awarded to a Chinese firm, China Harbour Engineering, from funds gathered from the Gabonese government and private investors (StauchVorsterArchitects, 2016; AidData, 2013).[4]

Unfulfilled Dreams in the Republic of Congo

Located just south of Gabon, the Republic of Congo has also benefitted from an oil-for-infrastructure development model. In fact, the country's leadership and willingness to engage China so impressed Chinese President Xi Jinping that he visited the country in the summer of 2016 and announced a package of new investment agreements to help accelerate its industrialization and economic diversification. However, new building in and around the capital of Brazzaville will likely repeat the pattern of disconnection from existing urban fabric already evident in new development there. Among these projects is a newly opened university campus named after President Denis Sassou Nguesso that is composed of low-slung, widely spaced, International Style buildings surrounded by acres of parking.

In Congo much of the imagined modern makeover has also evaporated before it could be built. Particularly intriguing was the failure to realize an ultra-modern proposal for a series of venues and grounds for the 2015

Figure 12.8. Pan African Games Master Plan (Brazzaville, c. 2013). (*Source:* http://www.archdaily.com/383731/pan-african-games-masterplan-competition-entry-group-iad)

Pan African Games. Original renderings for the complex in northern Brazzaville showed a series of amoeba-like buildings floating over a surface of parking lots and ambiguous groundcover. Located on the urban fringe, the site was previously agricultural land with little connection to the city. Yet, even so, the design's fluid, swirling geometries were literally applied to the site without regard for context or connection to public infrastructure (figure 12.8).

Designed initially by the Paris- and Madrid-based Independent Architectural Diplomacy (IAD), the fluid shapes were intended to echo the morphology of the nearby Congo River. But closer examination of renderings and drawings reveal that this design approach could never have supported the staging of a real event. It included a pedestrian network twisted into a bottlenecked arcing geometry, perimeter parking lots stylized for show instead of traffic management, an almost totally unstudied connection to surrounding areas, and buildings designed to resemble sensationalized landforms without regard for function. Furthermore, considering the site's remote location and the lack of provision for public transportation from other areas of Brazzaville, spectators and contestants were given little choice other than to drive to the site. Alternatively, if they did not want to commute, they could dream of staying in the project's futuristic on-site hotel.

The aerial renderings used to envision and sell such fantasies of capitalist modernity must, however, be understood as inherently deceptive. The very sense of grandeur from which they derive their seductive power is a product of their ability to exude a sense of domination and control over the landscape. But to do so, they relate almost no information about the actual experience of place at a human level.

Imagery over Substance

Developments like the ones described here represent a new tradition of placemaking in west-central Africa. Hungry for natural resources, a resurgent China has moved in with its own traditions of development based on specialization, technology, and control. Chinese developers have co-opted local leaders who profit in this quest for aesthetic progress. What is not new, however, is the tradition of exploitation and subjugation. The powerful local elites thus continue to sell off their country's resources to the highest bidder, which in this case is China. It is ironic that a 'communist' country like China is operating under what is in effect a capitalist model that harkens back to the days of colonialism.

These projects also highlight the difficulty faced by African nations in reckoning with their history of colonial exploitation while simultaneously seeking to gain recognition as legitimate destinations for global investment. Meanwhile, nationalist leaders continue to insist on maintaining a tight grip on power through a mirage of aesthetic accomplishment, chains of business patronage, and cooperation with a neocolonial power.

In the past, the colonial powers in west-central Africa saw little benefit to educating the local populace. Indeed, only three Gabonese were known to have received college degrees at the time the country acquired sovereignty from France in 1960 (Podur, 2014). In west-central Africa, the past several decades have thus been as much about developing a functioning political economy as about the construction of cities and high-profile architecture.

Typically, one characteristic of a developed economy is a strong intellectual service sector that can support consulting and technology development. But without reliable primary and secondary schools and universities, countries in the region continue to have difficulty staffing high-level (and thus high-paying) service jobs.[5] Despite such obvious weaknesses, the construction of high-profile urban architecture continues as if there were a skilled workforce ready and able to benefit from and inhabit it. Meanwhile, the oil-for-infrastructure development model does little to build local capacity, and government spending on peripheral megaprojects takes resources away from social programmes such as education, healthcare, and government services. The present building boom, then, with all its attendant spectacle, has so far been a missed opportunity in terms of creating or sustaining an imagined middle class.

No doubt, this is a new version of an old story involving the struggle for independence. However, this time the role of imagined wealth and the aesthetics of consumerism directly implicates the work of urban planners and architects. New built environments (that promise modernity and prosperity) not only fulfil a functional purpose, but satisfy a key imaginary through their ostentatious display of recognizable objects of visual capitalism. This imaginary, however, comes with a steep price.

In the race for international status and prestige, or perhaps just to be acknowledged, the newly independent nations of west-central Africa persist in dreaming of themselves as modern actors. To do so, they are leveraging vast resources to fund the development of urban centres. But since much of the work is outsourced to China, these projects may have little or no economic impact on marginalized portions of the populations (Cain, 2014, p. 562). As Zafar (2007, p. 121) has pointed out, the risk here is that the new relationship between Africa and China, supposedly a mutually beneficial match between developing areas of the world, will merely reprise the failures of the colonial era, which was marked by resource extraction and the neglect for human capital. Meanwhile, the chance to build a new, more locally relevant architecture seems to have been totally abandoned in favour of neomodernist imagery.

Whose traditions are these?

Notes

1. The first general principle of the Constitution of the Confucius Institutes is to serve as a guide in '… enhancing understanding of the Chinese language and culture … [and] strengthening educational and cultural exchange and cooperation between China and other countries …' (HABAN, 2014).
2. This is a common paraphrasing of a statement by the mid-nineteenth-century British prime minister and foreign secretary to the House of Commons on 1 March 1848: 'I say that it is a narrow policy to suppose that this country or that is to be marked out as the eternal ally or the perpetual enemy of England. We have no eternal allies, and we have no perpetual enemies. Our interests are eternal and perpetual, and those interests it is our duty to follow…'.
3. The fact that this foundation, directed by England's Prince Charles, boasts of helping to prepare town plans for sites in former European colonies is itself ironic.
4. The most important byproduct of Chinese investment in Gabon may ultimately be the creation of national infrastructure. Projects that have commenced include new boulevards for public transit, the Trans Gabonese Rail Line (to improve manganese

export), the development of Port Gentil, new airports in Franceville and Port Gentil, and more than 3,500 km of new highways, such as the Owendo–Nkok road, which will allow heavy truck traffic to bypass Libreville to support its Special Economic Zone (Kimball, 2013, pp. 4, 10, 26; AidData, 2013). Most of this investment is primarily directed at improving export efficiency; however, it may also eventually boost the domestic economy.

5. However, all three countries studied here have recently invested in important educational projects. New national universities, for example, in Angola and the Republic of Congo and a new master plan for Université Omar Bongo in Gabon are a welcome trend.

References

AidData (2013) Chinese Company Signs Contract for Expansion of Port Mole in Libreville. Available at: http://china.aiddata.org/projects/30569.

Bado, N. (2012) Community-driven development: a viable approach to poverty reduction in rural Burkina Faso. *African Development Review*, **24**(1), pp. 34–40.

Benazeraf, D. and Alves, A. (2014) 'Oil for Housing': Chinese-built New Towns in Angola. SAIIA Policy Briefing 88. Johannesburg: South African Institute of International Affairs. Available at: http://www.saiia.org.za/policy-briefings/507-oil-for-housing-chinese-built-new-towns-in-angola/file.

Berman, M. (1982) *All That is Solid Melts into Air: The Experience of Modernity*. New York: Penguin.

Bernault, F. (2015) Aesthetics of acquisition: notes on the transactional life of persons and things in Gabon. *Comparative Studies in Society and History*, **57**(3), pp.753–779.

Bing, J. and Ceccoli, S. (2013) Contending narratives in China's African development. *Journal of Third World Studies*, **30**(2), pp. 107–136.

Burgos, S. and Ear, S. (2012) China's oil hunger in Angola: history and perspective. *Journal of Contemporary China*, **21**(74), pp. 351–367.

Cain, A. (2014) African urban fantasies: past lessons and emerging realities. *Environment and Urbanization*, **26**(2), pp. 561–567.

Çelik, Z. (1992) Le Corbusier, orientalism, colonialism. *Assemblage*, **17**, pp. 58–77.

Corkin, L. (2012) Chinese construction companies in Angola: a local linkages perspective. *Resources Policy*, **37**, pp. 475–483.

Emerging Gabon (2012) Emergence Work Projects for Tomorrow's Gabon. LeGabon. ORG, 10 December. Available at: http://www.en.legabon.org/news/1099/emergence-work-projects-tomorrow-s-gabon.

Esteban, E. (2014) Gabon: Angondjé small town model. *Jeune Afrique*, 9 January. Available at: http://www.jeuneafrique.com/135030/societe/gabon-angondj-petite-ville-mod-le/.

García-Rodríguez, J.L., García-Rodríguez, F.J., Castilla-Gutiérrez, C. and Adriano Major, S. (2015) Oil, power, and poverty in Angola. *African Studies Review*, **58**, pp. 159–176.

Gordon, C. (2016) Mapping Decline: St. Louis and the American City. Interactive website and supporting information. University of Iowa. Available at: http://mappingdecline.lib.uiowa.edu/.

HABAN (2014) Constitution and By-Laws of the Confucius Institutes. *Confucius Institute Headquarters*. Available at: http://www.haban.org.

Harris, D. (2001) *Cute, Quaint, Hungry and Romantic: The Aesthetics of Consumerism*. Boston, MA: Da Capo Press.

Harvey, D. (2008) The right to the city. *New Left Review*, No. 53, pp. 23–30.

Jameson, F. (1984) Postmodernism, or the cultural logic of late capitalism. *New Left Review*, No. 146, pp. 53–92.

Kabamba, P. (2012) A tale of two cities: urban transformation in gold-centered Butembo and diamond-rich Mbuji-Mayi, Democratic Republic of the Congo. *Journal of Contemporary African Studies*, **30**(4), pp. 669–685.

Kimball, W. (2013) Delivering the Vision. Bechtel Status Update for Autumn 2013.

Melvin, J. (2012) Perkins + Will's University Campus in Luanda, Angola. *The Architectural Review*, 24 April. Available at: http://www.architectural-review.com/today/perkins wills-university-campus-in-luanda-angola/8629302.fullarticle.

Munslow, B. (1999) Angola: the politics of unsustainable development. *Third World Quarterly*, **20**(3), pp. 551–568.

Naidu, S. and Mbazima, D. (2008) China-African relations: a new impulse in a changing continental landscape. *Futures*, **40**, pp. 748–761.

Ngare, E. (2015) Universidade Agostinho Neto / Perkins + Will Architects. *ArchiDatum*, 28 March. Available at: http://www.archidatum.com/projects/universidade-agostin ho-neto-perkins-plus-will-architects/.

Nossiter, A. (2009) Underneath palatial skin, corruption rules Gabon. *New York Times*, 14 September, pp. 1–2.

Podur, J. (2014) A Short Course on Development in 'Post-Conflict' Congo. *Radical Teacher*, **98**, pp. 52–57.

Power, M. (2012) Angola 2025: the future of the 'world's richest poor country' as seen through a Chinese rear-view mirror. *Antipode*, **44**(3), pp. 993–1014.

RMB Westport (2016) Available at: http://www.muximashopping.co.ao/aboutUs.asp.

Rodrigues, C.U. and Tavares, A.P. (2012) Angola's planned and unplanned urban growth: diamond mining towns in the Lunda provinces. *Journal of Contemporary African Studies*, **30**(4), pp. 687–703.

Sautman, B. and Hairong, Y. (2007) Friends and interests: China's distinctive links with Africa. *African Studies Review*, **50**(3), pp. 75–114.

StauchVorsterArchitects (2016) Port Mole Waterfront. Available at: http://www.sva rchitects.com/?project=port-mole-waterfront.

UN DATA (2016) *World Statistics Pocketbook*. New York: United Nations Statistics Division. Available at: http://data.un.org/CountryProfile.aspx?crName=angola.

World Bank Development Workshop (2012) *Angolan Urban Land Policies, Strengthening Citizenship through Upgrading Informal Settlements*. Washington DC: World Bank, p. 7.

Zafar, A. (2007) The growing relationship between China and Sub-Saharan Africa: macroeconomic, trade, investment and aid links. *The World Bank Research Observer*, **22**(1), pp. 103–130.

Reflections

Chapter 13

The Agency of Belonging: Identifying and Inhabiting Tradition

Mike Robinson

The provocation inviting us to consider 'Whose tradition?' is fascinating because traditions do not float freely in the ether but rather are constructed attachments to individuals, communities, nations, and cultures. It is central to understand these attachments not as given, unchanging relationships but as ones that ebb and flow in a wider context. Establishing and identifying a specific tradition is an attempt to *anchor* values expressed in various ways against agents of change and for specific purposes. This positions the concept of tradition as a process; some may view it as a strategy to resist change, some as a means to ameliorate and negotiate change, and others as a state of flux – bound up with the shifting sands of modernity.[1]

Over the years the discussion around tradition and the idea of the traditional has begun to move to a more flexible and discursive place that recognizes the subjectivity of its uses and the complexity of the environments it is used within. The conflation of process with progress has largely evaporated. The dark binaries that used to divide the world into either societies that have progressed/modernized/civilized or those that have not (and thus by default remain 'traditional') have certainly faded – though they have not fully disappeared. Change is no longer the mere diachronic passing of time but rather a much more complex and randomizing process that challenges certainties and problematizes tradition. What we once conceived of as solid is now fluid and harder to isolate, situate, and interrogate; it is within this fluidity that we can locate tradition.

Over the years, catalyzed in particular through the work of IASTE, the 'tradition' concept has indeed been interrogated, in part demonstrating its potency, pervasiveness, and persistence, as well as its semantic slipperiness. In no insignificant way, the concept is generally approached through its materiality – the structures and objects that signify meaningful continuities and the ways the urban and rural landscapes display valued trophies of the past. I have always found it telling that by far the longest chapter in Edward Shils's landmark text *Tradition* (1981) is the second, 'The Endurance of Past Objects'. For nearly 100 pages – almost one-third of the book – he deals with the materialities of tradition, though he recognizes that objects, be they buildings or books, are the mere vehicles of intangible intellect. It is indeed in the material world that we embed meaning, and it is sensible (in its most literal definition) that we look to objects and buildings as reference points for continuity. But, as Dell Upton (1993), among others, has suggested, the danger in this approach is that it tends to privilege a 'Western' hegemonic category, which speaks of an objectively determined 'authenticity' that can become stranded within a reality of emergence, adaptation and transformation. However, there is a fine ethical and epistemological line between the embodied traditional – which is worthy of preserving and maintaining – and that which essentializes and dislocates. One only has to examine the UNESCO World Heritage List – or the collections of European national museums – to see that the very denotation and display of 'tradition' (as architecture or as a series of exhibits) can refract our understanding of the present and the future as being fossilized.

Oscillating Desires

Central here is the notion of power – or, in a more active sense, the notion of empowerment: the capacity of communities to make decisions and interventions regarding the extent to which they mobilize the concept of tradition in the context of global change. Foucauldian notions of diffuse, enacted, and discursive power assist in our understanding of tradition as being embedded in social life, professional practice, and organizational scales and hierarchies. And within this context, it is easy to lapse into an idea of tradition as being 'authoritative', with its authoring power reflecting state-dominated discourses and, arguably, its position as an integral, if often uncomfortable, part of modernity. Positioning tradition within modernity itself disrupts both concepts and the binary that continues to structure our reflections. As Nezar AlSayyad (2014) has reminded us, in considering tradition, we need to think through modernity at the other end of the spectrum. But we can no longer see these as opposites; rather, they are merging and melding contingent categories. In his richly detailed analysis of craftsmen on the Greek island of Crete, Michael Herzfeld (2004) thus revealed that traditional skills flourish there not through their innate power to resist modernity but rather as a very part of the processes of globalization. Such traditions are played out for tourists and patterns of consumption that are defined through what Herzfeld termed a 'global hierarchy of value'. This can be seen as a framing device – arguably, almost a mode of entrapment – for nations and individuals and all that lies in between. Class, regional cultures, 'local' cultures, and notions of national identity swirl and spiral around in hierarchies from the dominant world systems and structures of capitalism, consumerism, the legacies of colonialism, and the ideas of a universal morality. The charm, the craft, and the deeply local practices of traditional artisans are as much a part of global capitalism as transnational hotel chains. Everyday life attempts to differentiate and associate – finding itself complicit in emphasizing extant hierarchies. It is thus caught up in reproducing what effectively become marginalities, creating new ways of working with old stereotypes, global imaginaries, and hegemonies.

Tradition implies some degree of continuity – what Foucault (2002) saw as the condition for making history possible – with continuity normally seen as being in *opposition* to processes of change, broadly categorized as modernity. This all-too-simple polarization comes with an obvious moral undercurrent that is easily reversed: it is dependent upon *who* is speaking, when, and from what position. Modernity has long been viewed as the desirable state of being and has widely absorbed a political, technological, and moral superiority. This is closely entwined with the economic promises that the modern is understood to offer: a state of betterment that spans right and left ideologies so that modernity – as the dominant discourse – can be wrapped up in concepts such as globalization and neoliberalism, or in the idea of sustainable development. It would appear a question of extent – of the pace of change and the ability and desire of communities to embrace such change. In a developed-world context, within a relatively short period, the promise of the modern was realized, only to then give way to a nostalgic engagement with the traditional as a sort of *desirable*, 'safe' premodern. Reflexively, in the humanities and social sciences, the idea of tradition, and particularly the tradition of the 'other', remains highly attractive to the modern subject, providing the researcher with a far more interesting place to visit. It comes with its own aesthetic: the irony of the ruined and the run-down, the admiration of craft and content, the authenticity of the subaltern, and the exoticism that distance generates – all captured in the drama of monochrome photography.

This is no doubt an unfair exaggeration, but nonetheless, tradition is a problematic category to clearly identify with from the position of the modern self. There is a danger of 'museumifying' communities and cultures by applying tradition as a label. At the same time the very reification of the traditional taps into an important and omnipresent uncomfortableness within ourselves as the constituent subjects of modernity. This is akin to a sort of mourning, of which nostalgic engagement is a frequent surface expression. Zygmunt Bauman (2006) thus described our fear of modernity and the collapse of order. Émile Durkheim (1984) also wrote of the threats of disorder and what he helpfully termed a 'fear of ambivalence'.[2] Are we afraid of modernity? Is this what draws us back to the category of tradition – as human subjects and also as researchers – precisely because we carry our angst about drifting into the unknown spaces of the future? To put it another way: if certainty could be identified in advance of change, and if desire was only focused on the future rather than what marks the past, would we value tradition in the same way?

The concept of tradition thus makes sense when continuities are made visible and are practiced self-consciously. Indeed, James Clifford (1988) located tradition as a response, a reaction to the historical experience of loss; but he challenged the idea of continuities. The persistent question that follows all discussions of tradition relates to the *extent* to which continuities can, and are willing to be, maintained in social and cultural life. The boundaries between tradition and modernity, however defined, are constantly being negotiated, with appropriate concessions and adaptations made to make any sense of loss bearable. Such negotiations are located in the practice of everyday life. While governments – at all levels – may be complicit in the making of modernity, they nevertheless recognize the public power of tradition and its solidifying effects. In studying tradition, we are drawn into its objectification and the distance this brings. We can observe that what constitutes continuity in the context of tradition, and our desire to maintain it, oscillates widely and relates to what communities and societies consider as possessing value at any given time.

Tradition as Home

Conceptions of 'home' are varied and morph into adjacent ideas of 'homeland' and territory, each with physical and rhetorical dimensions (Morley, 2000). Mary Douglas (1991) thus made the point that home is not necessarily located in space but is more of an organizing concept whereby we bring space under control. Anthony Giddens (1991) made a similar point in recognizing the home as a site for building routines that assist us in maintaining control in everyday life. This regulatory aspect is interesting, as it implies an authority to which we can defer, as a set of 'tested' values that we don't feel the need to question – a sort of lived, comfortable structure that provides meaning. I suggest that in the concept of tradition we are implicitly identifying something that symbolically and emotionally is very close to the idea of home. Like 'home', tradition offers a historical benchmark for change (though often only in retrospect), and also a geographical and sociological comparator when we travel from it – in both space and time. Tradition is a 'place' to which we *feel* we can return. It is what Robin Middleton (1983) termed 'a whole system of values'.[3] We frequently use the idea of 'traditional' as a reference point, not only as an academic measure or punctuation point in the creep of modernity, but also in an evaluative sense as something 'good' – that which has value and is worth retaining. It is the morality we accord to tradition that frequently stimulates the passions when we see it being 'misused' or 'misrepresented'. Distorted representations of the 'classical' tradition in architecture and surface references to, and pastiches of, traditional forms are criticized as much for their lack of reverence as for the aesthetic outcomes.

'Home' plays an important part in structuring our lives, and much like the idea of tradition, it provides a space for understanding our being in the world. It is distinguished by its intimacy; it is a sense of human contact that acts to bridge the sensible and the intelligible worlds. In various examinations of tradition, it is noticeable that we default to the idea of the intimate and the ability to connect, physically and intellectually, to senses of place, feelings of belonging, and of contributing to collective memory. We associate tradition with the human scale, and the personal stories it can yield tend to be those of individuals and small communities, usually in counterpoint to the non-personal meta-narratives of globalization. Indeed, in both fiction and academic study, dealing with tradition has been characterized by ongoing struggles that reveal differing levels of access to knowledge and power. This provides for a particular dramaturgy that permeates many studies of tradition and straddles cynicism and humanistic optimism. To over-romanticize tradition – as, arguably, Amos Rapoport (1969) did in considering the notion of the 'vernacular' – is to risk ignoring the structural realities of neoliberalism which can result in a political distance, a form of commodification, and a denial of creative hybridization. At the same time, to ignore the influence of nostalgia, the impact of the indigenous imaginary, and that feeling of intimacy, is close to accepting those structural realities.

While accepting that there are multiple traditions and multiple modernities, scale (or more precisely sense of scale) cuts across all as a marker of power (or lack of it) and a signifier of subjectivity (Roy, 2001). But beyond scale is the notion of attachment. In understanding conflicts that arise between communities and the state, or between communities and corporate business, the researcher quickly identifies the ways and histories by which people are *attached* to their environments and what such attachments mean in terms of identity. The term 'attachment' (or belonging) seems to be a more apposite term than 'ownership' or 'possession' – though clearly these aspects are important. Such terms transcend the idea of legal possession, so that while we may 'own' a house, we may not form an attachment with it and consider it 'home'. We can thus form attachments to small or large dwellings, to old and new, to single properties or streets and neighbourhoods. While we may express, in a shorthand way, our attachment as a sense of ownership, as something that belongs to us, belonging unravels as a complex concoction of identity, place, intimacy, personalization, continuity, security, safety, support, and – critically – recognition among our immediate peers and the wider world. What home provides in both real and symbolic terms is a *source* of belonging and a framework, which we adopt and carry through life. Tradition, in its material and immaterial forms, is an expression of belonging and something that can feed into and feed off identity – or what James Tuedio (2009) termed 'cultural authentication'.[4]

In this volume, Tim Bunnell thus speaks to a sense of attachment that is both real and imaginary, and that manifests itself in the idea of home that is somewhere we travel from and return to, but against a backdrop of socioeconomic change and major political shifts. Bunnell relates how the sense of home for Malay seafarers in the mid-twentieth century altered as they travelled from Malaysia to the port of Liverpool in the United Kingdom, and then back to Malaysia. Over the course of their lives, these journeys took the sailors into, out of, and back into modernity. The traditions of home in Malaysia were thus initially exchanged for the relative modernity (defined more by household bathroom facilities than architectural development) in the port cities of Liverpool and Cardiff. However, for those returning to Malaysia in the 1980s, in moving away from a then-deindustrializing Britain, they returned to a newly developing and highly visible modernity that exuded political dominance and Islamic identity. Notions of home, as with the desire to be there, also move through generations relative to where we are in the world.

In part, reflecting on the work of Christian Norberg-Schultz (1985), by widening the concept of 'home' to include that of *dwelling*, it is possible to open up a much wider engagement with social and economic worlds, and with the natural environment.[5] 'Home' spills out into wider community subjectivities that absorb understandings of pasts and the processes/evaluations of social and environmental change. Thus, in Gauri Bharat's chapter in this volume, which reflects on her work with an indigenous community (the Santal) in eastern India, traditions, as expressed through domestic architecture and architectural knowledge, are linked to daily life practices; but they are not privileged, nor do they solely define Santal identity. Dwelling, as perceived from an emic perspective, thus crosses many boundaries of what we consider as categories of tradition: tangible and intangible heritage, indigenous and non-indigenous identities, and that which belongs to the past, the present, and the future. Bharat emphasizes in conclusion that it is the local voice of the community that is effectively the agent of tradition and thus needs to be taken into account.

Notwithstanding ideas of invention and reinvention, tradition has mostly been viewed as rooted and cultural transmission as following lines of generational change. As Oliver Morin (2016) has pointed out, the transmission of traditions is not inevitable, nor is it comprehensive; rather, it is selective and partly reconstitutive. Nevertheless, we largely view continuities as place-specific and bound symbiotically to a kind of interactive identity-constructing territorialism. Challenges to tradition thereby emerge from changes over time without considering place. This assumption of geographical rootedness infers that when considering the question of 'Whose tradition?' we can almost intuitively locate traditions and to whom they belong. However, as is widely recognized, global mobilities are redefining notions of place (see, for instance, Sheller and Urry, 2004). Home, more than ever, is a mobile concept, and ideas of belonging are disrupted through the crossing of real and virtual physical/cultural borders, new partialities and temporalities – voluntary and enforced. Yet, the idea and the ideal of home remain embedded in these hypercomplex global flows. Indeed, it takes on a new imperative as an antidote to transient uncertainty. So, too, is this the case with tradition. Thus, AlSayyad (2004) pointed out that in the context of globalization and new configurations of modernity, tradition has not ceased to exist, but rather its basis as a 'static authoritative legacy' has given way to something rather more contingent.

Partial and Temporal Inhabiting

The need to belong to communities, groups, society, and the 'world' has not gone away. On the contrary, it continues to surface and shape our experiences of, and attachments to, tradition – while at the same time it fluctuates and flows with increasing mobilities and shifting desires and aspirations. But we have become increasingly adept at negotiating our sense of belonging and inhabiting traditions that are not our own. Thus, Pico Iyer's (2000) autobiographical account of himself as a 'global soul' not only explores his own hybrid identity but how identity itself is continually tested in a constantly shifting world. Belonging, for Iyer, would seem to be a test – a feeling that is residual, partial, and conditional (as to where he is in the world) all at the same time. Traditions lapse into memories, as different places and cultural spaces are crossed. Even if we don't travel – as most of the world does not – we are tested with the changing cultures that now travel to us.

We move more easily than ever through the traditions of others. Anthony Giddens (1994), in an analysis of the tensions and connections between what he termed 'institutional reflexivity' and a process of 'de-traditionalizing', argued that tradition was closely bound to authority, and he spoke of guardians and experts of tradition as agents of knowledge, and hence power and control. However, Giddens highlighted the ways expertise has become decentred and decontextualized and thus somewhat detached from notions of place. Certainly, if we see tradition as increasingly constructed and animated through practice and participation, rather than as a territorial project (national or regional), then there are fewer systems of authority (or, at least, the systems in place are more easily bypassed). In one sense, this is a sort of liberation; it is reflective of the liquid modernity that Bauman (2000) discussed and that allows for self-defining traditions in changing places. It also allows for a process of adaptation, so that we can evaluate and select which and 'whose' traditions we wish to adopt. Rather than feeling trapped by traditions, we can temporarily inhabit them while moving through life, as if we were tourists experiencing a temporary sense of belonging. Of course, as practicing rather than 'metaphorical' tourists, we do move through the traditions of others, though not always with a feeling of ease or with an awareness of whose tradition. Rather, we tend to mobilize our vacations as a means of reflecting upon our own identity, benchmarking the traditions of others against our own.

In another sense, the dislocation of tradition from place, and particularly from the idea of a nation, disrupts the concept of identity and, paradoxically, can catalyze the retrenchment of tradition and ignite reattachment – particularly through tangible, material culture. In relation to the Western world, Steven Vertovec (2007) used the term 'super-diversity' to make reference to a wide range of geo-socio-political changes, including the end of the Cold War, postcolonialism, and late modernity, that have allowed new transnationalism to take root, particularly in large cities. Here, immigration displays itself as multiple-origin, scattered, and of small communities – all transnationally connected and socioeconomically differentiated. These communities dwell in the traditions they came from as best they can; and at various levels of organization they continue these traditions (front and backstage), aided by whatever aspects of material culture and mobile heritage they have brought with them or have been able to reconstitute. However, simultaneously, they have to inhabit the traditions of their new 'home'. Noticeably, this is a process of ongoing negotiation not only between cultures, but also between generations whose relative accumulations and articulations of tradition are often very different. It also involves a very direct and physical inhabitation of someone else's built and embedded environment, where communities are constituted largely outside of legal ownership and any deep-rooted emotional attachment to the fabric of a city. The processes of re-creating 'new' traditional spaces and structures in or next to old ones are thus slow and frequently contested. In her work on mosque construction across European states, Jocelyne Cesari (2005) made the point that contestability comes about when immigrant groups seek to move out of private space and into public space. And in the case of Muslim communities, it is precisely the visibility of the mosque and its signifying role of Islamic tradition that can generate conflict and contestation within urban settlements.

Susanne Cowan, in her discussion here of neighbourhood politics in St. Louis, highlights the ways in which tradition, visibly expressed in the social and aesthetic character of an area, can be appropriated in the struggle to belong to the city. She conveys how the power to preserve and gentrify the traditional housing stock of the city became embedded and legitimized in preservation policy while increasing both the social and economic capital of the dominant classes. This power serves to exclude other residents (non-white, Eastern-European, and lower-income) not only from property ownership but also from a sense of belonging. The visualization of tradition is also the visualization of identity. However self-defining these aspects may appear to be, within the competitive context of diverse and 'super-diverse' urban space, they are nevertheless bound to dominant discourses of power.

A complementary example is provided by Anne-Marie Broudehoux's contribution, which examines the super-diverse city, Rio de Janeiro, and the impacts of what may be termed a 'mega-tradition' of the 2016 Olympic Games. Here, the intervention of a top-down, reinvented tradition is shown to have the effect of disturbing communities to the point of creating both formal and informal spaces of social exclusion. In such a case, it is easy to see how the trajectories of modernity, as demonstrated through the neoliberal practices of aggressive urbanism, the privatization of space, 'legal exceptionalism', and increased surveillance – all compressed to deliver the Olympic event – act to overthrow notions of community belonging. Even when sites of attachments are the 'no-go-area' *favelas* of the city, the sheer force behind the 'mega-eventism' acts to further fragment communities and preclude any hope of bottom-up traditions establishing themselves.

Sitting somewhat in counterpoint to claims of deterritorialization and global liquidity, Craig Calhoun (2007) maintained that both the nation and nationalism remain a reality, though one in need of redefinition and transformation. There may be increased permeability between borders, but the nation still maintains political and cultural prominence. And while warning against the notion of tradition as being fixed and discrete, Calhoun also emphasized the everydayness of tradition, its centrality at the base of social relations, and its cosmopolitanism through what he termed 'the co-mingling of older traditions and the production of newer ones'. However, while accepting the *possibilities* of tradition, the nation – as both a historic entity and a contemporary space – still provides an important screen onto which identity is persistently projected.

Somewhat understandably, debates about what constitutes a national tradition are hotly contested between and within expert and non-expert communities. This is highlighted in Palazzo and Moura's discussion here of how a sense of Brazilian-ness was forged and hotly debated in the nineteenth century by artists, writers, and architects attempting to reflect a 'national character' for the country. In part, such debate captures the spirit of the time and place by selectively drawing on indigenous and vernacular traditions. But, as the authors point out, the debate itself has agency, in that it, too, continues to surface in contemporary understandings of Brazilian national identity.

Jennifer Gaugler also takes up the role of experts as translators of tradition in her overview of African architects. In the years following independence in Nigeria and Tanzania, these architects were influential in generating new expressions of modernity, not as something imposed through European colonialism but as something rooted in traditional identity and a sense of regionalism.

Architects, developers, and commissioning agents are powerful filters through which concepts of tradition pass. And Marvin Brown's contribution picks up on this influence in relation to the construction of Government House on the island of Guam. He explains how key elites on this colonized Pacific island played out its history, blending an indigenous and somewhat imagined Chamorro style with Spanish colonial and American interpretations of tradition and modernity, to produce an architectural form that speaks to the fundamental hybridization of its cultural heritage.

In the context of 'Whose tradition?' the nation still matters – indeed, arguably more so for those countries that have emerged/are emerging from years of colonial scripting (Gregory, 2002).[6] The concept of the 'national' frames many of our traditions; nations struggle to preserve traditions through contrived structures and organizations designed to link reciprocally tradition, entwined with heritage, to a national idea. And questions regarding 'Whose nation?' are intimately linked with 'Whose tradition?'. For instance, national tradition as a point of differentiation is the first face of international tourism, which significantly still works with reductionist but recognizable typologies of place and peoples.[7] Despite cosmopolitan churnings and the complexities (also possibilities) that 'super-diversity' presents, there remains a duality in terms of those traditions that are presented and displayed and those that are experienced by host and guest alike.

Trapped in Tradition

While for tourists and migrants the conception of tradition has become increasingly fluid – allowing for different types of attachments and different relations with modernity – in situated parts of the postcolonial world, whose residents cannot or do not travel, communities live on a day-to-day basis with inherited and imposed traditions. For communities inhabiting cities and towns constructed in various parts through imperial pasts, the relationships that exist with these remnant buildings and monuments have long been under scrutiny. For example, for the British tourist walking through the streets of present-day Chennai (formerly Madras) in India, the municipal buildings and the urban townhouses will be reminders of any large nineteenth-century industrial city in the United Kingdom (Scrivner and Prakash, 2007). This is at once both a reminder of 'home' and a reference point for colonial history. There is no longer any sense of 'possession' on the part of the tourist but merely a feeling of distant and perhaps uneasy connection. But encounters with the British traditional, colonial architecture are overlaid by layers of otherness and distance: the heat, the language, the social practices, and the relative and visible poverty that stands in stark contrast to the edifices of former colonialization. In such locations the notion of 'Whose tradition?' is highly problematic for the local population, who are in some ways metaphorically trapped in the built and highly symbolic tradition of the colonizers.

This theme is picked up by Jayde Lin Roberts's contribution, in which she discusses the ongoing processes of negotiation regarding the legacy of British colonial buildings in Yangon, Myanmar. In the context of a country and city moving into a new globalized future, she highlights the tensions involved around what she terms a 'tradition of modernity' and how these may best be mobilized. The built environment established by the British in what was then Rangoon could play a role in the relaunching of the city as a focal point for heritage and an attractive asset for adaptive reuse and development. At the same time, the colonial architecture and urban morphology serves as a reminder of not only oppression and resistance, but also of denying Burmese identity and tradition while preventing the leap into the modernity that is displayed in most Southeast Asian capitals.

In the case of Yangon, as in other cities which struggle with the legacies of colonial/foreign incursions into 'home', the re-evaluation of tradition also generates debate around ownership and property rights. Questions of ownership, attachment, and belonging are not restricted to the traditional, but also relate to modernity. Often characterized as an anonymous, faceless, almost self-propelling force, modernity (as with tradition) is simultaneously *owned* by everyone and no one. Claims of attachment are political claims that permeate and challenge belonging. As Partha Chatterjee (2004) has suggested, struggle and the project of social transformation in postcolonial cities are not only a question of modernity or a relative transition from tradition, but are also an issue of democracy. However, democracy is not an automatic guardian of tradition, and neither can it be relied upon to offer a mechanism for its (re)interpretation.

It is in this regard that Tiago Castela's contribution discusses the memorials and monuments to and of colonialism in Mozambique and in present-day Portugal as these relate to the democratization of the former colonizer. The narratives that accompany such monuments in Lisbon persist in speaking of a 'violence of spatial division' and inequality. In contrast, in Mozambique, the post-independence government mobilized the memorials of conquest and empire as part of the decolonization project. Many of the statues and sculptures that celebrated the conquest were removed from the capital, Maputo, and have been placed in the central Fortaleza of the city as an open-air museum. In part, as Castela seems to suggest, this is a function of blending these objects into the wider 'heritagescape' of the city, and thus bypassing their political significance. These remainders and reminders of division thus become absorbed almost uncritically into other traditions.

Breaking out of the tradition trap is problematic and invokes processes of introspection and socio-political fracture among communities as to how far they are prepared to trade, or rather reappraise, their attachments to markers of *their* identity. Shu-Mei Huang explores this 'opening up' and interrogation of community histories in her examination of the politics of 'traditional' house building in the New Territories of Hong Kong. Here the power play of tradition, as expressed through 'rights' to build, uncovers tensions between (imposed/invented) indigenous and non-indigenous peoples, between the rural and the urban, between the formal and the informal (Roy and AlSayyad, 2004), and between male and female (in terms of inheritance rights). Tradition in this case is very much one of process; moreover, it is a process that reflects the precarious and contested dual identity of Hong Kong and what Homi Bhabha (1994) termed 'post-colonial ambivalence'. In recognizing tradition as process, we acknowledge a multiplicity of forms of governance that oversees, participates in, and shapes, implicitly and explicitly, the negotiations between interest groups representing various points along the conceptual tradition-modernity continuum. Tradition is the stuff of politics, particularly in the dynamic, competitive spaces of the urban. Traditions carry value, not only in terms of real estate prices but also in terms of political capital. In considering 'Whose tradition?' we are invariably led to the way politics apprehends and allocates value in real and symbolic terms, and the way it builds and disrupts constituencies that attach themselves to particular traditions. In the city it is inevitably a politics of space that pervades, and in a sense, urban politics itself is the trap for traditions.

Thus, in his contribution here, Abidin Kusno writes of the ways that the formal and particularly the informal traditions of urban politics operate in the contested and pressured spaces of Jakarta, Indonesia. These political traditions, which over the past several decades have spanned the authoritarian and bureaucratic to the decentralized and complicit informality, demonstrate both a positive and negative impact, particularly on marginalized communities, and are closely tied to the political character of the changing governors of the city. What Kusno's analysis demonstrates is that behind the visible expressions of tradition in the built environment lie more invisible, intangible traditions that exert agency and have the capacity to shape not just urban fabric, but notions of belonging.

Claiming and Feeling Belonging

As with much of the discourse surrounding the concept of tradition, the terrain is tricky and punctuated by some intractable questions, including that of 'Whose tradition?'. However, the debate has moved on considerably from viewing tradition as something solid, continuous, and disconnected from modernity – and indeed, a host of other factors relating to globalization, new mobilities, and social change. Moreover, tradition is no longer the sole territory of the nation, but now performs real, symbolic, and imaginary functions for local groups and communities. As AlSayyad (2004, p. 40) wrote: '… tradition should also be viewed as an arena of mediation between the hegemony of national or local cultures and the exercise choice by some members or groups of that society'. Groups and individuals have always claimed tradition(s) as a point of reference, as an expression of power, and as a way of challenging power. Increasingly, however, such claims are made as a way of belonging to old and new communities alike, both within and beyond the nation-state. While we may still instinctively look for tradition in its material form (in art and craft, in the built environment, etc.) we truly find it in the relationships that are formed between communities and the material world, and between people. We find (feel) it in the processes of searching for identity, of negotiating, of political manoeuvring, of large and small economic transactions, and in the very act of belonging.

Ultimately, all the chapters within this volume deal with the ways belonging and its articulation, through planning, constructing, adjusting, inhabiting, and searching for 'home', is constantly negotiated. The intricate processes of negotiation (economic, political, etc.) take place simultaneously at the meta-level and the personal level, and develop their own momentum, which redefines the meanings and expressions of tradition. This constantly shifting landscape continues to demand the attention of scholars.

Notes

1. The shift from seeing tradition as an 'ancient' and unchanging entity to more of a process was liberated by Hobsbawm and Ranger's (1983) work on the invention/inventiveness of tradition. A more pragmatic notion of tradition, which allows its mobilization and strategic use, has, however, been picked up in the works of numerous anthropologists – e.g. Smith (1982), Toren (1988) and Sahlins (1999).
2. Durkheim's prescient notions of anomie and ambiguity through social change were developed in the context of the postmodern world by Bauman (1993).
3. These views were presented in a lecture to the Royal Society of the Arts. At the time Middleton was Head of General Studies at the Architectural Association School of

Architecture and Librarian at the Faculty of Architecture and History of Art, University of Cambridge.
4. The idea of cultural authentification is rooted in what James Tuedio (2009, p. 289) has referred to as '… nostalgic concepts of domestic identity. These material or spiritual constructions of home speak of a familiar, self-evident atmosphere of trust and belonging'.
5. Norberg-Schultz (1985) used the concept of dwelling as a guiding concept for architectural practice and the construction of 'place'.
6. The term 'scripting' is taken from Derek Gregory (2002) in his examination of how colonial travel writing reflects the power to impose a particular narrative and construct an otherness that is prone to essentialize traditions.
7. An important but often overlooked point that reflects upon the travelling world, in terms of tourism and despite a few exceptions, is that tradition sells better than modernity, indicating – for the developed world anyway – the role that tradition plays in social life.

References

AlSayyad, N. (2004) The end of tradition or the tradition of endings, in AlSayyad, N. (ed.) *The End of Tradition?* London: Routledge, pp. 1–28.
AlSayyad, N. (2014) *Traditions: The 'Real', the Hyper, and the Virtual in the Built Environment.* London: Routledge.
Bauman, Z. (1993) *Modernity and Ambivalence.* Cambridge: Polity Press.
Bauman, Z. (2000) *Liquid Modernity.* Cambridge: Polity Press.
Bauman, Z. (2006) *Liquid Fear.* London: Polity Press.
Bhabha, H.K. (1994) *The Location of Culture.* London: Routledge.
Calhoun, C. (2007) *Nations Matter: Culture, History and the Cosmopolitan Dream.* London: Routledge.
Cesari, J. (2005) Mosque conflicts in European cities. *Journal of Ethnic and Migration Studies*, **31**(6), pp. 1015–1024.
Chatterjee, P. (2004) *The Politics of the Governed: Reflections on Political Society in Most of the World.* New York: Columbia University Press.
Clifford, J. (1988) *The Predicament of Culture: Twentieth-Century Ethnography, Literature, and Art.* Cambridge, MA: Harvard University Press.
Douglas, M. (1991) The idea of a home: a kind of space. *Social Research*, **58**(1), pp. 287–307.
Durkheim, E. (1984 [1893]) *The Division of Labour in Society.* London: Macmillan.
Foucault, M. (2002) *The Archaeology of Knowledge*, translator A.M. Sheridan Smith. London: Routledge.
Giddens, A. (1991) *Modernity and Self-Identity: Self and Society in the Late Modern Age.* Stanford, CA: Stanford University Press.
Giddens, A. (1994) Living in a Post-Traditional Society, in Beck, U., Giddens, A. and Lash, S. (eds.) *Reflexive Modernization: Politics, Tradition and Aesthetics in the Modern Social Order.* Cambridge: Polity Press, pp. 56–109.
Gregory, D. (2002) Scripting Egypt: Orientalism and the cultures of travel, in Duncan, J. and Gregory, D. (eds.) *Writes of Passage: Reading Travel Writing.* London: Routledge, pp. 114–150.
Herzfeld, M. (2004) *The Body Impolitic: Artisans and Artifice in the Global Hierarchy of Value.* Chicago, IL: University of Chicago Press.

Hobsbawm, E. and Ranger, T. (eds.) (1983) *The Invention of Tradition*. Cambridge: Cambridge University Press.

Iyer, P. (2000) *The Global Soul: Jet Lag, Shopping Malls and the Search for Home*. London: Bloomsbury.

Middleton, R. (1983) The use and abuse of tradition in architecture. *Journal of the Royal Society of Arts*, **131**, pp.729–739.

Morin, O. (2016) *How Traditions Live and Die*. Oxford: Oxford University Press.

Morley, D. (2000) *Home Territories: Media, Mobility and Identity*. London: Routledge.

Norberg-Schulz, C. (1985) *The Concept of Dwelling: On the Way to Figurative Architecture*. Milan: Rizzoli.

Rapoport, A. (1969) *House Form and Culture*. Englewood Cliffs, NJ: Prentice-Hall.

Roy, A. (2001) Traditions of the modern: a corrupt view. *Traditional Dwellings and Settlements Review*, **4**(2), pp. 7–19.

Roy, A. and AlSayyad, N. (2004) *Urban Informality: Transnational Perspectives from the Middle East, Latin America, and South Asia*. New York: Lexington Books.

Sahlins, M. (1999) Two or three things that I know about culture. *The Journal of the Royal Anthropological Institute*, **5**(3), pp. 399–421.

Scrivner, P. and Prakash, V. (2007) Between materiality and representation: framing an architectural critique of colonial South Asia, in Scrivner, P. and Prakash, V. (eds.) *Colonial Modernities: Building, Dwelling and Architecture in British India and Ceylon*. London: Routledge, pp. 3–27.

Sheller, M. and Urry, J. (2004) *Tourism Mobilities: Places to Play, Places in Play*. London: Routledge.

Shils, E. (1981) *Tradition*. Chicago, IL: University of Chicago Press.

Smith, M.E. (1982) The process of sociocultural continuity. *Current Anthropology*, **23**(2), pp. 127–142.

Toren, C. (1988) Making the present, revealing the past: the mutability and continuity of tradition as process. *Man*, **23**(4), pp. 696–717.

Tuedio, J.A. (2009) Ambiguities in the locus of home: exilic life and the space of belonging, in Johansson, H. and Saarikangas, K. (eds.) *Homes in Transformation: Dwelling, Moving, Belonging*. Helsinki: Finnish Literary Society, pp. 284–310.

Upton, D. (1993) The tradition of change. *Traditional Dwellings and Settlements Review*, **5**(1), pp. 9–16.

Vertovec, S. (2007) Super-diversity and its implications. *Ethnic and Racial Studies*, **30**(6), pp. 1024–1054.

Chapter 14

Process and Polemic

Dell Upton

'Whose tradition?' is a question that grows thornier the more one handles it. Both words in this short sentence embed assumptions that may not bear up under scrutiny. 'Whose tradition?' frames the traditional as a finite commodity, one that can be owned, treasured, lost, borrowed, or stolen. It grants traditional sites and practises a coherence, a boundedness, that raises all sorts of intellectual problems, but that, in the political realm examined in many of the contributions to this volume, can be a powerful weapon.

Our colloquial understanding of tradition derives from the work of anthropologists, folklorists, architectural historians, and material-culture scholars of the late nineteenth and early twentieth centuries. These scholars studied people whom they imagined to live outside historical time or in an earlier stage of cultural evolution. For anthropologists, the subjects were almost always people in colonized societies remote from Euro-America. Folklorists turned to internally colonized members of their own societies whom they thought had been excluded from modernity – isolated farmers, ethnic and racial minorities – to find survivals of past cultural practices. In both cases, the assumption was that some cultural practices were anachronisms, and that to survive they needed to be isolated from the broader society. Tradition was regarded as a closed, static and holistic system, its nature memorably summarized in the anthropologist Robert Redfield's classic *The Little Community* (1960, p. 4), which portrayed self-contained, self-sufficient societies.

Tradition as commonly imagined has roots in an unspecified, often indeterminate, past. As James Deetz (1967, p. 61) once put it from an archaeological perspective, tradition has great time depth but narrow spatial (we might also substitute social) distribution: it is 'a configuration of traits with a very long life'. Yet as our thinking has developed, we have come to understand that not all traditions are what they appear to be. Eric

Hobsbawm's and Terence Ranger's influential exploration of 'invented' traditions made this point forcefully; but in all other respects the essays in *The Invention of Tradition* (1983) still adhered to traditional *tradition*. They continued to assume coherent bodies of practices that were initiated fairly recently but that claimed to be ancient, usually for broadly political purposes.

Moreover, tradition is always viewed in relation to something else. Deetz (1967, p. 59) contrasted a tradition with a horizon, 'a set of traits which links a number of cultures over a broad area in a short time'. Such rapidly disseminated cultural innovations could be the result of missionization or conquest, he thought; but they could also be seen to resemble the process of modernization as it has been elaborated over the past half-century. As many scholars have noted, the concept of tradition is a complement to, and meaningless without, the concept of modernity. Indeed, the idea of tradition was created by people conscious of, and sometimes discomforted by, the experience of modernity. Tradition was the reverse image of everything that the modern was thought to encompass.

The more we scrutinize tradition and modernity, the more difficult it is to differentiate the two ideas. I often think of a life-sized portrait photograph of the Meaders family, potters from northeastern Georgia, that I once saw at the Atlanta History Center. The family members held face jugs and other vessels in prized 'folk' forms. But they were wearing sneakers, baseball caps, blue jeans, and Atlanta Braves t-shirts. How might we understand tradition as enacted in this image?

One way would be to see the photograph as an image of tradition on life support. According to John Burrison, the principal scholar of the Meaders's work, their pottery was a product of:

… an age in rural Georgia, not so long ago that it cannot be vividly recalled by people still living, when time was not measured by the ticking of a clock but by the rising and setting sun, the phases of the moon, and the changing seasons. This was a time when men and women had a close – and often hard – working relationship with nature. Each farm and settlement was a self-contained, diversified organism, producing for itself out of the natural environment most of the necessities of living which now, in our machine age, require hundreds of specialists and a complex distribution network.

People then relied on the teachings of the past, traditional ways of doing things that had been handed down from generation to generation, changing slightly to remain relevant but always preserving the basic patterns so long as they proved useful…

This was an age of hands, when local craftspeople produced the bulk of material goods needed on the farm… (Burrison, 1983, p. 3)

As modernity encroached on people such as Burrison's Georgia farmers, folklorists and anthropologists believed, tradition inevitably collapsed. Much folkloristic practice from the late nineteenth to the late twentieth century was thus devoted to recording and, if possible, salvaging traditional cultural practices that were always disappearing but that seemed never quite to disappear (Upton, 1995). The assumption was that modernity is irresistible. Confronted with the power and promises of the modern, traditional societies quickly abandoned their old ways in favour of new ones. Similarly, when certain practices were maintained – crafts, music, foodways, architecture – it was assumed that a few people had made a *choice not to change* in those limited corners of their lives. They were *resisting* the modern. We could interpret the Meaders photograph this way: allegiance to tradition in pottery-making endured despite the incursion of the 'hundreds of specialists and a complex distribution network' that produced the family's clothing.

Another way to look at the encounter of tradition with modernity is to see the Meaders's modern clothing as products of a *choice to change*. In this light, modernity expands the range of material possibilities rather than sweeping away earlier ones. Thus, as the Meaders entered the modern economy, they found many of its products useful to their lifeways and chose to incorporate them into their everyday lives. But there was no reason to stop making pottery (or eating certain foods, or singing certain songs, or believing certain religious doctrines).

Henry Glassie's (1999*a*, pp. 36, 39) discussion of the Meaders points to a third possible reading of the photograph. John Milton Meaders founded the pottery in 1892. At that time, few people even in the poorest and most remote areas of the United States were unaffected in some way by the modern economy and its cultural products. Nevertheless, John Meaders's butter churns and other utilitarian vessels continued to be useful to local farmers. But by the 1930s, this was no longer so, and production languished. Fortuitously, this was about the time that modern artists and architects invented 'folk' art and architecture as inspiration for contemporary design. Cheever Meaders, John's son, was thus elevated to the status of folk artist, and the family business revived. In the 1970s Cheever's son Lanier quit his job in a mobile-home factory to take over the work. Lanier's children and nieces and nephews now run the pottery.

Seen in this light, there is no tension to be resolved in the Meaders family photograph. Pottery-making provided an income in the local agricultural economy, and it continued to do so in the modern, consumer economy. The Meaders responded to their changing clientele by reviving 'folk' forms of the nineteenth century, such as face jugs, a synthesis of familiar European, African, and West-Indian ceramic forms first made by African-American potters in nearby South Carolina (Vlach, 1978, pp. 81–85). They also created new shapes and new glazes that appealed to the aesthetic sensibilities of their new audience. To succeed in the contemporary economy, the Meaders donned the mask of the folk, even if their costumes were modern.[1]

As we consider successive ways to interpret the modern dress of the Meaders in the photograph, and through it the relationship of the traditional and the modern, tradition's apparently self-contained, cohesive nature dissolves under scrutiny, as does its time-anchored, static nature. The social and material practices that we call traditional meld into the variety of ever-changing habits of varying ages to which we attach the equally slippery label *culture*. If we must use the word tradition, it might be better to think of it less as an entity than as a process through which new ideas and practices are integrated into, rather than sweeping away, older ones. Tradition is an assemblage of disparate, learned practices that operate, and can change, independently. We see this everywhere around us in the choices individual actors make. At the same time, these independent variables, imagined as a cohesive entity, are often comfortable ways of organizing social life or convenient fictions that can be evoked strategically. (I'll come back to this point later.)

The reified idea of tradition nonetheless retains its hold both among scholars and the public at large. In a recent press release, the Merriam-Webster dictionary company identified *culture* and *nostalgia* as 2014's most searched words.[2] The modernist polemic that viewed the preindustrial landscape as a repository of superior aesthetic and sometimes moral values has been reinforced by broad popular nostalgia for a premodern, usually pre-urban golden age free of the tensions of the present.[3] Thus, shelter magazines and bookstores are full of advice about using 'traditional' or 'ethnic' or 'folk' imagery in contemporary urban settings as an aesthetic and ethical gesture, while architects turn to the reified traditional as a touchstone for authentic design.[4] Consider, for example, this blurb advertising the book *African Style* (Guibourge et al., 1998) on the Barnes and Noble website:

What is modern today? Cutting-edge decoration is about plundering the past and crossing geographical boundaries in order to combine furniture and objects from disparate times and places. This series on interior design focuses on contemporary trends incorporating furnishings from different cultures throughout the world, showing how to achieve authentic atmosphere with just the right touch.[5]

Among scholars, this way of seeing the traditional leads to an emphasis on the visual and the internally consistent as authenticators of tradition. Nezar AlSayyad alluded to this habit in his opening remarks to the IASTE 2014 conference in Kuala Lumpur (at which much of the work in this volume was first presented), when he spoke of a tendency to emphasize 'image over experience'. His point is underlined in the chapters here by Pedro Paulo Palazzo and Ana Amelia de Paula Moura and by Jennifer Gaugler, which recount architectural debates over the cultural authenticity of recent buildings. The same might be said about Gauri Bharat's contribution, which reveals the divergence of perception about local architectural history between scholars and the village communities they study.

An index of the continuing power of image as a guarantor of tradition is the tenacious regard among architects and scholars with architectural training for Bernard Rudofsky's *Architecture without Architects* (1964). Rudofsky's book was published a half century ago, and it was *written* almost 30 years before that. It is as much a modernist tract as Sigfried Giedion's *Space, Time, and Architecture* (1941), which was written at about the same time.[6] Both were part of a project to define a new basis for architecture outside the canons of classical and historicist thought – one to be found in the ahistorical truths of engineering and technology in Giedion's case, and in the ostensibly timeless design principles of indigenous cultures in Rudofsky's. In this regard, I have always wondered why Rudofsky's book retains its credibility while Sibyl Moholy-Nagy's *Native Genius in Anonymous Architecture* (1957), published only a few years before, is mostly forgotten. The reason, I think, may be that Moholy-Nagy focused as much on 'anonymous architecture' in industrialized societies as in preindustrial ones, while Rudofsky celebrated a romanticized pre- or extra-industrial primitivism. Romanticism assumes the superiority of traditional practice because it seems more visually appealing.

The power of traditional *tradition* may thus be seen to lie not only in aesthetic nostalgia, but even more in the concept's political usefulness. Tradition (and its derivative *heritage*) have been transformed from the sentimental values of antiquarians to powerful weapons in struggles over urban development and the differential rights of urban, rural, and national sub-communities. If ethnic identity is, as some anthropologists argue, a means to channel the distribution of scarce resources, tradition is its rubric in modernized societies. Tradition lends one's claims clarity and the authority of time. As the two essays in this volume on the New Territories of Hong Kong and the Soulard neighbourhood of St. Louis demonstrate, it gives one group of residents leverage over another. In Hong Kong, people accorded recognition as 'indigenous' retained land and development rights that were not available to other residents. They then used these not to maintain a 'traditional' way of life but to profit in a burgeoning real-estate market. In St. Louis, it was, by implication, the original residents of the neighbourhood who were the privileged group. Since they no longer lived there, the new, elite owners of their former houses assumed the privilege of speaking for them by resisting the changes wrought by lower-class newcomers from the rural South.

The evocation of time-sanctioned privilege is not new. It could even be observed in Neolithic Europe where, some scholars argue, the construction of tombs that allowed continued access to ancestors' remains supported claims to territory. Other archaeologists have argued that barrow tombs placed on the ridges of hills were meant to equate the monuments of current residents with the antiquity of the natural landscape (Bradley, 1984, p. 15; 1988: pp, 50–58). And in contemporary Guam and Yangon, as Marvin Brown and Jayde Lin Roberts show in this volume, the architecture of colonial powers, constructed in the relatively recent past, has been redefined as local tradition in the face of more recent colonializing influences. None of these instances of the use of tradition as a political strategy depends on visual authenticity for its power.

To claim ownership of tradition is thus a polemical position. If tradition is a process of adaptation, there is nothing to own. Every person or group will adapt idiosyncratically. But if it is a reified body of practices and images, then we can speak of origins and ownership.

Our scholarly understanding of tradition inclines us to side with these assertions of traditional privilege, for if our predisposition is romantic, it is also populist. Studies of tradition thus often tell a tale of good guys versus bad guys. Even though the details of individual accounts focus on the decision-making process, the power of elites, and other social grounds, each party is treated as a monolith, rather than as a collection of individual actors. That is, the story of the traditional landscape is customarily told in a Marxian mode of class struggle, of a proletariat against a bourgeoisie. Our scholarship is grounded in the left-liberal assumptions and attitudes of the 1960s with their appeals to 'the people'. Indeed, the work of founders such as Henry Glassie (1968; 1999*b*) in the United States (and later in East, South, and West Asia) and Paul Oliver in the developing world grew out of these impulses. Oliver, for example, was trained as an architect; but he made his first, and most widely known, reputation as a student of the blues at a time when white scholars were seeking to redefine this form of popular expression as folk music (O'Connell, 2015; Wald, 2005).

I have no quarrel with analyses of class struggle. But if we tell that tale in the language of tradition, it has the effect of deflecting concrete politics. Conflicts that have to do with the play of economic and political power, as Abidin Kusno details here, are often retold as stories of apolitical values or culture, of generalized depredation or oppression. Tradition is thus positioned as superior to modernity because it is conceived as the condition of the downtrodden – even when, as has often been pointed out, the older buildings that we often treat as traditional were built by local elites. Analyses in the register of tradition thus have no power to explain or to offer solutions, which must be political and economic.

A major problem with this stance is that it becomes difficult for us to analyze struggles among people who all claim the mantle of tradition. Events such as the 1969 Kuala Lumpur riots or the more recent 'communal' conflicts in South Asia are all political struggles framed as struggles over traditional rights and privileges. And across the American South one may find monuments to the nineteenth-century Civil War Confederacy right next to those marking the freedom struggle of black Americans in the twentieth century, which aimed to eradicate vestiges of the very white supremacism the Confederate monuments celebrate. In the South, for the moment, there is a standoff: Southerners have crafted the fiction of dual, parallel heritages that do not intersect or contradict one another. In this way, heritage rewrites history as the property of a particular group, removed from broader social conflict to the realm of the sacred and thus the unchallengeable. It deflects critical scrutiny and becomes a way to recast the disgraceful, the embarrassing, the outmoded, the criminal as tradition, and so to hold on to it without shame. If so, it may be that the study of *tradition*, however we might define it, is more suitable to examining other aspects of social life than political struggle, except in cases where tradition is presented unabashedly as a fiction to counter other fictions (Upton, 2015, p. 15).

These observations have a very direct effect on our preferred methods. We are inordinately fond of categorizing. We like to identify characteristic building types such as Southeast Asian shophouses, Gulf Coast shotgun houses, or Shanghai *shikumen* houses, treating them in isolation, divorced from their contexts or conditions of formulation. At their most extreme, these ways of thought lead to absurdities such as the 'Katrina cottages', based on a kind of single-storey house popularly known as a shotgun. The designers of Katrina cottages, who proposed them as reconstruction shelters for post-Katrina New Orleans, assumed that all of New Orleans was composed of this one kind of house. Not only was it only one kind of house among many built over the nearly 300 years of the city's history, but it was typologically unstable. The logic of social life and architectural form that produced the one-storey, one-room-wide, several-room-deep shotgun house could be doubled horizontally, raised partially or wholly to two storeys, and even made of houses customarily treated as entirely different types. More importantly, many residents of shotgun houses hoped to escape them whenever their economic prospects improved. Meanwhile (at the other end of the social scale), large shotgun houses have often been built by gentrifiers for their external 'typicality' as a New Orleans form, while these new residents have simultaneously altered their interiors completely to fit new bourgeois lifestyles (Upton, 2006).

We often call this kind of action 'hybrid', but it represents an attempt to cling to categories. As many scholars have noted, the term *hybrid* assumes the distinctiveness and the stability of the disparate cultural ingredients that go into the hybrid stew. A better strategy might be to understand everyday lives and landscapes as a-categorical.

Let me refer to another mid-century book that still retains currency: Thomas Kuhn's *The Structure of Scientific Revolutions*, first published in 1962. Kuhn gave us the widely used terms 'paradigm' and 'paradigm shift'. 'Tradition' and 'modernity' are, in Kuhn's model, paradigms, with traditionalists being the holdouts, while 'modernists' are those who grasp the new paradigms and whose thinking is transformed by them. In the history of science, Kuhn's paradigm has been strongly challenged by Peter Galison, a historian of physics. According to Galison (1997), there is no 'golden thread', no single strand or tradition that unites the history of science. Instead, he has written of scientific change as involving the 'intercalation' of discrete strands of varying lengths that begin and end at different times and for varying reasons. Tradition is that rope, and that realization has deep implications for the ways we as historians ought to think about our subject matter.

Architect Roger Sherman's study (2010) of property and land use in Los Angeles seems to me to exemplify Galison's model. Sherman depicts a fluid landscape of 'negotiation', in which mixtures of building forms and land uses flow through and across property boundaries. It is an exemplary study that stresses process over form, as I have been proposing here. It also seems to offer a way to understand the process of cultural engagement and change that we call tradition without casting it in the reified form that polemics and romanticization demand.

Nevertheless, however faulty traditional *tradition* might be, it remains persuasive because, as has so often been demonstrated at IASTE meetings, it has acquired an economic value – or rather, its cultural capital has been monetized. Putatively traditional environments (sometimes even newly created ones) can be marketed to affluent people seeking novelty in an imagined escape to the authentic – either in their residences, as in Soulard, or temporarily, through travel.[7] The economic value of tradition real or imagined is often the only strategy capable of countering unchecked development, whether it be poor neighbourhoods or affluent NIMBYs making the claim. So the tension between theoretical and practical definitions of tradition – between process and polemics – will not disappear soon.

Notes

1. Similar stories could be told about other so-called traditional practitioners. With regard to other potters, see DeNatale *et al.* (1994) and Baldwin (1993).
2. '2014 Word of the Year; Merriam-Webster Announces "Culture" as 2014 Word of the Year.' Viewed 15 May 2016, at www.merriam-webster.com/press-release/2014-word-of-the-year.
3. Raymond Williams (1973) explored the idea of a golden age that for every era was 'just over the last hill'. For an amusing exploration of the peasant aesthetic as a modern bourgeois ethic, see Brooks (1998).
4. See, for example, Dani (2013), Woods (2001), Kelly (2006), Cliff and Rozensztroch (1998), and Habibi and De Meulder (2015).
5. The blurb was viewed 9 August 2016, at http://www.barnesandnoble.com/w/african-style-stephane-guibourge/1003893464?ean=9782080136817.
6. Note that the subtitle for Giedion's book was 'The Growth of a New Tradition'.
7. See, for example, the efforts of the Committee on the Conservation and Development of Traditional Villages, organized in 2012 under the auspices of the Chinese government's Ministry of Housing and Urban-Rural Development, which seeks to revitalize rural life by bringing tourism activity to rural locations that are rapidly losing population and economic base. It sponsors an annual Conference for the Revival of Chinese Villages. Some of the group's efforts are detailed in the newly launched *Traditional Chinese Villages Bulletin*.

References

Baldwin, C.K. (1993) *Great and Noble Jar: Traditional Stoneware of South Carolina.* Athens, GA: University of Georgia Press.
Bradley, R. (1984) *The Social Foundations of Prehistoric Britain: Themes and Variations in the Archaeology of Power.* London: Longman.
Bradley, R. (1988) *The Significance of Monuments: On the Shaping of Human Experience in Neolithic and Bronze Age Europe.* London: Routledge.
Brooks, D. (1998) Conscientious consumption. *The New Yorker*, 23 November, pp. 46–47.
Burrison, J.A. (1983) *Brothers in Clay: The Story of Georgia Folk Pottery.* Athens, GA: University of Georgia Press.

Cliff, S. and Rozensztroch, D. (1998) *Caribbean Style*. New York: Potter.
Dani, N. (2013) How to decorate your home with an ethnic touch. *Economic Times*, 7 January. Available at: http://economictimes.indiatimes.com/slideshows/spending-lifestyle/how-to-design-and-decorate-your-home-with-an-ethnic-touch/slideshow/17923500.cms.
Deetz, J. (1967) *Invitation to Archaeology*. Garden City, NY: Natural History Press.
DeNatale, D., Pryzbysz, J. and Severn, J.R. (1994) *New Ways for Old Jugs: Tradition and Innovation at the Jugtown Pottery*. Columbia, SC: McKissick Museum.
Galison, P. (1997) *Image and Logic: A Material Culture of Microphysics*. Chicago. IL: University of Chicago Press.
Giedion, S. (1941) *Space, Time and Architecture: The Growth of a New Tradition*. Cambridge, MA: Harvard University Press.
Glassie, H. (1968) *Pattern in the Material Folk Culture of the Eastern United States*. Philadelphia, PA: University of Pennsylvania Press.
Glassie, H. (1999a) *The Potter's Art*. Philadelphia, PA: Material Culture and Bloomington, IN: Indiana University Press.
Glassie, H. (1999b) *Material Culture*. Bloomington, IN: Indiana University Press.
Guibourge, S., Morellec, F. and Desgrippes, A. (1998) *African Style*. Paris: Flammarion.
Habibi, R. and De Meulder, B. (2015) Architects and 'architecture without architects': modernization of Iranian housing and the birth of a new urban form Narmak (Tehran, 1952). *Cities*, **45**, pp. 29–40.
Hobsbawm, E. and Ranger, T.O. (eds.) (1983) *The Invention of Tradition*. Cambridge: Cambridge University Press.
Kelly, A. (2006) *Casa Mexicana Style*. New York: Abrams.
Kuhn, T.S. (1962) *The Structure of Scientific Revolutions*. Chicago, IL: University of Chicago Press.
Moholy-Nagy, S. (1957) *Native Genius in Anonymous Architecture*. New York: Horizon Press.
O'Connell, C. (2015) *Blues, How Do You Do? Paul Oliver and the Transatlantic Story of the Blues*. Ann Arbor, MI: University of Michigan Press.
Redfield, R. (1960) *The Little Community and Peasant Society and Culture*. Chicago, IL: University of Chicago Press.
Rudofsky, B. (1964) *Architecture without Architects: A Short Introduction to Non-Pedigreed Architecture*. New York: Museum of Modern Art.
Sherman, R. (2010) *L.A. under the Influence: The Hidden Logic of Urban Property*. Minneapolis, MN: University of Minnesota Press.
Upton, D. (1995) The story of the book, in Stotz, C.M., *Early Architecture of Western Pennsylvania* (orig., 1936). Pittsburgh, PA: University of Pittsburgh Press, pp. ix–xxvii.
Upton, D. (2006) Understanding New Orleans' architectural ecology, in Birch, E.L. and Wachter, S.M. (eds.) *Rebuilding Urban Places After Disaster: Lessons from Hurricane Katrina*. Philadelphia, PA: University of Pennsylvania Press, pp. 275–287.
Upton, D. (2015) *What Can and Can't Be Said: Race, Uplift, and Monument Building in the Contemporary South*. New Haven, CT: Yale University Press.
Vlach, J.M. (1978) *The Afro-American Tradition in Decorative Arts*. Cleveland, OH: Cleveland Museum of Art.
Wald, E. (2005). *Escaping the Delta: Robert Johnson and the Invention of the Blues*. New York: Amistad.
Williams, R. (1973) *The Country and the City*. New York: Oxford University Press.
Woods, S. (2001) *Santa Fe Style*. New York: Rizzoli.

Index

Accountability 22, 31, 67, 261
Adivasi v, 8, 111, 113–116, 120, 125–126
aesthetics 43, 136, 138, 157, 204, 214–215, 223, 226, 231–232, 244, 265, 271, 275, 279–281, 299
    architectural acquisition 265
Africa i, vi, xi–xii, 12, 14–16, 78, 188–189, 201–206, 236–239, 242–243, 250, 252–265, 267, 269, 271, 273–275, 277–279, 281
    African architects 14, 237–240, 242–243, 254, 294
    African architecture 15, 237–238, 244, 252, 254, 256–257
    African Style (Guibourge, Morellec and Desgrippes) 304
Agamben, Giorgio 63
Akenzua Cultural Center 245, 252
Alexander, Robert 154, 157
Almeida, Anthony 237, 243, 247–252, 255
AlSayyad, Nezar iv, 21, 24, 25, 90, 98, 106, 128–129, 139, 193, 214, 255, 286, 291, 298, 305
ambush marketing 68
    archipelagos of exception 67, 77
American ix–xii, xiv, 11–12, 39–40, 60, 72, 75, 79–80, 128, 147, 150–151, 153, 161–162, 164, 166–167, 169, 175, 177, 182, 185, 203, 220, 222, 234–235, 257, 271, 274, 280, 295, 304, 307, 310
Amuli, Beda 15, 237, 239, 243, 250–252, 255
ancestors 113, 123, 222, 306
Angola 16, 200, 203, 205, 259–260, 265–268, 270–271, 280–281
    Baia de Luanda Marginal 266
Appiah 42, 52, 59
architect-researcher 8, 111, 124
architectural history v, vii, xi, xiii, 8, 111, 115–116, 123–125, 158, 305
    architectural historian xi, 124, 206, 238, 301
    architectural styles 178, 217, 247, 268, 271
Architecture without Architects (Rudofsky) 305
aspirations xi, 123, 135, 173, 190, 209, 292
Ath-chala 116–118, 126
attachment 56, 285, 290, 292–297
authenticity 2, 5, 98, 107, 166, 170, 175, 233, 286–287, 305–306
authorship 1, 3, 8, 21, 87, 188, 204–206
    authoring power 286

Barra do Dande 269
Barradas, Jorge 203
Beaux-Arts 12, 168, 182
belonging vi, 16, 125, 283, 285, 287, 289–300
Benin City 15, 245
Bharat, Gauri 305
Bhitar 116, 118, 125
Bongo, Omar 267
Bordallo, Madeleine 164, 166
Bordallo, Ricardo 'Ricky' 11, 152, 158–164
brand-exclusion zone 68–69, 77
Brazil i, 11–12, 65–66, 70, 73–74, 77, 79–80, 168–169, 171–172, 174–175, 177–178, 182–185, 202, 205
British Malaya 129, 131–132, 134–135, 142
Brown, Marvin 306
building practice 124
bureaucracy 4–5, 28, 42, 49
  bureaucratic 28, 31–32, 35, 297
Burma/Myanmar 58
Burrison, John 302–303

capital 5, 12, 14–15, 22, 28, 30–31, 34, 36, 41, 44, 47, 49, 55, 58–60, 64, 68, 77, 79, 129, 133–139, 141––142, 149–150, 153, 159, 163, 174, 176, 186, 188–191, 197–198, 215, 232, 234, 253, 261, 265, 268, 272, 276, 279, 293, 296–297, 309
capitalism 6, 16, 36, 42, 54, 57–58, 64, 78, 80, 169, 239, 258, 264–266, 279, 281, 287
cattle 114, 116, 118, 122, 124–125, 169

Caxito 269
Chamorro 11, 147–148, 150–154, 157–159, 161–166, 295
  indigenous architecture 150
  language 148, 168,
  public feasting 148
Chamorro-Spanish architecture 148–151, 158–164
Chennai 295
Choy Yuen Village 101–102, 104
Christian 15, 22, 55, 249, 252, 290
citizenship 58, 72, 74, 78, 143, 215, 281
codes 209, 214, 226–227, 229–233
colonial i, xi–xii, xiv, 5–6, 8, 10–14, 21, 27–29, 37, 39, 41–50, 52–61, 87–91, 93, 99–100, 102, 105–107, 109, 120, 126, 128, 140–142, 147–148, 150, 152, 156, 158, 160–164, 166, 168–171, 173–174, 176–177, 180–182, 184–186, 188–193, 196–201, 203–209, 236–238, 250, 253, 256, 259–261, 263–268, 272, 278–279, 295–296, 299–300, 306
  colonial government 8, 90–91, 93, 100, 102, 120, 126, 140
  colonial rationality of rule 188
colonialism i, vi, 2–3, 10, 12–13, 30, 30, 50, 52, 99, 110, 145, 153, 155–156, 158, 162–163, 166, 188–189, 196–197, 199, 201, 204–205, 209, 238, 240, 242, 257, 260, 278, 280, 287, 294, 296
  Spanish 11, 148–152, 155, 159–164, 166–167, 295

colonialization 296
comprador intelligentsia 42, 52
Congo 16, 162, 166, 205, 259, 267, 276–277, 280–281
consumerism 265, 269, 275, 279, 281, 287
  globalized modernity 265
cosmopolitanism 42 170–171, 239, 294
Costa, Lucio 12, 168, 179–186
courtyard 116–120, 154, 160
crisis 24, 29–30, 63–64, 90, 143
critical regionalism 15, 241–242, 256
culture x, xii–xiv, 8, 12, 14–15, 23–24, 32, 35, 38–39, 58, 60, 66, 69, 80, 97, 109, 114–115, 120, 126–127, 136, 138, 140, 143–144, 148, 162, 165–167, 169, 171–174, 176–177, 182–186, 206, 214–215, 220, 222–223, 231–232, 236–238, 241–245, 247, 250–251, 253–254, 256–258, 279, 285, 287–288, 292–293, 298–302, 304–305, 307, 309–310
  cultural authentification 299
  cultural evolution 301
  cultural transmission 291
  culture and anthropology 301
  culture as popular word 304

Dar es Salaam 15, 248–250, 256
  Central Library of Dar es Salaam 15, 248–249
decentralization 22
decolonization xiii, 162, 165, 189, 205, 296;
decolonization of urbanity 189
Deetz, James 301–302
demolition 70, 75, 218, 230, 253
development vii, xiii, 3, 8, 10, 13, 15–16, 24–25, 35, 39, 42–43, 46, 50–51, 54, 56, 58, 60, 63–64, 67, 72, 79–80, 86–88, 91, 93–94, 104, 106, 108–109, 116, 118–120, 123, 126–127, 132–136, 138, 141–142, 151, 154, 156, 159, 166, 171, 173, 176, 179–180, 182–184, 190, 208, 213–216, 222, 224, 227–229, 231, 234, 239, 252–254, 256–257, 259, 261–264, 266–268, 270–274, 276, 278–281, 287, 290, 296, 305–306, 309
  uneven development 133
development model 16, 261, 263, 266, 276, 278
  credit 68, 170, 268
  meg-project 253, 257, 268
dialogue 1, 14–15, 63, 120–121, 123–125, 237, 245, 254
Direcção dos Monumentos Nacionais (DMN) 191
disjuncture 121, 143
displacement 2, 72, 102, 148, 214, 224–225
dissent 7, 66, 71, 77, 79–80
division 92, 132, 166, 189–191, 204, 209, 219, 281, 296–297, 299
  unequal urban division 189–190
Duque, Gonzaga 12, 168–174

Elvidge, Anita 152, 156–158
Elvidge, Ford 152, 156–158
Empire square 199, 207
enclave 7, 62, 67, 76–77, 221, 225, 274
ethnocracy 137
ethnographic xii, 9, 122, 126–127, 200
European 13–14, 45–47, 54, 59, 131, 148, 169–171, 174–175, 182, 188–189, 192–193, 205–206, 220–222, 236–239, 242–243, 245–247, 252–253, 259, 279, 286, 293–294, 299, 304
everyday x, 6, 52–53, 55–58, 90, 100, 111–112, 114, 120–121, 124–125, 158, 193, 196, 233, 250–251, 287–289, 303, 308
　everyday life x, 6, 55, 57, 90, 100, 112, 114, 120, 124–125, 250–251, 287–289, 303, 308
　everydayness of tradition 294
eviction 33, 36, 38, 70, 72, 74–75, 79, 190, 227, 230, 233
exception v, 6, 31, 62–65, 67–81, 97, 114, 126, 299
　city of exception v, 6, 62–65, 67–69, 71, 73, 75, 77, 79, 81
　exceptionalism 65–67, 73, 77, 294
　legal exceptionalism 65–67, 77, 294
　regimes of legal exceptionalism 77
　space of exception 31
　state of exception 63–64, 67, 77–78, 80

exclusion 6, 62–63, 68–69, 74, 77, 79, 97–98, 205, 215, 232, 294
excremental transition 141–142
EXIM Bank 262
expectations of modernity 132–133, 141, 143
extraterritoriality v, 6, 62–63, 65, 67, 69–71, 73–75, 77, 79–81;
　extraterritorial 67, 74

fantasy Middle Eastern architecture 143
farming 99, 101–105, 107–109
favela 74–76, 80–81, 294
Ferguson, James 132
fieldwork 58–59, 121–123, 125
FIFA 6, 65–70, 73
　World Cup 6–7, 62, 65–66, 68–70, 76, 78
filtering 66, 71
forest 114–116, 120, 122, 203
　forest-dwelling 114
Forjaz, José 193
Fortaleza museum 190–198
fragmentation v, 6–7, 62–63, 65, 67, 69, 71, 73, 75, 77–79, 81
Frampton, Kenneth 241–242

Gabon 16, 258–259, 265, 267, 272–276, 279–281
　Cité de la Démocrati 273–274
Galison, Peter 308
Galvão, Henrique 200
Gaugler, Jennifer 305
gaze 8–9, 32, 87–88, 99, 106, 120, 124, 126

gentrification xii, 14, 213–214, 216, 231, 233–234
Giedion, Siegfried 305
Glassie, Henry 303, 306
global hierarchy of value 287, 299
globalization 1–2, 42, 79, 98, 109, 141, 167, 287, 289, 291, 298
Gonzaga Duque Estrada, Luiz 12, 168–174
Government House vi, 10–11, 145, 147–149, 151–167, 295
grain storage 118
Guam i, vi, xi, 10–11, 145, 147–161, 163–167, 295, 306

Hagåtña (Agaña) 148, 150
heritage ix, xii–xiv, 2, 8, 10, 13–14, 41–43, 52–53, 57–58, 60, 70, 98, 106, 110, 122, 136, 159, 162, 171, 176, 180, 182–183, 188–189, 193, 197, 199, 204, 206, 208, 213–215, 219–222, 229–230, 232–235, 242–243, 245, 264, 286, 291, 293, 295–296, 305, 307
  built heritage 10, 13, 188, 197
  built heritage of colonial occupation 197
Heung Yee Kuk (HYK) 85
high-technology 268
historic preservation vi, x, xiii, 13, 166, 178, 213–214, 216, 219, 230–231, 234
Hobsbawm, Eric 302
home, i, 9, 16, 51, 74–75, 110, 115, 132, 141, 166, 204, 216, 218–219, 224–230, 235, 239, 247, 249, 255, 272, 288–291, 293, 295–296, 298–300, 303, 310
Hong Kong i, v, xii, 7–8, 83, 85–91, 93–95, 97–110, 297, 305
  handover, 90, 95, 99;
  New territories of Hong Kong 297, 305–306
human capital 279
human-centered modernism 271
hybridity 308

IASTE vii, ix–x, xii, 1–3, 214, 285, 305, 308
identity, ethnic 305
immigrants 14, 174–175, 178, 215, 217–218, 220, 223
India i, x, 8, 43, 46, 59, 111, 115, 126–127, 134, 140, 205, 239, 247–248, 257, 291, 295, 300
indigenous v, 7–8, 41, 48, 60, 70, 83, 85–91, 93–111, 122, 124–125, 127, 136–137, 143, 150, 190, 201, 237–238, 243, 251–252, 255, 257, 267, 289, 291, 294–295, 297, 305–306
  indigenous modernities 60, 237, 251, 255, 257
inequality 6, 13, 43, 48, 52, 62, 77, 189, 199–200, 204, 233, 296
  aesthetic of inequality 199
  pedagogy of inequality 189, 200
informal settlement 74–75, 266, 272, 274, 281
infrastructure 10, 15–16, 51–53, 64, 71, 73, 75, 87, 94, 131, 134, 141, 197, 253, 259–264, 271, 276–279

inhabitation 219, 293
institutional reflexivity 292
intimacy 289–290
Invention of Tradition, The
  (Hobsbawm and Ranger) 302
Islamization v, 9–10, 128–129, 131, 133, 135, 137–141, 143

Jahira 112–113, 125
Jakarta v, xiii, 4, 19, 21–29, 31–40, 55, 166, 297
Jharkhand 8, 111, 126–127
Joint Christian Chapel 15, 249, 252

Kahn, Joel 137
KaMpfumo 192
Kampung 4, 30–31, 33–36, 131
Kariakoo Market 15, 250–252
Katrina cottages 307
Kilamba Kiaxi 270
King, Ross 136, 139–140
knowledge 2, 13, 52, 119, 144, 178–179, 190, 201, 204, 240, 243, 264, 289, 291–292, 299
  circuits of knowledge 190
Kuala Lumpur i, v, vii, xii, 1, 9, 60, 128–129, 133–135, 139–143, 305, 307
  1969 riots 307
  IASTE at 305
Kuhn, Thomas 308
Kultermann, Udo 243, 252
Kumbaha 116–119
Kusno, Abidin 4–5, 297, 307

Laclau, Ernesto 24
Lai, Chee Kien 134

land politics 99
Le Corbusier 247–248, 255, 267, 280
Lee, Julian 139
legitimacy 2–4, 26, 87, 97, 267
Libreville 258, 265, 272–276, 280
  Port Mole 275, 280–281
  Stade d'Angondje 275
  Université Omar Bongo 258, 273
lifeworlds 123
Lisbon 12, 189–190, 200–201, 203, 207–208, 296
Little Community, The (Redfield) 301
Liverpool 9, 129–133, 135, 141–143, 290
Los Angeles, California 308
Lourenço Marques 189–193, 206–208
Luanda 265–266, 268–269, 271–272, 281
  Muxima Shopping Center 269

Machel, Samora 196, 198
Malay 9–10, 129–144, 290
Malays 132, 136, 138, 142
Malaysia vii, xi, 9, 128–129, 131–144, 290
Malo, Manasse 25
Manjhi 113, 125
Manjhithan 112–113, 125
Maputo 12, 189–190, 194, 197–198, 205, 207–208, 296
Maracanã stadium 69–70, 75
Marianno Filho, José Marianno Carneiro da Cunha Filho 168, 176, 183–185

marketing 57, 68
Meaders family 302–303
mega-events v, x, 6, 62–81
Merseyside 131–132, 142
middle class 16, 35, 37, 47, 218–220, 225, 265, 269, 279
Miss Pearce Chapel 245–247
modernism 2, 15–16, 151, 153, 161, 179, 183, 185, 237–239, 241–243, 245, 247–248, 250, 253–255, 271–272
modernist architecture 11, 242
modernity vi, xi, 5, 9–10, 14–16, 21, 41–44, 47–54, 57–60, 98, 128–133, 137–143, 162, 165–166, 171, 176, 236–239, 241, 243, 245, 247, 249, 251–255, 257, 259, 264–267, 274, 278–280, 285–296, 298–303, 307–308
modernization 5, 13, 15, 33, 42, 48, 57, 80, 133–135, 141, 156, 171, 173, 180, 236, 241, 243, 268, 275, 299, 302, 310
Moholy-Nagy, Sibyl 305
Monteiro Lobato, José Bento 12, 168, 172–176, 184–185
monuments 9, 43, 52, 56, 182, 185, 191, 196, 205, 220, 234, 273, 295–296, 306–307, 309
American Civil War 307
Morales de los Ríos Filho, Adolfo 12, 168, 182, 185
Moser, Sarah 139
Moura, Ana Amélia de Paula 305
Mozambique vi, xi, 12, 188–189, 191–194, 196–198, 200, 204–209, 296

multiple modernities 290
multiple traditions 4, 290
museumifying 288

Nas, Peter 25
nation-building 23, 41, 49, 55, 58, 134–135, 169
national art 170–171
national character 11–12, 168–173, 175, 180, 182, 185, 294
nationalistic romanticism 169
National Fine Arts School (Brazil) 182
national identity 10, 12, 41, 136, 140–141, 143, 166, 185, 238, 287, 294
nationalism 15, 29, 47, 55, 108, 137, 174, 238–239, 256, 294
Native Genius in Anonymous Architecture (Moholy-Nagy) 305
natural resources 15, 57, 120, 258, 261, 267, 278
neighbourhood 213–214, 218, 224, 229–230, 233–235
neocolonial 12, 16, 168–169, 176, 179–183, 185–187, 259, 261, 263–264, 266, 272, 278
neocolonialism 50, 259
neoliberal 6, 32, 35, 42, 57, 63–64, 69, 77, 79, 294
neoliberalism 6, 52, 54, 57, 80, 265, 287, 289
Neutra & Alexander 11, 153–154, 156, 165, 167
Neutra, Richard 11, 152–158, 160–163
New Orleans, Louisiana 221, 307–308

new urbanism xiv, 274
New York iv, xiv, 60, 72, 81, 130, 144, 166, 208, 233–235, 257, 280–281, 299–300, 310
Nigeria 14, 237, 242, 244–245, 254, 257, 260, 269, 294
nostalgia, as popular word 304
Nu, U 49
Nwoko, Demas, 237, 239–240, 243–249, 252

oil 15–16, 258–260, 262–264, 267–268, 273, 276, 278, 280
oil-for-infrastructure China 16, 263-264, 276, 278
Oliver, Paul 306
Olympic Games 78–80, 293
　International Olympic Committee (IOC) 66
Ong, Aihwa 128–129, 137
Orak 116–119, 126

Palácio Atlântico 202
Palazzo, Pedro Paulo 305
paradigm shift 308
Pearn 44, 47, 60
Penang 128–130, 135
policing 71, 76
police pacification 76, 79
Porto 12, 72–73, 76, 79–80, 186, 189–190, 199–204, 207–209
Porto Maravilha 72–73, 76, 79–80
Portugal i, vi, xi, 12–13, 174, 177, 183, 188–189, 191–194, 198–199, 202, 204–205, 207–209, 270, 296
post-global 3
postcolonial Africa 264

postcolonialism 161, 208, 293
post-coloniality 42
pottery, traditional 302–304
preservation vi, x, xiii, 5, 13–14, 52–53, 57, 87, 166, 176, 178–180, 213–216, 219, 229–234, 247, 293
privatization 63–64, 69, 72, 294
prosperity/progress 259, 264, 272, 279
public-private partnership (PPP) 64, 72–73
Putrajaya 139–141, 143
Rakyat 4–5, 27–34, 37–38
Rancière, Jacques 205
Ranger, Terence 302
redevelopment 72–73, 104, 264, 275
Redfield, Robert 301
regionalism 15, 137, 171, 241–242, 256, 294
　regionalist architecture 136, 138, 241
Republic of Congo 16, 259, 267, 276, 280
　Brazzaville 276–277
　Pan African Games complex 277
resistance 1, 7, 30, 32, 38, 66, 75, 77, 79, 102, 108, 110, 143, 193, 226, 231, 236, 241, 256, 296
revitalization 14, 72–73, 219, 221, 223–226, 232
rights iv, 6, 21, 65–69, 74–75, 77–79, 86–87, 91, 94–99, 102, 104–110, 158, 165, 220, 223, 229, 234, 260–261, 263, 270, 296–297, 305–307
　bargaining- 65
　civil- 74, 78, 220, 234

human- 66, 75, 260, 263, 271, 278–279, 288–289, 309
Rio de Janeiro v, x, 6, 62, 66, 69, 72, 74–75, 78–81, 171, 176, 186–187, 293
Roberts, Jayde Lin 306
Roy, Ananya 24, 96
Rudofsky, Bernard 305

sacred grove 111–112, 122
Santal i, 8–9, 111–127, 291
Sassa Bengo 269
Sassou Nguesso, Denis 267, 276
seafarers 9–10, 128–130, 133–135, 137, 140–141, 290
security regime 71, 76
segregation 6, 62–63, 272
self-representation 114, 121
Severo, Ricardo 12, 168, 173–176
Shenzen 8
Sherman, Roger 308
Silva, Joaquim Areal 191–193
Simmel, Georg 31
Singapore xi–xii, 5, 9, 39, 46, 51, 53, 56–57, 59, 109, 129–135, 142–143, 256, 264
Singhbhum 115, 119–120, 124, 127
Skinner, Carlton 152–158, 163
slums (*musseques*) 269, 271
small-house policy (SHP) 86, 90, 99
Soulard 13–14, 213–235, 305, 309
Southeast Asia xi–xii, 5, 9, 24, 27, 39, 42–43, 51, 54, 57, 60, 129–132, 135, 143
Southern Africa xi, 188–189, 205
sovereignty 55, 67–68, 80, 107, 278

sovereign law 67
Space, Time, and Architecture (Giedion) 305
Spanish colonial architecture 163
spatial pedagogy 189, 196, 199, 204
  postcolonial spatial pedagogy 189, 196, 199, 204
spatial violence 13, 189–190, 204
spirits 112–113, 125, 143
sponsor 6, 64, 66, 68–69, 71–72, 80, 309
St. Louis, Missouri 213
  Soulard neighborhood 306
State Law and Order Restoration Council (SLORC) 58
state of emergency 6, 63, 79–80
State Peace and Development Council (SPDC) 58
Structure of Scientific Revolutions, The (Kuhn) 308
subcontracted 4, 26–27, 30
subjectivity 1, 3, 16, 21, 121–122, 124, 188–189, 191, 197, 204, 255, 285, 290–291
super-diversity 295, 300
surveillance xii, 39, 71, 294
sustainability x, 64, 271

Tagore, Rabindranath 47, 60
Tajuddin, Mohamed 140
Tanzania 15, 205, 237, 247–250, 256–257, 294
territoriality 6, 39, 62, 67, 77
  territory of exception 74, 76
tombs 306
  Neolithic 309
tradition, definition of 301

invented 302
tradition of anticolonial struggle 188
tradition of colonial domination 190
ownership of 306
traditional art 174, 176
traditional architecture 136–137, 174–175, 178, 180
traditionalism 105, 108
tropical garden 189, 200–201
tropical modernism 242

Universidade Agostinho Neto 271–272, 281
urban design i, ix, xi–xii, 162, 205, 230, 269
urban memorials vi, 188, 199, 205, 209
urban planning 13, 21, 25, 79, 154, 189–190, 197, 204–205, 208, 268

venues 67–68, 71, 276
vernacular xi–xii, 185, 203, 242, 264, 289, 294

village house 86–87, 91–93, 96, 98, 104
village school 112–114
voice v, 1, 3–4, 8, 47, 52–53, 71, 110–111, 113, 115, 117, 119, 121, 123–125, 127, 214–215, 291

Weizman, Eyal 67
Widodo, Joko (Jokowi) 4–5, 22–26, 29, 31–36
Win, Ne 49, 54
working-class 14, 207, 214–216, 218, 222, 232
World War II 11, 14, 41, 49, 90, 151, 164, 166
Yangon v, xiii, 5–6, 41–43, 45, 47, 49, 51–61, 296, 306
   Yangon City Hall 47
   Yangon Heritage Trust 42, 52
   Yangon, Myanmar 296
   Yangon/Rangoon 41–57
Yuan, Lim Jee 137

Zaria Art Society 242–244, 257